# The RoutledgeFalmer Reader
# in History of Education

*The RoutledgeFalmer Reader in History of Education* brings together a wide range of material to present an international perspective on topical issues in history of education today. Focusing on the enduring trends in this field, this lively and informative reader provides broad coverage of the subject and includes crucial topics such as:

- higher education
- informal agencies of education
- schooling, the State and local government
- education and social change and inequality
- curriculum
- teachers and pupils
- education, work and the economy and
- education and national identity.

With an emphasis on themes that provide a historical understanding of modern and contemporary institutions and issues, this book represents the research and views of some of the most respected authors in the field today. Gary McCulloch also includes a specially written Introduction which provides a much needed context to the role of history in the current education climate.

This will be an essential resource for students of history and history of education who will find this Reader an important route map to further reading and understanding.

**Gary McCulloch** is Professor and Brian Simon Chair of History of Education at the Institute of Education, University of London.

# Readers in education

# The RoutledgeFalmer Reader in History of Education

Edited by
**Gary McCulloch**

Routledge
Taylor & Francis Group

LONDON AND NEW YORK

First published 2005
by Routledge
2 Park Square, Milton Park, Abingdon, Oxon OX14 4RN

Simultaneously published in the USA and Canada
by Routledge
270 Madison Ave, New York, NY 10016

*Routledge is an imprint of the Taylor & Francis Group*

*British Library Cataloguing in Publication Data*
A catalogue record for this book is available from the
British Library

*Library of Congress Cataloging in Publication Data*
A catalog record for this book has been requested

ISBN 0–415–34569–3 (hbk)
ISBN 0–415–34570–7 (pbk)

# CONTENTS

**Curriculum**                                                                                    161

10   Eton in India: the imperial diffusion of a Victorian
     educational ethic                                                                           163
     J. A. MANGAN

11   Catholic influence and the secondary school curriculum
     in Ireland, 1922–1962                                                                       179
     THOMAS A. O'DONOGHUE

     *General background 179*
     *The Church's pursuit of its interests through the*
        *secondary school curriculum 181*
     *An historical explanation for the Church's great influence*
        *over the secondary school curriculum 182*
     *Changes since 1962 186*


**PART VI**
**Teachers and pupils**                                                                          193

12   The symbiotic embrace: American Indians,
     white educators and the school, 1820s–1920s                                                 195
     MICHAEL C. COLEMAN

13   Classroom teachers and educational change 1876–1996                                         214
     PHILIP GARDNER

     *Three generations of teachers 214*
     *Classrooms and pedagogies 216*
     *Practical autonomy 218*
     *Post-war change 220*
     *The second-generation legacy 223*
     *New expectations 224*
     *Interviewees 227*


**PART VII**
**Education, work and the economy**                                                              231

14   Entering the world of work: the transition from youth to
     adulthood in modern European society                                                        233
     JOHN SPRINGHALL

15   Politicians and economic panic                                                              246
     ALISON WOLF

     *Introduction 246*
     *The current panic: players and panaceas 246*
     *Education and the CBI 251*
     *An older panic: the findings of the Samuelson Report 255*
     *The 1880s and the 1980s: why the same – and why so*
        *different? 259*

# HISTORY OF EDUCATION

Gary McCulloch

There are surprisingly few collections of previously published work in the history of education, and this Reader is an attempt to help fill this gap in the field. Yet there is so much work that has been published in this area that the task of selection is almost overwhelming. It is also a major responsibility, since the very act of selecting some, and therefore also of excluding the majority, serves to reify the field and to define it in a particular way for the future. In this editorial introduction, I will seek to explain the criteria on which the collection is based, and to discuss its potential role as a resource for students and researchers.

One of the rare examples of such a collection to have been produced in Britain was that of P.W. Musgrave, published in 1970 and accepted as a text book at the newly established Open University.[1] This work included twenty-two pieces by a range of authors, all previously published over the preceding 20 years. These were focused mainly on education in England, although a number developed a broader treatment or embraced a comparative dimension. The framework of the collection consisted of four general sections into which the contributions were allocated: definitions of the child and of education, education in society, the relationship between education and other social institutions, and the organisation of education. Even this is not wholly a precedent for the current collection, since it was explicitly an attempt to draw together sociology and history in the study of educational and social change. Moreover, Musgrave made it clear that he had a specific agenda to promote a theoretical model to explain the historical development of the educational system in England, based on changing definitions that have, at different times, indicated the forces at work in the sphere of education.

A more recent example is the four-volume collection of work in the history of education edited by Roy Lowe.[2] This comprised 111 contributions to the field, mainly though not all originally published in article form, published between 1957 and 2000, and totalling some 2146 pages of text. The separate volumes dealt with historiographical debates about the nature of the field, education in its social context, studies in teaching and learning, and a range of different national education systems. It was a genuinely international collection, although two-thirds of the items included were focused either on the United Kingdom (mainly England), or on the United States of America. Lowe's introduction to this collection reflected his underlying view that the field of history of education had experienced 'little short of a revolution' since the 1960s,[3] and he represented it accordingly in his selection, although again in particular ways that might be open to some debate.[4]

These earlier works offer some sense of the challenges and opportunities that await the present volume. Like Musgrave, I will concentrate principally on Britain, although with more emphasis on comparisons and contrasts between England, Scotland, Wales and Ireland. The selection also reflects the broader international and comparative context of the history of education in Britain. In addition, it evokes the nature of international influences, often reciprocated as between Britain and the rest of the world. A few of the chapters chosen examine broad issues in interesting ways with a focus on developments outside Britain. Nonetheless, I would not claim that this collection aspires to represent the global field as was open to Lowe's much larger selection. Like Musgrave also, I have concentrated mainly on the scholarship of the past 20 years, and especially of the past decade, to reflect recent and continuing debates in the field. The present collection seeks therefore to provide a complementary resource to Lowe's massive production, more limited and modest in scope but by the same token more convenient and accessible for students and researchers. For the same reason, I have tried to avoid selecting the same chapters as those in Lowe's work, which are already available for study both there and in their original forms. My ability to achieve this says much about the quality of a large amount of published work in this field, and there are many other chapters that I should also have liked to include, and I am sorry that I could not.

The selections in this Reader also reflect, as they are bound to do, my own personal development and professional interests as a historian of education over the past 25 years. My own research has been especially about secondary education, about the school curriculum, about education policy change, and about teachers; these topics are well represented in the following chapters. I have taught and researched in this field mainly in Britain, but also for a number of years in New Zealand, where I learned not only to appreciate the educational history of another country, and to relate national developments to broader international and global changes, but also to understand Britain's educational history in different ways. I have also been the Editor of the international journal *History of Education*, from 1996 until 2003, and this has further enhanced my awareness of new developments in the field. In particular, I have been increasingly conscious of theoretical and methodological debates in the history of education, and I expect that this is also evident in the present work. This is not to say I agree fully with the interpretations and treatments of the chapters that I have included in this Reader. Nevertheless, I would regard each of them as representing significant contributions to the history of education. All of them have interesting things to say and to add to our understanding. Together, they constitute an impressive range of important contributions to the field of a kind that has rarely been assembled together in a single volume.

The current selection, then, is but one starting point to an understanding of the history of education. If it has a straightforward rationale, it is to explore relationships between education and the configurations of society as these have played themselves out over time. This indeed has been the prime avowed purpose of historical studies in education for at least the past generation, in Britain as in many other countries around the world. Until the 1960s, the main thrust of published accounts in the history of education was to celebrate the growth and spread of national education systems as a testament to social improvement and economic prosperity. Since that time, as criticisms of the nature and effects of schooling have become increasingly marked, so historians of education have tended to dwell on the problematic aspects of the relationship between education and the wider society. Revisionist, generally Marxist critiques that vilified schooling for its alleged role in reproducing social class control were highly fashionable in the 1960s and 1970s. Towards the end of the twentieth century and into the twenty-first, a number of different aspects in the relationship between education and society have emerged in historical writings. These have often been more complex and in many ways more ambiguous, and arguably more interesting, than either the earlier liberal–progressive celebrations or the more recent vogue for Marxist critique.[5]

In Britain, for example, the late Brian Simon led the way in the 1960s in refashioning historical studies of education. He complained that 'It is the present tendency to review the past development of the English educational system, and of particular institutions within it, as if this took place by its own momentum rather than in relation to changing social pressures and needs.' The usual consequence was, according to Simon, 'a somewhat indigestible mass of dates and facts, orders and Acts'. By contrast, Simon argued, attention should be given to education as a 'social function', with primary importance in every society. He continued:

> It should be one of the main tasks of historical study to trace the development of education in this sense, to try to assess the function it has fulfilled at different stages of social development and so to reach a deeper understanding of the function it fulfils today.[6]

Nearly 30 years later, indeed, Simon could still insist that 'A crucial issue to which historical study can and should make a direct contribution, is that of the relation between educational and social change.'[7]

Simon was not alone in this preoccupation with social change. To the leading social historian Asa Briggs, writing in the early 1970s, the history of education should be regarded as 'part of the wider study of the history of society, social history broadly interpreted with the politics, the economics and, it is necessary to add, the religion put in'.[8] This in itself indicated a number of divergent approaches. The potential for complexity and argument was further adumbrated by another major figure in the field, Harold Silver, who noted that the history of education had become increasingly complicated by the recognition of relationships with other social phenomena:

> An older history of institutions and of ideas has become subject to an awareness of the ambiguous or controversial nature of historical interpretations in other and related fields – including economic history, the history of political institutions and ideologies, the history of class formation, social welfare and reform.[9]

The outcomes of these developments in the history of education were themselves open to debate. On the one hand, Lowe could suggest that,

> In recent years, History of Education has become clearly identified as a full and proper element in the study of history more generally, with a central role to play in the development of social, economic and political history, and this development can be only for the good.[10]

Crook and Aldrich, also British historians of education, similarly insisted that 'British history of education entered the twenty-first century in a relatively strong position.'[11] On the other hand, some observers of the field are more critical of its development. For example, Jurgen Herbst has stressed that in his view the 'revolution' launched in the 1960s has now run its course, to such an extent indeed that it has become stale and repetitive, with 'little genuine fresh input'. According to Herbst,

> Most writings tend to fill gaps in the record or bring to our attention groups or issues that have been overlooked in the past.... We endlessly repeat old mantras – class, race and gender being the one [*sic*] most often heard – but we are no longer sure just where and how we are to apply them.[12]

Another critic, Kevin Brehony, contends that insufficient attention has been given to social theory, in particular postmodernism.[13] Marc Depaepe, a senior figure in the European field, has directed particular criticism at historiographical trends in Britain.[14] Further concerns have been raised by David Vincent, a leading historian of literacy, who claims that in Britain, and perhaps to a lesser extent in North America, the history of education has 'almost collapsed as a subdiscipline'.[15] This Reader, personal and selective though it is, should afford some opportunity at least for readers to assess the state of the art and its current level of health.

I have chosen to define education broadly for the purposes of this work; that is, to include not only national systems of schooling and formal educational institutions for children and young people, but also more informal processes and practices throughout life and society. Educational systems for the mass of the population, organised by national states, became widespread during the nineteenth century. As Pavla Miller has observed, 'Sometimes earlier, sometimes later, but above all in the last third of the nineteenth century, systems of mass compulsory schooling were established in most countries of the Western world.'[16] Miller points out that between 1869 and 1882, schooling was made compulsory in Ontario, British Columbia and Manitoba in Canada, in 14 American states, in Victoria, South Australia, Western Australia and New South Wales in Australia, in New Zealand, Scotland, the 15 crown lands of the Austrian Empire, in the Netherlands, Switzerland, France and England. Many of these represented a break with previous practice and expectations, and in particular

> an international acceptance of the rational, compulsory-schooling model, a commitment of substantial proportions of public funds to the schooling enterprise and, over three or four decades (a brief period in historical terms), irreversible breakthroughs in the actual enforcement of what came to be understood as the one model of efficient schooling.[17]

It is a major task to assess the causes, characteristics and outcomes of these systems of schooling, and a great deal of energy has been expended in attempting to do so. Embracing a broad range of other educational processes and practices in addition to this is a most ambitious venture. Such was the intention of the American historian Bernard Bailyn, who defined education for his purposes as comprising 'the entire process by which a culture transmits itself across the generations'.[18] Another American, Lawrence Cremin, declared in similar style that education involved 'the deliberate, systematic, and sustained effort to transmit or evoke knowledge, attitudes, values, skills, and sensibilities'.[19] Indeed, in such work, schooling can come to appear to be of lesser significance than the many different institutions and processes that have developed with such properties over the years.[20]

There are two social institutions especially that challenge modern mass schooling in terms of their significance for an understanding of the history of education. The first of these is the family, an agency that has had primary responsibility for education in most societies and which continues to assert a major role. The changing nature of the family over many centuries has had an important bearing on this key educational function.[21] So too, for example, have underlying shifts in gender dynamics that have affected the relative positions of mothers and fathers as parents, and of sisters and brothers as future providers.[22] The second is the church, whether in societies where particular forms of devotion and religious practice are the accepted norm, or in periods when religious controversy has flared into social conflict, or at times when particular denominations or religions promote distinctive outlooks on faith or political action.[23]

This broad interpretation of the history of education, to include a wide range of institutions and processes besides those that have characterised modern systems of schooling, also carries implications for the potential time frame for historical study in this area. A concentration on schooling might suggest an exclusive focus on the past two centuries, with further backward glances to determine the longer term origins of these national systems. A more extended definition of education implies some deeper consideration of educational and social changes over many centuries. The scholarship of the past 20 years has tended to neglect these earlier epochs. In practice, the present collection stretches back to the invention of the modern printing press in mid-fifteenth-century Europe, and the Renaissance and Reformation of the sixteenth century. In some ways, these major developments form a helpful starting point for an understanding of modern ideals and practices of education. Lawrence Stone's pioneering essay documented the significance of what he described as an 'educational revolution' in sixteenth-century England.[24] More recently, Briggs and Burke have presented a wide-ranging survey of the technological developments that have marked the social history of the media from the Gutenberg Revolution to the invention of the Internet, while Burke has separately explored the social history of knowledge itself in the early-modern period to the mid-eighteenth century.[25]

Nevertheless, in many respects even this expanded conception of the history of education is insufficient. Even a timespan of six centuries cannot provide adequate scope for a full historical understanding of education. The medieval period might also be taken more fully into account especially for an appreciation of the origins of universities, or for an awareness of how Latin retained such a potent role. For example, Nicholas Orme has persuasively discussed the continuing significance of changes in medieval education.[26] Indeed, according to Orme, 'the history of education since 1500 has been, in one sense, simply the widening of this basis' as was developed in the medieval period.[27] Moreover, while Philippe Aries' formulations of the ideals of childhood have long been disputed and superseded, they did point to key developments affecting education prior to the Renaissance.[28] Earlier phases and debates in education also warrant detailed attention. Educational developments in ancient Greece and Rome were of fundamental importance in originating many of the ideas and practices of later centuries.[29] Global influences in education have also been active for thousands of years, for example in the ideals of traditional China which have found echoes and imitators in the British context and elsewhere.[30]

The 17 chapters selected for inclusion in this Reader are organised into eight distinct sections, each section representing a key theme in recent and contemporary writing in the history of education. The first relates to higher education, which itself has a long history originating in antiquity.[31] A number of institutions of higher education in different parts of the world have existed for several centuries, including, in the British context, the universities of Oxford and Cambridge (together often described as Oxbridge), and also Edinburgh. In a publication that marked the six hundredth anniversary of the foundation of Edinburgh University, the social historian Lawrence Stone surveyed the changing aims and functions of universities in relation to the wider social and historical context over hundreds of years (Chapter 1). In doing so, he also effectively points out the major significance of the State, the Church and parents in the history of education. Moreover, the similarities and differences of specific institutions of higher education over the long term are investigated in depth. By comparison, Carol Dyhouse's work (Chapter 2) focuses on a brief period, from 1918 until 1939, to appraise the social backgrounds of students at English universities during this time, and how they were able to finance their study. This in itself reflects a historical shift from elite higher education, reserved for a select few, to mass higher education, intended to provide for those deemed capable of benefiting from it due to individual merit. The full implications of this fundamental shift continue to be debated in the twenty-first century.

Part II examines informal agencies of education. The first contribution, by Harvey Graff, considers the historical characteristics of literacy, with particular reference to the Renaissance (Chapter 3). This chapter indicates a number of key features of literacy that have been explored further in more recent research, although all too rarely in the integrated fashion or with the scope achieved here by Graff.[32] Second, Stephanie Spencer explores the ways in which teenage girls in England in the 1950s understood the city, especially through magazines and novels, as a means of providing informal education into adulthood (Chapter 4). In both these cases, although they deal with very different historical and social contexts, key issues are raised and developed about the extent to which schools and schooling have interacted with other, more informal institutions and processes in the socialisation of the young.

In Part III, the modern development of national schooling systems assumes centre stage. Historians in many different countries have expended a great deal of attention on trying to explain this major phenomenon. The Marxist writings of the 1960s and 1970s emphasised the potential role of schooling in maintaining social control over an unruly and potentially dangerous urban working-class population.[33] Some more recent treatments have concentrated on the changing requirements of modern nation states. Andy Green, for example, has argued that the formation of national systems of schooling took place first and fastest in those countries where the process of state formation was most intensive, and he also relates this to the nature of social class processes in different countries. According to Green, in the British case, it was the relative weakness of the State that was crucial in ensuring that the education system was developed later than elsewhere, for example in France, Prussia and the United States, and with an emphasis on diversity and independence. On this view, the outcome was not only that Britain became the 'last to create a national education system', but also that it 'never quite completed the job'.[34]

The chapters selected here pursue these important themes further in helping to understand the emergence and development of modern systems of schooling. Pavla Miller and Ian Davey develop connections between the State and class issues, on the one hand, with gender relationships and the family (Chapter 5). They argue that a crisis of patriarchy in Western societies in the eighteenth and nineteenth centuries was no less responsible than the crisis of social class relations for the rise of compulsory schooling. This historical interpretation raises important issues about the role of gender and age relationships, and also suggests new questions about the involvement of the Church.[35] Andy Green investigates the implications of state formation for the development of technical education, with a particular focus on nineteenth-century England and France (Chapter 6). In this chapter, Green also provides an important critique of the thesis proposed by historians such as Martin Wiener, who have argued that Britain's relative economic decline since the nineteenth century has been principally due to an anti-industrial culture, rooted in turn in its educational values and practices.[36] Finally, Jane Martin examines the development of the London School Board, in its time the largest educational authority in the world, from its inception under the Elementary Education Act of 1870 until it was dismantled following the Education Act of 1902 (Chapter 7). In particular, Martin evaluates the role of women who were elected to serve on the London School Board, and relates their work to local government and national politics and policy issues.

Part IV of this Reader provides scope for general considerations as to how education has related over time to social change and social inequality. Brian Simon assesses the extent to which education can change society, recognising that even where the authorities have sought to use education in a particular way, the outcomes may be unexpected and even opposite to those that were intended (Chapter 9). Roy Lowe examines how far formal education systems have effectively promoted social mobility by identifying a meritocracy and communicating knowledge and skills that generate economic skills leading to social transformation (Chapter 10). Lowe contends that the key historical tendency of schooling has been towards the suppression of social mobility and the intergenerational defence of social and economic advantage. Much work has elaborated further on this theme, including William Marsden's detailed discussions of the influence of the social geography of urban communities in promoting educational inequality.[37] Gary McCulloch has also demonstrated the long-term social effects of the structural divide between 'public' and 'private' education in the English context.[38]

In Part V, we witness some of the ways in which the curriculum or content of education, as distinct from the administration of institutions and systems, has been a significant factor in the history of education. A number of scholars, such as Ivor Goodson and Barry Franklin, have emphasised the potential importance of curriculum history.[39] The connections between the curriculum and the promotion of educational 'standards', especially through testing and examinations, have also come under close scrutiny.[40] Similarly, the role of textbooks in representing the knowledge and values of different subjects and of the curriculum as a whole has attracted historical attention.[41] Moreover, historians have been able to document how the cultural values embodied in the curriculum have often served to resist and undermine major initiatives in educational policy reform.[42] In the present collection, J.A. Mangan demonstrates the processes by which the curricular values and practices of the English public (independent) schools were transmitted to India, for instance in Mayo College, Bombay (Chapter 10). The values of the 'hidden' or moral curriculum are no less significant than the distinctions represented in the formal school timetable, as is also evident in Mangan's other writings.[43] Thomas O'Donoghue follows this with an examination of the nature and scope of the influence of the Catholic Church over the secondary school curriculum in Ireland, in the four decades after its independence from Britain, from 1922 until 1962 (Chapter 11).

One basic issue that has concerned historians of education increasingly over the past decade is the experience of educational interactions in the classroom. How have pupils learned or failed to learn their lessons? How have teachers sought to pass on their knowledge, and through what pedagogical principles? These concerns have generated a growing interest in the social history of teachers and pupils in their schools and classrooms,[44] and this is reflected especially in Part VI of the present Reader. First, Michael Coleman inspects the development of schooling for native Americans in the United States from the 1820s to the 1920s, and finds an interactive, symbiotic relationship between the white educators and the pupils in the schools (Chapter 12). He acknowledges the controls imposed on the schools, but attempts also to understand the support shown by parents and pupils for the schools, and the character of the pupil culture. Second, Philip Gardner traces the changes that have affected school teachers in England and Wales from 1876 until 1996 (Chapter 13). He examines in particular teachers' changing understanding of their own professionalism, especially in terms of their autonomy in the classroom and their relationship with parents and the State over this time.[45]

Preparation for the world of work has been a prime motive for the growth of systems of apprenticeship as well as for the development of modern schooling.[46] Part VII of this Reader focuses on the vocational and economic purposes of education and the assumptions that underlie them. John Springhall discusses occupational choices and the transition from youth to adulthood in modern European societies, with particular reference to Germany and Britain (Chapter 14). Alison Wolf reviews the increasing emphasis that has been placed on the economic relevance of schooling towards the end of the twentieth century, and attempts to draw comparisons and contrasts with the educational policies of the late nineteenth century (Chapter 15). She identifies the role of different interest groups in influencing such policies, relating their involvement to the detailed findings of policy reports in different contexts, including the report of the British Confederation of British Industries (CBI), *Towards a Skills Revolution* (1989), and the Samuelson reports on technical instruction in the 1880s.

Finally, this Reader addresses the character of national traditions as incarnated in their educational systems, practices and values. According to Hobsbawm and Ranger, traditions are invented or constructed for specific social and political purposes.[47] A number of historians have examined the implications of this insight in relation to educational traditions, especially those developed in specific national contexts. Robert Anderson, for example, has investigated in depth the formation of an egalitarian Scottish myth, while other work has recently begun to untangle the characteristics of the English tradition of education.[48] For the purposes of the present collection, Gareth Elwyn Jones' historical perspective of education in Wales identifies the distinctive features of an educational culture and tradition that has often been much less well recognised than either its English or Scottish counterparts (Chapter 16). Finally, Ian Grosvenor analyses the meanings of four texts to comprehend and query the nature of national identity in the British context and its implications for education in the future (Chapter 17).

The chapters included in this collection therefore illustrate many of the key substantive issues in the history of education at the present time. What is more, they also represent a wide range of methodological approaches that may well be of interest to those who wish to develop research of their own in this area of study, or to consider possible strategies to enhance their research. Recent publications have begun to explore in depth the advantages and limitations of different methods in the history of education. For instance, McCulloch and Richardson have surveyed the general field of historical research with respect to education, and McCulloch has developed a further critical guide to the use of documentary research in education, history and the social sciences.[49] The chapters in the present collection may be used to illustrate the discussion provided in these works. All of the chapters selected draw on a range of documents from the period being studied to develop their arguments. In addition, some of these chapters make particular use of specific kinds of sources and methods to develop their findings. For example, Dyhouse (Chapter 2) provides a detailed study of questionnaires; Spencer and Gardner (Chapters 4, 13) discussion of interviews; Spencer (Chapter 4) an appraisal of novels; Martin and Coleman (Chapters 7, 12) reviews of autobiographies; and Wolf (Chapter 15) an investigation of policy reports. Several also make use of archives of different kinds, public and institutional, sometimes on their own but often in combination with other types of source.

What is offered here therefore is a rich mix of recent writings in the history of education, a cross-section of work that is nationally based, comparative, international and intercultural, informed by a wide range of theoretical perspectives, concerned with several types of problems, and based upon a large number of historical sources and research strategies. Overall, they indicate continuing engagement on the part of historians of education with major issues in education that should be of use to historians, educators and social scientists in general, and will stimulate renewed interest in developing the field further in years to come.

## Notes

1  P.W. Musgrave (ed.), *Sociology, History and Education: A Reader*, Methuen, London, 1970.
2  Roy Lowe (ed.), *History of Education: Major Themes*, RoutledgeFalmer, London, 2000.
3  Ibid., vol. I, p. xlii.
4  See Gary McCulloch, review of Lowe (ed.), *History of Education: Major Themes*, in *History of Education*, 31/3 (2002), pp. 303–7, for a brief discussion of these issues.
5  For a general discussion of these trends, see Gary McCulloch and William Richardson, *Historical Research in Educational Settings*, Open University Press, Buckingham, 2000, especially Chapter 3.
6  Brian Simon, 'The history of education', in J.W. Tibble (ed.), *The Study Of Education*, RKP, London, 1966, p. 91.
7  Brian Simon, 'The history of education: its importance for understanding', in B. Simon (ed.), *The State and Educational Change: Essays in the History of Education and Pedagogy*, Lawrence and Wishart, London, 1994, p. 9.
8  Asa Briggs, 'The study of the history of education', *History of Education*, 1/1 (1972), p. 5.
9  Harold Silver, *Education as History: Interpreting Nineteenth- and Twentieth-Century Education*, Methuen, London, 1983, pp. 7–8.
10  Roy Lowe, 'Writing the history of education', in Lowe (ed.), *History of Education: Major Themes*, vol. I, p. xlii.
11  D. Crook and R. Aldrich, 'Introduction', in D. Crook and R. Aldrich (eds), *History of Education for the Twenty-first Century*, Institute of Education, London, 2000, p. x.
12  Jurgen Herbst, 'The history of education: state of the art at the turn of the century in Europe and North America', *Paedagogica Historica*, 35/3 (1999), p. 739.
13  Kevin Brehony, review of T.S. Popkewitz, B. Franklin and M. Pereyra (eds), *Cultural History and Education: Critical Essays on Knowledge and Schooling*, RoutledgeFalmer, London, 2001, in *History of Education*, 32/4 (2003), pp. 441–3.
14  Marc Depaepe, 'What kinds of history of education may we expect for the 21st century? Some comments on four recent Readers in the field', *Paedagogica Historica*, 39/1–2 (2003), pp. 187–98.
15  David Vincent, 'The progress of literacy', *Victorian Studies*, 45/3 (2003), pp. 419–20.
16  Pavla Miller, 'Historiography of compulsory schooling: what is the problem?', *History of Education*, 18/2 (1989), p. 123.
17  Ibid.
18  Bernard Bailyn, *Education in the Forming of American Society*, University of North Carolina Press, Waterloo, Ontario, 1960, p. ix.
19  Lawrence Cremin, *American Education: The Colonial Experience, 1607–1783*, Harper & Row, New York, 1970.

20  See for example, Lawrence Cremin, *American Education: The Metropolitan Experience, 1876–1980*, Harper & Row, New York, 1988.

21  See for example, Lawrence Stone, *The Family, Sex and Marriage in England 1500–1800*, Weidenfeld and Nicolson, London, 1977; and Linda Pollock, *Forgotten Children: Parent–Child Relations from 1500 to 1900*, Cambridge University Press, Cambridge, 1990.

22  Kenneth Charlton, ' "Not publike onely but also private and domesticall": mothers and familial education in pre-industrial England', *History of Education*, 17/1 (1988), pp. 1–20; and Richard Aldrich, 'Family history and the history of the family', in R. Aldrich (ed.), *Public or Private Education? Lessons from History*, RoutledgeFalmer, London, 2004, pp. 127–43.

23  See for example, V.A. McClelland (ed.), *The Churches and Education*, History of Education Society, Leicester, 1984; and John Coolahan, Richard Aldrich and Frank Simon (eds), *Faiths and Education: Historical and Comparative Perspectives*, Paedagogica Historica supplementary series vol. V, Gent C.S.H.P., Belgium, 1999.

24  Lawrence Stone, 'The educational revolution in England, 1560–1640', *Past and Present*, 29 (1964), pp. 41–80.

25  A. Briggs and P. Burke, *A Social History of the Media: From Gutenberg to the Internet*, Polity, Cambridge, 2002; P. Burke, *A Social History of Knowledge: From Gutenberg to Diderot*, Polity, Cambridge, 2000. See also Rosemary O'Day, *Education and Society 1500–1800: The Social Foundations of Education in Early Modern Britain*, Longman, London, 1982; and Helen Jewell, *Education in Early Modern England*, Longman, London, 1998.

26  See for example, Nicholas Orme, *From Childhood to Chivalry: The Education of the English Kings and Aristocracy, 1066–1531*, Methuen, London, 1984; and Nicholas Orme, *Education and Society in Medieval England*, Hambledon Press, London, 1989. See also Jo Ann Hoeppner Moran, *The Growth of English Schooling 1340–1548: Learning, Literacy, and Laicization in Pre-Reformation York Diocese*, Princeton University Press, Princeton, 1985; and Michael van Cleave Alexander, *The Growth of English Education 1348–1648: A Social and Cultural History*, Pennsylvania State University Press, London, 1990.

27  Orme, *From Childhood to Chivalry*, p. 238.

28  Philippe Aries, *Centuries of Childhood*, Penguin, London, 1960.

29  On education in ancient Greece and Rome, see for example, H.I. Marrou, *A History of Education in Antiquity*, Sheed and Ward, London, 1956; Kenneth J. Freeman, *Schools of Hellas: An Essay on the Practice and Theory of Ancient Greek Education from 600 to 300 BC*, Macmillan, London, 1907; Frederick A.G. Beck, *Greek Education, 450–350 BC*, Methuen, London, 1964; Stanley Bonner, *Education in Ancient Rome: From the Elder Cato to the younger Pliny*, Methuen, London, 1977.

30  See for example, Thomas H.C. Lee, 'Introduction: Ideals and major themes in Chinese education', in T.H.C. Lee (ed.), *Education in Traditional China: A History*, Brill, Leiden, 2000, pp. 1–29; Rupert Wilkinson, *The Prefects: British Leadership and the Public School Tradition. A Comparative Study in the Making of Rulers*, Oxford University Press, London, 1964; and Margaret Mehl, 'Chinese learning (*kangaku*) in Meiji Japan (1868–1912)', in *History*, vol. 85, no. 277 (2000), pp. 48–66.

31  See for example, Christopher J. Lucas, *American Higher Education: A History*, St Martin's Griffin, New York, 1994.

32  For other major contributions to the history of literacy, see for example, Lawrence Stone, 'Literacy and education in England, 1640–1900', *Past and Present*, 42 (1969), pp. 69–139; David Vincent, *Literacy and Popular Culture: England 1750–1914*, Cambridge University Press, Cambridge, 1989; *History of Education Quarterly*, 30/4 (1990), special issue on the history of literacy; Carl Kaestle *et al.*, *Literacy in the United States: Readers and Reading since 1880*, Yale University Press, New Haven, 1991; and David Vincent, 'The progress of literacy', *Victorian Studies*, 45/3 (2003), pp. 405–31.

33  See for example, in the United States, Michael Katz, *The Irony of Early School Reform*, Harvard University Press, Cambridge, MA, 1968; and in Britain, Richard Johnson, 'Educational policy and social control in early Victorian England', *Past and Present*, 49 (1970), pp. 96–119. A key paper by David Tyack, 'Ways of seeing: an essay on the history of compulsory schooling', *Harvard Educational Review*, 48/3 (1976), pp. 355–89, discusses competing explanations for the rise of compulsory schooling with particular reference to the American case.

34 Andy Green, *Education and State Formation: The Rise of Education Systems in England, France and the USA*, St Martin's Press, New York, 1989, p. 316. See also Andy Green, 'Education and state formation revisited', special combined issue of *Historical Studies in Education*, 6/3 (1994) and *History of Education Review*, 23/3 (1994), pp. 1–17; and Andy Green, *Education, Globalisation and the Nation State*, Macmillan, London, 1997. For further reflections on the developing influence of the State in education in the British context, see also for example, Clyde Chitty, 'The changing role of the state in education provision', *History of Education*, 21/1 (1992), pp. 1–13.

35 See also for example, Ian Davey, 'Capitalism, patriarchy and the origins of modern schooling', *History of Education Review*, 16/2 (1987), pp. 1–12.

36 Martin Wiener, *English Culture and the Decline of the Industrial Spirit, 1850–1980*, Cambridge University Press, Cambridge, 1981.

37 W.E. Marsden, 'Education and the social geography of nineteenth-century towns and cities', in D. Reeder (ed.), *Urban Education in the Nineteenth Century*, Taylor & Francis Ltd, London, 1977, pp. 49–73; W.E. Marsden, *Unequal Educational Provision in England and Wales: The Nineteenth-Century Roots*, Woburn, London, 1987; and W.E. Marsden, 'Social stratification and nineteenth century English urban education', in R.K. Goodenow and W.E. Marsden (eds), *The City and Education in Four Nations*, Cambridge University Press, Cambridge, 1992, pp. 111–28. See also for example, Gary McCulloch, 'Constructing the community: secondary schools and their neighbourhoods in twentieth century Auckland', *Australian Journal of Education*, 36/2 (1992), pp. 143–56.

38 Gary McCulloch, 'From incorporation to privatisation: public and private secondary education in twentieth-century England', in R. Aldrich (ed.), *Public and Private Education: Lessons from History*, RoutledgeFalmer, London, 2004, pp. 53–72.

39 Ivor Goodson, *International Perspectives in Curriculum History*, Croom Helm, London, 1987; Barry Franklin, 'Review essay: the state of curriculum history', *History of Education*, 28/4 (1999), pp. 459–76.

40 For example, Richard Aldrich, 'Educational standards in historical perspective', in *Proceedings of the British Academy*, 102 (2000), pp. 39–56.

41 For example, Chris Stray, 'Paradigms regained: towards a historical sociology of the textbook', *Journal of Curriculum Studies*, 26/1 (1994), pp. 1–29; and Stuart Foster, 'The struggle for American identity: treatment of ethnic groups in United States history textbooks', *History of Education*, 28/3 (1999), pp. 251–78.

42 See for example, William Reid, 'Strange curricula: origins and development of the institutional categories of schooling', *Journal of Curriculum Studies*, 22/3 (1990), pp. 203–16; David Tyack and Larry Cuban, *Tinkering Toward Utopia*, Harvard University Press, MA, 1995; and Ron Brooks, 'In a world set apart: the Dalton dynasty at King Alfred School, 1920–62', *History of Education*, 27/4 (1998), pp. 421–40.

43 For example, J.A. Mangan, *Athleticism in the Victorian and Edwardian Public School*, Falmer, London, 1986; and J.A. Mangan and J. Walvin (eds), *Manliness and Morality: Middle-Class Masculinity in Britain and America, 1800–1940*, Manchester University Press, Manchester, 1987.

44 See for example, Kate Rousmaniere, Ian Grosvenor and Martin Lawn (eds), *Silences and Images: The Social History of the Classroom*, Peter Lang, London, 1999; Jonathan Rose, 'Willingly to school: the working-class response to elementary education in Britain, 1875–1918', *Journal of British Studies*, 32/2 (1993), pp. 114–38; and Philip Gardner, 'The giant at the front: young teachers and corporal punishment in inter-war elementary schools', *History of Education*, 25/2 (1996), pp. 141–63.

45 This theme is developed further in, for example, Gary McCulloch, Gill Helsby and Peter Knight, *The Politics of Professionalism: Teachers and the Curriculum*, Continuum, London, 2000; and Peter Cunningham and Philip Gardner, *Becoming Teachers: Texts and Testimonies 1907–1950*, Woburn, London, 2004.

46 See for example, Keith Snell, 'The apprenticeship system in British history: the fragmentation of a cultural institution', *History of Education*, 25/4 (1996), pp. 303–21.

47 Eric Hobsbawm and Terence Ranger (eds), *The Invention of Tradition*, Cambridge University Press, Cambridge, 1983.

48 See Robert Anderson, *Educational Opportunity in Victorian Scotland: Schools and Universities*, Oxford University Press, London, 1983; see also Robert Anderson, 'The idea of the secondary school in nineteenth century Europe', *Paedagogica Historica*,

40/1–2 (2004), pp. 93–106; Gary McCulloch and Colin McCaig, 'Reinventing the past: the case of the English tradition of education', *British Journal of Educational Studies*, 50/2 (2002), pp. 238–53.

49 Gary McCulloch and William Richardson, *Historical Research in Educational Settings*, Open University Press, Buckingham, 2000; and Gary McCulloch, *Documentary Research in Education, History and the Social Sciences*, RoutledgeFalmer, London, 2004.

# PART I

# HIGHER EDUCATION

## CHAPTER 1

# SOCIAL CONTROL AND INTELLECTUAL EXCELLENCE

## Oxbridge and Edinburgh (1560–1983)

### Lawrence Stone

In N. Phillipson (ed.) *Universities, Society and the Future (1983)*, Edinburgh: Edinburgh University Press, pp. 3–30

Dr. Kettle, the vigilant President of Trinity College, Oxford, said that the great arcanum of government... was to keep down juvenile impetuosity.

(Aubrey, 1972)

## Introduction: the functions of a university

Presidents, Vice-Chancellors and Principals of major universities usually tell the world that the institutions over which they preside have two functions and only two: first to advance the frontiers of knowledge by the pursuit of original research; and second, to convey a prescribed body of knowledge to undergraduates either in the form of a so-called liberal arts and sciences curriculum for general educational development, or specialised training for a particular profession or occupation. In fact until recently only the liberal arts aspect of this prospectus has ever been a part of the official agenda.

The phrase 'liberal arts' is to us today something of a misnomer, since the word 'liberal' has fundamentally changed its meaning over the centuries. Today, by a liberal education we mean a study in breadth rather than depth, of a wide range of subjects, and a deliberate encouragement of autonomous thought and judgement. An open mind, in theory at least, is the end product of the liberal education of today.

Until very recently, however, the liberal arts and sciences served no such function. On the contrary, their purpose was careful indoctrination in right thinking, based on the study of a very narrow range of materials. For centuries, all knowledge was thought to be embodied in the classical texts, and all wisdom in them and the Bible. Innovation was therefore the last thing a university should be concerned with. At Cambridge in 1824, for example, the object was defined as turning out 'an annual supply of men whose minds are... impressed with what we hold to be the soundest principles of policy and religion'. Innovation was especially to be resisted in religion since 'the scheme of Revelation we think is closed' (Rothblatt, 1974: 292). All that was required, therefore, was to teach those old and established principles which were beyond the reach of argument. Thus the examination in ethics was dropped since it allowed too much scope for controversy.

In my own university, Princeton, in 1854 President MacLean in his inaugural address announced firmly 'we shall not aim at innovation. No chimerical experiments in education have ever had the least countenance here'. In fact, however, President MacLean was wrong, and was merely reflecting a conservative and didactic trend which had set in again in about 1800, after half a century in which Enlightenment ideology had opened a window to allow some fresh air into the stuffy and authoritarian atmosphere of the Renaissance university. In 1760, President Samuel Davies of Princeton had written:

> In the instruction of youth, care is to be taken to cherish a spirit of liberty and free enquiry; and not only to permit, but to encourage the right of private judgment, without presuming to dictate with an air of infallibility, or demanding an implicit assent to the decisions of the preceptor.
>
> (Schmidt, 1957; Princeton, 1978)

Thus over the centuries the self-image of the university has fluctuated wildly between that of an authoritarian dictator of established wisdom in religion, politics, philosophy, morals and all academic topics, to that of an intellectual liberator which has deliberately set out to encourage a spirit of free enquiry. The latter periods have, however, historically been few and fairly short.

Nor has learning always been the prime aim of university education in the past, which is why there were no regular and serious examinations before the late eighteenth century, and only about half the students took degrees. In the late seventeenth century, when John Locke wrote his highly popular and influential book on education, he defined as its first priorities the inculcation of virtue, wisdom, and good manners. 'I put learning last', he said (Locke, 1968). I hope I do not shock you when I say that I think Locke was right. These educational ideals are a far cry from the virtual abandonment at Oxbridge today of attempts to inculcate virtue, wisdom or good manners, and the intensive concentration on a single narrowly specialised field of study throughout a student's university career, in preparation for an examination in the very latest research minutiae on this single topic. In Scotland, something of the older ideal of a broad-based education still prevails, as indeed it does in America, although few faculty today would dare to admit to be attempting to inculcate virtue, wisdom or good manners.

If the patent functions of the university are therefore far from immutable and agreed upon, the latent ones are virtually ignored. A central – perhaps *the* central – one of these has been the difficult task of keeping adolescents out of mischief at their most impossible age, when they are most likely to run wild. These disciplinary problems are happily shifted by the parents to the university faculty and administration, who are supposed to act *in loco parentis*.

There are also other latent functions, often conflicting ones, which I will only touch on. One is to provide a new generation of elite with those skills and values deemed necessary for future leadership roles, and to allow these elite to make influential friends and contacts who will come in very useful in later life. In this respect, great universities are instruments of hierarchy and social stasis. On the other hand, they also serve to open up channels of upward social mobility for bright and ambitious sons of the poor, supported by scholarships; and also a shelter for the germination and fruition of new and possibly subversive ideas. I can think of no revolutionary ideology over the past 400 years, from sixteenth-century Puritanism to twentieth-century Terrorism, which has not begun and taken root in a university.

Another enduring latent function of the university has been to provide the undergraduate with access to a luxuriant and an exciting adolescent subculture. Success in sport, sex, social climbing or love has always counted more than academic success for the bulk of liberal arts students (Rothblatt, 1974). The faculty has seen only the surface of these deeper waters, and thus has partly misunderstood the significance of a university experience. Only for the most intelligent, dedicated and academically ambitious of students has class work been the central focus of his life, before the advent in the late nineteenth century of a new over-riding purpose, namely the acquisition of scientific or technological knowledge as a step towards a career.

My theme is an exploration of violent oscillations over time in the most prominent of the many latent functions, namely the enforcement of extremely strict social, moral, religious and intellectual controls. My argument is first that this function rose to dominate almost all others, both patent and latent, in the two older English Universities in the sixteenth and early seventeenth centuries; that it then collapsed from 1670 to 1770; that it rose again from the ashes in the nineteenth and early twentieth century; and collapsed once more in the late 1960s and 1970s. And second that there is a curious relationship between discipline and intellectual excellence. The problem is first to establish the facts and then deduce the causes. As I proceed, I propose to contrast developments in England with the conditions and evolution at Edinburgh, about which I know only what I can glean from secondary literature, and to draw some conclusions from the differences which emerge.

## The rise of the Oxbridge College tutorial system (1560–1660)

As is now well known, the three most striking social developments in English Universities during the period from 1560 to 1660 were the massive influx of students from middle or upper class background who were paying their own way and not planning on taking a degree; the residential concentration of this expanded undergraduate population within Colleges; and its subjection to close tutorial supervision (Curtis, 1959: 36; Stone, 1974: I, 34). By 1600, in theory, and perhaps in practice, no student any longer lived unsupervised in lodgings, and none was without a tutor.

The problem that faced the University authorities was how they, who were lower-middle class clergymen, usually in their twenties or thirties, were going to discipline the crowd of arrogant young gentlemen who were flocking in. The answer lies in the development of the Collegiate tutorial system in the Elizabethan period, and to see how it worked we should look at its principle features in its prime, say in about 1600. In theory, and to a considerable extent in practice, the tutorial system involved the subjection of the adolescent sons of wealthy laymen to a set of physical, moral, mental, religious, psychological and financial controls more intrusive than anything which had ever before been attempted in the West.

The system evolved from two sets of interacting causes, one external, the other internal. Let us start with the more important of the two, the external forces, and the principles which guided them.

First, of course, there was the overwhelming influence of religious faith in the late sixteenth century, and especially the universally-held doctrine of Original Sin. All men were sinners, and the only hope of avoiding sin was thought to be to remove all occasion for temptation. Above all this meant avoidance of idleness, which was almost universally regarded as the principal cause of sliding down the slippery slope. As Ben Jonson made Touchstone observe in 1605:

Of sloth comes pleasure, of pleasure comes riot,
Of riot comes whoring, of whoring comes spending,
Of spending comes want, of want comes theft,
Of theft comes hanging.

(Jonson, n.d.)

The best hope of avoiding such a declension, especially among sin-prone adolescent males, was thought to be hard academic work under the closest moral and religious supervision. The agent of such a discipline was to be a new breed of teacher, the college tutor of the late sixteenth century. Young college Fellows now suddenly found themselves with an important and exciting new role to play as the absolute masters of a handful of young adolescents. It was a role thrust upon them by the first of the external forces, namely the parents of wealthy elite children aiming at a secular career. The appointment of a tutor was a purely private contract between the parent and an individual Fellow for the supply of certain supervisory and educational services in return for a negotiated fee. Basically the parents wished to transfer to others the responsibilities and anxieties and annoyance of handling adolescents at their most truculent and turbulent age. This question of governance was of critical importance to parents, which explains their insistence upon the twin elements of social control: the college as a living place and the tutor as a disciplinarian. So far as the parents were concerned, a principal – perhaps the principal – duty of the tutor was to keep his pupil out of mischief. Thus in the early sixteenth century, a parent asked a college head 'Please find him a severe and grave tutor, who will keep him from excess and stimulate him to good letters' (Grosart, 1887; Pantin, 1972; Brasenose College (a)). Note that morals come first and learning second.

A father expected four things in return for the fee. First he expected the tutor closely to supervise his pupil's morals, and many of the richest and most influential parents insisted that the pupil actually sleep in the tutor's room so that he was under his eye both day and night. Thus in the late seventeenth century, John North, the son of Lord North, slept in his tutor's room (North, 1890). Second, he demanded that the tutor supervise his pupil's religious education. The tutors were responsible for seeing to it that their pupils regularly attended College chapel twice a day, that they studied the Scriptures, that they absorbed the contents of the sermons they heard, that they imbibed the appropriate doctrines of church government, and that they developed habits of regular private prayer. It was while about to start prayers in his tutor's room at Cambridge that young Simonds D'Ewes and his tutor Holdsworth noticed out of the window the first appearance of the great comet of 1618 – which no doubt put an end to prayers for that evening (Clarke, 1677; Marsden, 1851: 54; Thompson, 1900; Trinity College). Third, a parent expected a tutor to receive and spend every penny of his pupil's money (Penton, 1688; Edwards, 1899: 101; tutors' accounts for the expenditure of pupils in the archives of Christ's College, Clare College and St Catherine's College, Cambridge, and Brasenose College, Oxford).

Fourth, a parent expected the tutor to supervise the academic education of his pupil by prescribing reading and supervising preparations on an individual basis, quite apart from the lecturing facilities supplied by the College, which were primarily intended for those preparing for a degree. Nearly all the sons of wealthy laity, however, had no intention of taking a degree, and therefore needed personal attention for designing a more general curriculum better suited to their needs (Looney, 1981).

An early-seventeenth-century student would therefore spend a good part of every day in his tutor's chamber. When David Baker came up to Oxford in 1590, he 'daily resorted to his tutor's chamber for teaching, and there remained almost all the day's space, save only for mealtimes'. In the 1620s and 1630s, Joseph Mead at Christ's gave daily lectures plus private instructions to his many pupils, and saw them individually every evening to check their progress (Mede, 1664; Baker, 1933; Curtis, 1959: 108).

The second set of external forces were the State and the Church. The State intervened mainly through the Chancellor, who was always a leading political figure at Court. In 1567 the Cambridge Chancellor, Sir William Cecil, warned the University to tighten up its discipline and to repress 'the lightness and disorder of your youth, as well in apparell as other behaviour'. As a spur to action, he used a new argument, that the flow of endowment income from the rich depended on the good reputation of the University and the Colleges as instruments for the strict control of morals and religion. Here was a new and important incentive behind the drive for discipline, that is the need to attract new endowment funds for scholarships, fellowships and building. What Cecil and the prospective donors wanted to encourage was learning combined with 'godliness, modesty, and the glad embracing of good orders' (Cooper, 1842–53: II, 230).

In 1570 at Cambridge and in 1636 in Oxford the State intervened directly in University affairs by issuing new Statutes which drastically modified their medieval constitutions. Power was shifted from the large number of young Regent Masters to a tight little oligarchy of the Vice-Chancellor and the College Heads, all of whom were in practice, if not in law, subject to appointment by the state through letters mandatory.

Nor did the State confine itself to these general constitutional issues, and sometimes its intervention in University affairs took bizarre forms, for example the action in 1542 of the Cambridge Chancellor, Bishop Gardiner. In his desperate efforts to prevent the spread of the new Erasmian pronunciation of Greek, he ordered that any student using it was to be publicly whipped before his fellow students in College. Emphasis on the external appearance of a student took on special significance as political tensions rose in the 1630s, and the new Oxford Statutes of 1636, written by the embattled Chancellor, Archbishop Laud, went out of their way to insist that part of a tutor's duties was the supervision of 'the dress, the boots, the wearing of hair, etc.' (Cooper, 1842–53: I, 76; Ward, 1845).

Religious indoctrination was a matter of particular concern to the State, which realised very well that if the country was to be effectively weaned from its traditional Catholicism, it could only be done by the production of a generation of zealously protestant clergymen, and of gentry patrons willing to provide them with church livings. The State and the Church saw the tutor and the College chapel as the two critical elements in a great missionary endeavour to mould the minds of the leaders of the new generation. The purging of the universities of papists, and the inculcation of the right religious ideas by tutors, were of central concern to the Elizabethan government and church. Judging by the shift in one generation of the English elite and clergy from Catholicism to Protestantism, this moulding process was highly effective. On the other hand, one can also plausibly argue that it was primarily the failure to stamp out Puritan ideas and practices among the tutors and in the chapels of the Colleges that prevented the unchallenged acceptance of the Anglican Church in England.

The University authorities were equally anxious to cooperate with parents, Church and State, to enforce discipline among the students, and also to internalise deference to superiors, not least to themselves. They were only too willing to cooperate in repressing vice and disorder. A classic, if rather odd, example of the trend is the Cambridge edict of 1571, which forbade students under the degree of BA to swim in the river, under penalty of whipping or placing in the stocks. The 1580 prohibition on football outside College was more reasonable, since this was a mass sport with few or no rules, which often degenerated into a bloody intercollegiate riot (Cooper, 1842–53: II, 277, 382; Marsden, 1851: 94; Mullinger, 1873–84: II, 60).

The major disciplinary control over the undergraduates, however, was exercised not by the University, but by the Colleges. Values were for the most part success-fully internalised by intensive tutorial indoctrination, but when that failed, recourse was had to the birch-rod. Publicity added to the punishment in this shame society, and some colleges had a special time set aside each week for the purpose of a public collective display of the whipping of undergraduates. In Balliol it was in the hall on Saturday nights, and in Caius, Cambridge, it was in the hall at 7 p.m. on Thursday nights (Venn, 1897: III, 180–1; Davis, 1900).

An alternate shame punishment, which fell slowly into disuse in the late sixteenth century, was placement in stocks. In the 1560s, Dr Caius, in his quarrel with the Fellows did not hesitate to place some of them in the stocks in the hall. Yet another shame punishment was public confession. In 1633 a student at Exeter College, Oxford, was 'enjoined first to cut off his hair and then publicly in the hall by a declamation to confess going without his tutor's leave from College' (Venn, 1901; Exeter College).

So far we have only discussed the external forces – parents, State and Church – which encouraged the University and the Colleges to tighten the disciplinary system. The linch-pin of the system was the college tutor, hired on private contract by the parents. But here internal forces came into play, since the College had a direct and urgent interest in seeing that this *ad hoc* system was made obligatory and universal.

There were two reasons for this, the first being financial, the need to secure the prompt payment of college bills. By custom, the college bills for room, board and extras were not paid in advance but at the end of each term. The bursars, who were responsible to the College for all monies due to it, became increasingly alarmed by the mounting size of the terminal credit extended to these rich lay students, and also by the problem of enforcement of unpaid debts. The solution adopted was to make it obligatory for every undergraduate to have a college tutor. Clare and Trinity were the first in the field in Cambridge in 1551–52, Balliol and Brasenose were the first Oxford colleges to follow suit in 1572 and 1576. These tutors were made legally responsible for the payment of their pupils' debts to the College. Instead of dunning the parents, the bursar was now able to deduct the money owed by the pupil from his tutor's college allowance and stipend. It was this which turned a private contract into an obligation enforced by the College (Mullinger, 1873–84: II, 598–9; Victoria, 1954).

The second way in which internal college politics became involved in private tutorial contracts with parents was over the allocation of rooms. If the tutor could not get the Master to assign him rooms for his pupils, he would have to reject requests by parents to take their sons under his supervision. The number and quality of pupils a tutor could accept – and therefore his income, status and future prospects – thus depended on the arbitrary decision of the Master about how many college rooms, of what size and comfort, would be placed at his disposal.

The Heads of Colleges inevitably seized this golden opportunity to increase their power, for they could make or break a tutor's career by granting him or depriving him of rooms for his pupils. In the 1610s, the wily Dr John Preston at Queens' College, Cambridge, assiduously cultivated the President, Dr Davenant, so that 'it was commonly said in College that every time Master Preston plucked off his hat to Dr Davenant, he gained a chamber or study for one of his pupils' (Slingsby, 1836; Fuller, 1840; British Library).

Between 1560 and 1660 there was thus a near-perfect match between the external desires of patrons, parents, Church and State and the internal willingness of the Heads and Fellows to extend the College tutorial system. All parties, for their own different reasons, had an interest in developing and sustaining the system.

Such was the theory. How effective the system was in practice is a much more difficult question to answer. Given human nature, and the nature of adolescents in particular, there was naturally considerable slippage between the ideal and the actual. Some tutors were more diligent than others, and some College Heads were more careful about the well-being and reputation of their Colleges than others. But some took their duties so seriously that they went to bizarre lengths to ensure diligence and order. President Kettel of Trinity, Oxford, used 'to go up and down the College and peep in at the keyholes to see whether the boys did follow their books or no', and Master Batchcroft of Caius, Cambridge, did the same. It is significant of the character of thought control that when the latter found a student studying a Jesuit mathematical treatise, he ordered him to 'read Protestant mathematical books' (Aubrey, 1962).

Even so, the control system was not perfect, the main weakness being that the students could not be forbidden to go into town during the daytime, since they had to go to university lectures and exercises. They were therefore not totally insulated from contaminating influences from outside. On the other hand the students' lack of pocket-money, which was usually securely in the hands of their tutors, and the need to be back in College before the gates shut at 9.00 p.m., severely limited their capacity to lead a life of unbridled dissipation. It is remarkable how relatively few complaints there were about University discipline between about 1580 and 1660. It looks as if the Oxbridge College at that time was as successful in shaping the mind and character and values of the ordinary boy planning a secular career as any institution the Western world had ever seen, or was to see again before the development of the Victorian Public School. It provided serious academic training; it imprinted lasting religious opinions; and it created behavioural norms which closely conformed to the 'Puritan Ethic' of piety, thrift, hard work and self-discipline. The gentlemen and clergymen exposed to this experience then went out into the world, and in their capacities as MPS, JPS and preachers attempted the far more difficult task of converting the population as a whole to their ideals. This was an effort whose culminating point was reached in New England in the 1630s to 1660s, and in England in the 1650s.

Moreover it was precisely at this time that the intellectual and cultural Renaissance of England was at its apogee, many of the leaders of which had been trained at Oxford and Cambridge. It was perhaps lucky that Shakespeare was never exposed to an intensive classical education, since this would have ruined his extraordinary capacity to handle the vernacular. But a very high proportion of the other intellectual, cultural and political leaders of England were certainly deeply influenced by their university experience, mostly for the better.

## Edinburgh (1583–1660)

Meanwhile what was happening at Edinburgh? (The following account is drawn from secondary sources: Crauford, 1808; Grant, 1884; Horn, 1967.) While the predominantly classical curriculum was virtually identical with that at Oxford and Cambridge, the educational structure evolved in a very different manner, for a number of reasons. The first was financial. For the first two hundred years of its existence, the University never had enough money, and could therefore never afford to build itself a residential College. Indeed it did not even have any communal dining facilities until the early nineteenth century or even later. The lack of residential quarters meant that the students were obliged to live with families – often their own – in the town. In a strictly Calvinist city, it was thought to be more natural and more morally secure for adolescents to live 'in the presence of their friends'. Be that as it may, the faculty carried heavy staffs with which to beat the students, so that discipline, as in England, was on the rough side (Horn, 1967: 9, 25).

The second difference was that the prescribed religion was Presbyterian, not Anglican. Both faculty and students were expected to take the Covenant, and there was a Divinity School attached to the Arts College to cater for that 50 per cent or so of the students who graduated and went on to become ministers in the Kirk.

The third difference was that the College was run by, and financially supported by, the city corporation, rather than being an independent and autonomous body governed by the faculty under a royal charter. Despite these differences, the College before 1640 seems to have flourished, just as did the well-endowed, constitutionally independent, and wholly residential Colleges of Oxford and Cambridge. It was, however, a College which seems to have catered for the middle and lower middle class, mostly from Edinburgh town itself, rather than for the nobility and gentry of the country. Moreover it showed the same basic educational weakness as did the English Universities, namely that the same tutor – in Edinburgh called regent – taught the same group of students all subjects over the whole 4-year cycle, which is hardly the best way to encourage specialised teaching or scholarly research. As in Oxbridge, however, there was no lack of learned Professors in Edinburgh in the first 80 years of its existence.

## The fall of the Oxbridge College tutorial system (1670–1770)

Now let us turn to the second problem – the causes of the collapse of the institution of the Oxbridge College tutorial system. After 1670 the system degenerated into the usual *ancien régime* pattern of sloppy and corrupt enforcement of stereotyped rules which left the individual student free to structure his work and his play, his morals and his religion, very much as he pleased (Stone, 1974: 52–6). To explain this decay raises very difficult problems, since there seems to be no specific and chronological, although certainly a vague and general, relationship between changes in the external demands of society, and changes in the internal operation of College discipline. I want to argue that if the causes of the rise were mainly external and social, the causes of the fall were mainly internal and institutional.

The first reason for the decay of the tutorial system is that it fell victim to its own success. In the late sixteenth century, each tutor had charge of no more than about six pupils at a time. This was because the task of tutorial supervision was widely shared and no Fellow was overburdened with too many pupils. By the 1610s, however, the first of the 'great tutors' had made his appearance at

Cambridge. Between 1612 and 1622 John Preston was a tutor at Queens', where he took on nearly one-quarter of the freshmen admitted. He was 'the greatest pupil-monger in man's memory', and may have been the first of his kind. But he soon had many competitors (Venn, 1897: III, 251–2; Edwards, 1899: 97; Fletcher, 1956–61; Morgan, 1957).

There were several reasons for the emergence of the 'great tutor'. The first was the growing stress by parents upon teaching as well as on moral, religious and financial supervision; this inevitably led to a singling out by parents of the most learned and diligent Fellows. These men became famous throughout elite society as successful teachers, and were therefore besieged by upper class fathers angling to enrol their sons under their tutelage. In the early eighteenth century a third stage was reached. In all Colleges for which records survive, all the students were now allocated to one (or sometimes two) tutors, who were formally appointed to their office by the College Head, who once again increased his power thereby. Statistics from one or two colleges show the effect of these successive stages in reducing tutoring from an occupation of nearly all Fellows to a monopoly of one or two. Thus where fifty-eight Fellows had been tutors at St John's, Cambridge, in 1632–35, only four were tutors in 1762–65, of whom only two held office at any one time (Mayor and Scott, 1882–1931).

It is easy enough to establish the facts of this transformation. To explain them is another matter. There were three interlocking developments taking place. First, there was a sharp decline in student enrolments between 1670 and 1730, which reduced the annual freshman intake by about 50 per cent (Stone, 1974: 6). Far fewer tutors were therefore needed. Second, there was a growing practice of allowing more and more Fellows to take leaves of absence in order to serve as curate, schoolmaster or private tutor to the son of a nobleman. Fewer Fellows were therefore resident and available as tutors. Third, there was the official concentration of the reduced amount of tutorial work available upon one or two Fellows.

The explanation which I favour is an internal one, that the tight monopoly was the outcome of a power struggle between the College Head and the senior Fellows against the junior Fellows, in which the first two defeated the second. The junior Fellows were excluded from any opportunity of tutorial work, which was monopolised by two senior Fellows, appointed at the direction of the Head. The Head thus increased his patronage powers, the senior Fellows became very rich, and the junior Fellows were left poor and merely waiting around impatiently for a college living to come their way.

The result was to wreck both discipline and education. The reason for this is that the reduction in the number of tutors was so enormously much greater than the reduction in the number of students that the pupil–tutor ratio rose by a factor of seven or more, from about six pupils per tutor to fifty or more. Personal tuition was no longer possible, so that teaching degenerated into boring public lectures read at dictation speed by the college tutors, geared inevitably to the diligence and ability of the most idle and stupid members of the class. The quality of teaching thus dramatically declined.

Discipline also collapsed at the same time. With fifty pupils per tutor, it was now impossible for the latter to manage every pupil's pocket-money, and he now gave up the attempt, confining himself to paying the college bills, as he was legally obliged to do (Bodleian Library (a); Brasenose College (b)).

After the mid-1660s, the practice of whipping students ceased in both Universities. The reason for this is obscure, but it seems to be part of a late-seventeenth-century movement against the beating of children and youths at home, in school, and at the university (Stone, 1977). But this abandonment of whipping meant that the means of controlling the sons of rich and influential parents were now severely limited.

Another important factor in weakening seventeenth-century standards of discipline was the rising age of the freshman, from sixteen-and-a-half to eighteen (Stone, 1974: 97–8). Inevitably, the 18-month rise in the age of freshmen profoundly altered their relationship with their tutor and their willingness to submit to severe financial and moral controls. They were more adult, and consequently more unmanageable.

As tutors got fewer and busier, students older, scholarship less regarded, society at large more easy-going, and university life more dominated by the pleasure-loving sons of the rich, College discipline became more relaxed in the late seventeenth and eighteenth centuries. No longer were the College gates shut tight at 9.00 p.m. and the keys handed over to the Head, thus immuring both Fellows and students for the night. The Head was now often absent, and the keys were left with the porter who, for a fixed fee, would unlock the gate to admit latecomers. The time of early morning chapel was shifted from 5 a.m. or 6 a.m. to the more comfortable hour of 7 a.m., and irregular attendance was now penalised by no more than a fine. Fewer and fewer Fellows bothered to drag themselves out in the early morning to attend, and the students naturally followed suit. Instead of praying with, catechising or instructing their pupils, the Fellows increasingly spent their time after dinner drinking in their own Common Room or Combination Room. Most Colleges set aside such a room sometime between 1660 and 1690 and continued to make it more convenient and elegant in the early eighteenth century. The wealthier students increasingly abandoned the Commons provided in Hall, ordering meals *à la carte,* or else arranging with the College cook for private parties in their rooms. They gambled with cards and dice, drank to excess and hired horses to take them hunting and shooting.

Most serious of all from the educational point of view was the end of any attempt to maintain regular residential requirements throughout term time. The story can be told from the Battel Books of Oxford and Cambridge Colleges which record individual daily residence and tell much the same story. Students were vaguely drifting in and out at all times of the year. Moreover, many did not even appear until after Christmas, presumably since they stayed at home to hunt in the Fall. If one looks at individual students, they came and went from week to week as they pleased, making any coherent course of study quite impossible. The tutors' lectures were now utterly tedious, as everyone admitted: in 1772 Gilbert Wakefield described them as 'odious beyond description' (Wakefield, 1804). This being the case, neglect of them was understandable, and perhaps not very important except as statistical proof of the bankruptcy of education in most (not all) colleges in Oxford and Cambridge between 1700 and 1770.

We may thus conclude that the Collegiate tutorial system was begun in the mid-sixteenth century in response to external demand by parents, Church and State for careful moral and religious supervision and personal academic tuition; and that it decayed primarily as a result of internal factors peculiar to the power structure and the economic organisation of the Colleges themselves.

This decay coincided with and was closely related to a major decline in the intellectual excellence of Oxford and Cambridge. Despite a few men of outstanding talent, like the classicist Bentley at Cambridge or the lawyer Blackstone at Oxford, the period 1680–1780 was in general one of apathy and torpor. It is no coincidence that Newton was the end of the line, and thereafter the lead in science shifted to France. Nor is it a coincidence that the catastrophic fall in student enrolment by 50 per cent, and the concurrent rise of private academies instead, was accompanied by a flood of complaints by parents that the Oxbridge Colleges were now places of uncontrolled debauchery, where their sons ran grave risks of acquiring bad moral habits that would permanently affect their lives (Stone, 1974: 52–3).

## The rise of Edinburgh (1660–1780)

An illuminating comparison is provided by the remarkably different path followed during these years by the University of Edinburgh. At first, in the late seventeenth century, Edinburgh seemed to be proceeding on the same downward slide as Oxbridge. By the 1690s discipline had declined. The regents lay in bed half the day, and drank or brawled among themselves, while the students rioted in the town, disrupted classes and haunted the taverns and brothels in the vicinity. They ceased to speak Latin among themselves in college, and reverted to English or Scots, and they ceased to wear their red gowns in the street. The regents so abused their privilege of beating the students with their staffs that the practice had to be abolished.

Thirty years later Edinburgh was one of the leading universities in Europe, far superior to Oxbridge, and comparable with or superior to the very best universities of the Continent. English and American students poured in, new chairs were founded and filled, distinguished schools of law and medicine were set up. Some scholars at Oxford might still be superior in classics, and some at Cambridge in mathematics, but the general quality and range of the education offered and the sense of intellectual excitement provided, were both infinitely higher at Edinburgh. So successful was Edinburgh that though a very much smaller institution, it educated nearly half as many men as Oxford or Cambridge who were distinguished enough to earn a place in the *Dictionary of National Biography*. In 1789 Thomas Jefferson declared that for science 'no place in the world can pretend to a competition with Edinburgh'. Between 1726 and 1785 Edinburgh was indeed producing far more eminent scientists than either Oxford or Cambridge – and this despite the ingrained eighteenth-century prejudice of the English against the Scots, and the much smaller size of the student body (Hans, 1951; Horn, 1967: 64. The figures are thirty-eight for Oxford, forty-eight for Cambridge and sixty-six for Edinburgh).

How was this miracle achieved? The answer seems to be that in 1708 the Edinburgh City Council, which ruled the College, took charge and restructured it on a Dutch model, in a manner radically different from that of Oxbridge. Where the English colleges shrank their teaching faculty down to two overworked and non-specialised tutors, Edinburgh abolished the regent system of indiscriminate Jack-of-all-Trades teachers, and began appointing professors for each discipline and speciality. Many new chairs were created to expand the offerings, and the curriculum was modernised to include the latest scientific, philosophical and medical advances. The curriculum was freed from its degree-oriented straightjacket, and the students were left free to attend what courses they wished, in what order they wished, in a kind of intellectual smörgåsbord, known in America today as the elective system. Since only a minority of students graduated, and so were tied to preparation for the final examination, the rest were liberated to study how and what they pleased. Finally the City Fathers, who ran the College, deliberately sought to fill the chairs with men who possessed the highest qualifications of scholarship, moral rectitude and teaching ability. They paid them small salaries, but allowed them to charge per capita fees for every pupil who attended their classes, which was a remarkable stimulus for raising the quality of the lectures. These fees were £3.3.0 per student per course, so a lecturer who could attract 300 students, as some did, could earn as much as £1000 a year, which made him a rich man. It is no coincidence that moral philosophy at Edinburgh only took off in the mid-eighteenth century, when the professor was at last allowed to charge per capita fees. As a result, not merely did many of the professors enjoy international reputations as scholars, but they also won the admiration and respect of their students. The Edinburgh professor was being described as 'an example of civility and good manners, as of morality and virtue...though all of them are men of letters and skilled in the sciences they profess', at much the same time when the Oxbridge don was being characterised as 'weak, obstinate, conceited, bigoted, unfriendly to man, ungrateful to God, melancholic, fretful, timid, cruel' (Horn, 1967: 60, 66; Rothblatt, 1974: 262). It was at Edinburgh and Glasgow that there was developed the Scottish Philosophy which crossed the Atlantic to my own university, Princeton, in the person of John Witherspoon, with enormous effect on the whole character of American higher education, as well as stimulating that salutary blow for democratic liberty, the American Revolution.

As for the students, they flocked to the lectures, put up with the inconveniences of the squalid physical side of the College and the total lack of residential housing, apparently avoided most of the temptations which, as we know too well from Boswell's *Journal*, were available at almost every street corner, and came away with a respect for the institution and for the broad range of learning that they had picked up. It helped that they were mostly middle-class boys, and that the idle and raffish sons of English aristocrats and gentry who dominated Oxbridge tended to stay away. As a place to obtain a free-floating, slightly chaotic, but intoxicatingly exciting liberal education, not deep but broad, there was perhaps nowhere in the world better than the College of Edinburgh in the last half of the eighteenth century. In its prime it was said that 'it is not easy to conceive a university where industry was more general, where reading was more fashionable, where indolence and ignorance were more disreputable. Every mind was in a state of fermentation' (Horn, 1967: 94; the author was Sir James Macintosh). A better description of a really distinguished university could hardly be penned.

When he visited Scotland in 1810, the Americanised Frenchman Louis Simond noted the two characteristic features of that College, the payment of the professors by results, and the lack of any kind of social control over the students. 'The professors,' he said, 'are soldiers of fortune who live by their sword – that is to say by their talents and reputation. They generally depend for their income on the number of students who attend their lectures.' Since the fee was £3.6.0 per course, and attendance rates varied between 30 and 400 students, a professor could be either a pauper or a very rich man. As for the students they

> do not appear to me to be subject to much, if any, collegial discipline. They board out, wear no particular dress, and make what use they please of their time. I understand, however, they are generally studious and I have certainly observed much zeal and emulation among them.
>
> (Simond, 1815)

By 1810, however, things were beginning to go wrong. For one thing, there at last started to be some competition from Oxford and Cambridge, and the English students began drifting away. But more important, it seems, were causes internal to the institution, just as had happened to Oxford and Cambridge in the late seventeenth century. The medical school was in decline by 1800, and a series of poor appointments made things worse. Thus, the anatomy chair became a hereditary place for the Monro family, grandfather, father and son, ending up with the last of the Monros reading his lectures from his grandfather's notes, which were by then some 80 years old. [In about 1820 he is said to have begun a lecture with his grandfather's words: 'When I was a student at Leyden in 1719...' (Horn, 1967: 108).] Infighting began between professors in competition for fees from students attending their courses. New chairs were blocked by professors fearful of inroads into their attendance and therefore their income. Next came the abandonment of the elective system and a return to the rigid curriculum of the sixteenth and seventeenth centuries, which was certainly in accordance with the trend of the time, but destroyed that flexible system of open choice which had formerly been so attractive. Finally, the faculties' energies were diverted into a ferocious and long drawn-out battle with the City Council over the issues of power and independence.

It must be admitted that there is a lot which is obscure to me about this decline of the College of Edinburgh so soon after its finest hour, but it certainly looks as if the causes were internal to the institution rather than pressures from outside. The cause of the earlier revival, however, is clear enough. Unlike the Oxbridge Colleges, Edinburgh was constitutionally ruled by an external authority, the City Council, which could and did intervene vigorously in 1708 to restructure the whole system of education. This was something which could only be done at Oxbridge by a Parliamentary Commission and Act of Parliament, that is by a major political effort, almost a revolution, which only became possible 150 years later, in the mid- and late-Victorian period. The story of the subsequent revival of Edinburgh to reach its present international eminence is beyond both my knowledge and the scope of this study. I do not mention it further, merely out of ignorance.

## The reform of Oxbridge (1770–1960)

From about 1770 onwards Oxford and Cambridge began slowly to put part of their house in order, the first priority being a restoration of discipline.

There were several causes for such a restoration. First and foremost was a religious revival which affected all classes except perhaps the rough and disreputable poor, who had no hope of going to college anyway. First Methodism, then Evangelical piety, spread rapidly through the middle and upper classes, and the dark but realistic concept of Original Sin returned. The only hope for salvation was once more thought to be the imposition of strict control, and soon after 1770 some university clergymen-dons were beginning to tighten up the reins of discipline once more. By the 1790s, this attitude was reinforced by not unfounded fears that if the elite did not put their house in order and show an example to their inferiors of piety and morality, the ideas of Tom Paine and the French Revolution might sweep the country. The Dons were now under heavy pressure to tighten up college discipline. Since fines were ineffective in penalising the rich, and flogging was not allowed, impositions, that is the writing out of hundreds of lines of Latin or Greek verse or prose, were substituted as a punishment. Rustication for a term or year was revived for more serious offences, and expulsion for the most serious of all.

By 1770 Brasenose was once more demanding that all students be in college by midnight, and the gates were closed at 9.00. After 1790 at Corpus, riot and drunkenness were severely punished, even if the accused were Gentlemen Commoners.

In every college a stream of regulations were issued. Compulsory early morning chapel was reinstated as an obligation on all; dress regulations were tightened up – pantaloons and trousers being forbidden in hall or chapel at Trinity and St John's, Cambridge. Rustication was imposed on any student found driving gigs and tandems, and blowing horns, firing guns or betting on horse races. After 1825 academic dress was once more to be worn at all times, on pain of severe punishment (Rothblatt, 1974: 270; Bodleian Library (b); Brasenose College (c); Cambridge University Library (a,b)).

So great was the stress now placed on discipline and obedience that the faculty were fearful of supporting even the most worthy cause proposed by undergraduates. In 1811 the clerical Vice-Chancellor of Cambridge was approached by some undergraduates with a request for permission to start a Bible Society. Despite his sympathies, he rejected the request since he was 'fully aware of the danger of encouraging, or of being thought to encourage, insubordination, by appearing as a leader in any plan which originated with undergraduates' (Rothblatt, 1974: 267).

Slowly, little by little, drunkenness is said to have declined, and earnest efforts – none too effectual, it seems – were made to clear the evening streets of prostitutes. Organised games, especially rowing, were instituted and encouraged in order to divert youthful energies into other channels. In 1818, one enthusiast at Cambridge suggested removing 'the disgraceful and licentious pictures exhibited in the FitzWilliam Museum', in an effort to deprive the students of the visual stimulus of 'naked women beautifully painted'. Others believed that while they were about it, it would be wise also to delete Ovid and Anacreon from the syllabus (Lawson, 1818; Maberley, 1818; Rothblatt, 1974: 270–1; Engel, 1979).

There remained, however, the critical problem of how to deal with the idle, ill-disciplined, extravagant and debauched Gentlemen Commoners and Fellow Commoners, whose numbers were actually increasing up to 1800. They regarded themselves as above the law, and indeed had been allowed to behave as if they were. But the records of several colleges make it clear that this special status for the rich, with its gold-embroidered gown, its special privileges, both social and academic, and its high fees, appeared more and more like the relic of a more easy-going period. First, the privileges were reduced in many colleges, beginning in the 1770s, and then the status was abolished altogether in college after college between 1810 and 1850, not because of egalitarian or meritocratic objections to the flaunting of social privilege by the rich, but because of the threat to tightened college discipline by the example set by these uncontrollable young men. (These observations are taken from the records of many colleges in Oxford and Cambridge.) The conflict of values between the new and the old Oxbridge created by the survival of the Gentleman Commoner is set out very clearly in Thomas Hughes's novel, *Tom Brown at Oxford*.

By 1810 these new attitudes, and the major changes to which they gave rise, had transformed the quality of Oxbridge life, and regular residence during term-time was once more the rule, as it had been in the 1660s. The Battel Books of Brasenose and Balliol show that undergraduates came up punctually at the beginning of term, and stayed to the end, making it possible once more to plan a coherent course of study, something which had simply not been feasible so long as students drifted in and out of residence at will. This in turn was both cause and effect of the most important innovation of all, the imposition upon all students of examinations of a serious nature to replace the old medieval tests which had long since become entirely ritualised and symbolic. It is difficult today, in our examination-ridden society, to appreciate the significance and novelty of this move. When serious examinations for all were first introduced into Yale in 1785, the students rioted in protest for four days, and broke the doors and windows of the rooms of the faculty. But the faculty won, as usual.

Serious honours examinations began at Cambridge in the 1770s and spread to Oxford by 1800. But these were only taken by a minority, and more important was the introduction in College after College in the early nineteenth century of terminal examinations for all, called 'collections'. The purpose of these innovations was evidently discipline rather than a stimulus to learning or as a step towards a modern meritocracy, since success in these exams did not lead anywhere, except possibly to election as a College Fellow. Their purpose was to keep the students from idleness, inspired by the spur of competition and the threat of humiliation.

But if discipline was effectively reformed, and idleness suppressed by the institution of constant examinations by Colleges and the University, the method of teaching was left entirely unaltered. The old system of teaching by one or two tutors per College remained entirely unchanged, despite the doubling in the number of students enrolled and the demand for more specialised tuition to prepare for the new exams. The encrusted vested interests of the senior Dons and the Heads were just too great to be overcome by any pressure for reform from within. Thus the college discipline could be radically improved, but the college teaching could not be changed at all.

In order to fill the vacuum there developed a new, unofficial and extra-collegiate educational body – the private tutors or 'coaches' hired by the parents but now wholly outside the College system. These private coaches were hired hacks, working long, dreary hours at low pay, coaching their pupils to pass their examinations – doing in fact what the increasingly wealthy college tutors were paid to do but did not (Engel, 1983: 4, 18, 39–41).

Between 1770 and 1850 the Oxbridge Colleges thus fully adapted to new *moral* and *social* needs by strengthening discipline, but allowed the new *academic* needs created by the disciplinary device of examinations to be filled by a parallel unofficial educational system of the private coach. It was the continuing failure of the Colleges to remodel their tutorial system to provide the necessary academic training for the new honours examination which exposed them to increasing and well-justified criticism. Oxbridge now had life-tenure professors who did not research, life-tenure lecturers who did not lecture, and temporary tutors who did not give tutorials. These were anachronistic hangovers of the ancien régime in a modernising society. This situation eventually led to forcible Parliamentary intervention in the middle of the nineteenth century. The result was the creation of a body of professional teachers and moral supervisors – the College Fellows and Tutors of the late nineteenth and early twentieth centuries, and also the creation of a minority of professional researchers advancing the frontiers of knowledge, namely the Professors. It was these latter, fashioned on the German model, who were primarily responsible for the restoration of a reputation of intellectual excellence to Oxford and Cambridge. By 1880 Oxbridge once more enjoyed both student discipline and academic distinction.

Since these major reforms imposed by Parliament through two Royal Commissions in the 1850s and 1870s, the two older universities have evolved in unexpected ways. The College Tutorial Fellowship, instead of being the first stage in a natural progression to a University Readership, and perhaps a Professorship, has become a permanent and increasingly burdensome life-time occupation. The reason for this is that the money intended for the creation of the new Readerships and Chairs was never forthcoming, because of the great depression of agricultural rents that lasted for nearly a century, from 1873 to the 1950s. Oxbridge never had the money to create a regular ladder of professional advancement (Engel, 1983: ch. v).

In the late nineteenth and early twentieth centuries, discipline tightened still further, as proctors prowled the streets, deans lurked in the dark to catch unlucky revellers climbing into college, and as new and extraordinary precautions were taken to limit the mingling of the sexes when women's colleges were established. For example, at one women's college at Oxford in the early years of this century, if an undergraduate wished to invite a young man to tea in her room, she had first to give his name to the college authorities to check that he was not on their black-list, and then to drag her bed out of the room and stack it in the corridor during his visit. Male students could become hopelessly inebriated inside their Colleges, but were subject to serious punishment if caught drinking a glass of beer in a pub. So long as the pass-degree existed, however, there were always a number of rich young men who could lead a life of idleness and frivolity, secure in the knowledge that their inherited position would secure them a comfortable place in life, regardless of their academic qualifications, or lack of them. It was the virtual disappearance of the pass-degree immediately after the Second World War which led to the final disappearance of these amiable but dissipated young wastrels. The Universities became more serious, but much duller, by the forcible removal of people like Brideshead and his friends.

By now, moreover, legal changes enforced by statute law were undermining many of the ancient symbols and rituals of that moral and religious training which had once loomed so large in the conceptualisation of the true function of a university education. Compulsory chapel, for example, became difficult to maintain in the face of the abolition of all religious tests, and the admission of Dissenters, Catholics and Jews. Only in America did compulsory chapel survive here and there into the 1960s, as at Princeton. Another survival from pre-modern times, the honour system of supervising examinations and preventing cheating still exists in a number of American universities and colleges. But its ethical requirements, involving putting the denunciation of a fellow student detected in cheating above loyalty to one's peer group, no longer conform to the moral standards of modern youth. The system is evidently failing.

## The decline of discipline

The final twist to the story has occurred in the last two decades. The strictly educational function of this new professional group of College Tutors has endured unchanged, and examinations are now the principal mode of social control of the student body. But the Tutors' disciplinary, moral and religious functions, their responsibility for acting *in loco parentis* – as moral tutors – have in the last 20 years been largely abandoned. This has occurred partly under the influence of the values of an agnostic, hedonistic and individualistic society, partly under severe pressure from the students themselves. Partly also it has occurred for internal reasons. The dons are now nearly all married, and it has become too much trouble for married men living out of college to enforce such regulations. They would rather go home, play with their children, and watch television. And so the ideal of the Oxbridge College and tutorial system as a 'total institution' for religious and moral control – although not as an excellent, but not ideal, educational system for preparation for an examination – has today virtually disappeared for the second time, even more completely than it did by the mid-eighteenth century. College gates are kept open, men and women live unsupervised side by side in the same colleges, and students are free to enter the pubs of the city. Provided they behave discreetly, no one bothers any more about how they conduct their private lives. If they get into trouble, they resort to the psychiatric counselling services of the local hospital rather than to the moral tutor – the result of the change being a significant decline in the suicide rate.

Thus the wheel of social control has spun full circle twice since the mid-sixteenth century, but the causes and consequences of the spin have varied widely over time.

## Conclusion

Several general conclusions may be drawn from this complex story:

1   The ostensible functions of a university often conceal equally or more important latent ones, the most critical of which is keeping adolescents out of trouble.
2   There is no grand social scientific theory that can be made to apply to changes in social control by institutions over time and space; thus, neither a purely externalist model, based on response to the changing values and needs of a society, nor a purely internalist model, based on changing fortunes in the struggle for power and money of the members of an institution, will suffice to explain the complex reality. Sometimes one and sometimes the other has predominated.
3   The *creation* and *development* of an institution for social and educational control tends to be mainly the result of *external* forces: parents, Church and State in late-sixteenth-century Oxbridge; Parliament in late-nineteenth-century Oxbridge; and the City Council in mid-sixteenth- and early-eighteenth-century Edinburgh. The functional decay of that institution tends to be mainly the result of *internal* pressures and contradictions, as in late-sixteenth-century Oxbridge and late-eighteenth-century Edinburgh.
4   The case of Oxbridge, but not that of Edinburgh, suggests that there is a clear correlation between student discipline and intellectual excellence, the former being a necessary pre-requisite of the latter. In the past, this discipline was imposed by the tutorial system and the use of physical punishment. Today, the honours examination system works even better, both as a disciplinary instrument and as a spur and goad to intellectual distinction. Its weakness is that, as operated in England, it suppresses that freedom of intellectual choice that was one of the glories of Edinburgh in the eighteenth century.

The contradictory history of both Oxbridge and Edinburgh from the sixteenth to the twentieth century thus not only provides two case studies in the rise and fall and rise again of institutions, but also offers a paradigm for examining the forces that first create and then erode such institutions, and studying the interacting roles of discipline, education and intellectual excellence.

## References

Aubrey, J. (1962) *Brief Lives* (ed. O. L. Dick), LXXIX, p. 183. Ann Arbor.
—— (1972) *Aubrey on Education* (ed. J. E. Stephens), p. 69. London.
Baker, A. (1933) *Memorials of Father Augustine Baker, O.S.B., Catholic Record Society* 33, p. 40.

Bodleian Library (a) Locke M S S, F.11.
—— (b) Gough, Cambridge 99, 67.
Brasenose College (a) Leigh Letters Transcripts, p. 11.
—— (b) M S S B.2.a.71.
—— (c) M S S A1/6.
British Library, Harleian M S S 389f.427; 390ff.203, 349, 225.
Cambridge University Library (a) Catalogue of Cambridge University Edicts.
—— (b) Cam c.500.
Clarke, S. (1677) *A General Martyrologie* ..., *sub* Herbert Palmer and Stephen Goffe.
Cooper, C. H. (1842–53) *Annals of Cambridge*. Cambridge.
Crauford, T. (1808) *History of the University of Edinburgh 1580–1646*. Edinburgh.
Curtis, M. (1959) *Oxford and Cambridge in Transition 1558–1642*. Oxford.
Davis, H. W. C. (1900) *Balliol College*, p. 58. London.
Edwards, G. M. (1899) *Sydney Sussex College*. London.
Engel, A. (1979) 'Immoral Intentions': the University of Oxford and the Problem of Prostitution 1827–1914. *Victorian Studies*, Autumn.
—— (1983) *From Clergyman to Don*. Oxford.
Exeter College M S S, Bursar's Day Book 1613–40.
Fletcher, H. F. (1956–61) *The Intellectual Development of John Milton*, II, pp. 38, 44–5, 52. Urbana.
Fuller, T. (1840) *History of the Worthies of England* (ed. T. A. Nuttall), p. 517. London.
Grant, Sir A. (1884) *The Story of Edinburgh University*, I. London.
Grosart, A. B. (1887) *Lismore Papers*, 2nd Series, I, p. 252. London.
Hans, N. (1951) *New Trends in Education in the Eighteenth Century*, pp. 18, 32. London.
Horn, D. B. (1967) *A Short History of the University of Edinburgh 1556–1889*. Edinburgh.
Jonson, B. *Eastward Ho*, IV, p. iii.
Lawson, M. (1818) *Strictures of F. H. Maberley's Account of the Melancholy and Awful End of Lawrence Dundas*, p. 30. London.
Locke, J. (1968) *The Educational Writings of John Locke* (ed. J. Axtell), pp. 200, 244–53. Cambridge.
Looney, J. (1981) Undergraduate Education at Early Stuart Cambridge. *History of Education* 10.
Maberley, F. H. (1818) *The Melancholy and Awful Death of Lawrence Dundas*, p. 27. London.
Marsden, J. H. (ed.) (1851) *College Life in the Time of James I*. London.
Mayor, J. E. B. and Scott, R. F. (1882–1931) *Admissions to the College of St John the Evangelist*. Cambridge.
Mede, J. (1664) *Works*, I, p. vii. London.
Morgan, I. (1957) *Prince Charles's Puritan Chaplain*, pp. 28–33. London.
Mullinger, J. B. (1873–84) *The University of Cambridge*. Cambridge.
North, R. (1890) *Lives of the Norths*, III, pp. 285–6. London.
Pantin, W. A. (1972) *Oxford Life in Oxford Archives*, p. 6. Oxford.
Penton, S. (1688) *The Guardian's Instruction*, pp. 57–67. London.
Princeton (1978) *Princeton University Chronicle* XL, p. 11.
Rothblatt, S. (1974) The Student Sub-culture and the Examination System in early 19th Century Oxbridge, in *The University in Society* (ed. L. Stone). Princeton.
Schmidt, G. P. (1957) *The Liberal Arts College*, p. 67. New Brunswick.
Simond, L. (1815) *Journal of a Tour and Residence in Great Britain during the Years 1810 and 1811*, I, p. 371. New York.
Slingsby, Sir H. (1836) *Diary of Sir Henry Slingsby* (ed. D. Parsons), pp. 302–3, 317. London.
Stone, L. (1974) The Size and Composition of the Oxford Student Body 1580–1909, in *The University in Society* (ed. L. Stone). Princeton.
—— (1977) *The Family, Sex and Marriage in England 1500–1800*, pp. 439–44. New York.
Thompson, H. L. (1900) *Christ Church*, pp. 74–7. London.
Trinity College M S S 10A.33, 'Rules of Dr. James Dupont of Trinity College, Cambridge'.
Venn, J. (1897) *Biographical History of Gonville and Caius College 1349–1847*. Cambridge.
—— (1901) *Caius College*, p. 56. London.
*Victoria County History of Oxfordshire* (1954) III, pp. 83, 109–10, 209, 328. London.
Wakefield, G. (1804) *Memoirs of the Life of Gilbert Wakefield*, I, pp. 82, 87. London.
Ward, G. R. M. (1845) *Oxford University Statutes*, I, pp. 155–67. London.

## CHAPTER 2

# GOING TO UNIVERSITY IN ENGLAND BETWEEN THE WARS
## Access and funding

Carol Dyhouse

*History of Education*, 31, 1, 1–14, 2002

The socialist politician Jennie Lee is probably best remembered for her vision of expanding popular access to university education in Britain through the establishment of the Open University in the 1960s. Writing as a young woman, some 20 years before this event, she reflected on her own educational experiences and entry into political life in a volume of autobiography entitled *This Great Journey*.[1] She noted that she had often been asked how it had been possible for her, as the daughter of a coalminer, to go to university (she had studied at the University of Edinburgh between 1922 and 1926). This had been possible, she explained, through a combination of 'public' support and private (i.e. parental) self-sacrifice. Fife Educational Authority provided schooling up to university entrance, and then presented her with a maintenance allowance of £45 per annum whilst at university. The Carnegie Trust took care of half of her class fees. She lived in a rented room rather than a women's hostel, a much more economical option at the time. Her parents struggled to help. There is a moving account of how her mother, normally cautious and risk-averse, defied her father's strict opposition to gambling in any form by putting a shilling each way on the Derby one year 'with a view to assisting Providence'.[2] Clothes suitable for college had to be obtained on credit – equally against the grain. Patricia Hollis, Jennie Lee's recent biographer, describes how on Saturdays, when Jennie's father was free from work, he would cycle the twenty miles from the family home to Edinburgh, bringing home cooked food supplies and freshly laundered clothes, and taking back clothes to be washed or mended.[3]

Scottish universities have long prided themselves on their 'democratic' tradition, and on having been able to offer access to talented youngsters from impecunious homes. Fees might be considered to have been less of a deterrent after the Carnegie bequest in 1901–02, which guaranteed the fees for students of Scottish birth attending universities in Scotland.[4] By 1938 the 'age participation ratio' (i.e. the proportion of the age group attending university) in Scotland was 3.1%, as compared with only 1.5% in England and Wales.[5] Although there were differences in the recruitment pattern between institutions – Glasgow, for instance, seems to have drawn from a wider social base than did Edinburgh – R. D. Anderson has suggested that the Scottish 'democratic myth' did indeed have substance, in that 'perhaps twenty percent of Scottish university students could properly be described as "working class" ',[6] whilst another 20% or so were the children of 'intermediate' or lower middle-class homes, the sons and daughters of shopkeepers, clerks and so forth. It is probably safe to conclude that at least 40% of the students in Scottish universities between the wars came from families beneath the stratum of the economically secure professional and managerial classes.

It has been much more difficult to generalize about the social background of those studying in English universities before 1939, given the patchy and incomplete evidence available. Studies of Oxford and Cambridge make it clear that these institutions catered for a social elite: students from working-class homes, and women, were very much outnumbered by those who might be seen as having regarded college life as something in the nature of a 'finishing school for young gentlemen'.[7] But if Oxford and Cambridge can in the main be seen as having functioned to confirm privilege rather than to offer opportunities for social mobility on any scale, can the same be said of England's 'other' universities? Between 1900 and 1935 the number of full-time students in the other nine English universities with charters and five university colleges that existed by 1939[8] more than trebled (Table 2.1) and many contemporary observers saw the university population as having been 'democratized'. Doreen Whiteley, who compiled a report on the 'system' of scholarships available for university study in 1933, estimated that over half of university entrants at that time benefited from some form of financial assistance aside from family support, and that going to university could certainly no longer be regarded as 'the privilege of the well-to-do'.[9]

This chapter will introduce material that will clarify our understanding of the social background of those who studied in English universities before 1939 and explore the ways in which they financed their studies. It will be suggested that, leaving aside 'Oxbridge', the social composition of the student body was not dissimilar to that in Scotland. Notwithstanding the differences in the age participation ratio mentioned earlier, the many differences in educational history and provision between these two countries, and differences in social structure, it would

*Table 2.1* Numbers of full-time students, England only, 1901, 1934–35, 1937–38

|  | All English universities | | Oxford and Cambridge | | Other English universities | |
|---|---|---|---|---|---|---|
|  | Total | % M/F | Total | % M/F | Total | % M/F |
| *1901* | | | | | | |
| Men | 11,755 | 84.9 | 5,367 | 90.9 | 6,388 | 80.4 |
| Women | 2,090 | 15.1 | 535 | 9.1 | 1,555 | 19.6 |
| Total | 13,845 | | 5,902 | | 7,943 | |
| *1934/35* | | | | | | |
| Men | 28,366 | 76.9 | 9,281 | 87.0 | 19,085 | 72.8 |
| Women | 8,526 | 23.1 | 1,383 | 13.0 | 7,143 | 27.2 |
| Total | 36,892 | | 10,664 | | 26,228 | |
| *1937/38* | | | | | | |
| Men | 28,409 | 78.1 | 9,380 | 87.0 | 19,029 | 74.3 |
| Women | 7,969 | 21.9 | 1,398 | 13.0 | 6,571 | 25.7 |
| Total | 36,378 | | 10,778 | | 25,600 | |

*Source*: UGC figures, 1929–30 to 1934–35, 1937–38

appear that the *proportions* of lower middle and working-class students in universities on both sides of the border were much the same.

Between 1995 and 1998 I distributed a total of 1900 questionnaires to graduates who had studied at a variety of English universities and university colleges before the Second World War. These four-page questionnaires sought information about social background, educational experiences and career histories. Respondents were asked to reflect upon why they had sought a university education, and how they had financed their studies. These questionnaires were completed and returned by just over 500 women and nearly 600 men. The women in the sample had studied at the universities of Manchester, Bristol and Reading, at University College, London, and at Royal Holloway and Bedford Colleges (now amalgamated) of the University of London. This choice of institutions stemmed from a desire to select different kinds of institution (older and newer foundations, institutions in different parts of the country, and mixed as well as single-sex colleges). The study of women graduates was made possible by a grant from the Spencer Foundation, and carried out in 1995. The survey of male graduates was carried out three years later, with funding from the Economic and Social Research Council. Women represented only about one-quarter of the student population in the 1930s. However, women have a longer life expectancy than men, many male graduates tragically lost their lives in the 1939–45 war, and a gap of three years between contacting the women and the male graduates in my sample meant that to achieve my goal of collecting a similar number of completed questionnaires from each sex I had to draw upon a larger sample of universities for the men. The male graduates were drawn from the universities of Manchester, Bristol, Reading, Liverpool and Leeds, University College London, King's College London, and the former University College of Nottingham (Table 2.2).

*Table 2.2* Numbers of questionnaires distributed to and completed by graduates

|  | Code | Nos distributed | Nos completed | Response rate (%) |
|---|---|---|---|---|
| *Women* | | | | |
| Bristol | BF | 123 | 88 | 71.5 |
| Manchester | MF | 225 | 136 | 60.4 |
| Reading | RF | 108 | 63 | 58.3 |
| Royal Holloway & Bedford* | RH & BD | 230 | 145** | 63.0 |
| University College London | UCF | 108 | 72 | 66.7 |
| Total | | 794 | 504 | 63.5 |
| *Men* | | | | |
| Manchester | MC | 260 | 120 | 46.2 |
| Reading | RD | 44 | 18 | 40.9 |
| King's College London | KC/KCX | 133 | 74 | 55.6 |
| University College London | UC/UCX | 150 | 93 | 62.0 |
| Bristol | BR | 97 | 59 | 60.8 |
| Leeds | LS | 164 | 96 | 58.5 |
| Liverpool | LP | 195 | 95 | 48.7 |
| Nottingham | NT | 42 | 22 | 52.4 |
| Total | | 1085 | 577 | 53.2 |

Notes:
  * Numbers distributed cannot be separated because of confidentiality.
  ** Royal Holloway 58; Bedford 87; some late returns from King's College (KCF) and Bristol (BX) were not counted in these responses; X in the code is for students from other universities finishing their qualification (e.g. in medicine).

Categorization in terms of social class is a process that is always beset with difficulties. In order to arrive at some kind of social profile of the graduates in my sample I decided to classify according to father's occupation into seven groups, following in the main the scheme devised by John Hall and D. Caradog Jones in 1950.[10] The categories were (1) Professional and High Administrative, (2) Managerial and Executive, (3) Higher Non-Manual, (4) Lower Non-Manual, (5) Skilled Manual, (6) Semi-Skilled Manual, and (7) Unskilled Manual. Where there were problems in grading occupations broadly designated, such as 'farmer' or 'engineer', I drew upon other information supplied by respondents that gave indications of social position, such as the kind of school attended or details of family finance. Only a small minority of respondents had mothers in regular occupation outside the home, but in cases where they did, particularly when mothers were widows or in the handful of cases where mothers worked in higher status occupations than fathers, this information was taken into account.

The results of this analysis of social class origins are given in Table 2.3, which shows percentages for men and women separately, giving percentages in each university by social class, and also percentages in each social class by university. There is an interesting pattern of variation between institutions in that the colleges of the University of London seem to have attracted a higher proportion of students from social classes 1 and 2 than did the 'redbricks'. Even allowing for the small numbers of men in the sample who studied at the University College of Nottingham, we can see that contemporary observations of Nottingham as having drawn a higher proportion of its student body from lower down the social scale than most other university-level institutions are well borne out.[11] The social profile is broadly similar for men and women, although there was a slightly higher proportion of women from social classes 1 and 2, and a slightly higher proportion of men from the semi-skilled manual group (class 6). (Although the numbers of graduates from Nottingham were small, there were no women from Nottingham in the sample.) Contemporary observers often suggested that the women students in the 'civic' or 'modern' universities came from slightly higher social class backgrounds than the men.[12] It should be remembered that a much higher proportion of men went to Oxford or Cambridge than did women: in the mid-1930s, one in three of the men attending a university in England went to 'Oxbridge', whereas the proportion for women was only one in seven. This may account in part for the difference. There is also the consideration that many sons from social classes 1 and 2 may not have contemplated a university education at all, but may have gone straight into family businesses.[13]

The aggregates in Table 2.3 suggest that just over half (54%) of the women and around 43% of the men in my sample were from family backgrounds that we can clearly designate as middle class. Leaving aside a small proportion of 'not givens', the rest, that is 52% of the men, 42% of the women, were from lower middle- or working-class homes. In representations of the social character of the student population at this time, obviously much will depend on whether one sees class 3, the group of students classified as having come from 'Higher Non-Manual' family backgrounds, as having had more in common with the 'middle' or 'working' class. I would suggest that the nature of the occupations represented in class 3, including commercial travellers, railway and post office clerks, small shopkeepers and the like, justifies their being grouped with the working rather than the securely middle-class families in this picture. This would certainly accord with the self-perceptions of those from this kind of background in my sample, who sometimes described themselves unequivocally as 'working class'.

*Table 2.3* Social class of origin of respondents in each university

| University | Percentages in each social class of origin, by university | | | | | | | | Total |
|---|---|---|---|---|---|---|---|---|---|
| | PHA | MEx | HNM | LNM | SKM | SSM | UM | ng | |
| *Men* | | | | | | | | | |
| BR | 14 | 24 | 17 | 19 | 10 | 12 | 2 | 4 | 59 |
| MC | 13 | 28 | 17 | 18 | 11 | 9 | 1 | 4 | 120 |
| NT | 0 | 14 | 36 | 14 | 14 | 14 | 9 | 0 | 22 |
| RD | 11 | 22 | 22 | 22 | 11 | 6 | 0 | 6 | 18 |
| LS | 13 | 32 | 22 | 10 | 7 | 11 | 1 | 3 | 96 |
| LP | 22 | 22 | 21 | 14 | 11 | 2 | 1 | 7 | 95 |
| UC | 30 | 26 | 23 | 2 | 14 | 3 | 0 | 2 | 93 |
| KC | 24 | 20 | 23 | 12 | 7 | 4 | 0 | 9 | 74 |
| Total | 18.2 | 25.1 | 21.0 | 12.7 | 10.2 | 7.1 | 1.0 | 4.7 | 577 |
| *Women* | | | | | | | | | |
| BF | 17 | 34 | 17 | 7 | 11 | 5 | 3 | 6 | 88 |
| MF | 16 | 26 | 28 | 5 | 12 | 7 | 1 | 5 | 136 |
| RF | 16 | 48 | 14 | 11 | 8 | 2 | 2 | 0 | 63 |
| UCF | 38 | 24 | 13 | 6 | 15 | 3 | 0 | 3 | 72 |
| BD | 29 | 37 | 15 | 3 | 11 | 1 | 0 | 3 | 87 |
| RH | 16 | 38 | 26 | 3 | 17 | 0 | 0 | 0 | 58 |
| Total | 21.4 | 33.1 | 19.6 | 5.8 | 12.3 | 3.4 | 1.0 | 3.4 | 504 |

*Keys:*

| | *Universities* | | *Social classes* |
|---|---|---|---|
| UC/UCF | University College London | PHA | Professional, Higher Administrative |
| KC/KCF | King's College London | MEx | Managerial, Executive |
| BR/BF | Bristol | HNM | Higher Non-Manual |
| RD/RF | Reading | LNM | Lower Non-Manual |
| NT | Nottingham | SKM | Skilled Manual |
| MC/MF | Manchester | SSM | Semi-Skilled Manual |
| LS | Leeds | UM | Unskilled Manual |
| LP | Liverpool | | |
| BD | Bedford College | ng | not given |
| RH | Royal Holloway College | | |

How much did it cost to go to university in the mid- to late 1930s? University tuition fees averaged around £40 p.a. (higher for science subjects, lower for arts). The cost of residence in a university hall or hostel varied considerably, from around £40 to £75 p.a. Fees for residence in London might be higher still. In 1933 Doreen Whiteley estimated that around £130 p.a. would cover the expenses of a student in arts or science (medicine was more expensive) at a provincial university, allowing £40 for tuition, £75 for residence and £25 for travelling, pocket money, laundry and books. This was considerably less than the cost of studying at a college in Oxford or Cambridge, which she estimated at from £160 to £240 p.a. for a woman, and from £200 to £275 p.a. for a man.[14]

However, it should be noted that a very large proportion of those studying at a provincial university in the 1930s 'got by' on considerably less than £130 p.a. by attending their local university and living at home. According to figures published by the University Grants Committee (UGC) just before the war, around half of those studying in the English universities (excluding Oxford and Cambridge) lived at home. The pattern of residence differed between men and women in that a higher proportion of men than women (33% compared with 18%) lived in lodgings. University authorities acting *in loco parentis* often insisted on women students living in halls or hostels if they could not live at home. The UGC figures show more than a third (36%) of the women students in English universities living in halls or hostels, as compared with only 14% of the men.[15] The remainder, 53% of the men, and 46% of the women, lived at home. Amongst the respondents in my survey, 43% of the women and 63% of the men recorded that they had lived at home whilst studying.

Even when students lived away from their parental homes in term time, their families were often obliged to support them during vacations. Only a very small number of my respondents indicated that they had been able to secure paid work during vacations – indeed, most of them responded to my question about vacation employment with incredulity, reminding me in no uncertain terms about the lack of paid work available during the Depression and pointing out that it would have been socially unacceptable for them to have taken jobs even if they had been available. Even leaving aside the 'opportunity' costs, to parents of modest means, of foregoing a son's or daughter's potential earnings whilst they were in higher education, a goodly proportion of the cost of a university education fell on families. Around 39% of the men in my sample and 41% of the women recorded that their families bore 'all or most' of the cost of their going to university, at least another third of each sex indicating that their families had borne 'some or part' of the expense. This is in line with contemporary estimates such as that by Whiteley in 1933, in her report *The Poor Student and the University*, which suggested that over half of university entrants at that time were benefiting from some kind of scholarship, bursary or support from public funds.[16] In what follows I shall look first at the kinds of scholarship and award available to those in my sample, then I shall return to the subject of family support.

My question about how respondents had financed their attendance at university often elicited an extraordinary amount of detail. This vivid recall of detail reflects the importance of the issue at the time and the ingenuity which often went into the piecing together of scholarships, and the finding of ways and means. The winning of particular scholarships, of course, was likely to be remembered with pride. The son of a mechanical engineer who studied the same subject at Manchester in the mid-1930s (MC120) wrote as follows:

> In the spring of 1934, I took the Manchester University Entrance Scholarship Examinations, and was lucky enough to be awarded a Beckwith Engineering Entrance Scholarship, valued at £60 p.a. for three years. I was also awarded a Cheshire County Scholarship, valued at £25 p.a. for three years, and at the end of my first year was given an Ashbury Scholarship of £35 p.a. for two years.
>
> After graduating in 1937, I was given a University Grant which enabled me to remain at Manchester for a further year; I was then awarded an MSc degree in 1938.
>
> My 'income' up to graduation was £(60 × 3) plus £(25 × 3) plus £(35 × 2) which comes to £325. The approximate cost of an Honours Degree in Engineering was £188.7, the cost breakdown being – tuition fees £143.3, examination fees £8, laboratory deposits £14, textbooks £15, and graduation fee £8.4. Up to graduation, therefore, the excess of my income over cost was £325 − £188.3, which equals £136.3 [*sic*].
>
> During my four years at university I lived at home, and travelled up to Manchester each day, as did more than half the students in my year.

My surplus of £136 up to graduation went a long way towards keeping me fed and clothed, and left a little over for tennis club fees!

This man was clearly fortunate. Others remembered having had more of a struggle. The son of an unemployed sheet metal worker, whose mother was reduced to taking in laundry to keep the family together, recorded that:

I sat for and won a studentship from University College Nottingham which covered tuition fees but othing else. My local authority was a very poor one, with only two grammar schools...I was the only student in my school to sit the Higher School Certificate in my year (which I passed at credit level in each subject), and to apply for a grant, but I was refused. As a consequence I had to inform UCN that I was unable to take up their offer, and I started 'Pupil Teaching' in the village school of a neighbouring village.

U.C. Nottingham responded by offering to grant me a further £25 p.a. if the local authority would do likewise. After considerable negotiating and pleading by my Mother on my behalf, the local authority finally agreed to *loan* me £25 p.a., interest free.

Finally a distant family relative (a spinster lady) agreed to loan me £2 per month, interest free. On the strength of this minimum amount of funding... I entered UCN some six weeks after the start of the Autumn Term.

(NT 8)

Financial support for university studies came from a variety of sources. The main sources of support for the men and women in my sample are shown in Table 2.4. The most prestigious awards were the State Scholarships. These were in short supply (300 per year in the 1930s) and hotly competed for. Whiteley estimated the proportion of successful candidates as less than one in fourteen in 1931.[17] Somewhat contentiously, more of these scholarships were allocated to boys than to girls (188 for boys, 112 for girls in 1930), and the majority of the awards went to students destined for Oxford and Cambridge.[18] The slightly higher proportion of women over men holding State Scholarships in my sample reflects the fact that fewer women than men went to Oxford or Cambridge. The most important sources of support were local authority scholarships and grants from the Board of Education made to students who declared their intention of becoming teachers.

Two reports on the system of local authority awards in the interwar period were compiled for the Sir Richard Stapley Education Trust by G. S. M. Ellis in 1925[19] and by L. Doreen Whiteley in 1933. Both emphasized that there was little consistency in policy and practice between authorities in various parts of the country. The value of awards varied considerably, as did application of a 'means test' in relation to parental income. Ellis drew attention to the fact that girls were far less well catered for than boys, noting that 'the supply of public scholarships for girls was lagging behind the demand for higher education in a most alarming manner'.[20] Whiteley felt that some progress had been made by 1933 and that local authorities were moving towards equity for girls, but pointed out that the percentage of women in the student population in Britain as a whole had actually diminished between 1924–25 (30.7%) and 1930–31 (27.2%), attributing this in part to the difficulty of girls obtaining scholarships, and in part to family attitudes rating girls' education as less important than their brothers' in a time of economic recession.[21] Just under a third (29% of the women, 31% of the men) of my sample recorded that they had received scholarships or awards from their local authorities. The amounts varied widely, from around £40 to £100 p.a. Respondents were

*Table 2.4* Source of external funds for university studies

| University | Percentages in each university obtaining each type of funding* | | | | | | | | Total |
|---|---|---|---|---|---|---|---|---|---|
| | SS | LA | BofE | SchSch | CollSch | Loan | Other | Pledge | |
| *Men* | | | | | | | | | |
| BR | 0 | 31 | 39 | 7 | 12 | 14 | 25 | 41 | 59 |
| MC | 3 | 34 | 20 | 10 | 18 | 3 | 25 | 20 | 120 |
| NT | 0 | 27 | 18 | 0 | 50 | 27 | 32 | 32 | 22 |
| RD | 6 | 28 | 44 | 28 | 6 | 17 | 28 | 44 | 18 |
| LS | 2 | 31 | 17 | 9 | 22 | 8 | 26 | 16 | 96 |
| LP | 4 | 26 | 14 | 9 | 11 | 8 | 19 | 14 | 95 |
| UC | 3 | 29 | 9 | 9 | 17 | 9 | 19 | 9 | 93 |
| KC | 7 | 35 | 11 | 5 | 16 | 4 | 23 | 12 | 74 |
| Total | 3 | 31 | 18 | 9 | 17 | 8 | 23 | 19 | 577 |
| *Women* | | | | | | | | | |
| BF | 3 | 31 | 42 | 8 | 1 | 5 | 8 | 43 | 88 |
| MF | 6 | 33 | 38 | 10 | 8 | 11 | 13 | 40 | 136 |
| RF | 8 | 27 | 29 | 6 | 6 | 10 | 6 | 25 | 63 |
| UCF | 6 | 19 | 8 | 1 | 11 | 8 | 11 | 11 | 72 |
| BD | 10 | 29 | 23 | 13 | 10 | 8 | 13 | 25 | 87 |
| RH | 14 | 34 | 16 | 19 | 36 | 9 | 17 | 19 | 58 |
| Total | 7 | 29 | 28 | 10 | 11 | 9 | 12 | 30 | 504 |

*Notes:*
Key to funding types: SS = State Scholarship; LA = Local Authority grant; BofE = Board of Education grant; SchSch = School scholarship; CollSch = College scholarship; Pledge = Pledge to teach.
* Totals do not add to 100% because of family sources, multiple external sources, etc. For the key to universities, see Table 2.3.

well aware of the vagaries and variations: certain local authorities had a reputation for being generous, others the converse. A woman who went from Hastings to Royal Holloway in 1935 noted that her local authority gave one scholarship a year of £50: the year she went to college there were two candidates with the same needs and qualifications, so the authority divided the scholarship, each receiving £25 (RH50). A man whose family lived in Dewsbury remembered that he had obtained the highest marks in his school (Batley Grammar) for Higher School Certificate, but that the grant of £65 p.a. which he had received from Dewsbury education authority had been conspicuously less than that of some of his classmates who had lived in the West Riding. Two of his friends had been able to go to Cambridge on the strength of the West Riding's generosity, whilst he himself had had to settle for living at home and studying at Leeds (LS59). Another issue that rankled was that some authorities made awards which could be held in addition to state or other scholarships, others did not. And many authorities in the later 1930s were moving towards a practice of substituting grants with loans, or coupling grants with loans, a practice noted and deplored by Whiteley in her study of 1933.[22]

Whiteley was critical of the idea of student loans on the grounds that the authorities offering them were ignoring their 'duties of providing equal opportunities to all classes of able students, accepting the less costly and less glorious role of moneylender'.[23] Those most needy of loans, she argued, were the most necessitous, and she found it 'strange logic that the more heavily handicapped student should be required to refund the additional help he needs'. Nevertheless, as Table 2.5

*Table 2.5* Social class of origin and external funding type

| Class | Percentages in each social class obtaining each type of funding* | | | | | | | | Total |
|---|---|---|---|---|---|---|---|---|---|
| | SS | LA | BofE | SchSch | CollSch | Loan | Other | Pledge | |
| *Men* | | | | | | | | | |
| PHA | 0 | 8 | 3 | 2 | 15 | 3 | 14 | 3 | 105 |
| MEx | 3 | 19 | 8 | 9 | 17 | 3 | 19 | 9 | 145 |
| HNM | 3 | 30 | 20 | 7 | 17 | 8 | 24 | 20 | 121 |
| LNM | 4 | 29 | 29 | 1 | 14 | 11 | 26 | 27 | 73 |
| SKM | 5 | 51 | 29 | 14 | 19 | 14 | 39 | 32 | 59 |
| SSM | 5 | 56 | 41 | 7 | 27 | 15 | 32 | 41 | 41 |
| UM | 0 | 50 | 50 | 0 | 17 | 33 | 33 | 50 | 6 |
| ng | 4 | 48 | 4 | 7 | 11 | 4 | 22 | 4 | 27 |
| Total | 3 | 28 | 17 | 6 | 16 | 7 | 23 | 17 | 577 |
| *Women* | | | | | | | | | |
| PHA | 4 | 10 | 12 | 6 | 7 | 1 | 7 | 12 | 108 |
| MEx | 5 | 29 | 28 | 13 | 13 | 5 | 13 | 26 | 167 |
| HNM | 10 | 33 | 36 | 8 | 11 | 9 | 10 | 37 | 99 |
| LNM | 17 | 41 | 41 | 14 | 7 | 17 | 7 | 45 | 29 |
| SKM | 8 | 44 | 37 | 6 | 15 | 18 | 18 | 45 | 62 |
| SSM | 12 | 59 | 29 | 18 | 12 | 24 | 24 | 59 | 17 |
| UM | 20 | 60 | 20 | 0 | 0 | 20 | 0 | 40 | 5 |
| ng | 12 | 24 | 24 | 6 | 6 | 18 | 12 | 18 | 17 |
| Total | 7 | 31 | 28 | 9 | 11 | 9 | 12 | 30 | 504 |

*Notes:*
ng = not given (indicators such as father's occupation inadequate to judge the class of origin). For the key to social classes, see Table 2.3; for the key to funding types, see Table 2.4.
* Totals do not add to 100% because of family sources, multiple external sources, etc.

(linking father's occupation and funding source) shows, local authority awards operated fairly progressively amongst my sample, and allowed many who would not otherwise have been able to afford it the opportunity of a higher education.

The same can be said of Board of Education grants to intending teachers. These were particularly important for women, who had fewer other sources of funding available to them, but they were also important for young men from working-class backgrounds between the wars (see Tables 2.4, 2.5). Awards from the Board of Education or local authority in aid of teacher training frequently required the recipient to 'pledge' her- or himself to a period of five to seven years' school teaching following graduation. I have described something of how this system operated for women in an earlier study.[24] The system was much criticized by contemporaries who argued that large numbers of young people with no inclination or desire for a career in teaching were driven to pledge themselves to such as the only way of financing themselves through college.[25] The evidence from my questionnaires shows that this was indeed the case. Joan Cooper, for instance, whose father was a commercial traveller, had always wanted to be a social worker, an ambition which she eventually fulfilled by building a distinguished career in social work and public service (MF15). However, she would not have been able to graduate (from Manchester, in 1935) without the support of a Board of Education grant, and saw herself as having no option other than to 'mark time' in schoolteaching, a profession which held no attraction for her, between 1935 and 1941. At least 50 of the men in my sample indicated that the Board of Education grant had been their only route to university, but many had been less than wholehearted about teaching, and some of them freely confessed that they had dreaded the prospect. One man who had wanted to study medicine at Cambridge, but failed to get the Kitchener Scholarship which would have made this possible, accepted a Board of Education grant which would enable him to study botany at Bristol University instead (BR21). Another, from a manual working-class background, set his sights on the ministry, but his headmaster advised him that his only way to get a grant for university would be by declaring an intention to teach first; 'many students, including me, became Board of Education protégés, without any burning desire to teach' (BR43).

There was much discussion about whether a 'pledge' to teach was legally binding or not. Kathleen Uzzell, who received a grant for teacher training which enabled her to graduate in English from Bristol in 1933 (BF20), described how when she arrived at university she was called into a room with others in the same position 'where we were told we had to swear an oath to teach for five years', but it was pointed out that it was 'a moral, not a legal oath'. The Board of Education's *Regulations for the Training of Teachers* included a 'Form of Undertaking to be executed by students' in receipt of financial assistance, and the highly legalistic language of this 'indenture' certainly impressed students who signed it with a sense of the seriousness of their commitment.[26] A more simplified 'form of declaration of intent' seems to have been used by some authorities in the 1930s. Percy Yates, who graduated from Manchester in French in 1935 (MC68) remembered signing a pledge to teach for three years after training, but added that the Professor of Education had assured the students that 'it was "a matter of honour"', and that the document had no legal value, 'since we were all "minors" at the time of signing'.

Understandings of the situation (and practices) seem to have varied considerably, and several of my respondents suggested that rulings were relaxed or abandoned in the build-up to wartime. However, a number of those in the sample who had accepted grants for teacher training but who subsequently decided against entering the teaching profession were required to repay their grants, and this had clearly caused heartsearching and hardship. One woman who graduated from Royal Holloway in 1936 (RH4) had been the recipient of a Board of Education grant, but all too quickly decided that 'teaching was not for me': she used a small legacy from her mother to pay back her grant from the Board. In one particularly interesting case Mr John Tollyfield, a graduate of King's College London (KC41), had been subsidized by the Board of Education, but had found himself quite unable to secure a teaching post after completing his training. When he found alternative employment (with the Safety in Mines Research Board) the Board of Education demanded repayment, although conceding that some reduction would be made in the sum required if he could show that 'genuine though unsuccessful attempts to obtain teaching posts had been made'. After the war Mr Tollyfield managed to secure a post teaching in a secondary school and applied to the Ministry of Education asking for a repayment of the sum that they had earlier required him to repay to them. His correspondence with the Board/Ministry of Education over this vexed question of repayment spanned the years 1939–47: he posted the whole collection to me when returning his questionnaire, as evidence of the administrative complexities which had bedevilled the whole system at the time.

The system of recruiting teachers by making awards for university education conditional upon a 'pledge' to teach had had its critics from the outset. As early as 1914 Professor Edith Morley argued that young people were being 'bound too early by a contract they [found] it hard to break', and that the teaching profession was ill served by being staffed by reluctant recruits. Morley drew attention to the need for more generous provision of grants: 'There should be other paths from elementary and secondary school to the University than that which leads to the teacher's platform'.[27] By the 1930s, voices were raised claiming that the teaching profession was 'overstocked', and competition for posts in secondary schools was intense. Many of my respondents described the difficulties that they had experienced in securing teaching posts, and what Brian Simon, as President of the National Union of Students in 1939–40, described as 'a modern system of indentured labour' seemed increasingly indefensible.[28] Nonetheless, the Board of Education awards widened access to universities in England considerably before 1939.

Aside from State Scholarships, Local Authority Awards and grants from the Board of Education there were other possibilities of support in the form of scholarships awarded by schools and individual universities, as well as those from Guilds, private charities and other public bodies. Lists of grant-awarding bodies were compiled and published by Morley and Whiteley.[29] Boys were eligible for many more of these awards than were girls. Kitchener Scholarships (for the sons of officers or ex-servicemen) and support from religious bodies for those studying theology or divinity were not available to girls. The relative importance of these other categories of support for the graduates in my sample can be seen in Table 2.4. Although there was little difference between the proportions of men and women benefiting from school scholarships, the awards going to the women were often very small; the older endowed boys' secondary schools were richer than most girls' schools and were able to offer more generous support to ex-pupils. There were more college scholarships for boys, and these were more commonly linked to the study of scientific and technical subjects. The profile of girls receiving some kind of college award in my study is skewed by the inclusion of ex-students from Royal Holloway, which was particularly well endowed by its founder, Sir Thomas Holloway and his family. Indeed, some of the women who studied there told me that they had been persuaded to turn down offers from other institutions precisely because they had been offered scholarships from Royal Holloway. University College Nottingham was fortunate in being in a position to offer scholarships to intelligent young people from needy backgrounds on the strength of endowments from W. H. Revis and Jesse Boot, and at least half of my respondents from Nottingham had benefited from college scholarships or awards. Unlike Board of Education and Local Authority awards, however, many of these 'other' forms of support tended to operate 'regressively' rather than 'progressively', serving to benefit those from the 'better' secondary schools, not least, one suspects, because the teachers in those schools were better informed and placed to direct their pupils' attention to the possibilities of applying for support.

What emerges very strongly from my evidence is an impression of the sheer chanciness of the circumstances that allowed many of those in my sample to embark on a university education. Stories of having inherited a small legacy from a distant relative, or having been offered a loan from a spinster aunt, were comparatively common. A handful of respondents mentioned receiving some financial support from their teachers. One man, whose father was a carpenter, had no grant, and could envisage no way of continuing his studies. A teacher from his Midlands grammar school went to see the boy's parents with the offer of meeting all the expenses of four years of study at Bristol University (BR19). This he did: his protégé secured a BSc in maths and physics and a teacher's certificate; sixty years later he told me that he had always referred to his teacher as 'St George'. Another example of fortuity came from Mr J. Horrocks, who retired as a consultant pathologist, and who had qualified in medicine from Manchester in 1939 (MC2). In 1926, ten years before he embarked upon his university course, he had won a national 'scholarship competition' organized by a newspaper, the *Daily Dispatch*. The young James won the boys' (8–10 years) scholarship of £100, and 'My old Council School got a "wireless set" capable of receiving the schools transmission on Station 2ZY. It cost a staggering £10, and got a civic reception at the school'. Mr Horrocks' parents decided not to take the award immediately; ten years later, their son at Manchester University, the newspaper paid them exactly £100.

Stories of parental sacrifice were a recurring theme in the questionnaires. There was much scrimping and borrowing. The son of a cloth overlooker in a cotton mill who graduated from Manchester in 1935 (MC42) recorded that aside from his tuition fees, which were paid by the local authority, his parents met all of the cost of his university education. His mother had not been earning, and his father's wage at the time had been under £3 per week. 'How they managed I do not know', he wrote, 'they sacrificed so much for me'. The son of an accounts clerk who graduated from King's College London in the early 1930s (KC33) remembered that his tuition fees alone had accounted for around one-third of his father's annual income. Both of these men had been only children. Larger families of course added to the burden of education, even amongst the more middle-class families. The son of a clerical executive working in the London County Council (LCC) Public Health Department remembered that his father had had quite a struggle to support three children through to graduation on a salary of £500 p.a. – even though the LCC had given help with fees. Those from larger families often reported that younger siblings had had to wait for older siblings to graduate, in order not to put too much strain on the family budget at any one time.

The son of a driller on Merseyside remembered his widowed father's anxiety when a headmaster suggested that the boy should go to college (BR43). 'It was with great misgivings, and much worry about the cost of it all that he allowed me to go to university'. There were many similar stories. There can be little doubt that the extraordinary amount of detail about costs recalled by many of my respondents stemmed from vivid memories of difficulty and feelings of obligation from that time. The networks of family obligation spread wide, and grandparents and godparents, aunts, uncles and other relations frequently gave support. Brothers sometimes paid for sisters when fathers died. Older sisters in teaching posts often contributed to the costs of their brothers' education. The son of an unemployed railway signalman thought he had no hope of studying medicine at university, but 'My teachers and my sister, newly trained to teach, made it possible. Everyone in my family rallied round', he recalled (MC119). A man who studied dyeing and colour chemistry at Leeds University – courtesy of a Clothworker's scholarship from his school in Gloucestershire – recorded that his parents had very limited means (his father worked as a chauffeur). Help with maintenance came from his grandmother who worked as a laundress; she sent him ten shillings or whatever she could afford in an envelope, each week (LS73).

Mothers were particularly important in making it possible for young people from working-class backgrounds to go to university. Many of my respondents emphasized their debt to their mothers. 'I have appreciated the opportunity to fill in this questionnaire' wrote one man, 'because it provides me with a chance to pay tribute to my widowed mother who toiled away as a school cook in order to make it all possible' (KC41). Only a small minority of the graduates indicated that their mothers had been in employment at the time when they went to college, but the range of ways in which mothers contrived to provide economic as well as moral support was quite extraordinary. Some took in lodgers or laundry, others did dressmaking, kept corner shops, or ran small businesses selling cakes, sandwiches and, in one case, ice-cream made in her backyard (LS1). One mother became a cook in the hall of residence in which her son lived at university (RD18). Widows had to be particularly resourceful if they were determined, as many of them were, to give their sons 'a good start in life'. The widowed mother of a man who graduated from Bristol supplemented her small pension by working as a domestic servant so that her son could complete his studies (BR21). Another mother became a publican when her husband (who had been a pharmacist) died so that her son could qualify as a doctor (MC71). No historian can possibly deny, that the odds were massively stacked against the likelihood of children from the working class acquiring a secondary education before 1939, let alone proceeding to any university.[30] But feats of self-sacrifice on the part of some parents, determined that their children should have a better life, made this possible in some cases.

## Conclusion

Before this research was undertaken comparatively little was known about the social background of the students attending English universities other than Oxford or Cambridge before 1939. R. D. Anderson suggested, in an article written in 1991, that 'the sources usually describe them as essentially middle class'.[31] This chapter has shown that the numbers of students from lower middle- and working-class homes who made it up the ladder (or greasy pole) from elementary school to university before the Second World War was quite considerable. England had fewer university students per head of the population than did Scotland (or Wales), but the social profile of those attending the universities in the two countries was not dissimilar. My sample of over 1000 graduates must be considered quite a large one given that the total population of English universities (leaving out Oxbridge) was around 25,600 in 1937–38. One of the hazards of doing historical research using the memories of the living, rather than archival sources, is that the researcher may be given instructions. One of my respondents, who graduated from Liverpool in 1938 (LP69), and who was the son of a department supervisor who worked in a factory, penned a little note on the back of his questionnaire: 'What I hope', he said, 'is that you will be able to undermine the myth that only the rich and the "posh" got to a university in the 1930s! This is far from the truth'. He was quite right. Jennie Lee's story of how she secured a university education in Scotland in the 1920s would have sounded very familiar to many of the graduates who shared their histories with me.

## Acknowledgements

My thanks to the Spencer Foundation for allowing me to carry out the study of women graduates, and to the Economic and Social Research Council for making it possible to complement this with a study of male graduates. I am extremely grateful to the Alumni and Development Officers who helped with this project, and to the graduates themselves, who so generously supplied information. Professor G. N. von Tunzelmann gave indispensable support with statistics and tables. All responsibility, of course, remains my own.

## Notes

1  Jennie Lee, *This Great Journey* (New York and Toronto, 1942).
2  Ibid., 56–9, 47–8.

3    Patricia Hollis, *Jennie Lee: A Life* (Oxford, 1997), 17.
4    R. D. Anderson, 'Universities and Elites in Modern Britain', *History of Universities*, 10 (1991), 230–6.
5    R. D. Anderson, *Universities and Elites in Britain since 1800* (Basingstoke, 1992), 23.
6    Anderson, *Universities and Elites in Modern Britain*, 234.
7    Anderson, *Universities and Elites in Britain since 1800*, 53. In *The Decline of Privilege: The Modernization of Oxford University* (Stanford, 1999), Joseph A. Soares argues that after the First World War, the 'not very academic sons of wealthy gentlemen were bumped aside by meritocratic scholars often from middle- or working-class homes' (p. 9), but nevertheless recognizes that even in 1938, 'state school alumni contributed only 19% of Oxford's freshmen' (ibid.). Of course, by no means were all of the latter from modest homes. The decline of the 'gentleman commoner' in Oxford between the wars is discussed in some detail by Daniel Greenstein in *The History of the University of Oxford, vol. VIII, The Twentieth Century*, edited by B. Harrison (Oxford, Clarendon Press, 1994), 52–9.
8    England's nine 'other' universities, with the dates of their charters, were: Birmingham (1900), Bristol (1909), Durham (1832), Leeds (1904), Liverpool (1903), London (1836), Manchester (1903), Reading (1926) and Sheffield (1905). The University Colleges, with their dates of foundation, were Exeter (1901), Hull (1926), Leicester (1922), Nottingham (1903) and Southampton (1905).
9    L. D. Whiteley, *The Poor Student and the University; A Report on the Scholarship System, with Particular Reference to Awards Made by Local Educational Authorities* (London, 1925), 19, 30.
10    J. Hall and D. Caradog Jones, 'The Social Grading of Occupations', *British Journal of Sociology*, 1 (1950), 33–40. See also C. A. Moser and J. Hall, 'The Social Grading of Occupations', in *Social Mobility in Britain*, edited by D. V. Glass (London, 1954).
11    E. M. Becket, *The University College of Nottingham* (Nottingham, 1928), 54. Becket quotes from a Treasury Inspectors' Report of 1901–02 which noted that 'Nottingham University College stood at the head of all English university colleges in the number of students who entered from elementary schools and that the opportunities offered to young working men of promise were very considerable'. 'We think', stated the Inspectors, 'that the College exhibits the nearest approach of all colleges we have visited to a People's University' (p. 54).
12    'Bruce Truscot' (E. Allison Peers), *Redbrick University* (London, 1943), 20, note 1.
13    Anderson, *Universities and Elites in Britain since 1800*, 56.
14    Whiteley, 59–61. For more detail on costs see C. Dyhouse, *No Distinction of Sex? Women in British Universities 1870–1939* (London, 1995), 27ff.; C. L. Mowat, in *Britain between the Wars*, 1918–1940 (Methuen, London, 1968), 490, estimated that in the mid-1930s, around three-quarters of all families in Britain could be described as 'working class', with an income of £4 a week or less (£208 p.a.).
15    Figures extracted from those published by UGC, *Returns from Universities and University Colleges in Receipt of Treasury Grant for the Academic Year* 1937–38 (London, 1939), Table 1.
16    Whiteley, 30.
17    Ibid., 33–5.
18    Dyhouse, *No Distinction of Sex?*, 31–2.
19    G. S. M. Ellis, *The Poor Student and the University, A Report on the Scholarship System, with Particular Reference to Awards Made by Local Educational Authorities* (London, 1925); Whiteley, op. cit.
20    Ellis, 9.
21    Whiteley, 23–5.
22    Whiteley was critical of the idea of student loans on the grounds that local authorities offering them were abandoning their 'duties of providing equal opportunities to all classes of able students, accepting the less costly and less glorious role of money-lender' (p. 78).
23    Ibid.
24    C. Dyhouse, 'Signing the Pledge? Women's Investment in University Education and Teacher Training before 1939', *History of Education*, 26, 2 (1997), 207–23.
25    See for example, H. G. G. Herklots, *The New Universities, An External Examination* (London, 1928), esp. Ch. 6, 'The Nemesis of Teaching'.

26 Board of Education, Regulations for the Training of Teachers (HMSO 1918) Cd. 9170, Appendix B, 55–7.
27 Edith Morley, *Women Workers in Seven Professions; A Survey of their Economic Conditions and Prospects, Edited for the Studies Committee of the Fabian Women's Group* (London, 1914), 11–12.
28 Brian Simon, *A Student's View of the Universities* (London, 1943), 46.
29 Morley, 82–136; Whiteley, 118–41.
30 In 1926 Kenneth Lindsay estimated that less than 1% (0.73) of elementary school children reached universities (K. Lindsay, *Social Progress and Educational Waste, Being a Study of the 'Free Place' and Scholarship System* (London, 1926), 193).
31 Anderson, *Universities and Elites in Modern Britain*, 238.

# PART II

# INFORMAL AGENCIES OF EDUCATION

## CHAPTER 3

# ON LITERACY IN THE RENAISSANCE*

## Review and reflections

### Harvey J. Graff

*History of Education, 12, 2, 69–85, 1983*

## Preface and overview

Renaissance. Literacy. How well these words resound when linked together. How naturally and intimately their relationships strike responsive chords in the minds and, perhaps even more deeply, the hearts of historians. That connection is not in the least surprising – not to persons familiar with the historiographical literature.

The age, or ages, of the great Renaissance rebirth of learning clearly impinges on manifold issues related to the social distributions and cultural conditions of literacy. The Renaissance was, in too many ways to note, profoundly an educational and a pedagogical movement. Although this has long been appreciated, recent scholarship in the Humanities has reinforced the point and deepened our understanding. Furthermore, the era witnessed the diffusion of printing, which also influenced currents in literacy and learning. Finally, this was an age of discovery and invention, marked by exploration and advancement manifest in science, medicine, technological innovations – eyeglasses, the compass, weaponry – and in the spread of what we now term the 'European world system'; all of these helped to reshape the known universe between the fourteenth and seventeenth centuries.

The contribution of literacy to these epochal transformations has been recognized, although its precise roles are, not yet well specified. Conversely, the changing configurations of European society, culture, and political economies equally, if not even more dramatically, affected the levels, roles, and meanings of literacy. That, while appreciated, is perhaps less clearly understood.

Despite these recognitions, which have achieved the safe (and sometimes stultifying) harbour of historical commonplaces, far too little is known about the basic facts of literacy during this key transitional era of 'early modernity'. Literacy, as a subject for direct historical analysis, is something of a novelty; its literature, though expanding rapidly, is hardly exhaustive or satisfying. As I have argued at length elsewhere, a general assurance of the nature of literacy's contributions, derived from a post-Enlightenment synthesis of 'normative' humanistic and social scientific 'wisdom', long precluded the direct study of literacy as a historical factor and a fresh questioning and critical stance toward our usual expectations and assumptions of its primacy and provenance.[1] For the 'pre-statistical' era, there remain, in addition, perhaps insoluble problems of evidence, although recent scholarship points to some ways around this complication.[2]

Conceptual problems, part theoretical, part historiographic, and part epistemological, plague efforts to comprehend literacy as a historical factor and force. Briefly put, what I term collectively the 'legacies of literacy' – centuries-old and much more recently – have culminated in expectations that literacy's roles are typically linear, direct, progressive, relatively unmediated, highly pervasive, and requisite and responsible for individual, societal, and national advancement. Literacy, in this common view, is not only intimately associated with progress and modernization, but also inextricably linked with *change*. Indeed, the sheer number of concomitants asserted to accompany changing levels of basic literacy and the processes of its acquisition could fill weighty tomes by themselves. Alas, the evidence – whether statistical or more substantive – typically is revealingly scarce. As an increasing number of students are beginning to recognize, new paths to conceptualization and understanding are needed; given contemporary perceptions of 'crises' and 'declines', the need is no less than urgent.[3]

These kinds of complications confound attempts to explicate the history of literacy during the centuries that comprise the European Renaissance. That is one of my arguments in surveying our knowledge of the contours of that history. There can be no doubt that the years spanning the fourteenth to the sixteenth centuries were critical in the long sweep of literacy's history. In the same way, there can be no doubt that this history differs from its usual presentations, whether in the hands of textbook authors or authorities like Professors Cipolla or Eisenstein.[4]

What I argue here is that literacy's courses, its determinants and its influences during this period can only be grasped with direct attention to (a) *contradictions* in the processes of social, economic, political, and cultural development; (b) *continuities*, as well as *changes*, in thought about literacy, agencies for transmission and dissemination, and realities of changing patterns of distribution, demand, and uses; (c) considerations of the variety of *outcomes* (sometimes opposing or conflicting) from such patterns; (d) greater than usual attention to literacy's associations with *hierarchies and inequalities* and, perhaps most importantly for historians; (e) more precise specification of what *qualitative levels* and what *different kinds* of literacy(ies) are under discussion. This, it may be noted, is hardly an exhaustive list of cautions. Rather, it is best taken as a set of origin points.

Perhaps the most intractable of all such problems impinges on issues of definitions of literacy, their relationships to levels and utilities of the skills, and, together, their relationship to the limited array of sources available to the student. Given such problems, for which no grand resolution is proposed here, I focus on levels of basic or elementary skills of reading and writing, *except as otherwise specified*, in this essay. The typical, if far from satisfactory indicator, is of course the presence or absence of a signature; such admittedly problematic sources only become available in a systematic if hardly sufficient fashion in this period. [The deficiencies of this measure are well-known. I shall not rehearse either the case against or in favour of its use in these pages. In the absence of alternatives, the historian must utilize, with caution and criticism, that which is available.] Signs of literacy in any language, and not solely in the learned Latin, are accepted; indeed, in his era, vernacular literacy not only takes on special importance but constitutes a force in its own right. Evidence of the uses and non-uses of reading and writing lends meaning to such measures. Literacy, finally, is viewed in terms that are not limited solely to the functional or its 'functionalities'. The import of such a perspective should be apparent.

From that beginning, let us consider the subject more directly. If the preceding is granted – and about that there may be some dissent – I wish to argue the following, in brief and highly schematic form.

i The centuries that comprise the Renaissance era were a critical period for literacy, but perhaps more so in ways that are not so commonly stressed.

ii Many of the major intellectual and broadly 'high' cultural events and advances of the Renaissance age have, perhaps surprisingly, relatively little to do directly with literacy *per se*. That point need not diminish the celebration of the achievements of the era, nor lessen their relevance (if conceived differently) for the history of literacy in that time or in the future.[5]

iii Regardless of the usually-emphasized changes and transformations of the period, literacy's history owes a major debt to social and cultural continuities. This does not imply that literacy's contours were unchanging; they were not. Instead, it demands a greater sensitivity to the Renaissance's relations to its own past and precursors. Continuities conditioned, shaped and limited the uses of literacy during the Renaissance. Thus, the simultaneity of change *and* continuity must be grasped and grappled with.

iv This was an era of marked advances in rates of literacy and in changing uses of literacy. To appreciate this, in the context suggested here, firm distinction must be made between levels, qualities and uses among elites (intellectual and other), middling persons, and the labouring and peasant orders. For some persons and places impressively high levels were achieved; for others little change transpired. Simple generalizations serve to describe or link neither the experiences of the different orders of society nor, for that matter, those of different geographic places. To the contrary, unevenness and often sharp differentiation are expected and found.[6]

v Change, sometimes major, *is* important in this period, yet it was probably not a common experience if the mass of European populations is considered. The major transformations, with many of which we are all familiar, were often slow to develop, and sometimes gradual, hesitant, and incomplete in their challenges and penetration. The early decades of printing, as well as the onset of pedagogical and cultural reforms, may be taken as examples.[7]

vi Literacy's roles, determinants, and influences or associations were seldom direct or unmediated. Literacy's history, in other words, can *never* be an isolated, abstracted history; it is *one* with the larger, complicated histories of society, culture, polity, and economy. This is marked in the case before us.

vii Potentially most significant *and* most difficult is the striking possibility that comprehending the history of literacy in this seminal age requires breaking the bounds of traditional definitions of literacy. As usually (and I also argue usefully) termed, literacy refers to reading and writing (decoding and reproducing, if you will, the products of writing and printing). The medium of exchange, to coin a phrase, is alphabetic. That, of course, is what we overwhelmingly signify when employing the term 'literacy', something better captured by the French *l'alphabétisation*. I recommend maintaining this usage, but going one step further in delimiting its employment: reserving 'literacy', *if* unqualified by modifiers or adjectives, for basic levels of so-called 'traditional' or alphabetic literacy. References to 'higher' or 'critical' forms of reading and writing skills, for example, can be made by qualifying the term 'literacy'; as one result, much historical (as well as contemporary) confusion may be reduced.[8]

My point with respect to the Renaissance is slightly different. In this, I follow the implications of recent thinking and, ironically, writing, in the arts and in science and technology. This is the significant recognition that there exist very different kinds of types of literacy or literacies: ranging, it seems, from numeracy to graphicacy, to various kinds of artistic, visual, aural, and perhaps even physical skills of and for 'reading' and expressing communicatively and meaningfully. More specifically, what I propose, although not wholly originally, is that some of the greatest achievements in the arts and in technology, and probably also in science and medicine, stemmed from advances in the uses of *non*alphabetic literacy, especially from forms of visual literacy or literacies.

These, then, are my major themes. Obviously, to fully develop or document them is impossible in a brief chapter such as this. Rather, in the remainder of this chapter, I wish to comment selectively on certain aspects of them. In so doing, I wish to suggest the outlines for a new approach to literacy's history and to hint at some speculations and hypotheses that strike one historian as worthy of investigation and reflection. I shall address the trends and levels of literacy, the patterns of uses and demands for literacy's skills, the 'meaning' of the Renaissance for literacy levels, the place of literacy in the contemporary culture(s), and, finally, achievements of 'visual' literacies. (I should note that only brief mention is made of the significance of print.)

## Trends and levels of literacy

The bewildering variety of literacy levels during the period we call the Renaissance, and the vagaries and limitations of the written record itself, preclude any simple survey or summary, yet that variety and vagary are themselves revealing. First, they reflect in fairly direct ways the uneven and often irregular patterns of socioeconomic, cultural, and political development of the late medieval and early modern eras; that development, often conjointly with the persisting impact of religiosity, underlay – although in no linear or simple causal sense – the contours and conditions of continental literacy. However trite it may seem today, the ages of the Renaissance were part of the epochal passing of a medieval world and worldview, and the onset of an incipient modernity. Levels and uses of literacy, and the forces and motivations that impelled and shaped them, were *transitional*. The meeting of new and old, of beginnings as well as endings, is found in European literacy of the period – not yet a fully literate world.

Variety – variability – is the first point to note, although students are forever limited by the paucity of sources that reveal, directly or indirectly, patterns of individual possession of literacy's skills, typically at an elementary level. That throughout Europe levels of adult elementary literacy cannot have surpassed something on the order of 5% is hardly surprising. That rural and agrarian areas (in a world that was overwhelmingly rural) had a largely non- or illiterate population is not a novel claim. Yet within the countrysides that were home to most Europeans, pockets of literacy and literate men (far less often of women, however) could be found. Although in the mass or aggregate, Renaissance Europe was neither a functionally nor culturally literate society, literacy was evidently expanding and beginning to break medieval bounds; the economies, polities, and cultures that comprised continental society were increasingly marked by the presence of literacy and the written word. Its context, however, more resembled the past than the future, regardless of some scholarly claims to the contrary.[9]

What must be stressed, though, is the *extent* of the diffusion of the skills of basic reading and writing and the *expanding patterns* of their uses. That extent *should* be seen as impressive, if not astonishing, and as unprecedented, despite being persistently restricted and uneven. Two brief examples establish my claim: the great centres of Florence and London. Florentine literacy levels have long, since G. Villani's time (1339), been celebrated; indeed, I believe that they have been exaggerated. Nevertheless, my demographic estimates suggest that perhaps as many as 50% of the school-aged population were in some form of education, with perhaps two-thirds of them male. Many of them gained some post-elementary schooling. Overall, adult basic literacy was conceivably as high as 25–35%, with, to be sure, sharp gender, class, status, and wealth differentials. This, I emphasize, was an astonishing achievement for a time before print or public school systems. Opportunities for schooling for local youths abounded, and the city's dynamism attracted migrants who were more likely to be literate than not. Of course, Florence's achievement, not sustained long into the future, was exceptional; it can only be explained in the specific contexts of social structure and relationships, economic developments and opportunities, benefactions, cultural vitality, political structures and the like which made Florence the jewel of the Italian Renaissance. This was perhaps the limits of the possible. In numerous ways, literacy was valuable, or perceived as important to large and growing numbers of Florentines in the Quattrocento.

Whilst Florence's literacy levels were exceptional and precedent-setting, they were not quite unique. Although lacking that plurality of conjunctures that made Florence so distinctive, other important centres of commerce and trade, finance and exchange, small commodity production, administration – civil and clerical, migration, education, religious and cultural production, and surplus wealth and luxury can be located among the *urban* lights of fourteenth-, fifteenth-, and sixteenth-century Europe. One or more such places can be found in most of the regions or incipient nations of the West. Further, these were places, relatively less scarred by the Black Death and other ravages of the first half of the period, which may have seen their literacy levels rise in partial consequence.

London is a good example, well studied in pioneering work by Sylvia Thrupp and more recently David Cressy. Thrupp was able to document impressively high literacy rates for the merchant class of late-medieval London, regardless of her tendency to extrapolate too readily from her rare but limited sources. Economic, religious, and cultural needs all provided a base for high levels of literacy – especially among the merchant class – as for increasing educational opportunities and their direct support – on that foundation were built more needs for cultural consumption, status symbols, and higher levels and more sophisticated uses of literacy. As in Florence and elsewhere, the maturation and more common use of vernacular language also underlay and stimulated such growth. Literacy was also achieving a pragmatic or practical value: a relatively new one for many persons, though 'traditional' uses and motives remained crucial. Crafts, professions, and women's culture were also positive forces. Thrupp presents evidence of a 40% literacy rate amongst 'employed' males: merchants achieved a significantly high level in a group skewed toward the higher ranking occupations. Cressy's sixteenth-century data suggest continued growth in the distribution of literacy. He stresses, perhaps a bit narrowly, more or less 'functional' or practical motivations as key.[10]

London and Florence, if not unique, were not representative of the fuller expanse of the continent or even their own regional and national territories. Many places continued to experience the presence of at best a small handful of literate persons (regardless of language of literacy); some remained much like LeRoy Ladurie's thirteenth-century mountain village of Montaillou or his largely illiterate

Languedoc of the sixteenth and early seventeenth centuries. In parts of this region, in the 1570s through 1590s, only 3% of agricultural workers and 10% of better-off peasants could sign their names; women were virtually 100% illiterate.[11] Parts of rural England were not much more often literate, as was much of Spain and eastern Europe. England, was, overall, one of the European leaders in literacy, although it was likely to have been passed by parts of Germany and the Dutch and Swedish lands by the later-sixteenth and seventeeth century, with the penetration of the Reformation.[12]

Europe is perhaps best viewed as extraordinarily variegated or 'crazy quilt', especially with regard to literacy levels. Cities and towns were regularly populated by a higher proportion of literates, and attracted more literate immigrants. They held more formal and informal opportunities for learning and for higher education. Literacy was definitely expanding, sometimes significantly. Nevertheless, the countryside was not static in terms of literacy, albeit with substantial, significant variations. Literacy, writing, and later print, and more educational opportunities (often at the level of parish priests and clerks) were penetrating, to some extent, a growing area. Naturally, the more advanced or developed regions moved farthest and fastest; medieval limits were being stretched, if not always broken. Regardless, with the rise of literacy levels (which, it should be noted, did 'take off' from medieval beginnings), real limits remained and were even reinforced. Most important were those of gender, social origins, social status and wealth ('class', if that term be allowed), places or regions of birth and residence, types of work or occupations, and similar factors. The links between literacy and stratification were growing, as were cultural divisions by states and regions. Within such a social framework, numerous forces could push or pull individuals toward or away from literacy. Yet, as Cressy, Spufford, and Laqueur all emphasize, individual motivations began to count for more and were able to overcome some obstacles.[13]

## Uses of literacy

The first generation of literacy studies, now largely completed, paid far less attention to the needs for and uses of reading and writing (the two are not always the same as narrow functionalism might otherwise suggest) than to measuring or estimating patterns of distribution. The many careful counts tell us relatively little, alas, about the larger significance and meanings of literacy. The issue is nonetheless vital.

In a nutshell, the Renaissance era can well be seen as a time of changes but also of continuities. In that intersection lies its relevance for literacy's history and that of literacy for it. About both, our understanding is far from complete; 'modern' assumptions have sometimes inadequately substituted for critical analysis and historical imagination. We are, I believe, only now gaining a grasp of the simultaneous circumstances of expanding and changing uses of reading and writing, reinforced and amplified by moveable typographic printing after the mid-fifteenth century; a strongly persistent 'traditional' and orally-based cultural mode of communications that limited the uses of literacy while also integrating literate with oral and aural modes, partially reshaping both; the continuing power of religion and the Church; and very real limits to both opportunities and needs for literacy's skills for most Europeans of the period. If this complicated, indeed transitional, cultural conjucture strikes you as contradictory, that, I believe, lies as much as in the history as in this interpreter (!) and constitutes an important recognition in itself.

The plethora of possible and actual uses of literacy defies simple listing or categorization; my commentary nevertheless demands such a simplification. At the grossest level, these observations seem most germane: for the largest mass of the population, there was, practically speaking, no special need for literacy. On the one hand, rural peasants, agricultural workers, and small holders who constituted the greatest share of the people, had no significant pragmatic need for individual access to reading or writing. Their work and welfare did not demand it; neither did religious adherence, especially for those on the land. On the other hand, their culture, as Natalie Davis in particular has argued, placed little primacy on it; and, in any case, the written (and more, perhaps, the printed) word worked its way into their minds through church readings by notables or officials, and by a literate reading to many others who were themselves unable to read in such settings as evening *veillées* and other collective occasions.[14] Readers and scribes seem to have been available in many, if not all places.[15] With the growth of a capitalized, commercialized market and rural production for market exchange and a possible expansion of private property ownership, to the contrary, did come more formal and direct needs for and uses of literacy. This was limited and selective, of course. According to Clanchy, this process of penetration and encroachment was underway in the twelfth through to the fourteenth centuries.[16] It spread even further during the next two or three centuries. The literacy levels of landholding peasants and yeomen in some parts of Europe do show the mounting utilities of literacy's skills: both to protect oneself and one's family and to use reading and writing toward one's own and one's family's advantage. Those of power, wealth, and status had many other motives and uses. Not all took up such possibilities, of course.

In addition to social, economic, and political changes that pushed increasing numbers of persons toward literacy, cultural and religious trends pulled more persons toward it. This was true before the Reformation, as Aston has demonstrated for Lollards, and more so after its onset.[17] The relationships tying literacy to such forces worked in complex ways; both sides of any equation are best viewed as at once causes and consequences; few such factors worked independently from one another. In the countryside, literacy's presence was becoming stronger from a number of motives. Yet, illiteracy remained the most common condition. Among other things, this serves to remind us that: (a) no linear or narrowly utilitarian interpretations will serve well; and (b) as Cressy (among others) observes:

> First, it should be stressed that people were capable of rational action, of acquiring and digesting information, and of making well-founded political and religious decisions without being able to read or write. Illiteracy was not necessarily a bar to economic advancement nor did it stand in the way of common sense. Second, we should not assume that people were wiser or more in control of their environment just because they had become literate. The skill could be squandered, used to rot the mind as well as inform it..., and might find no exercise beyond scanning an almanac or signing a receipt... We must distinguish the liberating potential of popular literacy from its more mundane reality... Literacy unlocked a variety of doors, but it did not necessarily secure admission.[18]

But that, as critical as it is, is only one dimension of the dialectic that literacy's realities comprised. The other more frequently (though not exclusively) urban pole was changing during this era, for reasons both old and more novel. Density, wealth, and better channels for communications underlay not only more opportunities for using literacy but also stimulated (and required, too) more demands and uses. Economics, politics, popular and scholarly culture, benevolence, concern for social order, and of course religion and its imperatives joined in this, as they came together in different ways and to differing degrees in the cities, towns, and sometimes the villages and countrysides of Europe: before and after the advent of printing. As Natalie Davis notes for sixteenth-century French cities, 'this press for literacy was associated with technological, economic, and social developments'.[19]

For Florence and Venice from the mid-thirteenth through the fourteenth century, J. K. Hyde points to the following uses of literacy: new employment for long-distance commerce and finance; accurate records of transactions in ledgers including the beginnings of double-entry book-keeping, correspondence, bills of exchange, contracts, and means to transport them thus creating a new class of 'professionally literate merchants' whose literacy differed from that of previously literate clergy and lawyers. Not needing Latin, they tended to stress numeracy and some degree of calculation. This could be a literacy active and broad; its remains are of enormous bulk, as the archive of Francesco Datini of Prato demonstrates. These uses of literacy at once overlapped with similar practices of civil and clerical administrators and large landowners as well as diplomats. They differed strikingly, however, from those of literary and scholarly elites. But, as Hyde usefully explicates, in one literary genre of the early Renaissance period,

> mercantile influence is unmistakable. This is the lay autobiographies and citizen family histories which grew directly out of the books of memoranda in which businessmen recorded their personal affairs...[and which] being essentially private, could be elaborated with a freedom impossible in more public documents.[20]

Importantly, the maturation, expansion, and popular (if not always scholarly) acceptance of the vernacular (as in this case, Tuscan) underlay and abetted many of these developments. With printing came a greater possibility for individual and improving uses of literacy. Such personal writing, of course, is only one sign of an emergent lay expressiveness, seen in other literary works of the period. This was also the age of Dante, his peers, and successors: another aspect of the transitional state of the era, and the forms of rhetoric that accompanied it. Diverse aspects of Renaissance culture were influenced, including forms of civic life and artistic creation, although many elites and scholars were revealingly ambivalent. Literacy was by no means an independent stimulus, as factors that propelled its increase also stimulated its diverse and sometimes novel employments. Histories, chronicles, political writings, philosophy, classical translations, in addition to literature – prose and poetic – and perhaps also to some extent medicine and science reflected this, and benefited. Great strides did not await the advent of printing. Importantly, oral culture – rhetoric, as spoken – was at least as great a beneficiary, if not even more so. This was one, but not the only, manifestation of Renaissance humanism. Nevertheless, the predominating religiosity of the age was not replaced; if anything, for prospering as well as popular classes, it may well have *increased* with expanding literacy and its uses. Early printing also demonstrates this. Of course, such important uses of literacy barely touched directly the truly popular classes, the *menu peuple*.

For the more 'ordinary' residents of towns and cities, the changing uses of literacy were different but still significant. Religion was one common, underlying factor. With the multiplication of manuscripts, vernacular writings, including religious materials, block prints, heresies and dissent and, then, printing and Reform, an earlier foundation typically above that of rural areas expanded. Crafts, by practical needs as well as by 'new' traditions, increasingly required literate workers. Apprentices were either to be able to read upon entry or were, in theory, to be instructed in letters as well as morality as part of their training. Guilds founded and supported schools; further, early welfare efforts by municipalities began to institute tutelage in elementary literacy along with religion and morality for their charges and inmates.

Literacy, not surprisingly, was not evenly distributed among urban workers. In Lyon, for example, according to Davis, in the late sixteenth century, there was a clear hierarchy of crafts by literacy rate which seems to parallel their status and wealth levels:

*Very high*: apothecaries, surgeons, printers.
*High*: painters, musicians, taverners, metalworkers (including gold).
*Medium (about 50%)*: furriers and leatherworkers, artisans in textiles and clothing.
*Low to very low*: artisans in construction, provisioning, transport; urban gardeners; unskilled day workers.

Levels varied from place to place; the facts of distinct hierarchies varied much less.[21]

City and town dwellers were also more likely to understand national vernaculars than rural folk. This not only gave an additional stimulus to their acquisition of literacy, but it also gave them access to more materials, individually or collectively, directly or indirectly. Nevertheless, although this category of evidence is ambiguous, urban artisans seldom owned books, or at least seldom were they listed in their wills. If they did, French studies indicate that the *Book of Hours* or the *Golden Legend*, a vernacular Bible, or a technical work such as a pattern book were most likely. They did not rush to personally acquire the products of the press. Costs, to be sure, limited their buying even after printing's advent, but it is more revealing that they found other ways to gain access to writing or prints. 'They bought a book, read it until they finished, or until they were broke or needed cash, and then pawned it with an innkeeper or more likely sold it to a friend or to a *libraire*.' Books were also shared in oral reading groups which brought together the literate and the illiterate, and some writings were clearly designed to be read orally rather than to be read silently. Perhaps the most innovative of such reading groups were the secret and secretive bands of religious dissenters: from the Lollards (well discussed by Aston) to Protestants. Such groups formed much deeper bonds, regardless of individual literacy abilities; they also more often crossed neighbourhood and occupational group lines. Cultural divisions were thus reinforced. Literacy was sought by an increasing number among virtually all social groups before the Great Reform of the 1520s and religiosity was both a motive and a consequence. Forms, influences, and results varied, to be sure.[22]

As Davis' French studies have taught us, some few among the urban *menu peuple*, not unlike Hyde's Italian merchants, expanded their literacy into writing. This was furthered by print, but print was not itself a cause. Surgeons and apothecaries wrote on health, medicine, and welfare; sailors on their travels; artisans and traders presented poetry; the potter Bernard Palissy wrote important dialogues on chemistry and agriculture; and there were the justly famed printer-scholars (as recently re-emphasized by Elizabeth Eisenstein). Some women also took to pen and print. On rare occasions, finally, groups spoke collectively through the literate medium, as did for example the *compagnonnages* of the journeymen of Lyon and Paris in a brief to the Parlement of Paris in 1572 objecting to a royal edict on printing and attacking their employers. Literacy, though not actually *causing* politicization or collective action, did prove a valued, useful vehicle for presenting, airing, and gaining larger audiences for grievances. This was no less true for advice literature, religious writings, creative literature, or, for that matter, scholarship – all amplified in important new, innovative ways with the addition of printing technology.[23]

## The Renaissance's relationships to literacy

Penetrating the textbook glosses of literacy as stimulus to the Renaissance and, conversely, the Renaissance as further stimulus to literacy is no simple task. Beyond the bounds of self-evident, partial truisms, often weak in explanatory or interpretive value – and the fact that the Renaissance was, chronologically, a period of generally rising levels of literacy – the connections are often less than clear or direct. In fact, the case I sketch emphasizes, on one hand, the contradictory nature of many connections, and, on the other hand, the limits of the Renaissance contribution to general levels of literacy; if, that is, we focus on it as a cultural and intellectual movement of the period, as I think we properly should. My position is sceptical, agnostic, if you like; it is not, I hope, heretical.

Several key distinctions must be made. First, we err if we are too latitudinarian in our use of the term 'Renaissance'. I wish to employ it in a fairly precise sense, which I think fits the historical case. Second, although we must be sensitive to variations over time and space, delimiting *too* many different Renaissances over the almost three-century period is as distorting as seeing the currents as constituting a seamless web. With respect to the Renaissance, of course, time and space *do* coalesce in essential ways. Third, and potentially most significant for the historian of literacy, we *must* distinguish (a) theory from practice; (b) impacts during the times themselves from those felt in later centuries – as in pedagogical reform, for example; and (c) actions and influences taken and felt by relatively small numbers of select, often elite, persons from those of and by the many.

With these provisos, the contradictions and the limits of Renaissance relations with literacy may be glimpsed. It should be clear, nevertheless, that literacy *was* very important; among those intellectual, artistic, and political elites who made and shaped the movements and their dynamics, the uses of literacy, novel and more 'traditional', were obviously enormously significant. Of that there can be no doubt; yet, that point is neither surprising nor original. Such uses derived in a general sense from the broadening diffusion of literacy skills and educational opportunities during the later Middle Ages and from the intellectual progress of that period. However, it is exaggerated and inadequate to presume that literacy *per se* 'caused' or stimulated the Renaissance. Such statements not only remove it from its far more complex and interesting historical context, but also misunderstand fundamentally the roles of literacy. What determined selected uses of literacy by special persons is a far more crucial matter.

Specifically, for the purposes of discussion, we may say that the primary emphases of the Renaissance were (i) the rediscovery of antiquity and the classical revival; (ii) civic humanism; and (iii) Christian humanism. These key elements overlap and interrelate, and contain within them most, if not all, of the period's major thrusts. In few direct or immediately consequential ways, however, did these epochal threads influence mass literacy or shape mass uses of reading and writing. In this, their roles differed instructively from those of economic change, trade and commerce, and the incipient expansion of the increasingly capitalized marketplace. This is not to argue, let it be said, that there were no impacts or that they were not consequential; rather, it is to postulate a limiting case.

The rediscovery of antiquity and its intellectual/artistic/cultural legacies and products was limited to the efforts and the *direct* benefits of the few. That argument should require the least qualification. This was an activity of the highly literate, whose own and whose successors' and adherents' learning and literacy usage only gained and deepened in the process. Their numbers surely grew, and they influenced much else: but not the conditions or opportunities for the literacy learning or usage of the greater mass of the population. Intellectual and cultural achievements of a high level, history shows, are never in any direct way a simple consequence of the extent of literacy, elementary, or even secondary schooling. They may occur in settings with a low level of literacy; a high rate is no guarantee, though it may assist. As in so much else, literacy was a contributor, *not* a cause; a beneficiary, *not* a consequence.

Indeed, their efforts may be seen as contradictory and limiting in that sense. One important issue is language. The Renaissance took place at a time of diffusing, maturing regional and national vernacular languages. Yet, with some important exceptions among literary figures, the classical revival did little to endorse or contribute to the vernacular's obvious potential for expanding lay and popular literacy and schooling. To the contrary, in many ways and to many influential minds, it was at best hesitant and ambivalent and sometimes actively opposed to use of the vernacular, especially in schooling and scholarly (and often literary) expression and creativity. Major authors in the vernacular (Petrarch, Boccaccio) scorned mass audiences. More popular literary work and more 'practical' kinds of schooling, as well as the persisting powerful presence of church-supervised education, never major thrusts of the Renaissance, were more consequential to general literacy levels. Vernacular translations did increasingly become factors conducive to more popular literacy. A widening cultural divide – based far less on literacy than on its uses and its linguistic vehicles – must also be associated with this period. Printing in no way reduced this widening split.

Civic humanism, the keystone of the great cultural contributions, had a wider scope than the classical revival and touched more lives. It too was limited and could be contradictory. Lauro Martines, in his *Power and Imagination*, presents an impressive case that humanism was a 'program for the ruling class'. Though he may overstate his thesis, he is not seriously in error, for that was not only the overarching emphasis of humanism, especially but not exclusively in Italy, but it was also the dominant, if not the sole impact. This is seen perhaps most starkly in humanist educational and pedagogical thought and theories, which dealt remarkably little with either elementary or literacy learning or training of the many. This is also seen in the practice of humanist education.[24]

If not the case for all such writing, this was the dominant perspective. Classical languages and their use was one prime theme; rhetoric, revealingly, was another. It was the pinnacle of education, toward whose advancement virtually all else was addressed. And rhetoric, a highly-valued political as well as cultural tool, reminds us that orality and aurality were hardly erased or eclipsed by literacy's increasing impact on the culture and communicative modes, nor by print's penetration for that matter. Walter Ong's seminal, idiosyncratic *The Presence of the Word* illustrates the persisting presence and power of oral speech and oral exchange into the early modern era. Much of formal education was so shaped, as was much of literature. Martines, among others, suggests the applications to power and control.[25]

Of course, humanism selectively but firmly fostered literacy's acquisition and uses, from sponsoring the upward mobility through schooling for some talented persons to increasing women's education and expanding job opportunities in administration, teaching, the professions, and cultural production. Investment in education was indeed promoted; although primary concern and support were addressed to post-literacy or post-elementary schooling, that foundation needed to be secured too. Surplus wealth, cultural consumption, political stability and ambitions, flowering of genius, and other factors equally underlay that set of developments. They were not the primary interests of leading humanists and their patrons.

Christian humanism is generally associated more with northern Europe and its later, so-called northern Renaissance. Such dichotomizing from the 'classical' or Italian Renaissance is only partially accurate, yet differences remain and were often significant. In some ways, Christian humanism had, at least in potential and theory, a greater relevance and relationship to literacy. That potential, I believe, lay more in the future than in the age itself. In most respects, the breadth of concern and action of Christian humanists, regardless of their geographic locations, were little broader than those of their Italian predecessors. Their programmes overwhelmingly related to the shaping of elites for properly enriched, cultivated, responsible, and godly-goodly works and lives. The writings of the major English, French, Dutch, Spanish, and German humanists all illustrate this. Formal religion was also very important to them. Precious little attention was accorded to literacy and primary schooling, especially for the commoners and the masses; the vernacular received only slightly less hostility and ambivalence than earlier in the south of Europe. Eramus of Rotterdam is a fitting case in point.

There is another side to Christian humanism, more important for literacy then and later both. More broadly mass or popular themes, more often proposed than enacted, are found here than in the more 'classical' thrusts of Renaissance humanism. They ranged from the bitterly-debated but nonetheless innovative vernacular schools and publishing of the Brethren of the Common Life, to municipal welfare and 'social reform' efforts – Catholic and Reformation Protestant – which sometimes included formal, required instruction of the poor charges in letters, along with moral and religious indoctrination. Such activities looked more to the future than the past. They also included farseeing, unprecedented, 'utopian' plans for mass welfare and mass education symbolized radically by Thomas More's *Utopia*, with its peculiar combination of modernity and medieval vistas, or by Vives' plans. A renewed focus on children and the young was part of these conceptions. Herein lay important seeds for the future of literacy – at once demonstrating its potential uses for control and hegemony and for individual and collective advancement and initiative and roles for formal institutions and the State – if relatively few strong initiatives before the sixteenth and seventeenth centuries. Precedents were being set for State and private philanthropic actions.

The Reformation of course attempted, on occasion came to compel, sometimes with striking success, mass campaigns and organizations for instilling literacy, in tandem with religion and morality, to large and growing populations. Counter-reformers made similar, if smaller efforts in these directions. Gerald Strauss' magnificent *Luther's House of Learning* demonstrates this and the contributions – and indeed contradictions – of humanism to the process. Regardless of place or sponsorship, however, a truly 'useful' literacy was seldom the goal. To be sure, as Strauss, among others, also illustrates, more than a few among the target populations took advantage of, and worked to expand, such opportunities for reasons not always dominated by concerns religious or humanistic.[26]

In either case, literacy's social and cultural relationships were expanded and reinforced. Furthermore, literacy's growth was indeed fostered. Numerical data only available from the mid-sixteenth century show this result. That this should derive from the diverse but often overlapping emphases of the Renaissance, in the ways it did, suggests the indirectness and contradictoriness of many of the most import relationships. For the Renaissance's and humanism's major interests did lay elsewhere and were more narrow socially. That should be one aspect of any interpretation of the period. For the endorsement of literacy, of differing levels and types, for differing persons and classes, and for divergent purposes, was cumulatively strengthened, and a set of legacies endowed for succeeding centuries.

## Literacies: alphabetic and visual

Mention of 'differing literacies' leads to my final theme and to another dimension of the Renaissance experience. This is the import of 'non-alphabetic' or, more precisely, 'visual literacy', a subject whose significance and scope, past or present, we are just coming to appreciate. As the strikingly original studies of Eugene Ferguson, William Ivins, and Peter Burke (and A. F. C. Wallace for a later period) together can teach us, Renaissance achievements, especially in the plastic arts and technology and probably also in science and medicine, owed a major debt to forms of literacy other than the traditional alphabetic type.[27] This is a difficult, largely uncharted area; we are, for example, ignorant of the relations that may tie visual with alphabetic skills. My comments are therefore hypothetical, but the significance of the subject demands its note.

Regardless of the connections among differing literacies, the visual, or what Ferguson has called, 'The mind's eye; nonverbal thought', seems both highly relevant and potentially seminally important to the Renaissance. Very different dynamics seem at work as compared to those with alphabetic literacy. And, if Burke's prosopographical data are representative, there may well have been strikingly different social origins, training and career patterns, and paths to productiveness and accomplishment between the two fields of endeavour, which may relate to, derive from, and result in acquisition of very different forms of literacy and their employment.

William Ivins notes:

> While both words and pictures are symbols, they are different in many ways of the greatest importance. So little are they equivalent to each other that if communication were confined to either alone, it would become very limited in its scope. All words need definition, names for them. Verbal definition is a regress from word to word, until finally it becomes necessary to point to something which we say is the last word in the verbal chain of definition means. Frequently the most convenient way of pointing is to make a picture. The word then receives definition, or, if one likes, the thing receives a name, by the association of a sensuous awareness with an oral or visual symbol.[28]

More specifically, after establishing striking distinctions in the social origins of 320 Italian Renaissance painters, sculptors, and architects, when compared to 231 writers, scientists, and humanists (much more artisanal), and also in their form of education, orientations, influences, and outlets, Peter Burke points to two rather distinct 'cultures': one rooted in a lengthy apprenticeship and workshops, the other in formal, higher education. Such differences likely resulted in different abilities and manners of 'reading' and 'expression'. (In grasping these possibilities, we should not be led astray by the virtually unique cases of a Michaelangelo or a da Vinci.) Living with their masters, such artists obviously emphasized the visual.

Although they surely had uses of the alphabetic, it was not primary to their forms of expression. Burke observes,

> an important part of the training was the study and copying of the workshop collection of drawings, which served to unify the shop style and maintain its tradition. A humanist described the process in the early fifteenth century: 'When the apprentices are to be instructed by their master...the painters follow the practice of giving them a number of fine drawings and pictures as models of their art'.[29]

How different this was from the training and practice of scholars and authors.

Ferguson, in a brilliant speculative article on technology and its cognitive concomitants, has taken this perspective a step further. Attempting to understand inventiveness and innovativeness during the Renaissance, and later, he explores their 'non-scientific' modes of thought, or the nonverbal thinking of the 'mind's eye'. He notes that many features and qualities of the objects that 'technologists' think about are not reducible to unambiguous verbal statements; 'they are dealt with in his mind by a visual, nonverbal process'. The developed, practised, and trained, 'mind's eye', he postulates, reviews one's visual memory and seeks to form new images as thought requires.

> If we are to understand the development of Western technology, we must appreciate this important, if unnoticed mode of thought. It has been nonverbal thinking, by and large, that has fixed the outlines and filled in the details of our material surroundings. Pyramids, cathedrals, and rockets exist not because of geometry, theory or structures, or thermodynamics, but because they were first a picture – literally a vision – in the minds of those who made them.

After reviewing the nature of design and invention, including important examples from the Renaissance and noting contemporary picture books, he concludes, 'Yet, science, when applied to engineering, is analytical... [Whereas] Nonverbal thinking, which is a central mechanism in engineering design, involves perceptions, the stock-in-trade of the artist not the scientist'.

> Much of the creative thought of the designers of our technological world is nonverbal, not easily reducible to words; its language is an object or a picture or a visual image in the mind. It is out of this kind of thinking that the clock, printing press, and snowmobile have arisen. Technologists, converting their nonverbal knowledge into objects directly...or into drawings that have enabled others to build what was in their minds...This intellectual component of technology, which is nonliterary and nonscientific, had been generally unnoticed because its origins lie in art and not in science.[30]

My speculation, my hypothesis, leads me to ask: how much of science itself and indeed of medicine, too, derives from the same or similar dynamics? Common sense, which I employ however misleadingly since I have no expertise in either field, suggests that it should be a great deal indeed. Burke's linking of Italian scientists with the scholars and writers, however justified on many grounds (a point that is significant), may mislead us on this one. By the sixteenth century, more and more scientists, physicians, and technologists, though certainly not all, were acquiring a relatively formal and advanced form of education; in this they differed from artists. In other ways and in key aspects of their training, it is possible that the difference remained less than might otherwise seem apparent. If that is in fact the case, a large number of important questions is opened to historians of science, medicine, and technology, as well as to those of the arts, and, of course, to students of literacy or, shall I now say, literacies. The roles of illustrations, and of printing's impact on reproduction, precision, accuracy, and like, recently pointed to by Elizabeth Eisenstein (though not considered in depth), is highly suggestive here. So is that of training. It may be the case that major scientists and physicians, among others, employed and practised, as they needed, visual as well as alphabetic literacies. Studies aimed at this question may provide one important path towards the relations and interactions of these, and perhaps other, literacies – an urgent priority on the scholarly (and contemporary) agenda.

[...]

A discussion like this one requires no conclusion or summation. Suffice it to emphasize the mixing and intricately interrelating variety of media, or communicative modes, that I have sought to introduce. In so far as literacy, traditional alphabetic literacy, that is, my major focus, is concerned, its understanding and interpretation can only be achieved with the appreciation of the other important modes, especially the oral and aural and the visual. Ong suggested something of this, when he wrote:

> The Renaissance fell heir to the medieval preoccupation with texts and to its lingering predilection for oral performance. In terms of the presence of the word to man, the Renaissance is one of the most complex and even confused periods in cultural history, and by that token perhaps the most interesting up to the present in the history of the word. An exacting devotion to the written text, a devotion which has been the seedbed of modern humanistic scholarship, struggled in the subconscious with commitment to rhetoric and to dialectic, symbolic of the old oral-aural anxieties and a sense of social structure built to a degree intolerable today on personal loyalties rather than on objectification of issues. Humanistic rhetoric as such was opposed to scholastic dialectic, and yet both belong to the oral-aural culture which typography was to transmute.[31]

Yet, to assume a complete transformation is to misread (to use a word) both literacy and communicative change.

## Notes

* This chapter as a paper was originally presented as a contribution to the Wellcome Institute for the History of Medicine's Conference, 'Medicine, Printing and Literacy in the European Renaissance'. It draws upon and is documented fully in my *The Legacies of Literacy: Continuities and Contradictions in Western Society and Culture* (New York and London, 1987).

1 See my 'The legacies of literacy', *Journal of Communication*, 32 (1982), 12–26, 'Reflections on the history of literacy', *Humanities in Society*, 4 (1981), 303–333, and *The Legacies of Literacy, passim.*, esp. Introduction.

2 As examples, see Franz Bauml, 'Varieties and consequences of medieval literacy and illiteracy', *Speculum*, 55 (1980), 237–265; Michael Clanchy, *From Memory to Written Record: England, 1066–1307* (London and Cambridge, MA, 1979); David Cressy, *Literacy and the Social Order* (Cambridge, 1980); Natalie Z. Davis, 'Printing and the people', in her *Culture and Society in Early Modern France* (Stanford, 1975), 189–226;

Francois Furet and Jacques Ozouf, *Lire et écrire* (2 vols, Paris, 1977); J. K. Hyde, 'Some uses of literacy in Venice and Florence in the thirteenth and fourteenth centuries', *Transactions*, Royal Historical Society, 5th ser., 29 (1979), 109–129; Thomas Laqueur, 'Cultural origins of literacy in England, 1500–1850', *Oxford Review of Education*, 2 (1976), 255–275; JoAnn H. Moran, *The Growth of English Schooling, 1340–1548: Learning, Literacy and Laicization in Pre-Reformation York Diocese* (Princeton NJ, 1984) and of course Lawrence Stone, 'Literacy and education in England, 1640–1900', *Past and Present*, 42 (1969), 61–139, among a growing literature. For bibliography to 1980, see my *Literacy in History: An Interdisciplinary Research Bibliography* (New York, 1981). For a selection of major studies, see my reader, *Literacy and Social Development in the West* (Cambridge, 1981).

3  See for example, my *The Literacy Myth: Literacy and Social Structure in the Ninteenth-Century City* (New York and London, 1979), esp. Introduction; as well as the literature cited earlier.

4  Carlo Cipolla, *Literacy and Development in the West* (Harmondsworth, 1969); Elizabeth Eisenstein, *The Printing Press as an Agent of Change* (2 vols, Cambridge, 1979).

5  *The Legacies of Literacy*, Introduction and *passim*.

6  See for example, Bauml, 'Varieties and consequences'; Davis, 'Printing'; Cressy, *Literacy*; Moran, *The Growth of English Schooling*. Compare with, for example, Eisenstein, *The Printing Press*; Hyde, 'Some uses'.

7  On printing, see Eisenstein, *The Printing Press*. Compare with Lucien Febvre and H.-J. Martin, *The Coming of the Book* (London, 1976); Rudolph Hirsch, *The Printed Word* (London, 1978). See also, Anthony Grafton, 'The importance of being printed', *Journal of Interdisciplinary History*, 11 (1980), 265–286; Michael Hunter, 'The impact of print', *The Book Collector*, 28 (1979), 335–352; Roger Chartier, 'L'Ancien Régime typographique: reflexions sur quelques travaux recents', *Annales: e., s., c.*, 36 (1981), 191–201; Susan Noakes, 'The development of the book market in late quattrocentro Italy', *Journal of Medieval and Renaissance Studies*, 11 (1981), 23–55; Anne Jacobson Schutte, 'Printing, piety, and the people in Italy, *Archive for Reformation History*, 71 (1981), 5–19.

8  Compare for example with the radically relativist viewpoint expressed in Robert Pattison, *On Literacy: The Politics of the Word from Homer to the Age of Rock* (New York, 1982).

9  Fuller documentation of this argument is presented in *The Legacies of Literacy*, esp. chs. IV and V; see also, the literature cited earlier.

10  Sylvia Thrupp, *The Merchant Class of Medieval London* (Ann Arbor, MI, 1962 (1948)); Cressy, *Literacy*.

11  E. LeRoy Ladurie, *Montaillou: The Promised Land of Error* (London and New York, 1978), *The Peasants of Languedoc* (Urbana, IL, 1974).

12  Egil Johansson, *The History of Literacy in Sweden, in Comparison with Some Other Countries* (Umeå, Sweden, 1977), 'The history of literacy in Sweden', in *Literacy and Social Development*, ed. Graff, 151–182; Gerald Strauss, *Luther's House of Learning* (Baltimore, 1979).

13  Cressy, *Literacy*; Margaret Spufford, 'First steps in literacy: the reading and writing experiences of the humblest seventeenth-century spiritual autobiographers', *Social History*, 4 (1979), 407–435 (reprinted in *Literacy and Social Development*, ed. Graff), *Contrasting Communities* (Cambridge, 1974), and *Small Books and Pleasant Histories: Popular Fiction and its Readership in Seventeenth-Century England* (London, 1981).

14  Davis, 'Printing'; see also, Peter Burke, *Popular Culture in Early Modern Europe* (New York, 1978).

15  See Spufford, *Contrasting Communities*; articles on scribes, for example, in *Local Population Studies*; Keith Wrightson and David Levine, *Poverty and Piety* (New York and London, 1979).

16  Clanchy, *From Memory*.

17  Margeret Aston, 'Lollardy and literacy', *History*, 62 (1977), 347–371.

18  Cressy, *Literacy*, 189; Davis, 'Printing'; Aston, 'Lollardy'; David Levine, 'Illiteracy and family life in early industrial England', *Journal of Family History*, 4 (1979), 368–380, 'Illiteracy and family life in the first industrial revolution', *Journal of Social History*, 14 (1980), 25–44; Graff, *The Literacy Myth*; Burke, *Popular Culture*; Roger S. Schofield, 'The measurement of literacy in pre-industrial England', in *Literacy in Traditional*

*Societies*, ed. Jack Goody (Cambridge, 1968), 311–325, 'Dimensions of illiteracy in England, 1750–1850', *Explorations in Economic History*, 10 (1973), 437–454 (reprinted in *Literacy and Social Development*, ed. Graff). Compare with Spufford, 'First steps', *Small Books*; Laqueur, 'The cultural origins'; Eisenstein, *The Printing Press*.

19 Davis, 'Printing', as reprinted in *Literacy and Social Development*, ed. Graff, 83.
20 Hyde, 'Some uses of literacy', 116, and *passim*.
21 Davis, 'Printing'. See also, Furet and Ozouf, *Lire*; Cressy, *Literacy*; Graff, *The Legacies of Literacy*, for additional data.
22 Davis, 'Printing', as reprinted, 85; Aston, 'Lollardy'; LeRoy Ladurie, *Montaillou*; Carlo Ginzburg, *The Cheese and the Worms* (Baltimore, MD, 1980).
23 Davis, 'Printing'.
24 Lauro Martines, *Power and Imagination: City-States in Renaissance Italy* (New York, 1979); Graff, *The Legacies of Literacy*.
25 Walter J. Ong, SJ, *The Presence of the Word* (New York, 1970); Bauml, 'Varieties and consequences'; Martines, *Power and Imagination*; among the literature.
26 Strauss, *Luther's House*; Johansson, *History of Literacy*; Kenneth Lockridge, *Literacy in Colonial New England* (New York, 1974); the major contributions of Natalie Davis, Harold Grimm, Brian Pullan, and Robert Kingdom on the development of social welfare in early modern Europe.
27 Eugene Ferguson, 'The mind's eye: nonverbal thought in technology', *Science*, 197 (1977), 827–836; William Ivins, *Prints and Visual Communications* (Cambridge, MA, 1969); A. Hayett Mayor, *Prints and People* (Princeton, 1981); Anthony F. C. Wallace, *Rockdale* (New York, 1978). On the psychology of literacy, the major work to date is Sylvia Scribner and Michael Cole, *The Psychology of Literacy* (Cambridge, MA, 1981).
28 Ivins, *Prints*, 158–159.
29 Burke, *Culture and Society in Renaissance Italy* (London, 1972), 53, *passim*.
30 Ferguson, 'The mind's eye', 827, 834, 835, *passim*.
31 Ong, *Presence*, 63.

## CHAPTER 4

# SCHOOLGIRL TO CAREER GIRL

## The city as educative space[1]

### Stephanie Spencer

*Paedagogica Historica*, 39, 1–2, 121–33, 2003

> They used to give me money for taxis to take me and wonderful garments to fashion shoots and I met David Bailey, who was just a greasy little studio assistant at John French's studio, and people like that. It suddenly threw me into the real world, from being a little mouse. And there was a fashion editor who – she was like a racehorse, a wonderful elegant woman. 'Oh my God!' she said when she saw me, and 'We must do something with you'. But she said it kindly. And they took me to a very posh hairdresser to have my hair cut and some of them in the fashion department gave me some clothes they didn't want. It sounds horrid but they were beautiful clothes…after three months the editor had me in and she said: 'We want to train a junior sub-editor, would you like it?' And they did, and I was so happy there, really really happy.[2]

This extract from an interview with a woman, who, as a teenager, left the suburbs in order to work in the centre of London, graphically illustrates the young girl's metamorphosis into an adult persona. This metamorphosis was achieved under the tutelage of city sophisticates, those who were already established in the urban lifestyle, and tutored also by the very environment itself and the influence of the 'posh hairdressers' and the photographic studios. In late 1950s' England this informal education into adulthood took place for a majority of girls, to a greater or lesser extent, in the few years between leaving school and embracing full-time domesticity. In this chapter, I explore the way in which the city acted as an educative space, as a finishing school for entry into the adult female role in postwar England at a time when very few girls went into further, or higher, education. The city took on the part of the wood in Shakespeare's *Midsummer Night's Dream* as a distinct space, a space away from close parental surveillance, where mistakes could be made in the process of growing up. The comparative anonymity of the city meant that there would be no sullied reputations which would cause long-term discomfort or embarrassment to the individual. The notion of the city as a space apart provided both the freedom and a containment for a rising generation to challenge convention, or boundaries, without undermining, or threatening, the stability of society as a whole.

This chapter is informed by the approach of Mark Gottdiener and Alexandros Lagopoulos who identify a socio–semiotic analysis of the representation of the city which: 'explicitly assumes that signification is a social product dependent for its sustenance on the interaction among individuals in society and between social groups and cultural codes'.[3] In addition to providing the site of training institutions or wider employment opportunities, I argue that the city acted as a representation of a world substantially different from the cloistered suburban environment in which girls grew up and attended school. The colleges or places of work within the city had a symbolic as well as a functional purpose. Gottdiener' and Lagopoulos' critique analyses which have ignored the articulation between semiotic and non-semiotic processes in the social life of the city. In the source material used for this chapter it is apparent that, while the city was important as an actual location for the process of entering adulthood, it was also a powerful representation of all that was opposed to childhood and suburbia in terms of sophistication and independence. In postwar Britain the Town Planning Act was part of the new Welfare State and its provisions served to emphasise still further the difference between areas of new tower blocks surrounded by ring roads and quieter country areas.[4] There was no place for children in the city of the imagination. It was this representation which informed the actions and expectations of girls on the brink of adulthood, which, like a good teacher, provided examples and role models for new recruits. James Donald writes of the 'pedagogy of the boulevards' in his analysis of the building of Paris and the 'exacerbated divisions between the centre and suburb, and so between public and home'.[5] The fictional glamour of the city as presented in girls' novels offered a site for further education both in the imagination and in lived experience. These boundaries have been described as 'fuzzy and porous' and the two areas discussed in the following pages – novels and oral accounts – reflect this 'traffic between the two, an economy of symbolic constructs which have material consequences and that are manifested in an enduring reality'.[6]

A job as a shop assistant might not have been quantitatively different in Oxford Street or deepest Surrey but the world of the West End acted as a beacon to hundreds of girls who spent their hard-earned money on a daily commute. Gottdiener and Lagopoulos suggest a methodological approach which embraces first: 'attention to historically and culturally established signification, realised through research into the general cultural traits of the society within which the settlement space is embedded' and, second, case study research: 'to document the codified ideology structuring the signifieds of space'.[7] This chapter will therefore consider briefly the 'cultural traits' which the city embodied in the late 1950s and then, using material from girls' career novels and oral history interviews as case studies, discuss the way in which these significations were both presented at the time, and remained powerful enough to be remembered at a distance of forty years. The girls' career novels enjoyed a decade of popularity, providing sound advice on training and careers within a fictional format. In drawing on fictional representations of the transition from girlhood to adulthood the chapter highlights the popular notions about the city, propagated by the media, which would have been familiar to the readers. The readership for the novels included parents and teachers who would also have been conversant with the city culture described by the authors of the novels.[8] Interviews offer an insight into the way in which this culture was inscribed in the memory of women who were school leavers at the time. The city provided an imaginary as well as an actual educative space for the passage from gawky schoolgirl to sophisticated career girl about town.

## The lure of the city

Many universities, colleges and teaching hospitals were, of course, situated in cities. Industries were located in urban environments and attracted those wanting to embark on both engineering and office work within large companies. Working on national magazines or newspapers held a higher status than journalism on a provincial publication. After a day's work the leisure activities available in cities offered an introduction to new worlds of jazz, ballet, theatre and art, all within a small geographical area. Dance halls and coffee bars also boomed in the postwar years with the influence of American popular culture and rock and roll. The palpable excitement of the learning curve of new experiences available in the city was clear:

> I had a lot of people I referred to as my platonics. I had a friend who was very keen on the ballet, a male friend, who used to book all these whole raft of tickets for the whole season, it was wonderful! So I saw all the Fonteyn and Nureyev and I became a bit of a culture vulture. The friend I went to the cinema with, we then started to go to the Academy Cinema every week so we saw early Polanskis and Antonionis and things like that and I felt rather grand you know seeing these subtitled films, it was just – I soaked it all up really. It wasn't all just mindless pop.[9]

Full employment meant that if mundane jobs became tedious it was easy to change work environments from one week to the next. Many of the interview participants talked about leaving a job on Friday and starting another the following Monday. Although London, as capital city, was the most cited in the texts used for this chapter, it is apparent that other large cities functioned in the same way. Foreign capitals, especially Paris, Rome and New York were presented in girls' literature as the epitome of glamour and sophistication.

For those embarking on creating their adult image in terms of their appearance, the newest fashions were available first in the shops of the big cities. The late 1950s saw a change from the rather staid dress shops of the immediate postwar period to smaller boutiques and the wooing of the new teenage consumer market.[10] Grammar school girls wore school uniform up to the age of eighteen and may have turned to magazines for advice on how to dress for their new adult role. Women's magazines confirmed that a more formal style of dress was required even for shopping 'in town' and those attending city centre universities were expected to live up to the sophisticated image. *Woman*, a widely read weekly magazine, devoted an article to student dressing, focusing on a fresher at Leeds University. Trousers were decried as: 'rarely worn for lectures and too informal for city streets'.[11] The emphasis on dressing formally for city life suggests an interesting contradiction in an argument which proposes that the city provided a space to *challenge* convention. The formality of dressing served however to emphasise the *difference* and separateness between city and suburban or rural, casual, styles. At the same time the imposition of formality by, in this case the media, also suggests an attempt to control an outward challenge to tradition.

In addition to its material advantages the city acted as a signifier of sophistication. Even in the decade before London's Carnaby Street and King's Road became acknowledged as the leaders of urban style, the 'yeastiness' in the air identified by Angela Carter implied that knowledge of the Zeitgeist emanated from the urban centre.[12] Sophistication also implied an independent lifestyle away from the surveillance of parents. The city provided a site where contemporary morals and values could be challenged. The notion of the city as site of corruption was a longstanding trope. Since at least the middle of the nineteenth century the city had symbolised the perils of industrialisation and the destruction of the rural innocence as epitomised in the novels of Charles Dickens and the engravings of Gustav Doré. Young women were seen as particularly vulnerable when they first arrived in the city before they had gained experience of living in an urban environment.[13] Parental concern over the move away from home was much more than the empty nest syndrome. The financial independence offered by a wage packet represented a new stage in a girl's move to adulthood, even if a majority of it was still handed to mother for board and lodging. Romance fiction in popular magazines suggested that girls were more likely to be susceptible to unsuitable relationships, away from the surveillance not only of parents but also of relations, friends and neighbours. However, in both the career novels and in the life stories constructed during interviews a pattern emerged whereby, after a fling in the city, girls, now women, returned to the suburbs to repeat the domestic pattern of their parents. The city had fulfilled its educative role and its alumni might return infrequently to renew the acquaintance, but only as visitors, on shopping trips or 'days out'.

This chapter now turns to a discussion of the way that this image of the city was portrayed in the girls' career novel and narrated in oral history interviews. James Donald suggests that the media provided a 'mediating pedagogy' between the reality of the metropolis and its imaginary place in mental life.[14] The novels provided a fictional representation of the city, which the interviews reflect, as women recounted how the experience of city work did not always live up to their expectations. Despite this initial disappointment there remained a sense that this experience was still a valuable part of their education for adulthood.

## The career novel

The girls' career novel was a genre which flourished in England in the late 1950s. The two main publishing houses, Chatto and Windus, and Bodley Head imported the idea from the United States and reworked it into an English model. The two publishing houses produced over fifty titles between them in the decade up to 1962. Historians of children's literature have been somewhat dismissive of the genre.[15] Yet its popularity and specificity of purpose in a clearly delineated time period demand that it is revisited, not for any literary worth, but because the novels provide a representation of widely held contemporary assumptions of female gender roles. Correspondence in the Chatto and Windus archive indicates that the books were widely distributed into libraries and sold well.[16] They were aimed at girls on the brink of leaving school and, under a fictional format, gave specific advice on a number of careers. Some of these were traditional female occupations, for example: *Young Nurse Carter*[17] and *Brenda Buys a Beauty Salon*.[18] Others covered more unlikely careers such as *Juliet in Publishing*[19] and *Anne in Electronics*.[20] Although not written to a specific formula the books had many common traits. Mary Dunn closely controlled the content, asking for rewrites if she thought that the heroine wore too much make-up or shopped in exclusive boutiques. It was agreed, after correspondence with the author of *Brenda Buys a Beauty Salon*, that the heroine should be permitted to wear make-up as part of her job, but not without misgivings on the part of the editor for fear that the novels would not be considered suitable for purchase by schools.

The novels were intended to be classless or cross-class, yet to a present-day reader they appear unremittingly (upper) middle class; mothers do not work, fathers have white collar jobs and brothers attend boarding school. It is significant that, in the final chapters of the novels, the return to suburbia did not herald the cessation of the chosen career. The notion of the stopgap in which the period of employment between school and marriage or motherhood was a self-contained unit, lost currency towards the end of the 1950s. It was still referred to in the novels, but in a rather dismissive fashion: 'I hate the type who only want to fill in time before they get married, and collect their pay packet at the end of the week, having done the minimum of work and that shoddily. After all every career girl plans to get married in good time.'[21]

Typically, a storyline would follow a young girl from her provincial home to her training in an urban environment, where after a few trials, she would emerge as an adult with a fiancé and a profession. This was specific editorial policy, as publisher Nora Smallwood wrote to Mary Dunn: 'The development of character should be shown indirectly and be the outcome of the girls' experience and reaction to the work'.[22] Margaret, trainee doctor, after accepting a proposal of marriage, announces that she envisages going into public health so that she can be on hand to get supper for her medical fiancé: 'And when we have children later on...I can resign from my job when they're young and need me, but later I'll work again. I don't think any doctor has the right to waste her training'.[23]

In the novels the heroines usually moved to the city for their training. Few of the heroines had flats of their own; they lived under surveillance in 'digs', nurses' homes or hostels. They were therefore rarely left to discover the delights of city life completely unrestricted. When Anne (in Electronics) goes to Darrington 'a big industrial town' to take a sandwich course, she compares it to the 'complacent middle-class dignity of Lindford'.[24] Social class is presented as an issue of concern to Anne's mother who is worried about the 'sort of people' Anne might encounter, as is Monica Anson's mother when Monica moves to London to train as a travel agent.[25] The girls themselves meet a wider variety of people in the city than their home circle of friends. This aspect of moving to the city was confirmed in the interviews, as one woman observed:

> I didn't grow up with any black people, and I met people, I met Arabs and Africans. I met all sorts of nationalities and made friends of them and they took us out to their Turkish restaurants and we went to East Africa House a couple of times in Hyde Park.[26]

A stock character who appeared frequently in the novels was the more sophisticated girlfriend, met on arrival in the city. Sara Gay (model) meets up with Betsy, who has the added glamour of being American.

> Betsy had learned modelling in America but because her father, a US colonel, was stationed in Europe, she had decided to work in England so that she could see him more frequently. Sara had learned a great deal from Betsy, whose casual disregard for conventions had done a great deal to lighten the hard work and tedium that Sara had experienced in this, her first job.[27]

The sophisticated friend also acted as a mentor in the choosing of new clothes or the selection of make-up. Wearing make-up became part of the mantle of sophistication bestowed by city life. Rather frowned on by mothers, it became part of the norm for the career girl. The novels described in detail the interview outfit and frequently commented on the lack of nail varnish as signifier of youth and naïveté. Before leaving home, girls accept fashion guidance from their mothers. Sheila Burton wears a 'clean, freshly ironed summer dress and clean gloves',[28] while Margaret Lang, destined to be a fashion buyer tells her mother:

> Mother I am glad you made me wear this hat and suit. One or two of the girls looked awful. One had dirty hands with bright red nails, long earrings and no stockings. Jean looked nice, she wore her blue coat with the velvet collar and her velvet beret.[29]

The transition from fresh-faced ingénue to sophisticated young woman was much promoted in women's magazines. Many beauty articles focused on the importance of light make-up for young teens but equally on the necessity of make-up as an indication of adult status. 'Congratulations' warbled *Woman's* beauty editor: 'You've made a good job of growing up sensibly! Your beauty life begins now, and make-up will play a big role'.[30]

Sarah Gay becomes her friend Beryl's mentor when Beryl decides to abandon her dull job in Frimpton and come to London. Sarah offers advice on what she has learned from her time living in the city. Beryl hopes that simply 'being in London' will teach her to become more fashion-conscious and stick to a diet.[31] They share a flat before Sarah moves to the even more sophisticated surroundings of New York where: 'The New York models took her breath away by their elegance and grooming, and how thin they were!'[32] However, after her adventures in New York, Sarah is ready to return home: 'There was now an extra gloss to her appearance that made everyone look at her twice', but the point of the story was that having achieved the extra gloss, Sarah was going home to: 'Home and my family. Home and Marc'.[33]

Alternatively, the apparent sophisticate is revealed as unreliable or underhand, emphasising the down-to-earth qualities of the heroine who, with her new-found confidence, is able to recognise the values of her upbringing. It is in Paris that the inefficient and devious ways of Miss Lock 'always dressed in sleek suits and frocks and nylons and high heels' come to light and Pan Stevens (junior secretary) learns the true worth of her own qualities of grit and steadfastness.[34] The gulf between childhood and adulthood becomes a geographical gulf in the novels between the cosy domesticity of the hometown and the excitement of the city: 'Anne realised that shuttling between Lindford and Starrington was going to be like shuttling between Earth and Mars.'[35]

The time spent as a single girl in the city was usually terminated in the novels by the appearance of Mr Right. Mr Right often originated from the home area and contrasted favourably with Mr Wrong from the city. The temptations, pitfalls and amorality of the city were often personified in the form of the smooth rival to the dependable boy-next-door. Pan Stevens is nearly side-tracked by the lascivious Michel Dubois in an interlude in Paris, before settling for nice dependable Larry from the home tennis club.[36] Margaret Lang trains as a fashion buyer in a department store in London. Her supervisor signifies the sophistication of the city: 'An immaculate woman with beautifully dressed greying hair, lovely hands and a detached imperturbability of manner which was a little alarming.' Margaret becomes entangled with John Derry, an 'older man' at work, who turns out to be a crook. She realises the error of her ways as she becomes more streetwise during her stay in the city.[37] Cookery Kate meets her future husband Peter from Suffolk, his clothes: 'all proclaimed country breeding and living'.[38] Peter remains steadfastly in the background while Kate finishes her training, shares a bedsit and works as a pastry chef in London. Eventually she returns with Peter, to a hotel in Suffolk to raise a family and start the cycle over again.

There is a clear indication in the career novels that the journey to the city is an established rite of passage. The introduction to *Sheila Burton, Dental Assistant* states:

> This is the story of the year Sheila spent as a student at the Vandaleur dental hospital in London, and of her subsequent appointment as a fully-fledged dental assistant – and it is also the story of her first experience of living an independent life away from the shelter of her provincial home.[39]

Sheila's mother, happily married to a G.P., is reluctant to allow Sheila to live on her own in London. The following extract sums up the popular notion of the single girls around town:

> We think you are far too young to have a room on your own yet. London is very expensive and we can't allow you much beyond your living expenses. If you live alone you will spend it all on cinemas and concerts and nylons and then come home after a hard day's work to revive yourself on half a tin of sardines. I know because I did it myself when I first worked in London and horribly spotty and anaemic I became too until I learned sense.[40]

In this extract the implication is that Mrs Burton had learned from her time in London, the author depicts her as by far the most efficient and forward thinking of the other mothers portrayed in the novel. Spotty or anaemic she may have been, but her training in the city left her ultimately a more organised and understanding individual.

## The interviews

Although Sheila Burton and her family belong firmly in the realm of fiction, women interviewed about their memory of leaving school and working in London in the late 1950s and early 1960s voiced similar sentiments and drew on a similar understanding of the place of the city as that found in the novels. These case studies illustrate the two-way process between the construction of the city as seen by those who also draw on its signification in order to narrate their own stories. As Donald suggests: '[W]ays of seeing and understanding the city inevitably inform ways of acting on the space of the city, which is again seen, understood and acted upon.'[41]

The interviews which are discussed in the second part of this chapter were from a series of twenty-three, conducted with women who had left school in Southeast London between 1956 and 1960. They left between the ages of fifteen and eighteen and either entered jobs immediately or, like the heroines of the career novels, underwent a period of training before entering employment. The interviews were part of a project which focused on career choice for girls in the late 1950s. The women were not asked specifically about their decision to work in the centre of London. They were asked more about their expectations of work and family than detailed questions about the type of work they undertook. It is all the more striking that so many of them chose to emphasise the location of their first job, in the centre of 'town', and the way in which this was held in higher esteem than local employment. In their case, 'local' employment would still have been on the outskirts of the capital city, but it was the centre which attracted young women looking for their first job. They may have been unsure what they wanted to do as a career but they quite decided where they wanted to do it. It was not only the case that there was more money to be earned in the centre (which was either largely taken up with fares or rent), as Penny observed: 'And you felt you were out of things. Everything was happening in London'.[42]

In contrast to the young heroines of the career novels, most of the women interviewed chose to remain living with their parents, commuting each day. This had its own problems as the new persona that the girls developed at work was constrained by the return to parental strictures each evening. The differences in values observed between town and home were similar to the gulf between home and school observed by Michael Carter.[43] In the interviews the city took on the mantle of 'school' allowing space for the questioning of established conventions and parents' expectations. Flat-sharing did not seem to be a common experience and the reservations expressed by the fictional mother of Sheila Burton were shared by the parents of several interviewees. Cathy, who is quoted at the beginning of the chapter, broached the subject of sharing a flat to her mother. Even at a distance of some years she justified the refusal, first on the grounds of moral panic, but then reflected that the decision was just as likely to have been an economic one. It is clear in the following extract that she initially draws on accepted notions of the city as sign of moral danger:

> Were you still living at home? Yes I was and I do remember I said to my mother..., some of the girls up there said: 'We are going to get a flat together. Would you like to do it?' And I went home and I said, and she was absolutely horrified. I do know now, in retrospect, it wasn't just my moral welfare she was interested in, although in retrospect she was possibly a little hard on me as far as strictness, as she was worried I'd go the same way as her and my grandmother also, whereas I wasn't a bit flighty. But it was partly because they quite liked the little bit of money I brought in. I know now that was what it was, because [my stepfather] still hadn't got much of a job and they would have lost that if I'd gone into a flat. I didn't know that at the time, I thought she was being mean. And again I felt isolated from other people who were, but on the whole people, didn't really do that sort of thing. The girls I left behind in M_, they didn't have flats, they lived at home and were going out with the boy they'd known for ten years or something. It wasn't very unusual, but I was in a different world by then.

As noted earlier in the chapter, the notion of the different world of work and home was similarly described in some of the career novels. The worlds of home and work were approximately fifteen miles apart for those interviewed, yet the imagined distance was considerable. In the following extract it is notable how the memories recalled draw on the same concerns voiced by the fictional mothers of the career novels. The extract also emphasises the transitional nature of the period spent in London. Although the flats that Janine lived in were still geographically away from the centre, they represented a quantum move away from parental influence and the mores of the suburbs. The purpose of the interview was to discuss the participant's career path, she nevertheless chose to digress in order to give a verbal portrait of living in London and the apparent freedom that it gave to allow space for self-development:

> And I left home and I got a flat, I got a bedsit and I really wanted to be on my own...My mother was very tearful but she was really driving me out at the same time. 'This is my house you can't bring your friends in at eleven o'clock.' And I thought I would get a flat. And it was really a bedsit. I got a bedsit in East Finchley...quite a lot of my friends in the bank were sort of in digs and things like that; Earls Court, Highgate and Hampstead and that sort of way. My first flat I got at East Finchley and then I had another flat at Greenwich for a while. It was Deptford I suppose, but I like to say it was Greenwich. That was with a girlfriend and then I went to Earl's Court for a while and by that time I was going out with Don I suppose... It was difficult. The bedsit wasn't too bad that was only two pounds a week, that was OK, that was living in a house with the owners living down below.[44]

The way that Janine changes her choice of words from 'bedsit' to 'flat' reflects the striving for independence that the move to the city represented. A bedsit is small, temporary and often part of a family unit. As the age of majority was twenty-one, the freedom and sense of independence could still be easily undermined. A flat, on the other hand, is a more substantial representation of independence and sophistication. Landladies and hostel wardens in part took over the role of surveillance from parents. Yet having a flat was still the key to experimenting with a different way of life from the expectations of the suburbs. Janine continued:

> The flat we got in Greenwich with my friend who also worked in the bank, our personnel manager had to personally guarantee us to the housing management...how old was I? 22? 23?...it was really like two rooms, one of which was the bedroom and one of which was a lounge and it was decided that I would put a bed in the lounge and we would have bedsits. I had to go and buy a bed, so I bought one of these fold-away type, it was only ten, twelve, pounds at the time and something to do with HP terms and there was an offer for cash discount. So I said: 'I'll have the cash discount'. They said: 'You don't get discount because you wouldn't qualify for HP'. And I didn't realise that [laugh] but it was man's world really. You know trying to get anywhere [laughter].

Janine's comment that it was a 'man's world' reflects James Donald's analysis of the city space at the beginning of the twentieth century as one predominantly gendered masculine and public.[45] Although by the 1950s women had claimed their right to walk the city streets with their reputations intact there was still a sense that young women were only temporary visitors. Having received their education into adulthood they would retire to the domestic spaces of suburbia. Janine's flats were part of her rite of passage. However much she and her contemporaries might have enjoyed being introduced to all that London had to offer, nobody suggested that, having claimed Mr Right they intended or had wished to remain in this environment.

In popular memory, the representation of London in the early 1960s is overwhelmingly one where youth reigned unchecked and old values were dismissed. Yet even Janine, who broke free from a suburban lifestyle, remained ambivalent about changing morals. Life in the city was acknowledged to be temporary; sooner or later there would be a return to the 'real' world:

> I was swinging yes! I had my hair done by Vidal Sassoon...I had all the short skirts and all the fashions really that I could afford. I wasn't wealthy but you know I was earning reasonable money. I was having to look after myself which was expensive. I just managed...Yes. I was independent. I did remember worrying...I wasn't promiscuous at all. I always joked I was saving myself for Prince Charles! Because in those days they said 'There won't be a virgin by the time he comes to...!!'...I think somebody gave me a bottle of sherry as a sort of moving-in present and I used to sort of look at this bottle and think I could become an alcoholic..., because there was no-one to say 'No' for the first time. And I did think to myself: 'I am going to have to be quite self- controlled here because it's a licence to do anything'. And I found myself becoming quite selective and almost prudish about how I conducted myself. And even when we moved to Greenwich and my friend was having an affair – which was why she got the room with a double bed! [Laugh] and I didn't have any feelings one way or another about that, except I did know

the wife of the chap she was having an affair with which made me feel a bit
sad. But I was never really tempted to, I think I was more concerned about
what my parents would say if I had to go back to them pregnant or something
like that.[46]

The difference between Janine's description of the avantegarde way of life
represented by the city and her memory of her own reticence in the face of this
representation is striking. She is at the same time part, and yet not part, of the
construction. She retells the story, perhaps even the myth, of 'swinging London'
and, in the retelling, confirms the representation that she both drew on and learned
to reject.

The interviews suggested that living and working in London did not always in
reality live up to the expectations promoted by the idea of the city as exciting, forward thinking and ground breaking. 'Dickensian' was used by both Hazel and
Deborah to describe their first jobs in the metropolis and the still-vivid memory of
spending days in front of ledgers or ancient adding machines. Yet an initially dis-
appointing experience did not seem to dull the excitement of working 'in town'.
Taking Mary's interview as an example it was clearly the location, rather than the
nature of the job, which was important. In the following extract she describes her
first few jobs before she went back to helping her parents in their business on the
outskirts:

> These four ledgers had to balance at the end of every day and I had to do it.
> And I used to go home in tears. There was nobody else young, the youngest
> person in the department must have been about forty...and the woman
> immediately above me must have been sixty if she was a day. They weren't
> cruel or unkind but you were just a junior clerk and I used to be in tears
> because I couldn't do it. It was an absolute nightmare. So I decided to leave.
> I found myself a job in Lilley and Skinner selling shoes, and I thought at least I'll
> get to meet people and I loved shoes...And I, that was in London, yes I didn't
> want to work out of London at all. And then I just drifted from one job to
> another, left Lilley and Skinner and went to Clarkes' shoes. I couldn't stand it
> all those green boxes staring at me, so I left.[47]

Mary described helping her father in his new shop as 'a novelty' but after a couple of months, and despite the rather nondescript nature of her previous employment in the city, she observed: 'I stuck at it two or three months but I missed the
girls, going out at lunchtime, so I went back into the West End, carried on doing all
sorts of jobs, switchboard, reception work – a whole string of things.'

Elizabeth was made to leave school by her mother, which thwarted her original
plan to train as a librarian. She presented working in London as a form of rebellion,
precisely for the amoral life it represented:

> At the time I think I thought in terms of a job because I was disgruntled. I didn't
> really want to leave at that stage...So I think that although I went into the BBC,
> I think part of that was: 'All right, if I'm going to be forced to leave school I shall
> go to London to work'. And I thought of it as going to work rather than a
> career, there were a very wide range of people. She was always convinced I was
> going to go off the rails, I didn't actually but she was always convinced I was.
> I remember going to a party in Charlotte Street which in her day was a street
> of prostitutes you know and she said 'Aarrrgh!'[48]

Once married, the interviewees took a different view of their careers. It was clear that domesticity, especially in the form of motherhood, demanded a different location, away from the excitement of the city. Penny was adamant in her statement: 'Everybody automatically worked in London. You didn't think. A local job at that time would have been thought to be so dead-end and boring you know'. Penny's learning curve to adulthood included the time working in Paris, which she remembered as a time of great excitement. Yet, even though she and her husband chose not to have a family, Penny's priorities changed with marriage and it was no longer so important to be working in the centre of town. The fun and camaraderie of city working was displaced by an emphasis on efficient housekeeping and the need to fit a job around domestic commitments.

This chapter has explored the idea of the city as a rite of passage for young girls on the brink of adulthood. The city, as a sign, was constructed by magazines and teenage novels and also by those who also drew on the representation to make sense of the period of their youth spent in the city. As well as being a physical space which facilitated independent living, studying and employment opportunities, the city represented an imagined educative space in which to form an adult female identity. This was especially marked in the England of the 1950s when rigid social codes constrained teenagers, especially young women, in their home environment. Fictional accounts made great play of the physical move away from home, which was constructed much more in terms of a psychological move by all but a few of those interviewed. Those women who did move away from home were still aware of the ties that bound them to existing moral standards and which, although fragile within a city space, were nevertheless apparently immutable in wider society.

## Notes

1  The author has been awarded the ISCHE-prize 2001 for this work. Throughout this chapter 'city' functions both as place and representation.
2  'Cathy'. Interview transcript in author's possession. Pseudonyms are used throughout as, prior to the interviews, we agreed that the women would remain anonymous. I would like to thank them for their enthusiasm and generosity with their time for the project.
3  Mark Gottdiener and Alexandros Lagopoulos, *The City and the Sign: An Introduction to Urban Semiotics* (New York, 1986), p. 12.
4  Mark Girouard, *The English Town* (London, 1990), p. 312.
5  James Donald, *Imagining the Modern City* (London, 1999), p. 49.
6  Ibid., p. 27.
7  Gottdiener and Lagopoulos, *The City and the Sign*, p. 18.
8  The archive of one of the main publishing houses, Chatto and Windus, contains detailed correspondence between authors, editor and publisher and readership surveys sent to schools and public libraries, University of Reading, Chatto and Windus Archive (CWA). I am grateful to Random House for allowing me access to these archives.
9  Janine, transcript in author's possession.
10  Mark Abrams, *The Teenage Consumer* (London, 1959).
11  *Woman*, 14 February 1959, p. 21.
12  Angela Carter quoted in Paul Ferris, *Sex and the British: A Twentieth Century History* (London, 1993), p. 247.
13  See Judith Walkowitz, *City of Dreadful Delight, Narratives of Sexual Danger in Late Victorian London* (London, 1992).
14  Donald, *Imagining the Modern City*, p. 73.
15  Humphrey Carpenter and Man Prichard, *The Oxford Companion to Children's Literature* (Oxford, 1984), p. 96; Marcus Crouch, *The Nesbitt Tradition. The Children's Novel in England, 1945–1970* (London, 1972), p. 186.

16 The editor's husband was a distributor of library books and was asked to complete surveys and questionnaires to gauge the market. Letters from schools and librarians indicate that the series was popular with secondary modern and grammar school girls.
17 Shirley Darbyshire, *Young Nurse Carter* (London, 1954).
18 Evelyn Forbes, *Brenda Buys a Beauty Salon* (London, 1954).
19 Elizabeth Churchill, *Juliet in Publishing* (London, 1956).
20 Louise Cochrane, *Anne in Electronics* (London, 1960).
21 Angela Mack, *Outline for a Secretary* (London, 1956), p. 120.
22 Nora Smallwood to Mary Dunn, CWA, 29 January 1957.
23 Joan Llewelyn Owens, *Margaret Becomes a Doctor* (London, 1957), p. 156.
24 Cochrane, *Anne in Electronics*.
25 Lawrence Meynell, *Monica Anson, Travel Agent* (London, 1959).
26 Interview with Janine, transcript in author's possession.
27 Janey Scott, *Sara Gay, Model Girl in New York* (Manchester, 1961), p. 8.
28 Anne Barrett, *Sheila Burton, Dental Assistant* (London, 1956), p. 36.
29 Mary Delane, *Margaret Lang, Fashion Buyer* (London, 1956), p. 2.
30 *Woman*, 4 April 1959, p. 13.
31 Scott, *Sarah Gay*, p. 40.
32 Ibid., p. 70.
33 Ibid., p. 184.
34 Pamela Hawken, *Pan Stevens, Secretary* (London, 1954).
35 Cochrane, *Anne in Electronics*, p. 41.
36 Hawken, *Pan Stevens*.
37 Delane, *Margaret Lang*.
38 Mary Dunn, *Cookery Kate* (London, 1955), p. 33.
39 Barrett, *Sheila Burton*.
40 Ibid., p. 32.
41 Donald, *Imagining the Modern City*, p. 27.
42 Penny, transcript in author's possession.
43 Michael Carter, *Home School and Work* (Oxford, 1962).
44 Janine, transcript in author's possession.
45 Donald, *Imagining the Modern City*, p. 49.
46 Janine, transcript in author's possession.
47 Mary, transcript in author's possession.
48 Elizabeth, transcript in author's possession.

# PART III

# SCHOOLING, THE STATE AND LOCAL GOVERNMENT

## CHAPTER 5

# FAMILY FORMATION, SCHOOLING AND THE PATRIARCHAL STATE

Pavla Miller and Ian Davey

In M. Theobald and R. Selleck (eds) *Family, School and State in Australian History (1990)*, Sydney: Allen and Unwin, pp. 1–24

Revisionist historians have, for two decades, explored the links between the origins of mass schooling, the rise of capitalism, and aspects of class relations. More recently, feminist historians have started to correct the blindness to the place of women and girls within nineteenth-century societies, and to construct a more adequate account of gender relations. Such feminist-inspired work is useful and long overdue. However, its influence has been largely confined to the rewriting of accounts of the internal dynamics of schools and has had little impact on explanations of the origins of mass compulsory schooling. We argue that a more fundamental reworking of revisionist historiography needs to take account of the profound transformation of patriarchal relations which accompanied the last stages of the transition to industrial capitalism. We also argue that accounts of patriarchal relations need to attend to their age and gender aspects.

Our argument revolves around four propositions. First, early debates about citizenship and liberal democratic theory, which underpin much theorising about schools, were of a patriarchal character. At stake was not an overthrow of the rule of fathers and kings and its replacement by a social contract of free men and women, but the ascendance of a new form of patriarchy – a fraternal social contract. Second, alongside a theoretically posited overthrow of patriarchalist political relations there occurred a widespread and prolonged crisis of patriarchal relations in everyday life, a crisis eventually resolved by the forging of a new form of patriarchy. Third, much feminist analysis has overlooked the fact that patriarchy is a concept that concerns age as well as gender relations: it was the overthrow of the rule of the father rather than that of the husband that liberal theorists stressed. Finally, we argue that patriarchal as well as class relations helped shape the state school systems which, in turn, were implicated in nineteenth-century state formation.

## Church and state

Until the 1970s, the accepted way of writing about the beginnings of mass compulsory schooling was to focus on the bitter conflict between the church and the state over who would educate the people and own the schools. Most authors traced the relationship between democracy, citizenship and education. More often than not, the history of schooling was seen as a vital component of the

Enlightenment project of replacing superstition and custom by rational thought and science, and preparing the population for modern industry and responsible citizenship. In such 'pilgrim's progress' accounts, little attention was paid to the genesis of new social interests and forms of organisation, or to new definitions of rationality. Since the account was dominated by chronicles of the struggles between institutional forms, ordinary men, let alone women and children, rarely appeared. In Australia, the 'Melbourne school', a group of historians at the University of Melbourne associated with formulating the church and state problematic, produced some of the first scholarly accounts of the history of education.[1]

## Revisionist critique: industrialisation, urbanisation and wage labour

By the late 1960s, and later in Australia, several aspects of these accounts came under challenge by a disparate group known in the United States as 'revisionist' historians, and were reformulated by various Marxist authors. First, the revisionists shared a commitment to an explicit use of social theory, and drew inspiration from Marxist writings. Traditional 'Whig' historians, the revisionists claimed, viewed the development of school systems as a triumph of democracy and enlightenment, a compromise between church and state or the diffusion of cultural ideas. The 'revised' histories, in contrast, put emphasis on industrialisation (understood as the emergence of large factories) and urbanisation as causal factors, and made explicit use of the theories associated with these.

Second, the existence of schools ceased to be taken for granted: the revisionist historians accorded primacy to finding out why and how the education systems were set up. Their answers varied, but most downplayed the role of the church and included some mention of class conflict and domination, social control, and a crisis of capitalist social relations. In their reworkings of modernisation theory and Marxism, authors focused on different aspects of nineteenth-century social change. Some stressed the need for new skills, created by industrialisation, which the education system alone could provide. Others, often taking their lead from Marxist theory, emphasised new forms of social conflict. According to them, industrialisation and urbanisation created a protracted crisis of social order. In these conditions, mass schooling was almost 'forced into existence' as a means of 'class cultural control' of the urban poor, the immigrants, or the insurrectionary, undisciplined and disrespectful working class.[2] This approach challenged the implicit view of the Whig historians that the liberal state was a good thing. For example, as Bannister argued, the state was not a neutral arbiter between a plurality of interests or a rational and secular opponent of the church, but an instrument of ruling-class interests.[3]

Third, following the lead of social historians, more emphasis was placed on examining the lives of ordinary people. Even school children began appearing in the histories of education systems alongside the inspectors, legislators, reformers and headteachers who sent and kept them there. Gradually, this work was enriched by new historical studies of the family (often making use of anthropological approaches), and later providing a link to feminist concerns with gender relations and the position of women in society.[4]

While revisionist historians have made a significant contribution to education history, their conclusions regarding the origins of compulsory schooling have been challenged. The tight link between industrialisation and mass schooling is made problematic by the fact that mass education systems appeared in countries such as Prussia, Ireland, Scotland, Canada and Australia well before they filled with factories. Equally awkward is the fact that in England, the greatest industrial power in the nineteenth century, a national education system was established after the major wave of factory industrialisation.[5] A later Marxist formulation diminishes the disparity in timing by arguing that the generalisation of the system of capitalist wage labour rather than industrialisation or urbanisation as such led to the development of mass schooling. Nevertheless, the problem remains that very similar education systems developed in regions with different levels (and even forms) of wage labour.

Whatever its shortcomings, there is now a useful literature on the way schooling systems were established to help shore up a class society, and on the way they set about producing individuals with appropriate class characteristics.[6] There is less work on the links between schooling and patriarchy. Existing research concentrates on the effects rather than the origins of mass schooling, and frequently subordinates explanations of gender relations to those of class.

## Feminist critique

Feminists have drawn attention to the fact that, until recently, the various accounts of schooling (revisionist or not) dealt almost exclusively with the history of men and boys and of boys' education.[7] From these histories, it is difficult to answer such basic questions as whether girls were allowed to enrol in and whether they actually attended the same educational institutions as boys, whether they were taught the same subjects, by the same teachers, in the same classes, from the same books and by the same methods. Neither is it possible to determine whether their attendance showed similar patterns to those of boys, whether they were examined and marked in the same way, and whether their success in examinations diverged from the pattern shown by boys from similar families. At the same time, although most of the early accounts dealt almost exclusively with the history of males, they said little about the formation of masculinity. In remedying these defects, feminists brought to light the gendered messages of school texts and teaching methods, and tried to reconstruct the dynamics of gender relations among pupils and teachers. They also reopened debates about the church, this time as a site of the reproduction of gender relations. Finally, some feminist historians began to ask why girls were sent to school at all.

The problems posed by the inclusion of girls are evident in discussions of citizenship, which have received renewed attention from historians of education.[8] In Whig and revisionist accounts, education for citizenship (however interpreted) motivates social reformers to press for the introduction of compulsory schooling.[9] Most late eighteenth- and nineteenth-century commentators, from the conservative Edmund Burke to the liberal J.S. Mill and the radical Karl Marx, argued that, under existing conditions, a universal franchise was incompatible with the preservation of capitalism. By the end of the nineteenth century, the verdict had changed. To the chagrin of radicals and the joy of their opponents a schooled working-class electorate did not vote to throw off the shackles of capitalism or to destroy what liberals and conservatives considered to be the best features of Western civilisation. Whether this development was welcomed or condemned, schooling was considered to have played an important part. The problem is that, for most of the period, girls were not seen as potential citizens (even though they *were* often seen as potential rioters and troublemakers).

## Patriarchalist vs liberal political theory

In the late seventeenth and eighteenth centuries, patriarchalists such as Sir Robert Filmer and social contract theorists such as Locke and Rousseau articulated themes which resonate in political life today. Generations of students of education (ourselves included) studied Rousseau's *Emile* to explore the issues of education, democracy and freedom. Most assumed that the author's precepts for the education of young Emile applied to all children. Few bothered to read book five, which concerns the education of Sophie. If they did they discovered that Rousseau's ideas about girls were entirely different. Young women, whether rich or poor, were not considered potential citizens by these champions of democracy.

According to Filmer, political hierarchy, obedience and authority were natural; just as children were born subject to their father (biologically, a curious assumption), all people were born naturally subject to their king. The contract theorists rejected most of these claims. Paternal and political rule, they claimed, were distinct; the family and the polity were fundamentally different; sons were born free and equal and, as adults, were free as their fathers before them; political authority and obligation were conventional rather than natural; and political subjects were civil equals.[10]

Filmer himself spotted a fundamental flaw in the expositions of the social contract. The logic of the argument applied to all people, male or female, yet Locke and Rousseau agreed with Filmer that women, as future wives, were born and remained subject to men and husbands. Rousseau could not be clearer. Men are told in *The Social Contract* that 'to renounce one's liberty is to renounce one's quality as a man, the rights and also the duties of humanity', while women, according to *Emile*, 'must be trained to bear the yoke from the first so that they may not feel it: to master their own caprices and submit themselves to the will of others'.[11]

Feminist theoreticians such as Carole Pateman, departing from orthodox political theory, argue that the debate between patriarchalists and social contract theorists is one between champions of two different forms of patriarchy, rather than one between patriarchalists and the proponents of civil equality (or of a society divided by class in a novel way).[12] Equality, liberty and fraternity should be understood literally; in political theory, a contract between free and equal brothers replaces the 'law of the father' with public rules which bind all men equally as brothers. Women remain subject to men, but under a different set of rules.[13] Democratic precepts should indeed have different consequences for boys and for girls, whether in schools or elsewhere.

Such conclusions are, however, complicated by the prevailing relations between generations, and here the new feminist analyses are less helpful. Most fail to explore a key theme of Rousseau's famous work: the relations between children and adults. Boys, as adults, become as free as their fathers. But what happens while they are children, and considered to be subject to their fathers (and to some extent their mothers), or to the state *in loco parentis*?[14] How do unfree young men become free citizens? The problem is not confined to feminist political theory. With a few exceptions, feminist writers have ignored the age dimension of patriarchal relations – and yet this is crucial if we are to make sense of schooling.[15] Even those who call for the examination of different historical forms of patriarchy show little interest in how gender and age relations were articulated in different historical periods.

The discussion of citizenship is a useful starting point for exploring the gender and age dimensions of compulsory schooling. To answer the key questions this discussion opens, however, it is necessary to move beyond political theory, feminist or otherwise. If we confine our critique to the realm of ideas, the revisionist analysis need not be challenged. Revisionists stress that material relations between people are far more important than ideology. We do not support any simple base-superstructure schemes, but agree that an examination of social relations is crucial. Was the rule of fathers overthrown in everyday life as well as in political theory? Did men in practice construct a fraternal social contract? How did this happen? Was this an instance of the transformation of one form of patriarchy into another? Were schools implicated? It will be some time before we have detailed research addressing such questions. Some of the key ingredients, however, have already been explored. Next to a feminist re-reading of political theory, there exists an expanding literature on the patriarchal nature of the modern state. In addition, several strands of historical and demographic research can be used to draw a preliminary map of material changes in patriarchal relations.

Over the last twenty years, family and demographic historians have focused on different stages of the 'proletarianisation' of the labouring population.[16] In their research on Western Europe and England, they describe several family forms whose internal dynamics had implications for gender, age and class relations. We argue that such research can help reconceptualise arguments regarding the origins of mass compulsory schooling.

But why should research on England and Western Europe be relevant to Australia or other colonial societies? First, in spite of their many distinctive features, the history of the colonies is inseparably tied to that of Europe. Australia not only inherited the white immigrants' taste for money, brick houses and straight roads, but also systems of familial, social and economic relations. These links continued to develop as relatives, colonial officials and businessmen migrated to Australia and back, trade flourished, and the Colonial Office scrutinised Australian legislation. To understand obvious facts of Australian life, such as compulsory schooling or the exclusion of women from skilled trades, we need to look beyond our shores. Finally, European research provides a model for urgently needed work on different family forms and waged and unpaid labour in Australia.[17]

## Proletarianisation and the demise of the patriarchalist family economy

The core of the 'patriarchalist' social system described by Filmer and affirmed in contemporary catechisms was the peasant household, common throughout medieval Europe. There was a number of productive 'niches' in a relatively stable economy; surplus people would be redistributed among households to ensure that wealthy farmers and masters had enough labour and the children of poorer families would not 'eat their parents out'. In the country, overlapping entitlements to land were a prerequisite for the formation of new families. In towns, where a minority of the population lived, a similar system operated: guild regulations ensured that journeymen would marry only when they finished their lengthy apprenticeship and a productive niche became available.

Since new households could be formed only when land (or a master's position) became available, the inheritance system provided a solid material basis for patriarchal authority: it was the father (and, if his wife outlived him, the mother) who decided who would inherit the 'living', and local notables who allocated the remaining niches. Young people who failed to secure a living were forced to migrate or stay on as servants in the households of wealthier neighbours, under the patriarchal control of their heads. For most people, 'coming of age' had little significance. Since servants, apprentices and other dependents remained, for most purposes, children, full adulthood was impossible to attain without parentally sanctioned entitlements to land or a trade – and, among women, widows formed the only significant group of property owners. In turn, waiting for a living usually meant late marriage, fewer children and stable populations. White settlement of Australia commenced long after this family form ceased to be dominant in Western Europe. Yet reactions to its gradual disintegration in Europe had a crucial impact on the making of colonial society.

From the seventeenth century, as peasant families in Western Europe lost their land and commons use-rights, they became increasingly dependent on wage labour and the production of commodities for sale, whether in cottage industry or as farm labourers. Individual remuneration was rare; rather, the head of the household received a lump sum, often accompanied by payment in kind, for the combined labour of the household. As children grew older, their contribution to household income became increasingly important, typically exceeding that of the father. As a consequence, except in times of economic depression, parents tried to keep their children at home as long as possible. From the children's standpoint, the logic worked the other way around: it made sense to marry young and get over the strain of supporting several unproductive toddlers while their own productivity was still at its peak.[18]

Economic existence outside a family unit was virtually impossible. New households, however, could now be set up to subsist on wage labour alone. Unlike their grandparents, children were able to withdraw their labour when they reached 'adulthood' and establish their own households without the parents' help or consent: the sons to become patriarchs in their own right, the daughters to pass from the patriarchal control of their father to that of their husband. In turn, the feasibility of forming new households on the basis of wage labour, combined with the expropriation of peasants' and smallholders' land, undermined parents' ability to make binding agreements with their children about subsistence in infirmity and old age. The centre of gravity in age-related patriarchal relations began to shift.

Earlier age at marriage and the incentive to have more children unleashed a population explosion. From 1750 to 1900, the population of Western Europe almost trebled. Moreover, it did so despite emigration to overseas colonies and settlements of some 45 million people between 1800 and 1914. In England itself the proletarian population grew from 2.5 million in 1700 to 16.5 million in 1871.[19]

In Australia, cottage industry had never been a significant part of the economy. However, tenant farming, based on a similar family economy, was widespread, and large families were seen as an economic asset by many working people. Although comprehensive research on the forms of family economies in Australia is not yet available, demographic studies of nineteenth-century Western Australia, Castlemaine and Horsham in Victorian and Boonah in Queensland all indicate that large families were the norm.[20]

## Industrialisation and the early proletarian family

In Europe, the proto-industrial economy was gradually transformed by capitalists seeking better returns on their investment. Gathering producers under one roof might reduce the pilfering of materials, allow the lengthening of the working day, speed up production and lead to the deskilling – and cheapening – of the work process. In early nineteenth-century England prices of products manufactured under the new system fell dramatically; cottage industry gradually ceased to be viable.

While the workforce of some of the new manufactories consisted of orphans or the destitute, in others whole families were employed. They continued to labour as a unit under the direction of the husband and father and the combined payment continued to be given to the head of the household. In turn, early factory design was influenced by gender relations in the wider society: it was modelled on traditional forms of patriarchal authority and subordination.[21] The separation of home and workplace made it increasingly difficult for married women to take part in wage labour, although many continued to work in such family teams in the fields, mines and textile factories.[22] Labouring men had not yet learned to regard themselves as sole breadwinners; indeed, many complained bitterly that the spread of the factory system took remunerative work away from their wives. For this type of family economy, early marriage and many children remained possible and desirable; the proletarian population grew, and patriarchal age relations came under more stress.

In early colonial Australia, a similar form of family wage labour existed. Pastoralists often employed whole families as farm servants;[23] family subcontracting was used by Cornish miners in South Australia and, among teachers, the employment of married couples (and sometimes their children) in one school was common.

## The fully proletarian family

By the early nineteenth century in England and some other Western European countries, the decline of family hiring and the rapid expansion of industrial employment for individual women and children brought existing tensions within patriarchal families to a head. Not only did female and juvenile workers seem to gain public presence, power and independence almost equal to that of males and even heads of families, but they were often employed in ways which undercut the material sources of patriarchal power.

Women and children now worked – and often lived – next to strangers and away from the supervision of family and kin. Alarmingly, some saw their individual wages as their own, rather than as part of a combined family income. Indeed, the new wage system made it easier for young people to set up independent households at a time when the parents still needed their economic contribution. The financial assistance of children allowed the household income to rise as the father's wage-earning capacity declined, and stood between many of the parents and destitution. While most young people in their teens, even when they did not live at home, turned over their whole pay packet to their mothers, they tended to marry young, and often people their parents thought unsuitable.

Moreover, according to critics, few factory women had the time or the energy to care for children or do housework. Worse still, as competition from cheap, mass-produced goods slowly strangled the cottage economy, men, women and children began to compete, as individuals, in an overcrowded labour market. Frequently, women and children were employed to tend machines or to perform newly deskilled tasks in competition with male craftsmen attempting to defend their traditional privileges and work organisation. Some manufacturers used female and child labour to defeat trade organisations and undercut male rates of pay. In some regions adult men, the nominal heads of families, could be unemployed for years, and depend for their subsistence on the wages of their wives and children. While we cannot document the extent of such developments in different countries, we know that identical complaints were raised in the Australian colonies as in England. Everywhere, they brought into question the remaining aspects of patriarchalist age and gender relations among the labouring poor. The natural order of things, with a male patriarch presiding over the labour of his family and other dependents, seemed to be turning on its head.

This uneven process of proletarianisation of the labouring poor can be seen as a gradual demise of patriarchalism parallel to that discussed in political theory, or even as a crisis of patriarchal relations. More detailed work on developments in different regions would need to be done before any such claim could be substantiated. Nevertheless, several other forms of evidence point in the same direction. First, writers such as Barbara Taylor stress that within the early labour movement in England, the place of women and children within the emerging system of wage labour was the focus of bitter struggles. While these struggles have been written out of most commentaries on 'utopian socialism', there is abundant evidence that in early nineteenth-century England (as well as on the Continent) competing strategies for rebuilding gender relations were discussed. While most of the labour movement eventually adopted a strategy modelled on the separate spheres recently elaborated by the men and women of the middle class, a significant minority of labour activists, male and female, advocated an alternative strategy based around equal pay for women workers, socialised childcare and housework, and a universal franchise. Some went further to advocate the abolition of marriage, which they hoped to replace by a free and equal union of men and women based on love.[24]

Second, in the 1830s and 1840s there developed a 'social panic' regarding the disintegration of the working-class family; and not only in Britain. On the right, writers stressed the moral unsuitability of factory work for women and children, the dangers associated with the improvident breeding of the poor, and the shining virtues of the bourgeois family. On the left, commentators such as Frederick Engels argued that the factory employment of women and children, coupled with the frequent inability of grown men to find work and the lack of any inheritance, made for the disintegration of patriarchal relations within working-class families.[25]

Third, such evidence has led some writers to argue that the tensions generated by the disintegration of familial patterns of patriarchal authority, and the inability of most families to adopt the new bourgeois model of patriarchal family relations, led to an increase in family violence. Such claims are difficult to substantiate; as in the case of social panics, we have to take into account changes in popular and official tolerance of different forms of behaviour, and the visibility of violence as affected by residential patterns and population density. Even so, some social historians argue that sexual antagonism and violence in proletarian families escalated dramatically during the nineteenth century. According to Taylor, for example, 'artisan households in which women replaced men as the major breadwinners were ripe for violent confrontation, as men attempted to assert authority which had lost its material basis'.[26] Such violence continued as the labouring population accepted the ideal of the male breadwinner when only a minority of men were in a position to support their wives and children.

## The proletarian family and the male breadwinner ideal

For a small minority of labouring families, however, the adult male did become the sole breadwinner, and could pride himself on keeping his wife at home, and his children at school, just like his employer. The wage form became fully individualised, and involved a doubly concealed form of unequal exchange. On the one hand, as Marx argued, the labourer seemed to make a fair bargain with his boss, but in fact was paid less than the value of his labour. On the other hand, as feminists have pointed out, the price he received for subsistence appeared to belong only to him and not to the wife (and children) who worked at home to reproduce his labour power.[27] For women, the latter was no mere theoretical issue. Combined with the demise of payment in kind, the new system set the stage for a bitter struggle by wives and children as they attempted to gain a rightful share of the 'family wage' which the employers handed over to the men.

While only a minority of men, and only during periods of prosperity, could earn enough to achieve the breadwinner wage ideal, it became one of the building blocks of a new model of masculinity and femininity. At the beginning of the nineteenth century, labouring men complained bitterly that women were being pushed out of family-based wage labour. Fifty years later, their grandsons felt ashamed if their wives had to work for wages, while a wife's 'fierce questions and taunts' would frequently call into doubt a man's masculinity if he were unable to provide for his family. However impractical or painful the male breadwinner ideal proved for individual families, it became part of working-class respectability, a keystone of labour struggles, and the basis of industrial and trades organisation. Although many (particularly single) women remained in the workforce, most were treated as marginal, paid less than subsistence wages, and excluded from skilled trades and technical education.

With the gradual exclusion of married women from paid work and the lengthening period of childhood dependency, the dynamic of family formation began to change again. Women acquired a powerful incentive to limit their fertility; by the end of the nineteenth century a demographic transition became visible throughout the Western world as the average number of children per family fell from more than six to less than three.

## The middle class and the remaking of the separate spheres

Any discussion of family formation among the labouring poor is incomplete without a close look at the families of their employers: each class made itself, just as it was forging new relations with the other. In their book *Family Fortunes* Leonore Davidoff and Catherine Hall deal with themes which are relevant to our argument.[28] First, they argue that the ideology of the separate spheres, which came to dominate middle-class life in England by the middle of the nineteenth century, was an achievement rather than an inevitable result of historical change. First formulated within Evangelical circles, the strategy of separating women and children rigorously from a public sphere tainted by greed and profit would reform the debauched aristocracy, tame the labouring poor and guarantee the moral standing of the bourgeoisie.

Second, the authors' emphasis on religious thought and association as a key site of negotiation and struggle about new gender and age relations brings back the importance of the church, albeit in a form considerably different from that used in the 'church and state' debates. A similar emphasis is present in Mary Ryan's study of the tumultuous process of industrialisation of Oneida County, New York, in the early nineteenth century. She argues that the confrontation was as much about gender and age as about class, and frequently mediated through the church. In particular, the painful transition between the older patriarchal household and the new middle-class home was expressed through religious experience. Indeed, the relations and values of the middle-class family were constructed not so much inside the family as in the social movements of the time – revivalism, associations, moral reform – and in all of these women and young people played a crucial part.[29]

Third, the ideology of separate spheres accorded women an important moral and practical role in their families. In the early nineteenth century, when institutions like banks and insurance companies were in their infancy, judicious economic alliances between families were essential if the family business was to survive and prosper. A mother's effort to establish and maintain the family's membership of 'polite society' and to secure suitable marriage partners for her children was a crucial link in the process of raising new capital, finding business partners, and securing new customers for the family business.

Fourth, Davidoff and Hall suggest that the same dynamic which made possible the emergence of the middle-class family systematically undermined the emergence of a similar family form among the poor. Charitable ladies and gentlemen did indeed hold up their families as a model for the poor, and were distressed when their exhortations were ignored. Yet they were loathe to pay wages high enough to enable male workers fully to support their 'dependents'. In addition, many employers profited so well from cheap labour that they were far from happy about excluding women and children from the workforce. And the ladies themselves could only remain ladylike if their housework were done for them by other women who worked for wages.

Finally, just as the male breadwinner wage became established as a labour movement orthodoxy by the end of the nineteenth century, significant numbers of middle-class women began publicly and successfully to challenge their exclusion from public life – albeit on the grounds that they were supremely qualified to represent, in public, the interests of the family. In the Commonwealth of Australia, women gained the vote in 1902, five years before the Commonwealth Arbitration Commission set the basic male rate of pay at a level sufficient to maintain a dependent wife and children in modest comfort.

## Industrialisation and urbanisation revisited

Revisionist and Marxist historians of education argued that mass compulsory schooling had its origins in a crisis of class relations and the attempts by the bourgeoisie to assert and maintain their economic, political and cultural dominance during a tumultuous process of industrialisation and urbanisation. More sophisticated versions of the argument tried to shake off the social control implications of some of the theories underpinning these accounts, and introduced Gramscian notions of hegemony and cultural contestation, or tried to use Foucauldian notions of power and governance. For their part, feminists have done much to correct the gender blindness of political theory and of historiography, not only through adding the history of women and girls within the education system to the general picture and utilising social histories of the family, but also through attempting to construct an adequate account of gender relations. We want to extend and rework this critique, emphasising the links between aspects of family formation and the genesis of school systems.

The proletarianisation of labouring families was associated with many developments which eventually influenced schools. Changed relations between men and women, and parents and children, coincided with the disruption of traditional marriage practices and the undermining of customary arrangements for the supervision of youth. Many young women, pursuing the traditional pattern of sexual activity on the solemn promise of marriage, found themselves deserted by their companions, whether because of callousness or inability to gain a livelihood. In turn, less rigidly supervised courtship combined with frequent failure to marry produced a sharp rise in illegitimacy rates. All these developments gave parents abundant motivation to try to protect their daughters from the new hazards associated with courtship.[30]

Paternalist control was disrupted not merely within labouring families, but between employers and workers. As the Rev. J.T. Allen put it in 1819, in a large and crowded manufactory 'it was impossible for the master to exercise the same patriarchal influence and authority over the moral character and conduct of those who are in his employ'.[31] And since workers no longer lived in their master's household, employers were less able – and concerned – to intervene in their employees' domestic affairs. Nevertheless, the autonomy of the workers' domestic sphere was limited, regulated by the factory whistle (and later the school bell) and by the need to make the daily journey to work. Gradually, the rhythms of housework, childcare, sleeping, eating and leisure were set by the dictates of capitalist work discipline.[32] For many bourgeois thinkers, however, such discipline did not go far enough. From their point of view, working-class parents were morally suspect and unfit to bring up their children. Men might have become brothers, but for many of them poverty demonstrated their failure as patriarchs and hence the need to 'improve' or to police them. It might not have been in the immediate interests of individual capitalists to control the workers' private lives, but to the bourgeoisie as a whole few things appeared more pressing.

Contemporary demographic changes sharpened these concerns. Both rich and poor were worried about rapid population increase. The supervision of children by family or neighbours was more difficult, and population pressure replenished the 'reserve army of labour', intensified competition for work, and reduced the bargaining power of workers. Combination of labour, sometimes coupled with the removal of women and children from the labour market, was put forward as one way of reversing the growing immiseration of workers. To the middle class, a different option held more promise: a general moralising of the masses was seen as a solution to the Malthusian nightmare of ever increasing numbers of degraded poor. Morality would replace traditional economic relations which had all but disintegrated as a means of population regulation. Understanding the shame and disgrace of child and female labour, the poor would defer marriage until the male breadwinner was in a position to support a dependent wife and family. In turn, the postponement of marriage and the changed family economy would reduce the birthrate; a tight labour market would eventually result in higher wages.[33] Moral education could replace the compulsion of patriarchalist age relations.

In Australia, concerns about the obedience of workers and young people were exacerbated by the conditions of early colonial society. The presence of large numbers of convicts put problems of governance to the forefront. Rapid immigration and demographic imbalance between men and women made orderly family formation difficult. Established families were disrupted as men left their wives and children to dig for gold, go shearing, or follow casual work. These trends made parents' (and in a different sense bourgeois) concerns over chastity and obedience more urgent, especially when democratic tendencies increased and manhood suffrage was granted. Importantly, this stress on patriarchal control was as clear in mining and pastoral communities as in the cities or in the vicinity of factories.

So far, however, our examples need not challenge a class-based account. After all, historians argue that economic changes associated with the rise of capitalism (or industrialisation and urbanisation) transformed the family, and that this family change was in turn relevant to the rise of schooling. We believe this account to be seriously flawed. First, the model involves a change from an extended to a nuclear family. Most demographic historians, in contrast, argue that there are distinct 'nuclear' family types associated with different stages of the proletarianisation of the labouring population in the West. Even here, the causality does not move simply from the economy to the family. Thus the working class made itself as much as it was made by external economic forces: the exponential population growth of eighteenth- and nineteenth-century Europe (coexisting with a huge exodus of people to the colonies) can be explained by the changing dynamics of family formation as much as by the proletarianisation of peasants and deskilling of craft workers. At the same time, both changing patriarchal and capitalist relations entered into the making of the division of labour outside the family. Feminist authors have argued that modern institutions are profoundly gendered; the design of technology and work organisation typically follows patriarchal as well as capitalist imperatives.

In summary, even if we retain a focus on industrialisation and the cities, the dynamics of gender and age relations were as important for the establishment of school systems as were those of class. The work of demographic and family historians suggests that changes within labouring families provided the rich and poor alike with motivation to experiment with institutional forms, including schools, to resolve the crises in which they were caught and to pursue their interests. There was, in other words, a close connection between family formation and the establishment of state school systems. Since an age-based crisis of patriarchal relations (related to parents' loss of control over inheritance and the labour of the younger generation) preceded a gender-based crisis, this hypothesis could help explain why the establishment of school systems frequently preceded factory-based industrialisation, was directed at girls as well as boys and often appeared as urgent in the countryside as in the cities. To refine this explanation we need to return, paradoxically, to the debate the revisionists believed they had permanently laid to rest.

## Church and state revisited

Two developments have been influential in bringing the church and the state back into focus: a growing sophistication of Marxist – and feminist – theories of the state, and a new emphasis on the role of religion within Western patriarchal societies.[34] The case for reopening the church and state debate – with different questions in mind – is strengthened if our suggestions about the links between a crisis in patriarchal age relations and the origins of mass schooling are taken up.

In feminist literature, the church has been portrayed as the major power underpinning a patriarchalist social order. While some feminist authors confine themselves to describing the role of the church in enforcing and reproducing patriarchal relations, others, such as Davidoff and Hall, and Ryan, present a more complex view of the different denominations struggling to deal with rapidly changing gender and age relations, partly by exploring new models of Christian association and family life.

In the English context, the demise of patriarchalism is associated with a crisis in the authority of the Established Church. The new Evangelical movements of the late eighteenth and early nineteenth century formed part of a wave of more 'democratic' and disparate forms of religion, united in their opposition to the hierarchy of the Anglican Church. These democratic tendencies inside religion were accompanied by a rise in secularism, both within the political sphere and in material life. E.J. Hobsbawm notes in *The Age of Revolution* that, though the nineteenth-century English working class were religious by our standards, they were more removed from religious supervision than any previous group in history.[35]

In spite of (or, perhaps, because of) the weakening influence of religion in social and political life, it was the church which was initially involved in attempts to establish new forms of patriarchal age and gender relations. This was particularly true of proletarian families, where the material bases of enforcing patriarchal authority between the generations had all but disappeared. One of the key concerns, in religious literature and in the writings of the founders of monitorialism, Lancaster and Bell, is a strong emphasis on children's obedience: the National Society, for example, saw its first object as making children 'pliant and obedient to discipline'.[36] These concerns can be understood to refer not merely to children's relations with their parents, but to relations of obedience in general, particularly those involving class and gender.

The origins of mass schooling, then, need to be located in the defensive experimentation by patriarchally structured churches, coping with a crisis in obedience originating in the gradual disintegration of patriarchalist social relations. The first remarkably successful invention was the Sunday school; in the long run, even more significant were the full-time schools conducted on the cheap and seemingly miraculously efficient monitorial systems of Bell and Lancaster. The next step is well known: as the idea of schooling all children was accepted, the state began to take over the emerging school systems, either because of a perceived inability of the church to get the job done, or because of a desire to curtail the spread of the 'wrong' faith.[37]

This reworking of the church and state debate can in part explain why women were included in the compulsory schooling enterprise, when they were not seen as potential citizens: it was because of a perceived crisis in age relations, irrespective of sex, which the church seemed unable to control. Our reconsideration of the church and state debate, however, does not end here. We now have more sophisticated accounts of the state than was the case in the late 1960s, particularly with regard to gender issues and to the creative role of state institutions.

Within these theoretical frameworks, the gradual transfer of power over social life from church to state should not be seen simply as a changing of the guard. Both sets of institutions were sites for creating new forms of social relations as well as policing old ones. The role of new state institutions is demonstrated by Curtis' *Building the Educational State*, which draws on Foucauldian notions of power and subjectivity to argue that state schooling was involved in the construction of a bourgeois state in mid-nineteenth-century Ontario. The hotly contested building of education systems was at one and the same time a process of building the state and moulding its citizens; the debates about the nature of compulsory schooling were simultaneously debates about the nature of the state. As Curtis argues:

> All the fundamental questions concerning educational organization – who needed to be taught, who could educate them, what they needed to know, how they should learn it, who should pay for it – these and other questions were answered only by answering at the same time questions concerning the state: who should rule, how, of what would rule consist, how would it be financed. The struggle over education was at once struggle over political rule.[38]

In addition, educational reform built state knowledge, and in a double sense. In systematic schooling, the state created a new field for information gathering. Inspectors' reports, statistics and bureaucratic expertise played a strategic role in the exercise of state power. At the same time, the children's appropriation of state-generated knowledge – the curriculum – became an important dimension of citizenship. The state-building force of education assumes more significance if we remember that the mid-nineteenth century was the period when most modern nation states were made; parcelled up, warred over and glued together out of hundreds of ethnic groups and contested pieces of territory. In such conditions, a common system of schooling would help create (not always successfully) a nation out of the collection of peoples inside the state boundaries.

Curtis' work recognises the importance of religion in state formation. He argues that Egerton Ryerson, the architect of Ontario's nineteenth-century school system, abstracted from Christian religion what he called 'our Common Christianity', embodying the moral regulatory dimensions of contemporary religious thought. Translated into educational practice, it meant a form of subjectification whereby people would govern themselves in accordance with particular moral precepts. For Ryerson, education was not a *means* to government; education *was* government: government of the self. The development of representative institutions demanded the development of individual self-government.[39]

Significantly, while he does not ignore gender, Curtis does not make a connection between his argument about religion and state formation and the issues of patri-archal governance. Two areas need to be looked at in this regard. First, there is the feasibility of one regime simultaneously producing male citizens about to enter the public sphere, and wives and mothers excluded from it. Did women's presence in public education systems, both as pupils and as teachers, lead to con-stant tension?[40] The second area of concern is the power of the new state institu-tions with regard to age and gender relations, particularly as the state acquired jurisdiction over patriarchal relations which was previously exercised by the church.[41]

Two examples illustrate the issues involved. The first relates to the state's gradual assumption of parental rights during the nineteenth century.[42] The compulsion to send children regularly to school, scrubbed and in clean clothes, was part of a process which eroded parents' discretion about the use of their children's time and labour. In practice, the expanding period of childhood dependency, coupled with more stringent school requirements, encroached significantly on women's hard-won citizenship rights. Not only was the mother's workload increased by the school's demands for clean, neat, punctual children who had done their home-work, but other aspects of her life were judged against the routines of an 'efficient' school. By the turn of the century, some 'child experts' exhorted women to feed and cuddle babies according to precise timetables, while others based their advice on the supervision and education of children provided by governesses in middle-class homes.[43] In the schools themselves, a family model of schooling, embodying some of the ideals of the private sphere, competed (and still does) with a military or industrial one, built around the instrumental rationality of the public sphere.

An equally pertinent example of the links between patriarchy, the state and schools is the debate about links between compulsory schooling and birth rates. Historians of education routinely make a distinction between legislative intentions and what actually took place in schools; between the legislation itself and the social conditions which made its implementation possible. For example, school enrolments were rising steadily in many localities before the introduction of compulsory schooling, and the new laws seemed to make little short-term difference to attendance rates. Why then did most children end up obeying the law?

Some authors have suggested that compulsory schooling, by forcing children out of the labour market, undercut many household economies, made children into an economic burden rather than an asset, and provided an incentive for women to limit their fertility.[44] The compulsory clauses, other authors argue, were enforced only as young people were pushed out of the labour market by other economic forces.[45] Was this contraction of the child labour market a primary force behind the restriction of fertility?[46] Or did smaller families enable parents to send children to school rather than to work? Whatever the cause, the effective introduction of compulsory schooling is linked with a family form built around the male breadwinner wage and limited fertility. This family form, in turn, was the result of a historical compromise concerning gender, class and age relations, a compromise favouring men over women and the patriarchal interests of capitalists against their interests as employers. The state – and schools in particular – helped shape gender and age relations within such families.

## Conclusion

In this chapter we have argued that a prolonged crisis of patriarchy reverberated through all levels of governance in Western societies in the eighteenth and early nineteenth centuries, and that this crisis is as important for explanations of the rise of compulsory schooling as are transformations of contemporary class relations. While in the long run such a hypothesis can only be tested in the light of theoretically informed historical work on the state and patriarchal relations in Australia, it promises to be equally relevant to the countryside as the city, where revisionist explanations hinging on urbanisation and industrialisation remained focused. At the same time, a historical account of changing patriarchal forms gives a purchase on both gender and age relations, and provides a new perspective on the intimate involvement of the church and the state in the complex search for new forms of institutional governance.

We have also argued that there was nothing inevitable about the resolution of this crisis. On the contrary, the demise of one kind of patriarchy and its replacement by another was accompanied by struggle and violence within the public and the private spheres. While the crisis provided all concerned with ample motives for seeking new forms of governance of social relations, there was no one clear logic, interest or course of action which seemed to suit all their concerns. Individually and collectively, men, women and children struggled to chart pathways through changing familial, economic and institutional landscapes which they in turn helped to construct. Mass compulsory schooling was one point where their paths crossed.

## Notes

1  See for example, J.S. Gregory, 'Church and state, and education in Victoria to 1872' in E.L. French (ed.), *Melbourne Studies in Education 1958–59*, Melbourne, 1960; A.G. Austin, *Australian Education 1788–1900: Church, State and Public Education in Colonial Australia*, Melbourne, 1961; G.M. Dow, *George Higinbotham: church and state*, Melbourne, 1964.

2  See in particular, M.B. Katz, 'The origins of public education: a reassessment', *History of Education Quarterly*, vol. 16, no. 4, 1976, pp. 381–407 and R. Johnson, 'Notes on the schooling of the English working class, 1780–1850' in R. Dale *et al.* (eds), *Schooling and Capitalism*, London, 1976.

3   H. Bannister, 'The centralisation problematic', *Australian Journal of Education*, vol. 24, no. 3, 1980.
4   For an overview of these, see I. Davey, 'Capitalism, patriarchy and the origins of mass schooling', *History of Education Review*, vol. 16, no. 2, 1987.
5   One interesting reminder of this is R. Johnson, 'Thatcherism and English education: breaking the mould, or confirming the pattern?', *History of Education*, vol. 18, no. 2, 1989.
6   For a review of some Australian work, see I. Davey and K. Wimshurst, 'The historiography of urban education in Australia: a survey, a case study and a commentary' in R. Goodenow and W. Marsden (eds), *Urban Education History in Four Nations*, Cambridge, 1992.
7   For an overview of the issues, see A. Mackinnon, 'Women's education: linking history and theory', *History of Education Review*, vol. 13, no. 2, 1984.
8   For an outstanding example, see B. Curtis, *Building the Educational State: Canada West, 1836–1871*, London, Ontario, 1988.
9   For an Australian example, see Austin, pp. 177–8.
10  C. Pateman, 'The fraternal social contract: some observations on patriarchal civil society' in J. Keane (ed.), *Civil Society and the State: New European Perspectives*, London, 1988.
11  Quoted in B. Thiele, 'Vanishing acts in social and political thought: tricks of the trade' in C. Pateman and E. Gross (eds), *Feminist Challenges: Social and Political Theory*, Sydney, 1986, p. 33.
12  See for example, C. Pateman, *The Sexual Contract*, Cambridge, 1988; L.M. Clark and L. Lange (eds), *The Sexism of Social and Political Theory: women and reproduction from Plato to Nietzsche*, Toronto, 1979; J. Elshtain, *Public Man, Private Woman: Women in Social and Political Thought*, Princeton, 1981; G. Lloyd, *The Man of Reason: 'male' and 'female' in Western philosophy*, London, 1984; S. Moller-Okin, *Woman in Western Political Thought*, London, 1980.
13  See for example, J.B. Landes, *Women and the Public Sphere in the Age of the French Revolution*, Ithaca, 1988, p. 164.
14  See J. Fitz, 'The child as legal subject' in R. Dale *et al.* (eds), *Education and the State: Politics, Patriarchy and Practice*, London, 1981.
15  One exception, dealing with contemporary issues, is A. McRobbie and M. Nava (eds), *Gender and Generation*, London, 1984.
16  See for example, D. Levine, 'Industrialisation and the proletarian family in England', *Past and Present*, no. 107, 1985; D. Levine (ed.), *Proletarianisation and Family History*, New York, 1984; D. Levine, *Reproducing Families*, Cambridge, 1987; W. Seccombe, 'Marxism and demography', *New Left Review*, no. 137, 1983.
17  A key contribution to this work is Patricia Grimshaw, Chris McConville and Ellen McEwen (eds), *Families in Colonial Australia*, Sydney, 1985.
18  The term proto-industrialisation has been used to describe this process. It was coined by Franklin Mendels in 'Proto-industrialisation: the first phase of industrialisation', *Journal of Economic History*, no. 32, 1972. See also P. Kriedte *et al.*, *Industrialisation Before Industrialisation*, Cambridge, 1981.
19  Levine, 'Industrialisation and the proletarian family', pp. 170–1; Levine, *Reproducing Families*.
20  Grimshaw *et al.* See also P.F. McDonald, *Marriage in Australia: Age at First Marriage and Proportions Marrying, 1860–1971*, Canberra, 1975.
21  See for example, W. Lazonick, 'The subjection of labour to capital: the rise of the capitalist system', *Review of Radical Political Economics*, vol. 10, no. 1, 1978; J. Lawn, 'Not so much a factory, more a form of patriarchy: gender and class during industrialisation' in E. Gamarnikov *et al.* (eds), *Gender, Class and Work*, London, 1983.
22  W. Seccombe, 'Patriarchy stabilised: the construction of the male breadwinner wage norm in nineteenth-century Britain', *Social History*, vol. 11, no. 1, 1986, p. 66.
23  See T.A. Coghlan, *Labour and Industry in Australia*, Melbourne, 1969, vol. 1, p. 444; vol. 2, p. 718.
24  B. Taylor, *Eve and the New Jerusalem: Socialism and Feminism in the Nineteenth Century*, London, 1984.
25  F. Engels, *The Condition of the Working Class in England*, London, 1892.
26  Taylor, p. 111; see also N. Tomes, ' "A torrent of abuse": crimes of violence between working-class men and women in London, 1840–1875', *Journal of Social History*, vol. 11,

1978 and E. Ross, ' "Fierce questions and taunts": married life in working-class London, 1870–1914', *Feminist Studies*, vol. 18, no. 3, 1982.

27 This analytical insight, for so long obscured in Marxist theorising, was transparently clear to early nineteenth-century feminists. See Taylor; see also Seccombe, 'Patriarchy stabilised'.

28 Leonore Davidoff and Catherine Hall, *Family Fortunes: men and women of the English middle class, 1780–1850*, London, 1987.

29 M. Ryan, *The Cradle of the Middle Class: The Family in Oneida County, New York, 1790–1865*, Cambridge, 1981.

30 It is in this context that we can see parents' and educationists' preference for single-sex schooling for older girls, and for married couples as teachers. M. Theobald, 'Discourse of danger: gender and the history of elementary schooling in Australia, 1850–1880', *Historical Studies in Education*, vol. 1, no. 1, 1989.

31 Quoted in P. Silver and H. Silver, *The Education of the Poor*, London, 1974, p. 4.

32 See for example, E.P. Thompson, 'Time, work-discipline and industrial capitalism', *Past and Present*, no. 38, 1967.

33 See for example, T. Chalmers, *The Christian and Civic Economy of Large Towns*, Glasgow, 1821, 1823, 1826.

34 See for example, J. Obelkevich, L. Roper and R. Samuel, *Disciplines of Faith: Studies in Religion, Politics and Patriarchy*, London, 1987.

35 E.J. Hobsbawm, *The Age of Revolution: Europe 1789–1848*, London, 1962.

36 Quoted in Silver and Silver, pp. 14, 8–9.

37 In Australia, the British colonial state had intervened to school the children whose parents were considered to be beyond redemption from the first years of white settlement, as it had done in early nineteenth-century Ireland where the majority of the population was from the 'wrong' faith.

38 B. Curtis, 'Preconditions of the Canadian state: educational reform and the construction of a public in Upper Canada, 1837–1846', *Studies in Political Economy*, no. 10, 1983, pp. 103–4.

39 Curtis, *Building the Educational State*, p. 110.

40 These issues have recently been explored in Theobald, 'Discourse of danger'.

41 For two different perspectives see K. Reiger, *The Disenchantment of the Home: modernising the Australian family 1880–1940*, Melbourne, 1985 and J. Donzelot, *The Policing of Families*, New York, 1979.

42 See Fitz, 'The child as a legal subject'.

43 Carolyn Steedman, 'Prisonhouses', *Feminist Review*, no. 20, 1985, p. 13

44 J. Caldwell, 'Mass education as a determinant of the timing of fertility decline', *Population and Development Review*, vol. 6, no. 2, 1980; E. Ross, 'Labour and love: rediscovering London's working class mothers, 1870–1918' in J. Lewis (ed.), *Labour and Love*, Oxford.

45 M.B. Katz, 'The origins of public education'; S.K. Troen, 'The discovery of the adolescent by American educational reformers, 1900–1920: an economic perspective' in L. Stone (ed.), *Schooling and Society*, Baltimore, 1976.

46 D. Levine, *Reproducing Families*.

## CHAPTER 6

# TECHNICAL EDUCATION AND STATE FORMATION IN NINETEENTH-CENTURY ENGLAND AND FRANCE

Andy Green

*History of Education*, 24, 2, 123–39, 1995

## Introduction

Modern economists generally see human skills as *the* key factor in economic competitiveness.[1] Vocational education has consequently been a high priority for policy makers, particularly in Britain where provision is seen to lag behind that of other competitor nations.[2] This situation has given rise to intense public debate about the causes of underachievement amongst young people in post-compulsory education and training. Current discussions focus on the narrow and over-specialized nature of academic study, the relative unpopularity and low status of alternative vocational tracks, and on the fragmented and incoherent nature of the post-compulsory system as a whole.[3] In addition to multiple institutional distinctions in the sector, and the fragmented and dispersed nature of control over these institutions and over the qualifications system, there is a deep and damaging divide between 'academic' and 'vocational' learning. This is often believed to impede access and achievement amongst students and to perpetuate the low status of the vocational routes which the government wishes to enhance.[4]

Although the current intensity of the debate over these issues is unparalleled in this century, there were similar debates in the nineteenth century. This was particularly the case during the period from 1870 when, as now, the country was undergoing an economic recession and also experiencing the first bitter taste of the relative economic decline which has dominated subsequent British history.[5] Contemporary policy making has much to learn from revisiting these historic debates to understand better the nature of this problem and the specific national causes which underlie it. A comparative analysis of the development of technical education in France and England can assist this process.

## The underdevelopment of scientific and technical education in nineteenth-century England

With the exception of pure science, which developed largely independently of formal educational institutions, England was, throughout the nineteenth century, notably backward in most areas of scientific and technical education by comparison with other major states in northern Europe. This judgement, shared by many late nineteenth-century commentators and the vast majority of subsequent economic and educational historians, applied not only to the state of science teaching, or the lack of it, in schools and universities, but also to post-school vocational education, whether in institutes, colleges or universities.[6]

For working-class boys and girls, elementary education was too sparse and narrow to provide a proper foundation for technical and scientific study and facilities for full-time post-elementary education were largely absent. State organized trade schools for artisans and skilled workers, which were common in continental Europe, had not developed in England where received opinion regarded the workshop as the only fit place for learning a trade.[7] There was also a virtual absence of those intermediate vocational schools, like the *Écoles des Arts et Métiers* and the *Écoles Primaires Supérieurs* in France, which trained students from the upper ranks of the working class and from the lower rungs of the middle class for supervisory and lower managerial positions in commerce and industry. Whilst in France and Prussia there was a plethora of such institutions by the 1840s, England had to wait until the 1880s for the development of the higher grade schools, and the first technical colleges, which would perform a similar function.[8]

Provision for the middle class was equally deficient in this area. Public and grammar schools remained frozen in the classical mould, and, until the last quarter of the century at least, universities contributed virtually nothing towards scientific and technical needs.[9] Engineering did not become an examination subject in Cambridge until 1894 and Oxford had no Chair in Engineering until 1908.[10] This again was in striking contrast to major continental states where not only was secondary and university education somewhat more scientific,[11] but where also a layer of higher technological institutions has emerged in the form of the *Polytechnique*, the French *Grandes Écoles* and the German *Technische Hochschule* (technical high school). Equivalent polytechnics and civic universities did not begin to emerge in England until the 1880s and then remained chronically underfunded until the beginning of the next century.[12] By 1910 Germany had 25,000 university students of science and technology compared with some 3000 in England.[13]

Until the last quarter of the nineteenth century England had thus not even begun to develop a system of full-time state technical schools, at either elementary, intermediate or higher levels, such as existed in many continental states and this was the true measure of its backwardness in vocational education. What it had instead was an apprenticeship system, which was the sole means of training for most trades and for many of the new professions, and a profusion of adult evening classes, first in the form of the popular Mechanics Institutes and later supplemented by the classes funded by the Department of Science and Art. However, the apprenticeship was often of dubious efficacy and rarely sought to train beyond the level of basic practical skills and the evening class provision was geographically uneven and often ineffective as training, hampered as it was by the lack of prior learning amongst students and the often desultory and unsystematic nature of the teaching.[14]

During the first half of the century, whilst Britain was still basking in the sunshine of its first successful industrial revolution and its still unchallenged economic supremacy, this state of affairs caused relatively little alarm. However, from the mid-century onwards it was increasingly apparent that continental countries were fast developing economically and this raised considerable concern about the state of Britain's education and training. This was fuelled by the reports of German and French technical achievements displayed at the various international Exhibitions and by the writings of educational lobbyists, such as Playfair, Huxley, Samuelson, Arnold, Thompson and Russell, who came back from their investigative travels on the Continent with dire warnings about the superiority of continental education and training and the dangers this posed for Britain's economic position.

These writers offered substantially different accounts of the problems inherent in English education and training. Some, like Huxley and Playfair, were strong supporters of workshop training and somewhat suspicious of the theoretical nature of continental trade schools;[15] others, like Sylvanus Thompson, the first Principal of Finsbury technical college, and John Scott Russell,[16] civil engineer and fellow of the Royal Society of London, were keen to adopt the school-based training model. However, they were unanimously agreed on two points: that English technical training was deficient and that this was endangering the economic health of the country. As Thompson put it in his book, *Apprentice Schools in France* (1879):

> The lack of technical education is costing us dearly – has cost us terribly dear – in spite of the oft repeated warnings of those who saw the efforts which continental nations were making to surpass us, as they could only surpass a nation possessing vast natural advantages, by organizing the technical education of their artisans, and by giving to the sons of the wealthier commercial classes and employers of labour that sound scientific training which alone would qualify them to use to the highest advantage the technical training given to the artisans.[17]

These warnings about the deficiencies in English technical education began with individual lobbyists and their beliefs were certainly not shared by all commentators or indeed, as far as we can tell, the majority of manufacturers at the time. However, in time they gained increasing credibility, reinforced by the verdict of successive Royal Commissions which noted the backwardness not only of technical training but of English education in general. The Schools Inquiry Commission reported in graphic terms to this effect in 1868:

> ...our evidence appears to show that our industrial classes have not even the basis of sound general education on which alone technical education can rest...In fact our deficiency is not merely in technical education, but...in general intelligence, and unless we remedy this want we shall gradually but surely find that our undeniable superiority in wealth and perhaps in energy will not save us from decline.[18]

The Royal Commission on Technical Instruction (1884), chaired by Bernhardt Samuelson, later reinforced the judgement about England's comparative disadvantage with a wealth of data on continental schooling. It found that the 'dense ignorance so common among English workmen' was unknown in Germany[19] and that the advance of continental manufactures could not have been achieved had it not been:

> ...for the system of high technical instruction in their schools, for the facilities for carrying on original scientific investigation, and for the general appreciation of the value of that instruction and of original research, which is felt in these countries.[20]

## Explanations of English underdevelopment

The most popular explanation of English backwardness in scientific and technical education is the so-called 'cultural critique' which focuses on the supposedly anti-industrial and anti-utilitarian culture of the Victorian political élite and the landed class from which they mostly came. Versions of this thesis have emerged both from the right and the left and can be found in the works of a series of eminent historians and social commentators – most notably: G. C. Allen, Perry Anderson, Correlli Barnett, Anthony Sampson, Martin Wiener and, most recently, Michael Sanderson.[21] The argument, broadly summarized, is that Britain, the first successful industrialized nation, never experienced a full bourgeois revolution and thus never fully displaced the landowner class from its dominant political and ideological position. The culture of the landed class, and of the old professions and sections of the bourgeoisie who became assimilated to it, was predominantly rural and conservative, suspicious and sometimes contemptuous of industry and commerce, and disinterested in science and technology and anything that smacked of base utilitarianism. Since this class continued to dominate the British establishment it fostered a style of political leadership which was more amateur than expert and policies which were hostile to modernization and economic development. The dominance of this 'anti-industrial' culture is said to have determined the resistance of the Anglican-controlled universities and secondary schools towards science and technology and the failure of governments to modernize the educational system.

The problem with the argument is that whilst these traits were predominant amongst the landed classes, and some of the older professional groups allied to them, they by no means constituted the dominant or hegemonic ideology of Victorian England.[22] Certainly there were aspects of the traditional landed ideology that remained distinctly influential in some areas, particularly in the Anglican Church, in the rural areas and in certain branches of the state, like the Army, the Home Office and the Foreign Office. There was also a powerful current of thought amongst sections of the intelligentsia which was overtly antagonistic to the dominant bourgeois ethos of the time. The romantic conservative tradition, which extended down from Coleridge to Carlyle, Ruskin and even Dickens in his later years, was deeply opposed to the narrow materialism and harsh self-interest of the liberal creed and at times appeared both unsympathetic to the urban world and hostile to industrialism itself. As both Wiener and Anderson rightly insist, these influences, combined with the lure of the gentlemanly, pastoral lifestyle, proved uniquely attractive to sections of the bourgeoisie and the old professional class.

However, the wide resonance and compelling attraction of this view of the world owed precisely to the very dominance of liberal and materialist values in this the most urbanized and industrial country in the world. It was an inevitable reaction and had important consequences, particularly in the later period, but it hardly dislodged the mainstream bourgeois values from their hegemonic position. The overwhelmingly dominant values of the Victorian era were those of individualism, enterprise and *laissez-faire* liberalism, at once both tempered and sharpened by religion. Whatever their antecedents, these were nothing now if not the values of a confident and predominantly bourgeois capitalism, and the heart of the metropolitan culture which held sway in the politics of the industrial cities. The Liberal governments of the middle decades of the century may have been dominated by landowners, but many of these had been won over to the values of the middle classes and where it mattered most succumbed to their wishes. For the most part, as Marx well observed, the 'aristocratic state' served as representative of the bourgeois interest.[23]

This bourgeois interest, though perhaps dominated more by finance and commerce than manufacture, was nevertheless, as Rubinstein has recently argued, triumphantly pro-business.[24]

Thus whilst it is certainly true that the anti-modern attitudes of the old élites still fashioned the character of the Anglican public schools and the grammar schools, and contributed towards their characteristic elevation of character over intellect and classics over science, it can hardly be said that the wholesale failure of the state to create other, more modern, institutions derived from this cause. After all, the old landed classes still maintained immense influence in most continental states during the nineteenth century, as Arno Mayer has demonstrated, but this did not prevent the development of technical education.[25] The remnants of the *ancien regime* in France, the *Junkers* and old bureaucracy in Germany, and the landowners and *Samurai* in Japan, all retained residual cultural traces of the old conservative values and were sometimes overtly hostile to modernization. All over Europe, the traditional humanist education, dominated by the study of classics, continued to retain the high status it had enjoyed since Aristotle first designated it as the only civilized education proper for the leisured classes, and it continued to be defined in opposition to utilitarian learning.[26] The German concept of *Bildung*, as defined by Von Humboldt, and the French concept of *culture générale*, as lauded by the likes of Victor Cousin, no less than Cardinal Newman's notion of learning for its own sake, were all anti-utilitarian and were used by the educational establishment in secondary schools and universities in all countries to resist the encroachments of professional or vocational education.[27] Where England differed from France and Germany was in the failure of the rising middle classes to secure reforms to these recalcitrant institutions or to ensure the development of alternative institutions. On the continent, and in *Meiji* Restoration Japan, these reforms were generally achieved through the action of a modernizing state. In England decisive state action was slower to occur, thus prolonging the retarding influence on education of the old cultural conservatism.

The underlying causes of the peculiarly delayed development of scientific and technical education in England should be sought, therefore, not so much in the culture of the old establishment but rather in the responses of the new industrial and bourgeois classes to it. The most striking aspect of this whole story is the failure of the bourgeoisie to secure adequate reforms in technical education despite the fact that they were clearly in favour of industrial development and in other respects quite capable of fighting for and winning those conditions which would secure it. The paradoxical fact is that majority of this pioneer class was neither generally aware of the singular importance of scientific and technical education to economic advance nor willing, when they became aware of it, to argue for the state to take the necessary remedies. Underlying this were two historical causes, which more than anything else constituted the peculiarities of the English situation: the first of these was the fact and consequences of having the first Industrial Revolution and the second was the nature of the liberal state and the individualist creed that underpinned it.[28]

In continental Europe industrialization occurred under the tutelage of the state and began its accelerated development later when techniques were already becoming more scientific; technical and scientific education had been vigorously promoted from the centre as an essential adjunct of economic growth and one that was recognized to be indispensable for countries which wished to close on Britain's industrial lead. By contrast, Britain's early industrialization had occurred without direct state intervention and developed successfully, at least in its early stages, within a *laissez-faire* framework. This meretricious industrial start had two consequences for technical education. First, state intervention was thought unnecessary for developing technical skills, where the initial requirements were slight and adequately met by traditional means. The customary empirical approach of the apprenticeship seemed adequate and eminently practical. In fact, Political Economy suggested that state intervention might be positively injurious. Not only would it offend against liberal principles and create an unwanted additional tax burden, but it would interfere in the market, undermine the manufacturers' own training provision and endanger trade secrets. Second, the very success of Britain's early industrial expansion encouraged a complacency about the importance of scientific skills and theoretical knowledge which became a liability in a later period when empirical knowledge, inventiveness and rule-of-thumb methods were no longer adequate.

The first cause of England's failure to develop scientific and technical education was thus a deeply entrenched complacency which derived from its uniquely fortunate position. As John Scott Russell put it in 1869:

> We have been enjoying the fruits of the inventions of a few men of genius who had created the whole system of modern manufacturing industry, and providence had also endowed [us] with the accumulated wealth of countless centuries shored up in the bowels of the earth in the shape of iron and coal.[29]

Such complacent confidence lasted well into mid-century and goes some way to explaining the lack of urgency felt in matters of technical education until this time. However, there was also another cause for inaction which outlasted the first for a further twenty years and this was the resistance to state involvement in education of any sort, whether elementary, secondary or technical.

The doctrine of *laissez-faire* and the minimal state, as first advocated by Adam Smith in the eighteenth century, became the fundamental tenet of nineteenth-century liberalism, permeating the culture and values not only of Dissent and the middle class but of all sections of society. When applied to education it provided powerful arguments against state involvement and led to the failure of countless reform initiatives during the first half of the century.[30] Although various liberal ideologists, such as Jeremy Bentham and John Stuart Mill, recognized that there must be exceptions to the rule of non-intervention, and particularly in the case of public goods like education, the predominant view of Political Economy during the first sixty years of the nineteenth century was that the state should let alone wherever possible, including in the field of education. State education was frequently condemned as a 'Prussian' heresy – as alien to the English national character and tradition.[31] As well as costing the taxpayers money, it was often claimed to be prejudicial to voluntary effort, detrimental to the family and enfeebling for the individual. Above all it was considered to be fundamentally illiberal and conducive towards state tyranny over the minds of individuals. Despite the small encroachments made by the state into education since the 1830s, this view was still widely held in the 1850s, as evidenced by the considerable popularity of Herbert Spencer's *State Education Self Defeating* and Samuel Smiles's *Self Help*, both of which eulogized the individualist creed and berated state involvement in education.[32]

When, in the decades following the Franco-Prussian war, *laissez-faire* ideas came to be increasingly questioned, and state intervention seen more favourably, there emerged a body of opinion which was frankly sceptical of voluntarism in education. By the 1870s both John Stuart Mill and Matthew Arnold had acknowledged that opposition to state intervention was a major cause of English educational backwardness. Although he saw good cause for not allowing the state a monopoly of education, Mill recognized in his later years that 'jealousy of government interference' and opposition to 'centralization' could be a mere prejudice and one to which the middle class was particularly prone.[33] Matthew Arnold, like his father a long-time advocate of state intervention, roundly condemned the English middle class for their opposition to state secondary education which he believed to be the only way to achieve schools for the middle class comparable in excellence to the *lycées* of France and the German *Gymnasien*. Writing on *Higher Schools and Universities in Germany* in 1892, he quite accurately linked this opposition to state action to the characteristic British hostility to expertize and science:

> ...our dislike of authority and our disbelief in science have combined to make us leave our school system...to take care of itself as best it could. Under such auspices, our school system has very naturally fallen into confusion; it has done nothing to counteract the indisposition to science which is our great intellectual fault.[34]

From a later vantage point Michael Sadler, who was certainly no supporter of unfettered state control, summed up the particular problem of English educational development by a series of contrasts with Germany:

> The crucial difference between the history of German education and that of English during the nineteenth century lay in the different use which the two countries made of the power of the state. In Germany that power was exercised unflinchingly, with great foresight and clearness of purpose and without any serious resistance from public opinion. In England it was used reluctantly, with deliberate rejection of any comprehensive plan of national reorganization and in the teeth of opposition which had to be conciliated at every turn. As a result, Germany has constructed an educational system which works with fairly simple machinery; England has a complicated machinery, but no well-defined system of national education.[35]

By the 1900s even the Board of Education could acknowledge, in retrospect, that voluntarism had failed, arguing, in its 1905/6 Report, that reforms had been held up by 'the formidable inertia of the nation reinforced by intense jealousy of state interference and dislike of public control'.[36]

English technical education, like elementary and secondary schooling, was a major casualty of voluntarism and *laissez-faire*, and by the 1870s there were increasing numbers who were prepared to acknowledge this. Few of its advocates were as sanguine about state intervention as Arnold in respect of secondary schools, and indeed it would not have been politic to be so given the importance of the industrial lobby in the cause. However, there were some, such as J. Scott Russell, whose analysis of the problems in technical education closely mirrored those of Arnold and Saddler. Russell identified the same popular impediment to reform as Arnold:

> ...we dislike System, organization, and methodical control...,We despise the paternal governments of foreign nations, and spurn interference, control or direction from the executive for our own government.[37]

The result of this aversion to systematic organization in English education, Russell argued, was all pervasive, affecting every branch of the system, including technical education. Most specifically, it had prevented the development of an organized system of full-time technical institutions, such as had developed in many continental states since early in the century.

## The development of French technical education

We can see more clearly the particularities of English technical educational development by comparing it with France. In France the development of vocational schools predated both the Revolution and industrialization by over a century. Technical education developed under the tutelage of the absolutist state from the time of Louis XIV onwards. It was an important part of the process of early state formation underscored by the mercantilist doctrines which argued for the enhancement of national wealth and prestige through the exercise of state power. The *ancien régime* established schools of art and design and also a number of higher vocational schools such as the *École des Ponts et Chaussees* (1747), the *École du Corps Royale du Génie* (1749), the *École Royale Militaire* (1753), the *École de Marine* (1773) and the *École des Mines* (1783). The Revolution which, as de Tocqueville argued,[38] perpetuated many of the centralizing tendencies of the *ancien régime*, destroyed many of the religious schools, but had positive results for vocational schooling. The Thermidorean regime set up the *Écoles Centrales*, which were arguably the pioneers of a modern model of secondary schooling; the Directory (1795–9) created the *École Polytechnique*, soon to become the foremost science faculty in Europe, and numerous *écoles d'application*. The latter provided training for a diverse range of occupations including sailors, agriculturists, pharmacists, veterinarians and midwives.[39]

After the Revolution, the centralized, étatist policies first promulgated by the absolutist monarchs, and later consolidated by the revolutionary regimes, continued to support the development of technical education. Napoleon, although the architect of the *Université*, the heart of the burgeoning French national education system, was notably conservative in his beliefs on education, abandoning the revolutionary principles of the *écoles centrales* for a quasi-meritocratic but still traditionalist classicism in the new state *lycées* which he founded.[40] More concerned with the creation of loyal and disciplined officers and expert public administrators than with the needs of industry and commerce, he gave little attention to technical education for civil occupations. However, he did give his support to the *École des Arts et Métiers*, which had originally been founded by the Duc de la Rochefoucauld on his estate at Liancourt for training war orphans in skilled trades. He also had two similar institutions set up at Chalons (1806) and Angers (1811) and, according to Frederick Artz, the Chalons school quickly gained the reputation for being the best elementary trade school in Europe.[41] Later in the century these schools, which combined practical training with theoretical instruction in applied science, became a key source of engineering skills. Their graduates, known as *Gadzarts*, often came to occupy key positions as managers and production engineers in small and medium-sized companies concerned with the design, construction, installation and maintenance of heavy machinery and power plants.[42]

After the ravages of the Napoleonic Wars France was far behind England in the development of industry and manufacturing. However, the Restoration brought a revival of economic activity which increased the demand for skills which would no longer be available from Britain which had banned the emigration of artisans to France. Initially, the Bourbon regime did little to promote technical education and the *Université* remained wedded to the ideas of classical education. However, there was increasing pressure from industrial and business leaders to provide more technical education and this received growing support from Liberals, such as the economist J. B. Say, and from technologically minded Saint-Simonians; the desire to see France catch up with English industrial development gave impetus to this movement. During the 1820s the main initiatives came from private individuals with encouragement from the state. In 1820 a group of Parisian capitalists, including Laffite, Casimir and Périer, set up the *École Supérieure de Commerce de Paris*. Initially encouraged by government officials such as Chaptal, this finally received government funding in 1839. Likewise the *École Centrale des Arts et Manufactures* was originally founded in 1829 by a group of private individuals including the Saint-Simonian Eugéne Péclet and scientists Olivier, Binet and Lavallée. The school was designed to train civil engineers for the private sector, originally recruiting from amongst unsuccessful but able candidates for the *École Polytechnique*. With a supremely talented scientific faculty the school was dedicated to promoting the new field of applied science (*la science industrielle*) as a holistic discipline. Its motto – 'industrial science is one, and every *industrielle* must know it in its totality or suffer the penalty of remaining inferior to this task' – well symbolized its novel and demanding aspiration to unite the theory of pure science and the practice of engineering and in so doing helped reinforce the high status already acquired by the engineering profession through its association with the state and public works.[43] In time it became one of the chief sources for highly trained civil engineers in France, becoming a state institution in 1857.

During the July Monarchy the state played a more active role in promoting vocational and technical education. The 1833 *Loi Guizot* did much to improve primary education and also required the creation in every commune of over 6000 people of an *École Primaire Supérieure*. These taught a modern curriculum with some commercial subjects. Whilst seen as inferior to the *collèges* by many, they grew in strength to 352 by 1841.[44] Although out of favour during the Second Empire they were revived during the Third Republic. By 1887 there were 700 of these institutions (about two hundred of which were for girls) providing children from petit-bourgeois families with a vocationally orientated education to fit them for work as small manufacturers, artisans and white-collar employees.[45] During the July Monarchy the state, both local and central, also created a wide range of elementary vocational schools. By the mid-century there were some 50 trade schools, 35 agricultural schools as well as numerous naval, mining and design schools.[46] Although some of these were private establishments the majority existed by virtue of state support.

The Second Empire took relatively few initiatives in vocational education but substantial progress did occur in the development of a more modern secondary education. Louis Napoleon instructed his minister Fortoul to create a modern scientific stream in the *collèges* but his bifurcation policy was fiercely resisted by the *Université* and the scheme was finally scrapped by Duruy. However, there was clearly a strong demand for a more modern secondary curriculum and local initiative saw to it that this was at least partly met. A survey by Gustav Rouland found that a sixth of all *lycéens* and 50% of those in municipal *collèges* were already involved in vocational courses during the 1850s.[47] In 1865 Victor Duruy's law on *l'enseignement secondaire spéciale* was finally successful in creating a viable modern programme in the *collèges*. This scheme flourished and in 1880 its status as a full secondary course was acknowledged by the creation of a *baccalauréat* for special education. By this time some 33% of children were following the special modern programmes which involved systematic science education.[48]

The Third Republic was most noted for its achievement in primary and secondary education, but there were also important new initiatives in vocational and technical education. Jules Ferry battled successfully against the traditionalists in the *Université* to create a new range of applied science faculties which could recruit students from the technical schools. Although their degrees did not at first have parity with the state diplomas, the faculties were popular and developed good links with industry. There were also important developments at the lower levels of technical education. During this period a strong lobby for technical education grew up around the Ministry of Industry and Commerce's *Conseil Supérieur de l'Enseignement Technique* and a tussle ensued between this ministry and the Ministry of Public Instruction for control over vocational education. The two ministries between them created a new network of vocational schools. From the 1880s onwards they instigated numerous *Écoles Manuelles d'Apprentissage* which later became known as *Écoles Pratiques de Commerce et l'Industrie*. These recruited the sons and daughters of workers and petit-bourgeois families from primary schools and trained them to be skilled workers and office employees. By 1913 there were some 14,766 students in such schools, one quarter of whom were girls.[49] The Government also set up four regional boarding schools, known as *Écoles Nationales Professionnelles*, for the training of foremen and supervisors as well as reviving the higher primary schools. Day estimates that these, together with the intermediate technical schools, were by 1914 enrolling at least 150,000 students.

Despite opposition from the *Université* and some of the old élites, the French state, in collaboration with progressive private individuals, had created a system of technical education probably only rivalled in Europe by that in Germany.[50]

## The development of technical education in England

In contrast with the state-led development of technical education in France, England relied for the greater part of the century on individual private initiative for the development of its skills training. Apart from the Government school of Mines, the School of Naval Architecture, Owen's College and a handful of agricultural and military schools, there were few full-time state-funded vocational schools during the first half of the century, and this reflected the deep hostility within liberal opinion for state intervention in education. For the greater part of the nineteenth century English training was based on the apprenticeship and this remained the paradigmatic form of all future technical education. Privately organized by employers and independent craftsmen, the apprenticeship system received no public funds and embodied a characteristically practical approach based on on-the-job experience rather than theoretical study. The same principle was adopted in training for professional engineering. Whilst vocational education for doctors and lawyers was widespread, particularly with the numerous medical schools, a scientific and technical education for engineers and manufacturers was hard to find, reflecting the bias against science and the new professions in much middle-class education. This contrasted strongly with the typical practice in continental states. The 1968 Report of the Institute of civil engineers noted:

> The education of foreign engineers is strongly contrasted with that in England in every particular. Practical training by apprenticeship is unknown; the education begins at the other end, namely, by the acquirement of a high degree of theoretical knowledge, under the direction, and generally at the expense of government.[51]

Where government intervention later supplemented this system it was in an ancillary role that left its fundamental features intact. State-assisted technical education was predominantly part time, practically orientated and in administration largely marginalized from mainstream educational provision. When anxieties about the superiority of French design in silk manufactures prompted the government to create a school of design and later to fund other such schools in industrial areas (of which there were seventeen by 1852), the council which administered them was characteristically located within the Board of Trade, insulated from contact with educational administration. The schools were bedevilled by bureaucratic and factional conflicts and represented a very inauspicious beginning for state intervention in technical education. They were intended as a stimulus to technical education, but never as an alternative form to the apprenticeship.[52]

By the 1850s the limitations of this approach were becoming increasingly evident. Industrial development was entering into a new phase which made different demands on education. As Eric Hobsbawm has written:

> The major technical advances of the second half of the 19th century were essentially scientific, that is to say they required at the very least some knowledge of recent development in pure science for original invention, a far more consistent process of scientific experiment and testing for their development and an increasingly close and continuous link between industrialists, technologists, professional scientists and scientific institutions.[53]

What was absent in England was precisely this link between pure science and its application, such as had been pioneered in the *École Centrale* and the *écoles des arts et métiers*. In short, technical education. The limitations of this were becoming increasingly obvious with the development of new technologies – the electric telegraph, the synthesis of aniline dyes, artificial fertilizers, and so on – which were highly dependent on scientific knowledge, particularly on chemistry, and in which Britain was at some disadvantage.

The pragmatic approach of on-the-job training appeared to be inadequate and a more rigorous and systematic form of training was required. However, private and voluntary initiatives were not responding sufficiently. This was not surprising, since there was an inherent limitation in the *laissez-faire* approach to training which lay in the very nature of the market itself. Capitalist enterprise was, by definition, competitive and individualistic and recourse to any collective strategies to improve technical skills, for instance setting up technical schools, went against the grain of entrepreneurial values. Competitive entrepreneurs would not sponsor schools for technical training because they feared for their trade secrets, suspected that others would poach their trainees, and reckoned the investment was not warranted by its potential return in immediate profit. Their judgement was not untypical of their class. In no country did individual capitalist enterprise produce a collective strategy for training without state intervention. In this, the area of education with most economic importance, the market principles of political economy were found wanting.

Thus by mid-century there was increasing anxiety about the state of technical education. The Great Exhibition of 1851 had alerted more far-sighted observers to the potential industrial challenge from the Continent. Lyon Playfair, a leading chemist and champion of scientific education, returned from a tour of the Continent to warn of the superiority of their technical schools. In a much publicized lecture entitled *Industrial Instruction on the Continent* (1852), he argued that as improved transport lessened the competitive advantage to be gained from an abundance of raw materials, so science and technical skills would become increasingly important. However, it was in this area of technology that:

> ...we English are weak. Philosophy we have in abundance. Manual skills we possess abundantly. But we have failed to bridge the interval between the two. On the contrary, there is a dead wall separating our men of theory from our men of practice.[54]

Changing economic circumstances and the agitation of men such as Playfair and Henry Cole, the recently appointed Secretary of the School of Design, prompted government intervention and in 1853 the Department of Science and Art was created under the Board of Trade. The aim was to create a more effective central body to stimulate and co-ordinate efforts in technical education, including existing schools and sundry public institutions such as the Government School of Mines and the Division of Practical Geology. However, the system it supported would remain 'local and voluntary...[and] in the main self-supporting'.[55] The department had mixed fortunes. Under Cole's energetic supervision the existing design schools were revived and by 1858 there were 56 flourishing schools of art with 35,000 students.[56] The science division was less successful, initially; most of the new science schools failed and by 1859 only 450 students attended courses. Aid to science classes from the department between 1853 and 1859 amounted to a mere £898. However, in the following decade, with Henry Cole as sole secretary of the department and Captain Donelly as Inspector of Science, a more energetic regime evolved and pupils in Science Schools and evening classes increased to 10,230.[57] Payment by results was instituted throughout the schools and classes receiving funds, and outside examiners were brought in to assess the school results.

However, this limited government action still left scientific and technical education in an inadequate state. The Department's schools, like the Mechanics Institute classes, with which they partially merged, were part time, and their effectiveness was undermined by the paucity of elementary education amongst their students and the desultory nature of the classes. Michael Sadler's later reflection on this tradition of evening schools was characteristically perceptive:

> Thus alike in their excellence and their effects, the evening classes have borne the characteristic features of the English educational organization. Free in their development, vigorous in some of their achievements, and often well-adapted to the requirements of the persevering and strong, they were unsystematic in arrangement, weakened by deficits in the early training of their pupils, and from a national point of view, insufficiently adjusted to the needs of the rank and file.[58]

Criticism of existing provision continued and intensified, as burgeoning economic realities kept this issue alive in public debate. The Paris Exhibition of 1867 had a chastening effect since the failings of Britain's industrial performance were now evident. In all of the ninety classes of manufacturers, Britain was pre-eminent in only ten. Lyon Playfair, who was one of the jurors, reported back on the exhibition with some foreboding and, in a much quoted open letter to Lord Taunton, warned that Britain was losing its industrial lead owing to the fact that continental countries 'possess good systems of industrial education and that England possesses none'.[59]

Growing anxiety about the scientific ignorance of foremen, industrial managers and proprietors and the deleterious effects of this on the economy prompted a series of public enquiries into the state of technical education. In the year following the Exhibition, the Select Committee on Scientific Instruction reported; this was followed by eight reports from the Devonshire Royal Commission on Scientific Instruction and the Advancement of Science (1872–5) and then in 1884 with reports from the Samuelson Royal Commission on Technical Instruction. Each report praised the achievement of continental education and noted the industrial advances that could not have occurred without it. While all reports defended the notion of workshop training, they each found many defects in English provision.

The primary concerns of the reports lay in the results of inadequate training for supervisors, managers and proprietors. Most managers and 'capitalists of the great industrial enterprises' were only educated up to higher elementary level, although in 'rare' cases they followed courses at institutions like the Royal College of Mines or Owen's College, Manchester. There was a great insufficiency of modern Grammar Schools. In Public and endowed Grammar Schools 'science is as yet very far from receiving the attention to which it is entitled'.[60] Although some improvements had been made since the Clarendon Committee reported, still only eighteen out of 128 schools investigated had more than four hours of science teaching. Various witnesses noted the effects of this inadequate scientific background in managers and proprietors; many of them did not understand the manufacturing process and thus failed to promote efficiency, avoid waste and instigate innovative techniques. Furthermore, having little interest in science themselves, they did not value it in their workmen.

The second area of deficiency lay in the ignorance of foremen and supervisors. Ordinary workmen were not thought to require much scientific education but since the foremen and sometimes the managers also were drawn from this class, it was desirable that there should be a pool of expertise there. The absence of this was put down to a number of causes. The Revised Code had narrowed the focus of elementary schools to such an extent that they imparted little scientific or technical knowledge. Their standards were inadequate as a foundation for further study. Continuation schools and evening classes were 'unsystematic' and 'desultory' in their provision and they were hampered by the lack of preparation and fatigue of their students whose efforts to acquire further education after work were not recognized by employers. Furthermore, there was a shortage of qualified science teachers, and the administrative separation of Department of Science and Art classes and the remainder of elementary and secondary education was a handicap.

As to the apprenticeship system, opinions expressed in the reports varied. The Samuelson Report acknowledged the benefits of continental trade schools, concluding that 'secondary instruction of a superior kind is placed within the reach of children of parents of limited means to an extent [of] which we have no conception in this country'.[61] However, a number of witnesses criticized the overly theoretical nature of these schools and maintained the superiority of the workshop as a means of imparting practical skills. Some of the most perceptive comments were offered in evidence given by Flemming Jenkins, a Professor of Civil Engineering at University College. Explaining that in his experience apprentice supervision was often very lax, he maintained that whilst the best apprentices learnt a good deal, the idle ones learnt nothing at all. Comparing the apprenticeship system with the continental trade schools Jenkins argued that, in terms of practical ability and commonsense, the English apprentice was a match for anyone, and even for the products of the Polytechnic. However, he continued:

> When in after life, the two men came to fill the higher stations, the English engineer would begin to feel the want of elementary training very severely, and he is at a disadvantage compared with the man abroad, in the judging of new problems which come under his eye.[62]

Other contemporary commentators, such as John Scott Russell and Silvanus Thompson, were less generous to the apprenticeship system, claiming that in all respects it was inferior to the continental trade school. Thompson, in his book, *The Apprentice Schools in France*, argued that the English apprentice spent six years in repetitive drudgery that failed 'to make anything but a bad, unintelligent machine'. By contrast the French trade school, with its combination of theoretical and practical training, had demonstrably better results with its students:

> They are more methodical and intelligent in their work, steadier in general conduct, have a far better grasp of the whole subject, and are pronounced to be more competent than the average workman at executing repairs, since they have learned the principles and have not been kept doing the same thing...all through the years of their apprenticeship.[63]

The Reports made various recommendations for the improvement of science teaching in elementary and secondary schools and the better training of science teachers. Most significant was probably the recommendation of both the Devonshire and Samuelson Commissions that means should be found to integrate the work of the Department of Science and Art and the Education Department. Samuelson found much to criticize in the confusion and overlapping between the two departments and suggested that scientific and technical education was best advanced in the context of a broad and integrated secondary provision. Unable to go beyond the technical brief the report recommended the creation of a central authority for all matters relating to scientific and technical education.

Despite widespread acceptance of the findings of the Commissions, their more wide-ranging proposals were not adopted immediately. During the next ten years technical education expanded within its existing structures. The Department of Science and Art, which had become linked to the Education Department in 1856 but still remained essentially separate, expanded its support and supervision of Science and Art schools and classes. However, these remained unintegrated with elementary and secondary education and the dual administration of these sectors became increasingly fractious, wasteful and inefficient.[64] With the instigation in 1880 of the independent City and Guilds London Institute for the Advancement of Technical Education and with the creation of the new polytechnics in the 1880s, this *ad hoc* proliferation of technical provision was becoming increasingly muddled and chaotic.

The last decade of the century did finally bring some important advances in technical education. The 1889 Technical Instruction Act allowed the new local councils to set up technical instruction committees which could be financed by a one penny rate. As often happened with such permissive legislation the take-up of this was very uneven at local level with only twelve amongst 108 councils using this provision by 1894.[65] However, the 1890 Local Taxation (Whiskey Money) Act also provided public funds which could be spent on technical education and this was more widely used. Together the measures contributed to considerable growth in technical education and encouraged many towns to build their first technical colleges.

This was the golden age of the English technical education movement. The changes it brought were made possible through reform in the structures of the state. There were two aspects to this. First, there was the reform of local government. Prior to 1888 England, unlike France and Germany, had no local state apparatus as such and this had been an enormous handicap in setting up a nation-wide education system. After the 1888 Local Government Act, this situation was rectified creating the basis for systematic development through local state initiative. Second, there was a general change in attitude towards the role of the state which occurred during the last quarter of the century.

The nature of this change has been much debated. Some contemporaries such as Dicey regarded the Liberal reforms of the late nineteenth century as a manifestation of the wholesale abandonment of *laissez-faire* for a new anti-individualist collectivism.[66] Later historians, such as Polanyi, have tended to see these changes merely as pragmatic responses by the state to the recognition of overwhelming social needs which could not be met by the market.[67] The truth is probably somewhere in between. There were strong immediate problems, both economic and social, whose solution seemed to require new responses. The economic challenge of Germany and the USA after 1870, along with the depression of that period, suggested the need for more vigorous state action to maintain Britain's economic supremacy, not least in the field of education. Likewise, the social problems, brought graphically to light by the investigations of Booth, Mearns and Rowntree, imposed themselves on the social conscience of the middle class which, given the political implications of the extended franchise and the rise of mass democracy, increasingly felt the need for decisive action. All these factors suggested the necessity for more government intervention.

At the same time new ideologies were emerging in the closing decades of the century which embodied new conceptions of the role of the state. Chamberlain's radical followers broke with orthodox liberalism to develop a new philosophy of 'social Imperialism'. This yoked together ideas of imperial strength abroad with national efficiency and social reform at home in a new reactionary collectivism under the sign of the strong state. The new Fabian Society, created in 1884, combined the Benthamite tradition of expert administration with notions of national efficiency in a top-down programme of gradualist social reform and municipal socialism. In the same year the Social Democratic Federation was formed which marked the rise of a more revolutionary socialist tradition. These political movements all, in different ways, echoed the emergence of new and more interventionist conceptions of the role of the state in academic disciplines from philosophy (T. H. Greene) to economies (Jevons and Marshall). Together they marked the beginning of what Harold Perkin has termed the 'rise of professional society'.[68]

The beginning of concerted government action, now made possible in a climate less hostile to state intervention, drove the reforms in technical education in this period, and their relative success only highlighted the limitations of the former voluntarist creed. However, despite this late outbreak of good sense, the long record of neglect left an enduring legacy. Technical education had been cast in a mould that subsequent legislation would find hard to break. Growing up as an extension of the apprenticeship system and reliant on employer initiatives, it developed in a fragmented and improvised manner: perennially low in status, conservatively rooted in workshop practice, and hostile to theoretical knowledge, publicly funded technical education became normatively part time and institutionally marooned between the workplace and mainstream education. A century later we have still not overcome the deep divisions between theory and practice and between academic and vocational learning which were first entrenched in these nineteenth-century institutional structures. Nor, it would seem, have we quite outgrown the voluntarist reflex which gave rise to them.

## Notes

1 M. Porter, *The Competitive Advantage of Nations* (New York, 1990).
2 A. Green and H. Steedman, *Educational Provision, Educational Attainment and the Needs of Industry: A Review of Research for Germany, France, Japan, the USA and Britain*, Report Series Number 5, National Institute of Economic and Social Research (London, 1993).
3 For a summary of these debates, see National Commission on Education, *Learning to Succeed* (London, 1993).
4 C. Ball, *Learning Pays*, Royal Society of Arts (London, 1991); D. Finegold, E. Keep, D. Miliband, D. Raffe, K. Spook and M. Young, *A British Baccalauréat* (Institute for Public Policy Research, London).
5 A. Gamble, *Britain in Decline* (London, 1981).
6 For economic historians, see for example, E. J. Hobsbawm, *Industry and Empire* (Harmondsworth, 1968) and D. Landes, *The Unbound Prometheus* (London, 1969). For education historians, see for example, E. Ashby, 'Technology and the academies. An essay on universities and the scientific revolution', in A. H. Halsey *et al.*, *Education, Economy and Society* (London, 1961); S. Cotgrove, *Technical Education and Social Change* (1958); A. Green, *Education and State Formation* (London, 1990); G. Roderick and M. Stephens, *Education and Industry in the Nineteenth Century* (London, 1978); H. Silver and J. Brennan, *A Liberal Vocationalism* (London, 1988); and M. Sanderson, *The Missing Stratum: Technical School Education in England, 1900–1990s* (London, 1994). A rare recent dissenter from this view is W. D. Rubinstein in *Capitalism, Culture and Decline in Britain, 1750–1990* (London, 1993).
7 T. Huxley 'Technical education', in C. Bibby, ed., *T. H. Huxley on Education* (Cambridge, 1971).
8 G. Roderick and M. Stephens, op. cit.
9 E. Ashby, op. cit.
10 G. Roderick and M. Stephens, op. cit.
11 F. Ringer, *Education and Society in Modern Europe* (Bloomington, 1979); R. D. Anderson, *Education in France, 1848–1870* (Oxford, 1985).
12 G. Roderick and M. Stephens, op. cit.; J. H. Weiss, *The Making of Technological Man: The Social Origins of French Engineering Education* (Cambridge, MA, 1982).
13 G. Roderick and M. Stephens, op. cit., 107.
14 S. P. Thompson, *Apprentice Schools in France, 1879*; M. Sadler, *Selections from Sadler: Studies in World Citizenship*, compiled by J. Higginson (Liverpool, 1979).
15 T. Huxley, 'Technical education', in C. Bibby, ed., *T. H. Huxley on Education* (Cambridge, 1971); L. Playfair, *Industrial Education on the Continent*, lecture at the Government School of Mines, Science and Applied Arts (London, 1852).
16 J. Scott Russell, *Systematic Technical Education for the English People* (London, 1869); S. P. Thompson, op. cit.
17 S. P. Thompson, op. cit., 4.
18 Quoted in Roderick and Stephens, op. cit., 205.
19 Quoted in C. Barnett, 'Technology, education and industrial and economic strength', in A. Finch and P. Scrimshaw, eds, *Standards, Schooling and Education* (London, 1980), 67.
20 Royal Commission on Technical Instruction, *Second Report* (1984), 508.
21 G. C. Allen, *The British Disease* (Hobart Paper, London, 1967); P. Anderson, 'The origins of the present crisis', *New Left Review*, 23 (1964); idem., 'Figures of descent', *New Left Review*, 161 (1987); C. Barnett, *The Audit of War: The Illusion and Reality*

of Britain as a Great Nation (London, 1986); A. Sampson, *The Changing Anatomy of Britain* (London, 1983); M. Sanderson, op. cit.; M. J. Wiener, *English Culture and the Decline of the Industrial Spirit, 1850–1980* (Harmondsworth, 1981).

22   A. Green, *Education and State Formation* (1990); H. Perkins, *Origins of Modern English Society* (1985).

23   Marx's Review of Guizot, in J. Fernbach, ed., *Surveys from Exile* (London, 1993).

24   W. D. Rubinstein, in *Capitalism, Culture and Decline in Britain, 1750–1990* (London, 1993).

25   A. Mayer, *The Persistence of the Old Regime* (New York, 1981).

26   H. Silver and J. Brennan, op. cit.

27   J. Albisetti, *Secondary School Reform in Imperial Germany* (Princeton, 1983); R. D. Anderson, *Education in France, 1848–1870* (Oxford, 1985).

28   A. Green, Education and State Formation.

29   J. Scott Russell, op. cit., 80.

30   B. Simon, *The Two Nations and the Educational Structure, 1780–1870* (London, 1969).

31   The classic statement of this case can be found in the polemical open letters written by Edward Baines Junior, the leading Dissenter and editor of the Leeds Mercury, to Lord John Russell: Letters to the Right Honourable John Russell, *On State Education* (London, 1946).

32   S. Smiles, *Self Help* (London, 1859); H. Spencer, *State Education Self Defeating* (London, 1851).

33   J. S. Mill, Chapter 7, in J. Stillinger, ed., *Autobiography* (London, 1971).

34   M. Arnold, *Higher Schools and Universities in Germany* (1892), quoted in Roderick and Stephens, op. cit., 6.

35   M. Sadler, op. cit., 93.

36   Quoted in Roderick and Stevenson, op. cit., 30.

37   J. Scott Russell, op. cit., 3.

38   A. de Tocqueville, *The Old Regime and the French Revolution*, trans. Stuart Gilbert (New York, 1955).

39   F. D. Artz, *The Development of Technical Education in France, 1500–1850* (Cambridge, MA, 1966).

40   R. D. Anderson, *Education in France, 1848–1870* (Oxford, 1985).

41   Ibid.

42   C. R. Day, *Education and the Industrial World: The École d'Arts et Métiers and the Rise of French Industrial Engineering* (Cambridge, MA, 1987).

43   J. H. Weiss, op. cit.

44   F. D. Artz, op. cit.

45   R. Grew and P. Harrigan, *Schools, State, and Society: The Growth of Elementary Schooling in Nineteenth-Century* (Ann Arbor, 1991).

46   F. D. Arts, op. cit.

47   C. Day, op. cit.

48   C. Day, op. cit.

49   C. Day, 43.

50   Ibid.

51   Quoted in G. Rodericks and M. Stephens, op. cit., 132.

52   A. S. Bishop, *The Rise of a Central Authority in English Education* (Cambridge, 1971).

53   E. J. Hobsbawm, *Industry and Empire*, 173.

54   L. Playfair, *Industrial Education on the Continent*, op. cit.

55   A. S. Bishop, op. cit., 161.

56   Ibid., 159.

57   Ibid., 167.

58   Quoted in G. Roderick and M. Stephens, op. cit., 21.

59   Quoted in A. S. Bishop, op. cit., 174.

60   Royal Commission on Technical Instruction, *Sixth Report* (1984), 1.

61   Royal Commission on Technical Instruction, *Second Report*, vol. 1, part 1, 23.

62   Select Committee, *On the Provision for Giving Instruction in Theoretical and Applied Science to the Industrial Class (1867–8)*, 130.

63   S. Thompson, op cit., 8, 44.

64  A. S. Bishop, op. cit.
65  G. Roderick and M. Stephens, op. cit.
66  A. V. Dicey, *Lectures on Law and Opinion* (London, 1905).
67  K. Polyani, *The Great Transformation* (London, 1957).
68  H. Perkin, *The Rise of Professional Society: England since 1880* (London, 1989).

## CHAPTER 7

# TO 'BLAISE THE TRAIL FOR WOMEN TO FOLLOW ALONG'

Sex, gender and the politics of education on the London School Board (1870–1904)

Jane Martin

*Gender and Education*, 12, 2, 165–81, 2000

## Introduction

In October 1876, Florence Fenwick Miller (1854–1935) received a letter from the Reverend Stewart Headlam on behalf of the Bethnal Green Commonwealth Club, inviting her to become a candidate for the Hackney division of the London School Board. Educated, socially aware and a member of the first women's movement in Britain, Florence accepted the offer because she was interested in the education of the working classes and wished to speak on behalf of elementary school girls and women teachers. She was also motivated by what she described as the 'scandalous shortage' of women with the drive and ambition to pursue interesting careers in the public arena. Florence had strong connections with pioneer doctors Elizabeth Garrett Anderson and Sophia Jex-Blake, was well known to the leaders of the major suffrage societies and had reached the point of enjoying an established reputation among the intellectual elite of the London Dialectical Society. At 22 years, she became the youngest woman ever elected to the largest and most powerful organ of local government then in existence.

Opportunities for women in local government increased greatly in the last third of the nineteenth century. Although civic policies and administration were complicated by a tangle of authorities and agencies, the Municipal Franchise Act of 1869 was the first of a number of measures that were to affect women's democratic participation. This piece of legislation restored the local vote to women ratepayers (a right they had lost under the 1835 Municipal Corporations Act). The following year the passing of the Elementary Education Act made women eligible for nomination and election to the thousands of locally elected school boards set up in and after 1870. The extension of Victorian state activity engendered new forms of public service and women were active in their localities as elected and appointed officials responsible for the administration of most education and welfare services. Thane has noted the unique quality of the British situation by highlighting the fact that no other major state in Europe or America offered women 'a comparable institutional role at such an early date' (1993: 351). Nonetheless, female involvement in the development of the state system of elementary education has been neglected in the traditional historiography of mass schooling. Besides debates about female invisibility, this is because the activities of the central state apparatus have been accentuated and 'these histories have been written from the records of the official central state run by male bureaucrats and politicians' (Koven, 1993: 94–95). Consequently, there has been little work on the often lengthy public careers of local activists. However, recent work by Hollis (1989), Hughes (1992), Martin (1991, 1995, 1999) and Turnbull (1983) aim to understand and rediscover the position of women in the process of local educational policy-making. Therefore, women's participation in the politics of schooling is beginning to be released from historical obscurity.

This chapter considers the issue of female involvement by focusing on the work of the 29 women elected to serve on the London School Board.[1] It is based largely on a quite new source of manuscript material (the unpublished autobiographical fragment written by Florence Fenwick Miller) among papers in the Contemporary Medical Archives Centre at the Wellcome Institute for the History of Medicine.[2] The object is to place Florence as a central character in the analysis. The availability of her memoir has thrown up issues pertinent to current debates about the history of English feminism and produced new interpretations of the friendship networks that made up the metropolitan women's movement. However, there is no attempt to categorise these women as feminists. As elected women, they all publicised the work of women in local government but this did not mean they were all motivated by interest in sex equality issues. The term 'feminism' was not widely used until the First World War (Caine, 1997: 8), and it will become clear that sexual politics needs to be considered alongside party politics. Different class interests were also important and this chapter seeks to emphasise the diversities amongst activist women considered in relation to thought and actions. These themes will be located within a discussion of the role of women as educational policy-makers.

The chapter is divided into three parts. The first part looks at the issue of women's representation. In so doing it will focus on the selection process, as well as the background and the political beginnings of these female politicians. The main focus is the recollections of Florence Fenwick Miller and a biographical method is used to make visible the links between private life and public practice. Part two considers the political culture of the institution itself. The London School Board was the world's largest educational authority and the presence of women immediately complicated and partly contradicted the general connection of authority with masculinity. Hence, the third part uses a historical methodology to explore women's careers as educational policy-makers. Overall, the chapter throws up the following questions. Did the involvement of women change the political culture; and what impact did they have on the education policy agenda?

## Political candidature

Up to a point, the school boards were democratic institutions. They were the first elected bodies to admit women on the same terms as men, but most people lacked the necessary resources and motivation to contest the elections. However, political conviction combined with the tradition of female philanthropy and, especially in the towns, school board politics provided an important field of endeavour for the women's movement (Turnbull, 1983; Hollis, 1989; Martin, 1993, 1999). This was because the new franchise allowed women with the necessary property qualifications to vote, while multiple voting and the possibility of giving all your votes to one candidate favoured the representation of electoral minorities. Created under the terms of the 1870 Education Act, factors of size and formation placed the London School Board in a unique position. Whereas other school boards were restricted to between 5 and 13 members, the first London Board had 49 members, rising to 55 by the mid-1880s. In addition, the metropolis was divided into 10 vast wards (except the inner square mile of the City itself), each of which returned a number of candidates. As might be expected, the School Board for London was a flagship institution and played a vital role in setting the educational standards for other school boards to follow. London was the centre and symbol of imperial and national power and the letters MSBL (Member of the School Board for London), served to convey a certain sense of prestige and social status among one's peers.

The conditions for public life will be investigated in terms of political background, socio-economic status, education, marital status and family commitments. Florence Fenwick Miller has supplied a vivid record, which, while it may not be wholly representative, is illuminating. Florence was the eldest child of John Miller, a captain in the British merchant marine, and Eleanor Fenwick, the daughter of a civil engineer. She grew up in London in the 1850s and 1860s, in comfortable middle-class surroundings (the family had an income of between £600 and £700 per annum). First educated at a dame school, her mother then gave her lessons at home before she entered a Young Ladies' Seminary at the age of 6; a year later, she was sent away to complete her education at boarding school. In her late teens Florence was attracted to medical training and it is noteworthy that her father supported her decision, whereas her more socially conservative mother was left feeling 'she had three sons and no daughter' (Fenwick Miller, ch. 4, unpaginated). One of the first seven women students at Edinburgh University in 1871, she enrolled at the Ladies' Medical College, London, in the autumn, finished with honours and gained a portion of clinical instruction at the British Lying-In Hospital. In the 1870s, she ran a practice for women and children from her parents' home in Victoria Park. In 1879 she married Frederick Ford (honorary secretary of the London Dialectical Society). He was not very successful in business and Florence had to rely on daily or weekly journalism to support herself economically. By the 1880s she was writing steadily for a variety of publications including the *Modern Review, Lady's Pictorial, Fraser's* and *The Governess*; as well as being the author of several teaching texts. Marriage was quickly followed by motherhood (the couple had two daughters, Irene, born 15 April 1880, and Helen, born 1 July 1881), yet Fenwick Miller managed also to occupy significant public positions. Possibly her ego helped. We learn that her 'success as a public speaker was from the first quite exceptional' and that despite maternal opposition she found the electoral contest 'most exhilarating' (Fenwick Miller, GC/228/15; GC/228/27). She also gained advantage from her participation in the suffrage campaigns and membership of a social-cum-intellectual circle who carried on public debate from a position of centrality in the capital city. Was this kind of experience a familiar pattern for women's public activity in the past?

For the most part the 29 women considered here were well connected and better educated than others of their sex and class. A certain sort of familial background was an advantage when embarking on a public career and they formed part of a social and intellectual stratum of London society whose families were largely drawn from the traditional genteel professions, as well as wealthy businessmen

(Martin, 1993). The one exception was the service of Mary Bridges Adams (nee Daltry), the daughter of an engine fitter, who represented Greenwich from 1897 to 1904. The pupil–teacher system enabled Mary to establish herself as an independent person and in the 1870s she held posts as a teacher and headteacher in Newcastle and Birmingham. The first women members, Emily Davies and Elizabeth Garrett, were associated with the first women's network in Britain, established in the late 1850s and named the Langham Place group after its cultural centre in London. This forum served as a conduit for political patronage and in the division of Marylebone, Elizabeth Garrett was succeeded by her younger sister, Alice Cowell who served alongside the educationalist Jane Chessar. All but written out of history, Jane Chessar had close connections with the Langham Place social network but was forced to retire from public life on the grounds of ill health. Alice Westlake was selected in her place. She also belonged to the Langham Place group, canvassed for Elizabeth Garrett in 1870 and went on to hold elected office until 1888 when her place was filled by Emma Maitland. Emma was unsuccessful at the polls in 1891 and this marked the end of Marylebone's record of continuous female representation. However, the biggest breakthrough in terms of female representation came in 1879 when 9 of the 50 successful candidates were female.[3] It is instructive to look more closely at the selection process in 1879, which suggests that there were clear divisions among activists over the question of tactics.

Florence Fenwick Miller left a detailed account of a campaign meeting attended by herself, Elizabeth Garrett Anderson, Elizabeth Surr, Helen Taylor and Alice Westlake (among others). What is especially interesting is that Florence describes a clash over tactics and among personalities, a story that runs counter to earlier representations of past and present women members acting as support networks (Turnbull, 1983; Hollis, 1993; Martin, 1993). In any event, Alice Westlake and Elizabeth Garrett Anderson both counselled against women standing, explaining how difficult and costly an election was. It is possible that they acted out of concern at the more strident political behaviour of the other elected women and certainly there were manoeuvrings over the selection of a female candidate for Hackney, where Florence was the serving woman member. In an attempt to split her vote, Sir Charles Reed (Board chair and divisional colleague) proposed that the local Liberal Party adopt Jane Chessar as their official candidate and when nothing came of it, Alice Westlake asked the middle-aged and highly conventional Rosamond Davenport Hill if she would contest Hackney. A clear example of recruitment by patronage, the criteria of political recruitment were hardly auspicious for anyone who did not play by the rules. As Norris and Lovenduski make clear, in political recruitment the key question is 'whether the applicant is "one of us": party loyalty and personal character are seen as more important than policy expertise or formal qualifications' (Norris and Lovenduski, 1995: 238).

In addition to the women's network, party organisations steadily increased their grip on school board elections. In London they were contested by two loosely organised groupings of individuals running as the Progressive and Moderate parties. The Progressives included all shades of liberal opinion, later fortified by the socialist groups. The Moderates were allied with the Anglican clergy and the Conservative Party. Only four Moderate women served on the London School Board – Eugenie Dibdin, Frances Hastings, Susan Lawrence and Mrs Wright. The rest were Progressives. Then, as now, it seems likely that the political bias reflected powerful social conventions. For instance, evidence drawn from the British Candidate Study in the 1992 election established that few Tory women came forward as applicants for political recruitment, despite the predominance of older women as party activists (Norris and Lovenduski, 1995: 248). The women who served in the 1880s and 1890s had strong party political connections. This pattern clearly fits in with the recruitment of Mary Bridges Adams, who was first selected as a candidate in 1894. In demand locally as a public speaker, she was sponsored by the Royal Arsenal Cooperative Society (RACS), 60 trade organisations and the London Nonconformist Council; 3 years later she was returned as member for Greenwich by a Progressive Election Committee that included the RACS, the Woolwich Trades Council and the local Radical Clubs (*School Board Chronicle*, 17 November 1894; 29 November 1897). Her election was a triumph for the organised labour movement and an extraordinary woman. But what was the specific organisational setting to which she had gained access? The next section looks at the institutional practices and cultures of the London School Board in order to consider the gendered division of labour and the efficacy of female interventions.

## The political culture of the London School Board

Feminist critics of contemporary British politics argue that the distribution of political power reflects a certain bias in the way society is organised that makes it easier for some individuals and groups than others to see their objectives come to fruition (Lovenduski and Norris, 1996). In this context, it is useful to draw on the concept of gender balance that is being developed for the Gender and New Urban Governance Project (Lovenduski, 1996). To simplify, this typology draws out the sex and/or gender biases of contemporary politics by distinguishing between positional, policy and organisational balances. First, positional balance 'refers to the numbers of men and women in organisations as a whole and, within those organisations, to their presence in decision-making positions' (Lovenduski, 1996: 5). Second, policy gender balance points up the extent to which public policies impact on women and men in somewhat different ways, as well as the question of who plays the majority role in the policy-making process. Finally, organisational bias alerts us to the biases integral to the rules, values, norms, structures and policies of a specific organisation.

Taking each in turn, male bias was evident in quantitative terms. This is so even though the lowest level of female representation, just over 4% in 1870 and 1873, contrasts favourably with the absence at that time of women from the House of Commons. Nonetheless, women were contained at the lowest levels of power and responsibility. The three most powerful posts were chair and vice-chair of the Board and chair of the School Management Committee, which were always held by men. Helen Taylor was the only woman to become chair of a permanent standing committee. Elected for the first time in 1876, she created a stir by adopting a more open and generalised popular appeal to the working-class electorate, which centred on questions of active participation and control. Opinions towards her were mixed. Emily Davies found her tactless and overbearing. Male opponents nicknamed her the acid maiden. Yet in June 1883, members set a precedent by promoting Helen to a position of authority as chair of the Educational Endowments Committee – even though recruitment by patronage is based on criteria of acceptability and she did not play by the male rules. It may be that the great majority of the men were afraid of the rivalry of women and that this was a way of containing her within a context they could deal with. Helen resented a rigid allegiance to party and for 6 years was part of a women's caucus consisting of herself, Florence Fenwick Miller and Elizabeth Surr. Eager to promote a non-party approach,

*Table 7.1* Party allegiance among school board women (sample = 27)

| Member | Service on Board | Attitude to party |
|---|---|---|
| A. Besant | 1888–1891 | Loyalist |
| M. Bridges Adams' | 1897–1904 | Independent |
| J. Chessar | 1873–1876 | Independent |
| A. Cowell | 1873–1876 | Independent |
| E. Davies | 1870–1873 | Independent |
| R. Davenport–Hill | 1879–1897 | Loyalist |
| E. Dibdin | 1897–1900 | Loyalist |
| M. Dilke | 1888–1891 | Loyalist |
| C. Elder | 1897–1900 | Loyalist |
| M. Eve | 1891–1904 | Loyalist |
| E. Garrett | 1870–1873 | Independent |
| F. Hastings | 1882–1885 | Independent |
| R. Homan | 1891–1904 | Loyalist |
| M. Lawrence | 1900–1904 | Loyalist |
| S. Lawrence | 1900–1904 | Loyalist |
| E. Maitland | 1888–1891, 1894–1902 | Loyalist |
| E. McKee | 1897–1904 | Loyalist |
| H. Miall–Smith | 1900–1904 | Loyalist |
| F. Fenwick Miller | 1876–1885 | Independent |
| V.H. Morten | 1897–1902 | Independent |
| H. Muller | 1879–1885 | Independent |
| M. Richardson | 1879–1885 | Loyalist |
| E. Simcox | 1879–1882 | Loyalist |
| E. Surr | 1876–1882 | Independent |
| H. Taylor | 1876–1885 | Independent |
| A. Webster | 1876–1888 | Loyalist |
| A. Westlake | 1879–1882, 1885–1888 | Independent |

Florence thought the relationship between the Board Chair:

> and the Chairmen of Committees in some sort resembled the Premier and his Cabinet, and looked to Members who wished to be 'in the swim' to vote very much to order as is done in the House of Commons.
>
> ('An Uncommon Girlhood', GC/228/28)

On the 1876 Board, these three women politicians sought to challenge institutional norms and certainly behaved differently to Alice Westlake *and* their male counterparts. But was gender the major fault line in school board politics? To examine gender differences in political behaviour, the 27 women who served for one full term or more are considered in terms of their attitude to party (Table 7.1).

I would argue that 12 women members attempted to adopt an independent approach to politics, albeit with different goals. Thus, Jane Chessar, Alice Cowell, Emily Davies and Elizabeth Garrett are labelled Independent, as the party machines were not in control on the 1870 and 1873 Boards. By the late 1870s, Henrietta Muller and Augusta Webster stood on Independent platforms, while Florence Fenwick Miller, Elizabeth Surr and Helen Taylor did not want to play by the rules:

> Anything was justifiable, so long as it was safe, that would tend to the success of a man's Party...We three women Members, Elizabeth Surr, Helen Taylor

and myself were a thorn in the side of the Party management of affairs. We were genuinely independent on which ground we had all been elected. We would deliberate and consider every question on its merits...and if we saw anything that ought to be blamed...exposed it regardless of the question of personality and Party ties.

('An Uncommon Girlhood', GC/228/34)

Mary Bridges Adams and Honnor Morten were elected for their radical views, which set them apart from the Progressives, and Frances Hastings did not always adhere to the Moderate party line. By contrast, the four longest serving female representatives, Rosamond Davenport Hill (18 years), Margaret Eve (13 years), Ruth Homan (13 years) and Alice Westlake (12 years) were Progressive party loyalists. These successful women gave high priority to their role as party representatives and won promotion to middle-ranking appointments. At 50, Ruth Homan became vice-chair of the Industrial Schools Committee and Margaret Eve was appointed vice-chair of the Evening Continuation Schools Committee in 1900 (*School Board Chronicle*, 22 October 1900; 16 February 1901). In terms of the gender balance, there was a distinct male positional bias on the London School Board. This certainly had an impact on the political culture of the institution and it is this aspect that will be considered next; policy gender balance will be examined later in the section exploring women's careers as educational policy-makers.

From the start, three parties were involved in the management of London's board schools – the Board itself (working through a School Management Committee), individual members and local school managers. The Board held open meetings every Wednesday, beginning at 3 p.m. and usually continuing until 6.30 p.m., although it was often much later. Their main purpose was to hear the recommendations set out in reports from the various committees that conducted the work of the Board; these were accepted, amended or referred back. Members had a right to propose alternate motions of policy, and debate them, before an open vote was taken, with each individual answering 'yes' or 'no' at the division. Overall, new members found an elaborately ritualised and formalised politics that followed 'the precedent of the customs of the House of Commons' (Florence Fenwick Miller, 'An Uncommon Girlhood', GC/228/28). The accent on parliamentary tradition meant that the male organisational bias was very apparent, and female members undoubtedly felt uncomfortable and out of place at times. For instance, Florence Fenwick Miller testified to a rather bizarre difficulty she encountered on her second attendance at the Board. She recalled that the boardroom porter approached her and said, 'The lady members of the Board always wear bonnets, Ma'am' (Florence Fenwick Miller, 'An Uncommon Girlhood', GC/228/28). Florence disliked wearing a hat and had left her bonnet in the ladies' dressing room:

He said no more; but when I came to reflect, I felt certain he would not have spoken on his own initiative; Sir Charles Reed must have ordered him to say what he did. This droll insistence on women's heads being covered no doubt owes its origin to St Paul's observation on the point. As that Eastern person had made a woman's wearing a covering on her head a symbol of her inferiority to her brother man.

('An Uncommon Girlhood', GC/228/28)

At other times, a culture of male fraternity was reinforced by the exclusion of women members from the annual Lord Mayor's Banquet. Previously, Jane

Chessar, Alice Cowell, Emily Davies, Elizabeth Garrett and Alice Westlake had acquiesced with male wishes by declining their invitation to attend what they were told would be an exclusively male event. On this occasion Florence Fenwick Miller, Elizabeth Surr and Helen Taylor accepted. According to Florence:

> It was then represented to us that our demand for equal rights could be met by our being invited on the distinct understanding that we would all three have a previous engagement that we regretted would prevent us from having the pleasure of accepting. But still we were stubborn and attended.
>
> ('An Uncommon Girlhood', GC/228/34)

Although the presence of women members immediately complicated struggles over power and advantage in public life, male and female territories and responsibilities reflected traditional notions of the sexual division of labour. Women dominated the membership of the Cookery, Laundry and Needlework Sub-Committee and this was the only subcommittee never to have a male chair. By contrast, female members rarely served on the Finance Committee or the Works Committee responsible for the purchase of school sites and school furniture, the erection and enlargement of school buildings and the general care of Board properties. Emma Maitland asserted that she wanted to bring a female perspective to all areas of the Board's work, but the great majority were more likely to subscribe to conventional ideas about women's skills and interests. Once again, the service of Mary Bridges Adams is a notable exception. In 1897 she joined the traditional male territory of the Works Committee. Three years later she brought her professional expertise to the service of the Teaching Staff Sub-Committee.

Irrespective of the social and political pressures on women members, they also had to adapt to the demands of public office. Many members regarded the School Board as the main business of their lives and an indication of the workload can be gauged by reference to the weekly timetables of Florence Fenwick Miller in the 1870s and Emma Maitland in the 1890s. Thus, Florence spent 2 or 3 days a week at the Board offices on the Embankment, while Emma found that Mondays, Thursdays and Fridays were taken up with central Board work, as were alternate Wednesdays. Financial worries pressed hard on Florence. She frequently went without food on Board days and thought it a 'wild extravagance' to lunch out, on top of the 2s spent on fares and 9d on a cup of tea at the Board's tearoom. She spent hours on committee work, especially the powerful School Management Committee:

> I remember once a long discussion over the request of a headmistress to be allowed a larger quantity of soap, because her school was in such a poor neighbourhood and the children came so dirty. At last I exclaimed: 'It would pay me better to supply this soap myself for the winter than to spend any more time over it', to which the Chairman answered wearily: 'But we all feel like that, you know!'
>
> ('An Uncommon Girlhood', GC/228/34)

Both women devoted the rest of the week to constituency work, which included the supervision of local schools, to which they nominated teachers, ancillary staff and resources. As Emma explained to Frederick Dolman during an interview for the *Young Woman* in 1896, she also played a part in developing schools for children with disabilities, taking advantage of a continental visit to investigate German and Austrian methods for teaching deaf and dumb children (*The Young Woman*, January 1896).

The next section explores the implications of the female presence. Of course, it was clearly an advance for women to be elected to positions of this kind of political responsibility, but did they bring important perspectives and priorities to educational policy-making? The focus here concerns the impact of women's contribution to the politics of education. In particular, what were their policy priorities and what did they set out to achieve?

## Women's careers as educational policy-makers

The evidence presented here shows a male gender bias along the different dimensions of positional balance and organisational balance. But does this mean women had little impact on the policy-making process? This chapter considers what Hunt (1991: 11) defines as the 'middle level of decision making which intervenes between government policy and actual school practice', taking the chance to focus upon the way female representatives sought to influence the decision-making process. Women's claims to political power were based on the distinctive character of the female contribution. In particular, they were contingent upon a gendered and classed construction of 'special needs'. Girls were regarded as having different requirements to boys (either physical, emotional or intellectual) and women candidates found it advantageous to campaign as being ready to champion the interests of girls and women teachers. Moreover, just as researchers today are finding evidence of a 'widespread popular conception that women politicians are more compassionate' than men, this was true in the period between 1870 and 1904 (Norris, 1996: 93). Then and now, these assumptions were based on deep-rooted social stereotypes, but gender was not the only factor shaping political attitudes and in fact, 12 of the 27 women who served for a minimum of one term were loyal to parties dominated by men. Here the varied influence and policy priorities of women members will be considered in relation to some of the 'women's questions' mentioned earlier. The elementary schoolgirls' curriculum and the interests of women teachers make it possible to assess whether they made a distinctive stand on the interests of girls and women. The final example of school attendance will be used to assess the policy gender bias in the politics of schooling.

## The schoolgirls' curriculum

Ostensibly co-educational, in London the new board schools frequently had different entrances for the sexes, as well as separate playgrounds and separate departments for older children (Turnbull, 1987). Concern about value for money led central government to impose payment by results in 1862, and although each pupil earned the school the same amount for successful examination performance (Weiner, 1994: 35), failing to teach girls needlework became one of the few offences for which an elementary school could lose its government grant (Davin, 1996). In 1878, theoretical domestic economy was made a compulsory specific (optional) subject for girls; 4 years later the Government gave grants for the teaching of cookery. By the 1890s, this sex-differentiated curriculum had expanded to include laundry work and housewifery. Despite the addition of handicraft (workshop instruction, woodwork or manual work), Turnbull (1987: 86) concludes that working-class boys 'did not receive practical instruction equivalent to the girls' needlework, cookery, laundry work and so on'. Thus, it has been argued that the purpose of mass schooling was to impose an ideal family form of a male breadwinner and an economically dependent, full-time wife and mother:

> This was an ideal that came broadly to be shared by the bourgeoisie and men and women of the working classes alike, each for their own particular economic, political, cultural and social reasons. That it was unattainable for most outside the ranks of skilled and unionised labour was seen as unproblematic; it integrated the goals of the powerful men of the working classes with those of the dominant social and economic groups and served as an aspirational ideal to the unskilled, unorganised work-force.
>
> (Gomersall, 1994: 238)

So, the intentions in educating boys and girls were different. Excluded from national politics on the grounds of their sex, it is important to explicate women's involvement in school gender training.

Female reformers served as elected members of school boards and as co-opted members of the Technical Instruction Committees set up following the Technical Instruction Act of 1889, and some tried to win friends and influential allies under the auspices of the domestic subjects movement (see Turnbull, 1994; Bird, 1998). Women spoke with different voices and the question of school gender training clearly exposes the tensions in the period 1870–1904 (see Dyhouse, 1981; Hollis, 1987; Bird, 1991; Martin, 1995). A minority wanted girls and women to have access to the same educational provision as boys and men but the female curriculum was generally discussed as if biology was destiny. Yet, any discussion of the purpose of education was complicated by enduring social and educational distinctions. Thus, Clara Collet, Labour Correspondent to the Board of Trade, submitted a memorandum to the Bryce Commission, investigating secondary education in the 1890s, which endorsed the principle of class-based educational provision. She argued strongly in favour of divided aims and touched on the theme of education versus instruction. This meant an emphasis on the cultivation of mental culture for middle-class girls, whereas 'any system of education for working girls should have as its object their training for the responsibilities of married life' (*British Parliamentary Papers*, Secondary Education, 1895 session: 380). To what extent her attitude was representative of women on the London School Board will be considered later in this chapter.

An analysis of the voting record of women Board members in the 1870s and early 1880s shows that Rosamond Davenport Hill and Alice Westlake were ready to concede the place of domestic economy in the curriculum. By contrast, Jane Chessar, Alice Cowell, Emily Davies, Elizabeth Garrett, Frances Hastings, Florence Fenwick Miller, Henrietta Muller, Elizabeth Surr and Helen Taylor all tried to limit this kind of training. After 1882, changes in government policy and the influence of Social Darwinistic thinking put female opponents on the defensive and they had difficulty in making their presence felt. However, the 1879 Board provides an interesting example of an oppositional alliance that crossed class and gender groupings. It included the two working men elected in the 1870s, the ex-Chartist and cabinet-maker Benjamin Lucraft and the trade unionist George Potter; as well as Florence Fenwick Miller, Henrietta Muller, Elizabeth Surr and Helen Taylor. These six stand out as the most persistent opponents of single-sex classes in cookery, arguing that the teaching was inappropriate to the realities of working-class life since the cooking was done on gas cookers that were quite beyond the reach of working-class housewives. George observed, 'the girls must be intended for service. Such knowledge would not be of much use to them in an artisan's home' (*School Board Chronicle*, 30 March 1878).

Cookery was a grant-aided subject when the Moderate, Frances Hastings, was first elected in 1882; 3 years later, she seconded Helen's unsuccessful motion to reduce the number of cookery classes (*School Board Chronicle*, 12 March 1885). She also attacked the time girls spent sewing. In her contribution to the debate on needlework, for instance, Frances argued that much of the practical instruction was unnecessary. She wanted the girls to receive 'a foundation of general knowledge' instead (*The Governess*, 17 November 1883: 138). Writing to Helen Taylor in March 1886, Elizabeth Surr expressed regret over her defeat at the polls:

> I am sorry Miss Hastings is off, and that she was not re-elected; but although she is upright and well-meaning she was decidedly harsh in her dealings with the poor so that they would not care to vote for her; and she is too honest to be supported by any of the parties.
>
> (E. Surr to H. Taylor, March 1886)

In terms of their impact on policy-making, the Independent women were always struggling against the odds but managed to score some victories. Thus, for example, Henrietta Muller 'sought and obtained a reduction in the number of stitches to the inch required in the schools' (*The Times*, 17 January 1906). Neither she nor Florence could see the necessity of this fine needlework and the teachers reported that it was damaging the girls' eyesight. By contrast, the more socially conservative party women supported and influenced these developments. In the late 1870s, Alice Westlake told female headteachers to reduce their workload by substituting cookery for classes in 'drawing and grammar' (*School Board Chronicle*, 3 March 1877). Her colleague Rosamond Davenport Hill also wanted to consolidate the teaching of practical subjects related directly to domestic work. By the early 1880s, Hill was promoted to the position of chair of the Cookery Sub-Committee and subsequently gave evidence to the Cross Commission investigating the effects and working of the Elementary Education Act (1870). When questioned as to whether any of the girls become cooks or domestic servants, she replied:

> We hope they do. I heard a little time ago that a girl had taken a place, and that her employer was quite delighted with her because she could cook the dinner while the family attended chapel on a Sunday morning.
>
> (*Royal Commission on Elementary Education [Cross] 1887*,
> evidence of Miss R. Davenport Hill: 712)

At the turn of the century, Ruth Homan used her position on the School Management Committee to debate the question of whether cookery should be taught to boys. Assisted by Emma Maitland, she mobilised support for a pilot scheme at the Bow Creek School in Poplar where she was manager. For a year the boys attended the cookery centre attached to the school and a copy of the Cookery Superintendent's report was sent to the Education Department, ironically referred to as the Board's 'upper house' by Florence Fenwick Miller. Significantly, the report notes the vocational aspects of the teaching, with its emphasis on naval fare and promises of employment at the seamen's home, and Ruth achieved a pyrrhic victory when the 1902 Elementary Education Code allowed for the instruction of boys in 'seaport towns' (*School Board Chronicle*, 3 March 1900; Bird, 1998: 127).

## Women teachers

This discussion will focus on three issues that were crucial to the career development of London's women teachers: pay, promotion and opposition to married women's employment. Once again, the Independent women pursued a distinct policy agenda; the rest supported the party line. Florence Fenwick Miller has left a narrative account of the decision-making process, showing a trend towards policy formation by the School Management Committee. This was true of promotions to headships:

> The Scheme was to appoint the headmaster of a boys' school Head Teacher also of the girls in the same block of buildings. It was necessary by the laws of the Board that every Head Teachers' name should be submitted, on his or her appointment, to the full Board for confirmation but in the case of the appointment of the men over the girls' schools I found that it was being made a practice to simply pass the Master's appointment through the School Management Committee and not to send it up to the full Board for confirmation at all.
>
> ('An Uncommon Girlhood', GC/228/34)

Florence saw this as discriminatory. It certainly confirms Copelman's (1996: 50) suspicion that those in positions of power and authority were more concerned to establish a career ladder for men than for women. In 1876, the average salary of the headmaster of a boys' school was £305 while the average salary of an assistant was only £104. Florence argued that if this situation was allowed to continue, the practice would effectively deny women teachers opportunities for advancement beyond the post of assistant. So, she successfully moved that: 'No male teacher should in future be appointed to be the Head Master of a girls' school, without the special sanction of the Board being previously obtained' ('An Uncommon Girlhood', GC/228/34).

In February 1878 there was an attempt to ban the employment of married women elementary school teachers with 'rapidly increasing families'. This time Elizabeth Surr led the successful opposition, saying she 'feared this suggestion emanated from gentlemen who wished to introduce the thin end of the wedge for the ultimate exclusion of all female teachers from Board schools' (*School Board Chronicle*, 9 February 1878). The following year, she and Florence were frustrated in their attempt to overturn a proposal that the Board receive 3 months' notice of maternity leave from married women teachers. Elizabeth thought it 'indelicate'; the vice-chair retorted she could have 'opposed the proposal in committee instead of doing so openly and publicly before the Board and the press' (*School Board Chronicle*, 15 November 1879). Gradually the regulations defining the position of married women teachers grew more stringent. By the 1880s, for example, those who took confinement leave had to arrange for their own replacement and pay them out of their own salary. Florence Fenwick Miller, Henrietta Muller, Elizabeth Surr and Helen Taylor opposed the changes; Rosamond Davenport Hill, Mary Richardson and Alice Westlake did not. Far from it. Alice Westlake led the attack on the employment of married women teachers when working in the School Management Committee and speaking in debate. In the winter of 1881, for instance, she seconded a committee resolution to bar married women teachers with children under 2 years of age (*School Board Chronicle*, 26 November 1881; *The Governess*, June 1882: 122). The *School Board Chronicle* offered a blow-by-blow account of debate within the School Board. Press reports show the adversarial nature of School Board politics, as well as the concentration on aspects of women's personal lives. In one debate, Florence launched a personal attack on the character of her childless colleague Alice Westlake:

> ...she had been waiting in expectation that the lady who was largely respon-sible for this resolution would justify it. The resolution had been brought for-ward three times at the instance of that lady. She (Mrs Miller) was thankful that this Board was not composed entirely of married ladies without chil-dren...The true womanly instinct and feeling and sympathy for children did not arise in a woman until she had had children of her own in her arms...it was not for the Board to say that every teacher who married should become a household drudge instead of continuing to engage in intellectual work.
>
> (*School Board Chronicle*, 26 November 1881)

The personal animosity is evident and exceptional because Florence was one of only two women Board members who married whilst serving (the other was Elizabeth Garrett); and the only woman who gave birth during her period in office. There were nine women on the 1879 Board and they each articulate differ-ent dimensions of women's experience. Unlike Florence, Rosamond Davenport Hill, Frances Hastings, Henrietta Muller, Mary Richardson, Edith Simcox and Helen Taylor were single, Alice Westlake was married but childless, whilst Elizabeth Surr was married with two grown-up daughters and two small sons. Evidently, there was no correlation between personal biography and attitude to the employment of married women. Attitude to party was a far more reliable guide. Even though they won the battle, Independents did not think they had won the war. Concern was expressed that the authority might yet attempt to dismiss married women and Florence and Helen helped launch the Metropolitan Board Mistresses' Association to support and protect women teachers (*The Governess*, June 1882: 122).

## School attendance

The final example is used to show the extent to which specific policies impact on girls and boys in somewhat different ways, as well as to examine the question of who plays the majority role in the policy-making process. The significance of the women's role has been analysed in earlier work (Martin, 1991, 1999); here new source material is used to highlight the issue of legislative styles.

Local authorities prioritised the issue because the size of government grants, and until 1883, teachers' salaries, depended directly on average attendance levels. However, many of the urban poor saw mass schooling as an intrusion into family life that reduced the household's earning capacity and imposed an extra burden in the shape of school fees. Then, as now, pupil absenteeism was a persis-tent problem. It also had a gender dimension. Girls' average attendance was consistently lower than the boys'; it was also more irregular because they often had to care for younger siblings. However, there was a tendency for girl absentees to be treated sympathetically, whereas boys were more likely to be defined as truants and dealt with severely. The ultimate sanction was committal to one of two types of corrective institutions. The first was a single-sex residential truant or industrial school. The second was a co-educational day industrial school provided for under the 1876 Education Act. Although the London School Board did not establish a day industrial school until 1895, it founded three residential schools in the 1870s, two more in the 1890s and a sixth in 1903. Five out of the six were for boys.

Further analysis shows that many women members prioritised this area of the Board's work. For example, on the 1876 Board, Helen Taylor promoted the establishment of babies' rooms as a way of encouraging the attendance of girls who were frequently kept home to 'mind baby'; in 1881 she and Elizabeth Surr persuaded the Board to press for government legislation to provide for the establishment of nursery schools and they were part of a deputation to the Education Department on the subject (*School Board Chronicle*, 14 April 1877; 24 February 1881). Henrietta Muller shared their anxiety over female attendance, and in August 1881 she unsuccessfully sought to encourage the girls by enabling them to qualify for a book prize on the strength of one, as opposed to two, complete attendance cards (*School Board Chronicle*, 4 August 1881). Social and cultural values were reflected in a tendency for the punitive aspects of Board policy to impact more heavily on boys. Thus, Home Office regulations refused to allow corporal punishment to be inflicted on industrial schoolgirls and Ruth Homan led the opposition to Athelstan Riley's campaign to change the rules in the mid-1890s. First elected in the Moderate election victory of 1891, he ardently supported the attempt to make religious instruction more denominational and Ruth Homan presumed the 'Rileyite floggers' wanted to 'thrash theology' into the girls. In a letter to the press she concluded, 'We know what the natural impulse of every manly, chivalrous Briton would be – and that is to birch the floggers' (Fawcett Library newscuttings, 'School Boards', London 1896–97). She also fought moves to reinstate the ritual of flogging boys as a punishment for being sent back to industrial school and in 1898 she joined forces with Honnor Morten in an attempt to ban the use of corporal punishment in the Board's reformatory institutions. There were eight women members of the 1897 Board, and aside from Emma Maitland, there was general agreement with Ruth that the punishments were too harsh. However, her proposal was successfully watered down by two male Progressives who thought the powers were necessary but recommended that the practice be carried out in private. Although Ruth Homan did not accomplish her objective, she did achieve recognition in the shape of promotion to vice-chair of the Industrial Schools Committee.

Twenty years earlier Elizabeth Surr gained a high public profile through her membership of the School Board's Special Committee on Incorrigible Truants, which later became the Industrial Schools Committee. With the support of Florence Fenwick Miller and Helen Taylor she was largely responsible for drawing public attention to overexpenditure on the *Shaftesbury* training ship, as well as exposing the cruelties practised by the superintendents of the Board's first truant school and a voluntary industrial school for boys owned by the chair of the Industrial Schools Committee, Thomas Scrutton. The debate over the *Shaftesbury* provides the clearest expression of gender issues because it sought to breach the male bastion of finance and public exposure (Dyhouse, 1987).

In 1878 the Board decided to refit a vessel for use as an industrial training ship with the aim of encouraging boys to develop a taste for life at sea, with lessons in seamanship and extra-curricular activities like gun, rifle and cutlass drill (London County Council, *Report with regard to Industrial Schools*, 1870–1904: 53). However, the cost of the refit soon exceeded the original estimate and there were mutterings of discontent from the women's caucus on the 1876 Board, supported by Benjamin Lucraft. In October 1878 members authorised the expenditure of a further £6000, the Industrial Schools Committee having exhausted the £28,000 already voted. Three months later they voted a further £2000, despite the note of caution sounded by Elizabeth Surr and Helen Taylor. Not unreasonably, the two women recommended that they wait to see the findings of a Special Committee appointed to inquire into levels of expenditure on the *Shaftesbury*. In the face of growing public concern, Alice Westlake gave high priority to sustaining the committee chair and defending party policy. An example of her role as a party loyalist is to be found in her behaviour as a standard-bearer of the party line at the next election. In a letter to the editor of *The Times*, Alice cast doubt on the veracity of Elizabeth Surr's information about Thomas Scrutton's expenditure on the refit. These two were the only female members of the Industrial Schools Committee and the day after, Elizabeth protested her colleague's intrusion into a difference between herself and the chair:

> I regret it lest the public might imagine that women on the School Board cannot work harmoniously together; therefore I deem it worth stating that nothing has disturbed the harmony with which two of my colleagues and myself have laboured, and that my behaviour to Mrs Westlake has always been courteous.
>
> (*The Times*, 26 November 1879)

Alice Westlake was a more conventional activist in the public sphere than Elizabeth, Florence or Helen. The more radical women were prepared to challenge institutional procedures in defence of a principle they believed in, and it was Florence Fenwick Miller who moved a vote of censure:

> It was not by my own design or desire that I took the leading place in this public duty. One of our Members, Mr Lovell, said to Mrs Surr that the women Members ought not to have taken the lead in censuring the Industrial Schools Committee on which she immediately compared him to Abimelech in the Bible. But she and I *had* to lead, simply because the men would not undertake the task of censure which appeared to us necessary.
>
> ('An Uncommon Girlhood', GC/228/34)

Ultimately, the strength of party discipline kept other members under control and the guilty parties clung on to their positions of authority on the Committee and the Board (*School Board Chronicle*, 22 March 1879). Significantly, Florence recalled that several who voted against her motion to dissolve the Committee only did so because Mr Scrutton was a prominent Liberal. Writing in the *Women's Penny Paper* a decade later, Henrietta Muller recalled Florence's power as a speaker in debate: 'I have seen men grow visibly pale, as she dissected – or rather vivisected – their halting arguments with her pitiless logic, leaving nothing but shreds behind' (*Women's Penny Paper*, 23 February 1889).

## Conclusion

For a 34-year period women members of the London School Board drew upon and developed the ideology of domesticity to create empowering public identities. It has been argued (Yeo, 1998: 12) that British women 'stretched various family roles precisely to ratify their public activism'. Thus, Mary Bridges Adams mobilised her identity as a mother in electoral addresses, while Helen Taylor told the Metropolitan

Board Mistresses' Association that she cared for the children 'from the point of view of a maiden aunt' (*The Governess*, June 1882: 122). On the same occasion Florence Fenwick Miller subverted the dominant ideas about femininity as domestic married motherhood to promote the work of married women teachers:

> I believed that mothers would be very likely to be the most efficient teachers, partly because the sympathy of young women is often dormant until they have children of their own, when they understand and sympathise better with all the little ones; and partly I urged, because the woman who is married and has made up her mind to continue her work is more settled in it, and less distracted by her personal emotions, than one who is still single.
>
> ('An Uncommon Girlhood', GC/228/34)

This quotation shows how elected women used the rhetoric of familial femininity to justify their political actions and to set forth an ideal for imitation in public life. They must have felt satisfaction at feeling a sense of power but the evidence suggests that there were tensions between those who gave high priority to their role as party representatives and those who challenged the direction of the policy agenda. Certainly, some female politicians preferred the quieter work in private committees while others liked speaking in debate and some gave greater priority to constituency matters. For instance, Eugenie Dibdin kept a low profile on the Board but Hugh Philpott (1904: 24), a contemporary chronicler of London education, was fulsome in his praise of her role as chair of the managers of the Drury Lane industrial school. Her daughter taught the girls to swim and she proved 'a most devoted and sympathetic friend, who knows every one' of the children 'by name and takes quite a motherly interest in them all'. But whatever activities they perceived as appropriate and whatever their political behaviour, the presence of women in local educational policy-making contested the idea that a woman's place is in the home and the case studies suggest that they secured a number of significant policy decisions.

Overall, school board politics provided some middle-class females with a position of authority and a position of fulfilment. These women were a powerful force in their local communities and the preceding discussion highlights a distinct and vocal minority who acted in a less institutionalised way. More competitive than the average woman, the youthful Florence Fenwick Miller found the environment of power scintillating. Her objective was 'to blaise the trail for women to follow along' and like the other women policy-makers, her presence made more than just a symbolic difference to the politics of education.

## Notes

1   The 29 women were Annie Besant, Mary Bridges Adams, Jane Chessar, Alice Cowell, Rosamond Davenport Hill, Emily Davies, Eugenie Dibdin, Margaret Dilke, Constance Elder, Margaret Eve, Elizabeth Garrett, Edith Glover, Frances Hastings, Ruth Homan, Susan Lawrence, Maude Lawrence, Emma Maitland, Ellen McKee, Hilda Miall-Smith, Florence Fenwick Miller, Honnor Morten, Henrietta Muller, Mary Richardson, Edith Simcox, Elizabeth Surr, Helen Taylor, Julia Augusta Webster, Alice Westlake and F.L. Wright.
2   With grateful acknowledgements to Carol Dyhouse for this reference. Archival references have been used, as the pagination of the original manuscript is inconsistent.
3   The nine women were Rosamond Davenport Hill, Florence Fenwick Miller, Henrietta Muller, Mary Richardson, Edith Simcox, Elizabeth Surr, Helen Taylor, Augusta Webster and Alice Westlake.

## Archival sources

### Fawcett Library, London

Newscuttings, 'School Boards', London 1896–97.

### London Metropolitan Archives

London County Council *Report on Industrial Schools*, 1870–1904.
*School Board Chronicle*, 1870–1903.
School Board for London, *Minutes*, 1870–1904.

### London School of Economics

Mill/Taylor Special Collection.

### Wellcome Trust Contemporary Medical Archives Centre, London

'An Uncommon Girlhood' by Mrs Florence Fenwick Miller.

## References

Bird, E. (1991) To cook or to conjugate: gender and class in the adult curriculum 1865–1900 in Bristol, United Kingdom, *Gender and Education*, 3, pp. 183–197.
Bird, E. (1998) 'High class cookery': gender, status and domestic subjects, 1890–1930, *Gender and Education*, 10, pp. 117–131.
Caine, B. (1997) *English Feminism 1780–1980* (Oxford, Oxford University Press).
Copelman, D.M. (1996) *London's Women Teachers: Gender, Class and Feminism, 1870–1930* (London, Routledge).
Davin, A. (1996) *Growing Up Poor. Home, School and Street in London, 1870–1914* (London, Rivers Oram Press).
Dolman, F. (January 1896) The lady members of the London School Board, *The Young Woman*, pp. 129–132 (London, Horace Marshall & Son).
Dyhouse, C. (1981) *Girls Growing Up in Late Victorian and Edwardian England* (London, Routledge & Kegan Paul).
Dyhouse, C. (1987) Miss Buss and Miss Beale: gender and authority in the history of education, in: F. Hunt (Ed.) *Lessons for Life. The Schooling of Girls and Women 1850–1950* (Oxford, Basil Blackwell).
Gomersall, M. (1994) Education for domesticity? A nineteenth-century perspective on girls' schooling and domesticity, *Gender and Education*, 6, pp. 235–247.
Hollis, P. (1989) *Ladies Elect. Women in English Local Government, 1865–1914* (Oxford, Clarendon Press).
Hughes, M. (1992) 'The Shrieking Sisterhood': women as educational policy-makers, *Gender and Education*, 4, pp. 255–272.
Hunt, F. (1991) *Gender and Policy in English Education 1902–1944* (London, Harvester Wheatsheaf).
Koven, S. (1993) Borderlands: women, voluntary action, and child welfare in Britain, 1840–1914, in: S. Koven and S. Michel (Eds) *Mothers of a New World. Maternalist Politics and the Origins of Welfare States* (London, Routledge).
London County Council, *Report with regard to Industrial Schools*, 1870–1904.
Lovenduski, J. (1996) Sex, gender and British politics, in: J. Lovenduski and P. Norris (Eds) *Women in Politics* (Oxford, Oxford University Press).
Lovenduski, J. and Norris, P. (Eds) (1996) *Women in Politics* (Oxford, Oxford University Press).
Martin, J. (1991) 'Hard-headed and large-hearted': women and the industrial schools 1870–1885, *History of Education*, 20, pp. 187–201.

Martin, J. (1993) Entering the public arena: the female members of the London School Board, 1870–1904, *History of Education*, 22, pp. 225–240.

Martin, J. (1995) Fighting down the idea that the only place for women was home? *History of Education*, 24, pp. 277–292.

Martin, J. (1999) *Women and the Politics of Schooling in Victorian and Edwardian England* (Leicester, Leicester University Press).

Norris, P. and Lovenduski, J. (1995) *Political Recruitment: Gender, Race and Class in the British Parliament* (Oxford, Oxford University Press).

Norris, P. (1996) Women Politicians: transforming Westminster? in: J. Lovenduski and P. Norris (Eds) *Women in Politics* (Oxford, Oxford University Press).

Philpott, H.B. (1904) *London at School* (London, T. Fisher Unwin).

Thane, P. (1993) Women in the British Labour Party and the construction of state welfare, in: S. Koven and S. Michel (Eds) *Mothers of a New World. Maternalist Politics and the Origins of Welfare States* (London, Routledge).

Turnbull, A. (1983) 'So extremely like Parliament': the work of the women members of the London School Board, 1870–1904, in: The London Feminist History Group (Eds) *The Sexual Dynamics of History* (London, Pluto Press).

Turnbull, A. (1987) Learning her womanly work: the elementary school curriculum 1870–1914, in: F. Hunt (Ed.) *Lessons for Life. The Schooling of Girls and Women 1850–1950* (Oxford, Basil Blackwell).

Turnbull, A. (1994) An isolated missionary: the domestic subjects teacher in England, 1870–1914, *Women's History Review*, 3, pp. 81–100.

Royal Commission on Secondary Education (1895) (Bryce Commission) *Report of the Commissioners. With Minutes of Evidence* (London, HMSO).

Weiner, G. (1994) *Feminisms in Education* (Buckingham, Open University Press).

Yeo. E.J. (1998) (Ed.) *Radical Femininity. Women's Self-representation in the Public Sphere* (Manchester, Manchester University Press).

# PART IV

# EDUCATION AND SOCIAL CHANGE AND INEQUALITY

## CHAPTER 8

# CAN EDUCATION CHANGE SOCIETY?*

Brian Simon

*Does Education Matter?* (1985), London: Lawrence and Wishart, pp. 13–31

The best laid plans of mice and men, wrote Robbie Burns, gang oft agley. Much the same thought, if in a different context, was expressed by Karl Marx. However carefully planned particularly social policies may be, he wrote, the outcomes will not be those desired by any one of the groupings concerned. Unexpected outcomes, in fact, are the rule, rather than the exception.

When the Russian monarchy in the early nineteenth century was concerned to ensure in an economical and tested way the production of administrators and bureaucrats to administer that vast and ramshackle domain, not unreasonably (in the context of the times) they took Prussia as their model, and established in the main cities the equivalent of the German classical gymnasia and, in St Petersburg and Moscow, both universities and higher professional schools (for instance, the famous Medical Academy and others, which reflected the French Grandes Ecoles). The outcome of this policy was, however, hardly that desired. Certainly these institutions did produce the officials and bureaucrats, the doctors, lawyers and military experts that were required. What was clearly not intended was the massive alienation and radicalisation of a large proportion of the students, leading to the great student strikes and related actions of the 1860s.

In *Training the Nihilists*, Daniel Brower analyses this striking social phenomenon, showing clearly that the radicalised students came roughly equally from all the privileged social classes, including the nobles.[1] Brower also describes the social forms and philosophic and social/political outlook of these students, the literature that they used for their own self-education (the French socialists, Saint-Simon, Fourier, and the English political economists in particular), and the way this student movement linked with the democratic thinking of the leading group of advanced radicals of the 1860s – Dobrolubov, Belinsky, Chernyshevsky and, in exile, of Herzen. Nihilism does not describe the outlook of the students of the 1860s, who were really children of the Enlightenment, deeply concerned with clarifying the nature of moral behaviour, especially as it concerns relations between the sexes, and whose social policies related to such matters as the establishment of small co-operative producer societies, seen as an alternative 'system' in much the same way as the early Owenites established co-operative communities in England some thirty years earlier. All this forms the subject matter of Chernyshevsky's *What is to be Done?*, a seminal and profoundly influential book which delineated the ideal type – the new man and woman – of the Russian democrats of that time.

Later, in an effort to link up with 'the people', these students turned to mass literacy campaigns among workers and peasants (a movement with which Tolstoy was closely connected in his old age). The terrorist policies which followed the failure of all these initiatives were policies of despair. But it is worth recalling that Lenin's brother, who participated actively in student affairs in the 1880s, was in fact executed as a result of activities in which he was closely involved shortly after leaving university.

Is there not a direct line of connection between the alienated students of the 1840s, 1850s and 1860s and the events of February and October, 1917? If the relations between education and society are now generally interpreted, by neo-Marxists and by sociologists, as ensuring social reproduction, and therefore the stability and perpetuation of existing social relations, does this mean that unintended outcomes no longer occur in this field? That policies of social control always achieve their objectives?

# 1

What is of particular interest to the historian is not so much what the consensus views are at any given moment in time, as *how and why these views change*. Views often stated with the utmost authority and certainty, and accepted without question in one period, are totally contradicted in another, the new interpretation now finding equally widespread acceptance, again being presented with authority and certainty. In 1961, for instance, there appeared a well known reader in the sociology of education, *Education, Economy and Society*, edited by A.H. Halsey, Jean Floud, and C. Arnold Anderson; a popular and massive textbook for students at least in the English-speaking countries.[2] The many contributors here unanimously expressed the view not only that education could be, but also that it certainly was, a major factor in bringing about social change. Specifically oriented to capitalist societies in the West, it argued that, through planned expansion of education, an egalitarian society could and was being constructed in Britain and the United States in particular.

The ideological basis of this outlook lay in human capital theory, then widely accepted. Investment in human capital – that is, in education – was the key to economic, and so to social advance. Wealth creation through this means gave the opportunity for a relatively painless redistribution, and so for the construction of a more equal society in which class and other social divisions might be overcome. Education, in this interpretation, was *the* tool for social change, though, it should be noted, without disturbing basic structural features of the economy. This view was widely accepted by policy makers in the West, and provided the ideological support or legitimisation for relatively massive educational advances, particularly in the tertiary sector, but also within the school system, leading to support for experimental 'compensatory' measures such as Headstart and Follow Through in the United States, and for such positive discriminatory policies as the Education Priority Areas initiatives in Britain – masterminded, incidentally by Dr Halsey, one of the editors and compilers of the 1961 reader.

But here again there were unexpected outcomes – specifically the coincidence with this policy of another student movement which took its most radical form, perhaps, in the United States, though Britain, Canada, and in particular France and West Germany were profoundly affected. This is not the place to discuss this new alienation, or student disaffection, which certainly deeply affected the subjective experience of two or more generations of students, because I don't want to lose sight of my argument, which concerns shifts in consensus interpretations of the relations between education and society. Reverting, then, to the sociologists – the discipline which is most directly involved in offering an interpretation of this issue – there appeared, in 1977 (i.e. only sixteen years after the volume just mentioned), another reader, more up to date and modern in style, with a very contemporary title, *Power and Ideology in Education*, this time edited and compiled again by A.H. Halsey, but with a young American partner, Jerome Karabel (not a mainstream sociologist, but a product of the New Left – and of the 1960' student movement as we are editorially informed).[3] And what now is the consensus view? That education can do nothing of any significance; that it must inevitably reflect the society which creates it, that, as mentioned earlier, its function is that of ensuring social reproduction. This tergiversation, and of course it is one (though nothing is said about this aspect in the book nor any reference made to the earlier reader), is also now reflected in the attitude of policy makers and in government actions. What is heard of human capital theory now? And what Western government pursues a policy based on this ideology?

The sixteen years between the publication of the two readers, of course, also saw the publication of several important empirical studies and of much theorising on this crucial issue. In the United States first Coleman and then Jencks produced their Reports, both analysing a mass of contemporary (i.e. non-historical) data using modern social science techniques.[4] Both reached the conclusion, as is well known, popularly encapsulated in the phrase 'Schools make no difference'. That is, schooling was shown to have no significant effect either on the pattern of income distribution or on life chances; these depended very specifically on parental status and income (though Jencks included a factor which he called 'luck', and for this was sharply criticised by the sociologist, Jean Floud).[5] Nothing on quite this scale was attempted in England, but the Coleman/Jencks thesis was influential here and elsewhere. Both studies chimed with the times, in that, appearing in 1966 and 1972 respectively, they coincided with the beginning of a traditionalist (and populist) backlash against educational change (the first of the series of so-called Black Papers appeared in England in 1969), and with the onset of what turned out to be a world economic recession.

Perhaps more important in the long run were the many new contributions in the field of theory. In 1970 the French Marxist, Louis Althusser, published his well known essay entitled, 'Ideology and Ideological State Apparatuses', used as a set reading text by the Open University in England and so widely influential.[6] Althusser advanced a highly abstract theory as to the inevitable dominance of 'established' ideology through the education system which, he argued, had in modern times taken the place of the Church as the chief means by which the dominant ideology of a class society was perpetuated, and so that society itself. Teachers and other workers within the field of education were inevitably subsumed as agents of ideological domination, and nothing they could do could have any significant effect. Those who took a radical stance, holding that their actions as teachers could have some effect on the nature of society, and even bring about social change, were, said Althusser, 'a kind of hero', but one can only pity the futility of their efforts.[7] Some would say that it is ironic that so fatalistic and mechanistic an interpretation should be contributed by a Marxist, since Marxism surely stresses the flexibility and the complexity of the interrelations between education and society, particularly when analysed historically.

Other important theoretical contributions were made in this decade. Samuel Bowles and Herbert Gintis, best described, perhaps, as neo-Marxists, contributed their close analysis. *Schooling in Capitalist America* in 1976, arguing very ingeniously what has come to be described as the 'correspondence theory'; that the educational structure and ethos 'corresponds' to the structure and ethos of the institutions of monopoly capitalism – the factory and the modern corporation.[8] For their historical support and evidence, Bowles and Gintis rely on the works of the revisionist historians in the United States, and this foundation may be regarded as a little shaky; however that may be, in essence Bowles and Gintis reached the conclusion that, as far as the United States is concerned, this relationship was fixed and inevitable. Many critics, of which I am one, hold that their final chapter entitled 'Education, Socialism and Revolution', which, in contradiction to the book's whole thesis, sets out a programme for social as well as educational change, carries little conviction.

*Schooling in Capitalist America* was another of the set books of the Open University, whose antennae are, no doubt rightly, beamed to pick up the most contemporary, or modern interpretations, and therefore are widely influential. But of course the most powerful intellect to have been involved in this issue is another Frenchman, the sociologist Paul Bourdieu. In his *Reproduction in Education, Society and Culture* and in other writings, Bourdieu has advanced a tightly argued set of logically related propositions which lead to the conclusion that the educational structure, together with the pedagogical processes embodied within it, operates to ensure the reproduction of existing social categories, classes or groups.[9] Nothing is said in Bourdieu's work of unintended consequences, in the sense I outlined earlier, nor of what Antonio Gramsci defines as 'counter-hegemonic' activities and influences arising from social forces resistant to the status quo; nor is attention given to the coincidence of educational and social change as experienced historically – though both of course have continuously occurred. Instead we have a highly stimulating analysis explaining with great precision why everything must remain exactly as it is – in terms of social relations; 'The School as a Conservative Force', to quote the title of one of Bourdieu's most influential articles.[10] Bourdieu's motivation for these studies, it appears, arose from disillusion following the May 1968 events in France, as that of Bowles and Gintis followed the decline of the radical student movement in the United States.

So, both the empirical researches of social scientists, and the theoretical work of sociologists and neo-Marxists occurring between the publication of the two readers pointed in the same direction: put crudely and briefly, that education reflects society, and is certainly not a force for social change. The fact that, through the 1970s and early 1980s, the Western world has experienced a growing economic crisis, with massive cuts in public expenditure including education, has provided a context in which such theories, even if advanced by Marxists, neo-Marxists and sociologists, provide no direct challenge to the social order or to education. These are interpretative theories. Their implications are that, if social change is what is aimed at in terms of greater egalitarianism, then it is necessary first to change the 'deep structures' of society and the economy; that is, to work for a socialist transformation of society. This is, in fact, overtly stated at the conclusion of the Jencks study, but no strategy for its achievement is advanced. In essence these studies, both theoretical and empirical, project a kind of frigid or pallid fatalism concerning the role of education and of the teacher.

Enough has been said, perhaps, to clarify my thesis, which is that interpretations of the relations between education and society are themselves subject to change, and that the degree of optimism or pessimism expressed, if one may use these value-laden terms, appears to vary with the economic situation: an expansionist phase appears sympathetic to concepts stressing the importance of the role of education, a recessionary phase the opposite. That, at least, might appear to cover the succession of contradictory theories over the past two decades. But if we extend our analysis historically, other strands in the argument may be elucidated or defined, extending the complexity of the situation beyond the simplistic conclusion just presented.

## 2

It was my contention, in the first of my historical studies covering the period 1780–1870, that many of the educational measures undertaken and supported by the industrial and commercial middle class in England in the early nineteenth century should primarily be regarded as a response, and a considered one, to the rapidly growing and perhaps increasingly threatening independent political and educational activity of working people at that time.[11] I am not suggesting that this was a deliberate exercise of social control as I do not find that this concept has serious explanatory power. But I am suggesting that the Mechanics' Institute movement of the 1820s and 1830s, for instance, the formation of the Society for the Diffusion of Useful Knowledge with its *Penny Magazine* and avalanche of cheap literature, the reluctant provision of Treasury support for elementary education and later for teacher training, and like measures, were, in the circumstances, seen by those in authority, both nationally and locally, as necessary or desirable in view of the widespread movement both towards independent political activity (especially after 1832), and towards strictly independent forms of education. I refer here to the whole radical tradition and movement starting with the Corresponding Societies in the 1790s, through the activities of the Hampden Clubs, the Political Protestants, and others (especially in the north of England), culminating in the Owenite Socialist and the Chartist movements in the late 1830s and 1840s.[12] If we ask the question, 'can education change society?' then we should ask this question not only in relation to formalised and state or local authority controlled *systems* of education, as we have them today, but also in relation to informal, if you like independent networks (to use Illich's phrase) whereby, as in the case just mentioned, whole generations of working people (or at least their leading representatives) educated themselves, in many cases consciously, in order to transform society more effectively – the outer world – to their desires.

It would be rash to deny that this experience had no effect in bringing about social change, because these were mass, popular activities which brought thousands, and, in the case of the Chartist movement in Britain, hundreds of thousand of people into new forms of social and political activity and were themselves educative and profoundly so. How do we explain the extraordinary deep and widespread change in the consciousness of large sections of the British people between, say, the early 1790s – when Church and King mobs could rampage around Birmingham destroying the Unitarian chapel and ransacking its Minister's (Joseph Priestley's) house, scientific equipment and personal belongings, forcing him and his family to flee the city – and, let's say, the events at Peterloo in Manchester in 1819 where a huge popular demonstration swelled by representatives from all the villages round about demanded the extension of the franchise and an end to the Corn Laws? Edward Thompson has, of course, chronicled and interpreted this change in consciousness in his well-known book, *The Making of the English Working Class*,[13] and this points to an issue that needs stressing in this context.

What do we mean by *education*? Are we to reduce the term only to the systems of schooling – at different levels – which, even in advanced industrial societies, are a product, generally speaking, only of the last century, or, at the most, a century and a half? This situation today profoundly affects our thinking, so that education is taken to consist solely in what goes on within these systems. And, because of their nature and social function, the *process* of education is ordinarily conceived (and certainly historically) as essentially didactic. I am reminded of the illustration in the preface to one of the earlier editions of Comenius's *Orbis Pictus*, which represents a grave and learned teacher and a child or pupil with the slogan, 'the teacher teaches, the child learns'. Within modern educational systems in general, teaching and learning is conceived of as a one-way process, and normally this is precisely what it is. This was strikingly confirmed in the ORACLE studies into primary education in England based on systematic classroom observation with which I was closely concerned.[14] Even when the teaching was maximally individualised, and indeed especially in this case, the teacher–pupil interactions were found to be overwhelmingly didactic.

But it is arguable, at least, that it is through their *activity* that human beings learn, and learn best; that the unity of consciousness and activity, mediated through language, is what differentiates human beings from the rest of the animal species and underlies the development of the higher mental processes peculiar to man. Education, as Joan Simon has put it, is *the mode of development of human beings in society*,[15] and, seen in this light, the *process* of education involves all those formative influences including the family, peer groups, the Church, apprenticeship and the village or civic relations with which all are involved from the earliest times; relationships growing in complexity, of course, as society itself becomes more complex. Within these sets of inter-relations, organised schooling, of course, plays a part, but one which only affected a small, even tiny, proportion of the population until very recently.

Reverting then, to the situation in Britain between 1790 and 1819 and beyond, was it not the case that a changed consciousness, resulting from new circumstances and new forms of activity, profoundly influenced social development? In his fascinating study of nineteenth-century autobiographies by working men, many of them not yet in print, Vincent shows that, as a result of bitter and deeply felt experiences, a profound effort at independent self-education was made, particularly by men who became leaders of the Chartist and later movements – best epitomised, perhaps, in the title of one of the best known of these: *The Life and Struggles of William Lovett in the Search for Bread, Knowledge and Freedom* (1876).[16] In his recent study of the Corresponding Societies of the 1790s, Professor Goodwin draws particular attention to the educational implications of this movement, and of the forms of activity associated with it – the intensive discussions, debates, and readings as well as the mass demonstrations and similar forms of activity.[17] From all this there developed a self-conscious and deliberate movement for political and social change; in particular for the extension of the franchise; for full and genuine citizenship; for the right to leisure – the ten hour and later the eight hour bill; for the right to education. The measures that resulted, though never gained in their pure form as originally demanded, certainly effected social change – and on a massive scale; nor was there anything inevitable about it. Further, those measures that were achieved, once gained, acted as spring-boards for further demands, for new perspectives.

## 3

We started by examining recent analyses of the relation between education and society, and found quite opposite interpretations within a very short time-span, sixteen years to be exact. We then broadened the concept of education and looked at the subjective experiences of working people in Britain over a longer time-span, and found (or posited) a long term but clear relationship between educational and social and political change. Can we now attempt a longer view?

It was the distinguished archaeologist, Gordon Childe, who gave to one of his influential books the striking title *Man Makes Himself*. This embodies the concept I am tangling with, and trying to unravel in terms of the role of education. Human beings, Childe argues, make themselves – have made themselves through their growing understanding of, control and so transformation of nature; people's actions on nature being the product of socialised labour on the one hand (the determining form of activity), and their growing knowledge, or what slowly came to be science, on the other. The crucial aspect of human activity in this context is that it increasingly takes place in a humanised world; a world in which people's knowledge, and abilities, as they develop, are crystallised, as it were, in a transformed external world, existing independently of them and so forming for him or her a humanised environment. The modern computer is a good example, but, as Childe showed, the earlier and crudest of tools in their time played the same formative role. So, through new forms of activity, the senses themselves are refined, new skills and new abilities are developed. In an important sense, the whole long transition from savagery to civilisation (another title in a series Childe edited),[18] and the process of human and social change involved is a result of this development in which language, closely related to consciousness, plays a vital part. Through language, culture and knowledge are, as it were, crystallised and may be handed on, or made available to each new generation. 'Language, mathematics, or other theoretical ways of structuring knowledge,' writes Jerome Bruner, 'capitalise upon innate capacities. But these skills, though they depend on innate capacities, originate *outside* the organism and memorialise generations of encounters by members of the culture.'[19]

Insofar as man transforms his external world, and by changing it changes himself, the whole historical process must be accounted essentially educative – and indeed this is why it is illuminating to refer to education as the mode of development of human beings in society.

But if this argument carries conviction, how is it that today the consensus appears to be fatalistic – allowing no scope for education to effect social, or for that matter, human change? Here we may, perhaps, remind ourselves of one of Marx's aphorisms when tangling with this precise issue. It was not, he thought, through the imposition from above of changed circumstances that human change was brought about (Robert Owen was his example). The coincidence of human and social change, he argued, can only be understood in terms of what he called 'revolutionising practice'. In changing his circumstances, man changes himself. The educator, he concluded, must himself be educated. The key to both sets of changes lay in human activity – or self-change.[20]

These are overall philosophic propositions but I think highly relevant to our problem. Marx was here concerned with a critique of the mechanistic materialism of the late eighteenth century which fuelled the Enlightenment, and to re-emphasise the importance of subjective experience, the contribution of contemporary German idealism – and to fuse the two in a new world outlook. Mechanistic materialism saw human beings as the simple product of external circumstances; their role was seen as purely passive, as the recipients of innumerable external stimuli which determined their disposition and development, intellectual, moral and aesthetic. So much is attested by all the literature of that period relating to education and human formation. This strand was later developed into the consistent schemata known as behaviourism, which denied the role of consciousness and so of all subjective experience.

But behaviourism has had a long life, based partly on a misunderstanding of the significance of Pavlov's seminal studies early in this century, and a failure to grasp the profound implications of his later work on language – what he called 'the second signalling system' – and its role in the formation of the higher mental properties. It was on the basis of this work in particular that Pavlov laid the greatest stress on the flexibility and adaptability of the higher nervous system. Summarising a lifetime of research, he wrote:

> the *chief, strongest* and *most permanent impression* we get from the study of higher nervous activity by our methods, is the extraordinary plasticity of this activity, its immense potentialities; nothing is immoveable or intractable, and everything may always be achieved, changed for the better, provided only that the proper conditions are created.[21]

It is my contention that the current critiques that I have referred to adopt as an unexamined assumption what amounts to a crude behaviourist interpretation of the relations between man and the external world, and that it is this that underlies their pessimism and, indeed, fatalism. The subjective experiences of those being educated within the modern systems, not only within schools, but in the whole course of life itself, is nowhere examined. Instead we are presented with analyses which simply *assume* that the intentions of the architects of these systems are inevitably achieved. But we saw in the case of the Russian universities and higher professional schools that these intentions, in that case, were at the most only partially achieved, and that, in some senses, the outcomes were diametrically opposed to the original intentions. Can we look a little more closely at all this?

## 4

There is no doubt that in Western Europe, and in a modified sense in North America, highly structured and hierarchic systems of education have been established; full systematisation, in Europe at least, being a feature of developments in the last three or four decades of the nineteenth century. The historian, Geoffrey Best, characterises mid-Victorian education in England as not only reflecting class differences, but as deliberately erected to perpetuate them. 'Educational systems', he writes, 'can hardly help mirroring the ideas about the social relationships of the societies that produce them.' Education became, at that time, a 'trump card' in what he called 'this great class competition'. The result was that 'the schools of Britain not only mirrored the hierarchical social structure ... but were made more and more to magnify its structuring in detail.'[22] Institutionalised education, in this view, acted to reinforce and exacerbate class differences. This view is widely held among British historians; Harold Perkin, for instance, describes developments in the 1860s as intended 'to put education in a strait-jacket of social class.'[23]

Such was certainly the intention – but how can we assess the outcome? Once the whole population was brought into the systems of schooling – and this was not really so long ago – new contradictions, new perspectives, inevitably arose. Among those relegated to the lowest rung in the elementary schools, new aspirations developed. These systems acquired a certain autonomy; in England local school boards, several of which developed very progressive policies, took a pride in their schools; a skilled and devoted teaching force, increasingly professional, was created, its material and spiritual interests bound up with its advancement. Parental support gradually developed. In England it was a mere thirty years after the establishment of universal elementary education that a political and social crisis arose closely related to the upward thrust of a system which had been intended (and, indeed, carefully designed) to preserve the social structure inviolate.

That crisis was dealt with by a fundamental restructuring and in particular by the belated establishment of secondary schooling as a *system* around the turn of the century. But no sooner was this achieved than new struggles arose, related particularly to the issue of access to this new system; and so new crises, new forms of legitimisation, new concessions. The conclusion of all this, in Britain, was the swing to comprehensive secondary education together with the revulsion from forms of early streaming and/or tracking which had fastened on the schools in the inter-war and immediate post-war years. This potentially radical move swept away (at least in theory if not altogether in practice) what was left of the divisions between elementary and secondary education, and between segregated and differentiated forms of secondary education. Today in Britain over 90 per cent of all pupils in the maintained, or state, secondary schools are in comprehensive schools. This experience has been reflected in other countries in Western Europe, in France, Italy and Scandinavia.

Of course these schools are now subjected to a great deal of criticism – it would be surprising if it were not so. And equally of course, the intentions of the pioneers who established them are not being realised in their pure form. It is worth noting, as significant for our thesis, that comprehensive secondary education was originally a grass roots movement in Britain, the first schools being established in the late 1940s or early 1950s by certain advanced local authorities in opposition to government policy and advice, whether that government was Labour (as it was from 1945 to 1951) or Tory (1951 to 1964).[24] This movement arose, in this sense, from the experience of those subjected to the harsh, and apparently arbitrary, decisions about the future of children taken at an early age in order to fit them into the mould of a system erected to preserve what Geoffrey Best called 'the hierarchical social structure'. Experience shows that the establishment of a new system of this kind, which certainly embodies changed values and changed objectives, holding out the prospect of universal secondary education for the first time, is inevitably a hard and difficult process, disturbing deeply engrained vested interests and, for some, quite traumatic. Further, as is to be expected, a new system has to contend with practices and attitudes both deeply entrenched and reflecting the values and outlook of the obsolescent systems of the past. Here the role of examination systems is particularly important in that even today, in England, a three-fold level of examination or non-examination still dominates the internal structures of schooling, placing severe restraints on the degree of transformation that may be achieved.[25]

These are all areas of conflict, as are, for instance, the Thatcher government's measures designed to shore up the private sector (still important in Britain) at the expense of the publicly maintained system of schools. Modern education systems, it seems to me, are an area where the interests and objectives of different social classes, strata and even groups meets and very often clash. Hence contradictions develop within these systems which have a degree, as is now generally accepted, of relative autonomy. In this situation, as the historical record surely makes clear, there is scope for a variety of solutions; which of these will be successful depending on the balance of forces at any particular time.

## 5

I want to suggest that the crucial feature we need to take into account is the subjective experience of the educand – his or her activity and its effect on consciousness; and this in the large historical sense. I would not myself expect education systems, deriving from (or embedded in) societies with sharp class divisions reflecting, if you like, the distribution of wealth in modern capitalist societies, to act directly and immediately to transform that society – say in a socialist direction. And while some degree of social mobility is necessary for the health and continued stability of such societies, a moderate increase or decrease in its degree seems to me of little significance in terms of social change; nor do I regard the degree to which, for instance, comprehensive secondary education in England (or similar measures elsewhere) may marginally affect this as a chief criterion by which the success, or other, of such a change may be judged or evaluated; though this is the measure commonly appealed to by those who espoused the egalitarian objectives of the sixties.

It is, in any case, far too early to arrive at any such conclusion in the case of the transformation referred to; and one of the very real problems in tackling an issue of this kind is precisely that outcomes take a long period to manifest themselves, and then of course, they are only one of the factors determining social change. But it is, I suggest, the long-term outcomes to which we should devote attention. Here the evaluation of the significance of what he called 'the old primary school' by the Italian Marxist Antonio Gramsci seems relevant. In his essay on education, far from criticising the narrowness and inadequacy of the system, Gramsci points to its long-term positive implications.[26] In this school system, he says, there were two elements in the educational formation of the children. 'They were taught the rudiments of natural science, and the idea of civic rights and duties.' 'The scientific ideas the children learnt', he writes, 'conflicted with the magical conception of the world and nature which they absorbed from an environment steeped in folklore; while the idea of civic rights and duties conflicted with tendencies towards individualistic and localistic barbarism – another dimension of folklore.' The school, then, in Gramsci's view, was not a prison for children, nor a simple measure of social control. In combating folklore and 'every residue of traditional conceptions of the world', as he put it, it taught a modern outlook relating to what he calls the 'objective intractable natural laws to which man must adapt himself if he is to master them in his turn'. The pupils also learn that there exist 'social and state laws which are the product of human activity, which are established by men and can be altered by men in the interest of their collective development'. All this, he writes, 'creates the first elements of an intuition of the world free from all magic and superstition,' providing a basis for a new, realistic conception of the world, one 'which understands movement and change...which conceives the contemporary world as a synthesis of the past...and which projects itself into the future'. 'This', says Gramsci, writing around 1930 in Mussolini's prison in Southern Italy, 'was the real basis of the primary school, though whether all this was achieved in practice', he adds, 'is another question'.

I have quoted Gramsci at some length both because his evaluation was based very much on his own experience, in that it was through his own education in childhood that he was able to throw off the folklorist and magical interpretation which surrounded him in Sardinia, and because, in view of current trends, it is perhaps salutary to quote a Marxist who in fact made so positive an assessment of the imposition of mass primary or elementary education, so often profoundly denigrated by radical critics. And I wonder whether it is not in terms of criteria of a similar order that historians of the future will evaluate the great leap forward in education, specifically secondary and tertiary, of the 1960s and 1970s, in spite of the crises and conflicts this gave rise to, and of the subsequent backlash. There cannot, of course, be any guarantee that education may not be misused, to reinforce mythical and mystical interpretations on the basis of nationalist ambitions, as was certainly the case in Germany from 1933 to 1945 and in other countries later; in this sense the struggle for education in its true sense is and must be continuous.

## 6

So we return now to the initial question – Can education change society? And with the broader definition that I cited earlier. It must be clear by now that my own answer to this question is in the affirmative – especially if one takes the long view, as I attempted to earlier. We will not, I think, find our answer from the techniques of contemporary social science since these studies, with their heavy reliance on statistical analysis, necessarily leave out of account, or lose sight of, the crucial human factor – subjective experience; and it is this which determines outcomes – not whether it can be shown statistically that schooling, and/or a particular innovation, has a marginally positive or negative effect on the distribution of income, or life opportunities, however measured, or on social mobility.

I started by stressing unintended outcomes – with the Russian example. And were the outcomes of primary education in Italy all those intended? I then looked at the long-term, though in a sense quite sudden and certainly unexpected, change in the consciousness of important sections of the British people early in the nineteenth century and subsequent social and political action bringing social change; as well as at developments in the late nineteenth century with its restructuring, new contradictions, struggles, culminating in Britain in the movement to comprehensive education. Certainly, it seems to me, contemporary theorising and empirical studies on this issue – that is, on the relation between educational and social change – are both seriously misleading and, in many ways, shortsighted. They ignore human subjective experience – people's capacity for movement, for acting on the environment, transforming it, and so for self-change. It is this process which is educative, and profoundly so. And it is this which we need to take into account when seeking an answer to our question. There is no joy here for the fatalists who claim that all such action is futile. On the contrary the future is open and undecided; and it is, I suggest, of supreme importance that those closely involved in education recognise, and struggle consistently to realise, its potential.

## Notes

\* Lecture delivered at the University of British Columbia, Vancouver, October 1983.
1 Daniel Brower, *Training the Nihilists. Education and Radicalism in Tzarist Russia*, Ithaca, 1975.
2 A.H. Halsey, Jean Floud and C. Arnold Anderson (eds), *Education, Economy and Society*, New York, 1961.
3 A.H. Halsey and Jerome Karabel (eds), *Power and Ideology in Education*, New York, 1977.
4 Christopher Jencks *et al.*, *Inequality: A Reassessment of the Effect of Family and Schooling in America*, New York, 1972; James Coleman *et al.*, *Equality of Education Opportunity*, Washington, 1966.
5 Jean Floud, 'Making Adults More Equal: The Scope and Limitations of Public Educational Policy' in Peter R. Cox, H.B. Miles and John Peel (eds), *Equality and Inequality in Education*, New York, 1975, pp. 37–51.

6  Louis Althusser, 'Ideology and Ideological State Apparatuses' in *Lenin and Philosophy and Other Essays*, London, 1971, pp. 121–73.
7  Ibid., p. 148.
8  S. Bowles and H. Gintis, *Schooling in Capitalist America*, London, 1976.
9  Paul Bourdieu and Jean-Claude Passeron, *Reproduction in Education, Society and Culture*, London, 1977.
10 Pierre Bourdieu, 'The School as a Conservative Force: Scholastic and Cultural Inequalities' in Roger Dale, Geoff Esland and Madeleine MacDonald (eds), *Schooling and Capitalism*, London, 1976, pp. 110–17.
11 Brian Simon, *The Two Nations and the Educational Structure, 1780–1870*, London, 1960, first published under the title *Studies in the History of Education*.
12 Ibid., chapters 4 and 5.
13 Edward Thompson, *The Making of the English Working Class*, London, 1963.
14 See Maurice Galton, Brian Simon and Paul Croll, *Inside the Primary Classroom*, London, 1980, especially chapters 4 and 5. Observational Research and Classroom Learning Evaluation – ORACLE – was a Social Science Research Council research study into primary education in England.
15 Joan Simon, 'The History of Education in *Past and Present*', *Oxford Review of Education*, Vol. 3, No. 1, 1977.
16 David Vincent, *Bread, Knowledge and Freedom: A Study of Nineteenth-Century Working Class Autobiography*, London, 1981.
17 Albert Goodwin, *The Friends of Liberty: The English Democratic Movement in the Age of the French Revolution*, London, 1979.
18 Graham Clark, *From Savagery to Civilization*, London, 1946.
19 Jerome S. Bruner, *The Relevance of Education*, London, 1972, p. 119.
20 Karl Marx, 'Theses on Feuerbach' in Karl Marx and Frederick Engels, *Collected Works*, Vol. 5, London, 1976, pp. 3–8.
21 I.P. Pavlov, 'A Physiologist's Reply to Psychologists' (1932) in *Selected Works*, Moscow 1955, pp. 446–7.
22 Geoffrey Best, *Mid-Victorian Britain, 1851–1875*, London, 1973, p. 170.
23 Harold Perkin, *The Origins of Modern English Society, 1780–1880*, London, 1969.
24 David Rubinstein and Brian Simon, *The Evolution of the Comprehensive School, 1926–1972*, London, 1973, chapters 3–5.
25 For more recent developments in this area see pp. 225ff.
26 Essay 'On Education' in Quintin Hoare and Geoffrey Nowell-Smith (eds), *Antonio Gramsci, Selections From the Prison Notebooks*, London, 1971, see especially pp. 33–5.

## CHAPTER 9

# SCHOOLING AS AN IMPEDIMENT TO SOCIAL MOBILITY IN NINETEENTH AND TWENTIETH CENTURY BRITAIN

## Roy Lowe

In C. Majorek, C.V. Johanningmeier and F. Simon (eds) *Schooling in Changing Societies: Historical and Comparative Perspectives (1998)*, vol. IV, pp. 57–67

In recent years there has been a resurgence of the study of social mobility in Nineteenth and Twentieth Century Europe. There have been numerous important publications, mostly involving the deployment of new technology to deal with large samples for analysis. These are identified in the references. The work of these 'number crunchers' raises important questions for historians of education. The purpose of this contribution is to respond to the challenge of that work by developing a hypothesis, a rough working generalisation, about the role of formal education, of schooling systems in the processes of social mobility and, at the same time, to take the chance to reflect on the implications of that quantitative demographic work and to reflect on the methodologies used by historians of education, the nature of the questions it is proper and appropriate for us to ask and the ways in which we set about answering them. What I am seeking to do here is to offer my personal response to the challenges set for historians of education by these quantitative approaches to the study of social mobility. At the same time I am seeking to set out the grounds for significant research development in our discipline during the next few years.

But first it is appropriate to provide some background on recent developments in social demography. The engagement of historians with social mobility has gone in fits and starts. There was important pioneering work by Stephan Thernstrom (1964, 1973) in USA. Then in the late 1970s and early 1980s the work of Kaelble and others in mainland Europe was also of note.

But in recent years there have been some attempts to compile and analyse extensive data sets. Van Leeuwen and Maas (1992) have undertaken a long-term study of social mobility in Berlin during the Nineteenth and Twentieth centuries. A similar period was covered by the work of De Seve and Bouchard (1994) on Quebec. Similarly, John Goldthorpe's work (1987) on social mobility in modern Britain drew on the use of data sets and a heavily quantitative methodology.

Since 1993 there have been attempts, largely stimulated by Andy Miles and John Vincent, to develop communication between separate investigators in order to explore the potential for historical cross-national comparisons and the HISMA project is the outcome of this initiative, the Historical Study of Social Mobility and Stratification, a major project to deepen our understanding of social mobility in a historical context. Although this work is charged with significance for us historians of education, so far we remain largely outside of this debate. It is this omission which is the starting point for this chapter.

A glance at the findings of these historical demographers highlights the vital questions they raise for historians of education. The British case is particularly pertinent, although much of the evidence so far available suggests that similar provisional findings are being made with respect to a number of European countries. John Goldthorpe's work on Britain, which draws on both historical and sociological modes of analysis, is suggestive of high levels of social mobility in the Nineteenth Century. In essence he argues that there was considerable social fluidity in Nineteenth Century Britain. In his book *The Constant Flux* (1993), co-authored with Robert Erikson, Goldthorpe argued that all industrial societies share common mobility regimes and stressed the fluidity of the situation in the Nineteenth Century. This view is supported by Andrew Miles: one of the life histories he has chronicled is that of George Healey, who, during a relatively brief working career in the mid-Nineteenth Century, changed employment thirty-eight times, and by working in eleven separate industries, spent parts of his life in four of the five social classes identified by the Registrar General (Miles, 1993).

These insights by Goldthorpe are the starting point for a recent book by Andrew Miles, Mike Savage and David Vincent entitled *Pathways and Prospects: the development of the modern bureaucratic career in Britain* (1996). In it they go on to examine the extent to which this high level of social mobility continued into the Twentieth Century. There are several elements to their argument. They suggest first that there was a slowing down of social mobility during the Twentieth Century, second that this was linked to the rise of the tertiary section of the economy, the growth both in absolute size and scale of the professions and the coming of credentialism, the process of using formal qualifications more generally for access to the workplace. And also they suggest that ironically in this process of the slowing down of social mobility the power of males to define the social standing of their female partners is enhanced rather than weakened. In brief that gender is a key element in this analysis. But all of this is done without any more than passing reference to the role played in these processes and in these transformations by formal schooling.

It is this lacuna which generates a challenge for historians of education. What is attempted here is an effort to sketch out the ground and the research agenda which is open to us as historians of education. The central questions are, in brief, what is the role of formal education systems in mediating rates of social mobility; and is schooling itself, in any case, a key element in these processes?

The enigma and the intrinsic difficulty which is central to this argument is that it sets a view of what is (viz. that the education system has had the effect of retarding social mobility) against a supposition of what might have been (viz. that schooling is not necessarily dysfunctional from social mobility and might in reality under certain sets of circumstances contribute to it). So, the problems it raises are particularly complex because they involve juggling several variables which are in some ways interdependent. Further, they presuppose a view of the social functions of education systems, which is necessarily founded in theory.

First, the theoretical basis on which the argument is founded has to be made clear. This is derived from the work of Fritz Ringer, which is itself heavily dependent on insights drawn from Pierre Bourdieu and Max Weber. Ringer argues (especially in *Education and Society in Modern Europe*, 1979) that during what he identifies as the second phase of European industrialisation (about 1860–1930) education systems across Northern Europe took on their modern form and assumed a set of social functions which are related to that form and which have persisted. In brief, education became inclusive in the sense that the vast majority of the population came to pass through one sort or other of schooling and education systems became segmented, with schools of different type being established. Usually, but not always and not exclusively, the grounds on which those differences were justified had to do with the curriculum and this obliges us to begin by attempting to explain the issues around curriculum differentiation. In practice, the curricula of competing schools may have differed far less than the supporters of particular schools may have intended at the outset, although almost every institution experienced internal curriculum differentiation of one sort or another. Similar developments took place in higher education. So, to take a specific example, in England in respect of higher education, each of the new accretions to the system was justified initially on the grounds that it would compensate for the deficiencies of existing curricula. This was true of the civic universities at the end of the Nineteenth Century, equally true of the local technical colleges, true of the new universities after the Second World War and applied also to the technological universities and to those technical colleges which were upgraded to Polytechnics in 1970. But, in the event, once they were all at work then pressures of similar funding arrangements, competition for students and views of what constituted a proper education meant that the curricular similarities between these institutions came to outweigh the differences. And in this process, certain kinds of knowledge came to be awarded higher status than others. This in turn has generated a situation in which education appears to be, almost necessarily, dysfunctional from the point of view of economic development. The facts that for long periods Classical studies were seen as more prestigious than modern, that nuclear physics was clearly more valued than motor mechanics, that by and large pure sciences were afforded a higher cachet than applied (throughout the Nineteenth and for much of the Twentieth Century), all point to the possibility that education performs some important social functions which are not those which might be immediately presumed (Muller, Ringer and Simon, 1987).

One possible explanation of this apparent oddity is that, while formal education bore little relationship to the earlier stages of industrialisation, it was of enormous importance for the development of the professions (Jarausch, 1983): one of the indices of professionalism, as it became widely understood, was that it involved acquaintance with what was seen as the most prestigious forms of knowledge, often in reality Latin and Greek. In this sense the arguments around school and college curricula may have related closely to the structure of society. One hypothesis would be that, at a historical moment when changes in the structure of the economy were beginning to make more direct demands of the formal education system, the participants in education, both users and providers, came to use the curricular differentiation which was increasingly necessary as a device to mark out social distinctions as well as preparing the labour force of the next generation. So, one key role of the education system became the transmission of cultural capital, and the ways in which this was done meant that schooling was more able to define social class and became a more powerful agent in determining the place of its products within the social order.

But it is difficult to believe that strongly contested struggles over curricula and the structure of the education system were about little more than the definition and defence of the developing professions. We are therefore left with the question of what exactly were the implications of the struggles over curriculum differentiation and how did they relate to the broader social functions of schooling: in brief, how do we explain the phenomenon of segmentation? Even if all institutions came to offer similar curricula, we still have to explain the phenomenon that particular parts of the curriculum seem to be the province of particular social groups. To pursue this it is necessary to follow Ringer's argument a little further.

He suggests that these segmented education systems also become tracked (Ringer, 1979). That is that, without there being necessarily any one to one correlation, particular social groups came to attach to particular kinds of school and to particular tracks within schools, using them to progress on to particular forms of employment and to particular institutions of higher education. This raises the possibility that the role of an education system in the modern period is to retard or minimise social mobility in the interests of those social groups which are already in other ways advantaged. And this consideration makes more sense of the problem of curriculum differentiation. In a nutshell, Ringer's working hypothesis, which I will try to relate to the English education system, is that during this key period of modernisation, schools and colleges became segmented precisely because this structure enabled them to provide differing experiences and differing acculturation to different social groups, thus damping down, rather than promoting social mobility. So, the argument, as it applies to education, needs to involve the concepts of universality, of segmentation, of tracking and of curricular difference and needs to contain within it understandings of the interrelatedness of these phenomena.

But any attempt to apply this rough-working hypothesis to any real historical situation immediately raises as many problems as it resolves. The first is that in respect of modern English society we are not dealing with a constant. Just as the schools change, so does society itself. This leads to the view that, in order to apply Ringer's ideas in any meaningful way to a modern industrialised society we need to take account of several other variables. These are fairly easily identified. First, the nature of the economy, and in particular the deepseated changes which are taking place within it over time. The steady shift from industrial production towards the tertiary sector of the economy, the changing nature of commercial enterprise and the demands which it makes of the labour force, the scale of economic units: these are three immediately identifiable factors which relate. The very fact that the economy at the close of the Twentieth Century is so different in its structure from that of the beginning of the Century makes precise analysis of the social functions of the education system notoriously difficult.

Second, changing social mores and lifestyles mean that the bases on which social class is analysed are necessarily themselves in constant transformation. The coming of affluence and of consumerism may minimise the significance of certain indices of social class and highlight others. Leisure patterns, patterns of private investment, tastes, cultural interests, diet, dress, and a host of other changing indices all mediate social class. Yet each of these is susceptible to the administrations of schoolteachers and lecturers, is actually the subject of education. This fact poses a second difficulty.

A third key factor has to do with space and the rise and fall of suburbs in modern Britain. This is not simply a question of whether a prestigious suburb such as Edgbaston in Birmingham carried the same meanings in 1970 as it had done a hundred years before (which, in the context of this discussion it patently did not). The contest for urban living space in modern Britain, overlaid by tensions between concepts of urbanity and ruralism, has generated a situation in which, as Harold Perkin has pointed out, suburbanisation led to England being 'more visibly graded into discrete social layers' (Perkin, 1989: 269). The difficulty which is faced by the analyst of modern society is that she or he has to grapple with shifting perceptions of suburbs which are themselves constantly changing. Yet it is in precisely such suburban locations that the very schools which are under analysis are located. In brief, the location of any educational institution is of importance for an understanding of its contribution to social mobility, but the bases of any evaluation of 'prestige' as related to location must vary from year to year.

Fourth, it is impossible to make any sense of the contribution of schools to social mobility without taking on board the extent to which they have been mediators of gender distinctions and of discrete gender roles in modern Britain. If, as is now frequently argued, gender has to be seen as one key element in the definition of social class, then there are several other characteristics of school systems which need to be taken into account in analyses of social mobility. The development of a number of secondary schools for girls during the late Nineteenth and early Twentieth centuries, their affiliation to particular social groups, the particular career and life destinations of their pupils, the use of the school system to establish distinct gender identities, and variations in these patterns by region and by suburb all relate. So, too, does the rise of coeducation.

Finally, no account of social mobility in modern England can be complete without considering ethnicity as another key factor. Here the question of which ethnic groups use which schools and with what effects is vital. If we take the obvious examples of Irish, Jewish, Afro-Caribbean and Asian immigrants to Nineteenth and Twentieth Century Britain, it is appropriate to ask about location of their schooling, its nature, and in particular whether education has been used as an instrument of assimilation or to sustain distinctiveness. There are deeper questions about intent as well as outcomes here. This enquiry is needed to throw light on whether an education system promotes social mobility among ethnic minorities or impedes it, and in exactly what ways. There is yet another detail which compounds the problem. Without understanding the nature of social class in the societies from which these immigrant groups are drawn it is impossible to make judgements on how they mediate and use their own experiences of formal education. If this leads to the question of whether schools come close to giving ethnic minority pupils the same chance of mobility as pupils from indigenous backgrounds, it is only part of a much wider problem, because implicit in it is the supposition that education systems may not promote social mobility evenly: so region, suburb, gender, class, parental occupation, family accident and other variables (including choice of school or college) all help determine what we might call differential benefit rates in respect of social mobility.

In brief, what is being proposed here is that any argument about the relationship of formal schooling and social mobility may well be too complex, unless one is prepared to deal in such small units as to give only a fragmentary picture of the social whole, to allow any straightforward numerical analysis. What Halsey, Heath and Ridge (1980) refer to as the English tradition of 'political arithmetic' can provide vivid and accurate description of parts of a historical process.

In order to establish this point I will try to develop a rough working hypothesis regarding the connections between the various social components that I have identified, but will argue too that statistical analysis may help to illustrate the pattern I describe but can never fully explain it, and might necessarily stop short of historical explanation. This adds up then, to a plea for a resort to an older tradition of historical interpretation, by which the generalisations made are based on insight and on empathy as well as on statistics. So, I will offer two very small-scale examples of the linkage of school systems with social mobility in modern Britain and will use them to try to devise a rough working hypothesis about how we might best set about analysis in this field. In doing this I will also attempt to develop my personal construction of what Ringer's hypothesis means in practice.

Each of the examples chosen relates to late Nineteenth Century Birmingham, in the West Midlands of England, although the patterns of development which are hinted at may well apply widely across Europe or even further afield since the West Midlands may be taken as a fairly representative example of a conurbation responding to the stresses of industrialisation for much of the Nineteenth and Twentieth centuries and coping more recently with the phenomenon of de-industrialisation which is common to the developed world.

The first 'case study' is of the coming of universal elementary schooling during the final thirty years of the Nineteenth Century. Although it is not uncommon for historians to write about the coming of universal elementary schooling as though there were little evolution of the concept of an elementary school during this period, a glance at the experience of one city quickly establishes that quite the opposite was the case. In 1870, when an Education Act decreed the establishment of school boards, the city of Birmingham was experiencing its first major phase of suburbanisation. The schools which were built in the immediate aftermath of the 1870 Act were all within a mile of the city centre (that was the then extent of suburbanisation) and all were modelled on the rural elementary school with no internal divisions and an underlying assumption that schooling took place in a 'schoolroom'. In 1861 the Newcastle Commissioners had found the single schoolroom to be 'the only arrangement sufficiently general to require distinct notice' and little had changed in the intervening decade. By contrast as early as 1880, when the headlong flight of the city dwellers to new domestic locations was at its height, the Birmingham School Board was anxious to follow the Prussian model and incorporate classrooms in its new buildings. Thus, at Hope Street in Balsall Heath, only ten years after the passing of the Act, and only one mile further distant from the city centre, Birmingham's first 'central hall' school, with classrooms arranged around a small hall, was opened. By the beginning of the Twentieth Century, new commuter transport systems were further revolutionising urban life. The new jobs which followed from 'second phase industrialisation' allowed unprecedented numbers of the new salariat to think in terms of a commuter lifestyle and several of the rural settlements closest to the city began to be transformed by the appearance of semi-detached villas and Edwardian terraces. Those who chose this residential location were offered yet another model of elementary schooling for their children. Whilst the 'first phase' central hall schools had often been three storeyed, allowing for separate schooling for infants, girls and boys, by the early Twentieth Century the emphasis was on hygiene, on space and light, and many central hall schools, such as that built on Colmore Road in Kings Heath, were afforded three separate buildings set in a large playground. So, by the time of the outbreak of the First World War, there were at least three models of an elementary school in use in Birmingham, each undergoing constant subtle modifications of their social class intake and each catering, at any one time, for groupings of social class which were identifiable, different and distinct (Seaborne and Lowe, 1977). It is the organic nature of the development of an urban education system which enables it to be one of the key arbiters of life-chances, and this certainly appears to have been the case in late Nineteenth Century suburban Birmingham. There must be a question mark placed over the extent to which a process as subtle as this can be subjected to meaningful numerical analysis. It is certainly true that any such analysis which fails to take into account the minutiae of suburbanisation, developing local transport systems and the myriad changes occurring in urban lifestyle cannot hope to do justice to the subtle ways in which an emergent system of popular education, such as that in Birmingham, contributed to the identification and development of social class and to the processes of social mobility. But this account, although brief, does give rise to the possibility that schooling may have been one important agency in retarding intergenerational movement between social classes.

Much the same point can be made through approaches which focus on the social class recruitment of particular schools. Much of the pioneering work in this field was undertaken by W.E. Marsden (1987) and his associates, working on case studies from the industrial north-west. Relating to my own example of suburban Birmingham is the work conducted by Chris Scudamore (1976) on the recruitment pattern of the first higher grade school opened in Birmingham at Bridge Street. On the basis of an exhaustive study of the social backgrounds of the intake at Bridge Street between 1890 and 1894, Scudamore concludes that:

> Bridge Street School was predominantly used by the skilled working classes ... highly mobile, quite well paid and proficient in the new engineering industries that were beginning to flourish. They lived in the outer suburbs, in recently built houses, and amounted to perhaps two-thirds of the total of all pupils.
>
> (p. 140)

Further, Scudamore argues, it was from the start the intention of the School Board that this school would cater for this tranche of the population. Their parents were often recent migrants into Birmingham; they were drawn largely from the new outer suburbs and many of them went on to pursue careers as skilled technicians. In brief, what emerges is the tantalising possibility that not only the schools were increasingly agencies for the stabilisation of society and key arbiters of life chances in a situation of social stratification, but that this was consciously planned and understood by the participants on both sides, the providers of education and the recipients. This raises the possibility that a school such as the Bridge Street Higher Grade School in Birmingham may be but one example of a phenomenon which is pretty well universal within an urban industrial society. Is it the case more generally that particular educational innovations come very quickly, if not immediately, to cater for a particular niche in society and soon lead towards particular groupings of employment and adult lifestyle?

So, whilst this account draws attention to the inherent difficulties which are implicit in approaches dependent upon the deployment of quantitative evidence to study the role of schooling in the promotion of social mobility, it does not deny the possibility of meaningful generalisation. My rough-working summary of the processes at work would go something like this.

During the late Nineteenth Century economic transformations involved a redefinition of jobs and a significant shift in gender relations. These processes of transformation involved the establishment of new forms of schooling and some modification of existing forms. What developed was a divided education system which had the effect of carefully distinguishing the young people it processed by class and gender. Its function became, increasingly, to fit them for particular niches in society which were increasingly preordained from birth. Only at moments of economic growth and transformation did this seem, if only briefly to offer chances of social mobility. But what was occurring might be better described as social change. The argument therefore goes that the acquisition of wealth was a far better index of social mobility than schooling. Once wealth was acquired, schooling came into play. Those who acquired wealth in the relatively fluid situation of the first phase of industrialisation were able to use it to sustain their position of advantage. One of the agencies available to them to achieve this was schooling; that which their own children received, and that of the less well-off. In the generation of new social classes and of new lifestyles, the school system was of enormous importance. But, always, at every turn the chances of self-improvement through education were severely curtailed by, not simply what the economy would stand, but how far the promotions involved would threaten those who were already, in one way or another, privileged. To this end several characteristics of the education system became of key importance. Definition of good and bad knowledge through control of curricula was vital. The location of schools was also important. Schools defined suburbs and suburbs defined schools. Interestingly, at moments of apparent democratisation, such as the opening up of grammar schools after the Second World War, or in the coming of comprehensives a few years later, the pupils who were most likely to benefit from a schooling which differed from that of their parents were already predisposed in that way by attitudes and expectations, often parentally inspired, which showed the untypicality of those parents within the class group or neighbourhood they inhabited. In a society within which gender was becoming increasingly an aspect of social class, the gender roles and attitudes which were imparted at school became an important element in minimising change. The 'cultural capital' which the schools invested in their pupils was necessarily part of a deeply conservative educational settlement which ensured that schools and universities posed the least possible threat to the existing social order whilst providing a necessary minimum of technological skills to fuel continuing economic development. The segmented and tracked nature of the education system was vital if it was to perform its function of minimising social mobility. By this analysis, education comes to be seen as, not dysfunctional in respect of social and economic change, but a key agent in the preservation of social stability. By promoting social change it pre-empted the need to promote social mobility.

# References

De Seve, M. and D. Bouchard (1994). *Long term social mobility in Quebec, 1851–1951.* Bielefeld: Paper to the ISA Committee on Social Stratification.

Goldthorpe, J.H. (1987). *Social Mobility and class structure in modern Britain.* Oxford: Clarendon Press.

Halsey, A.H., A.F. Heath and J.M. Ridge (1980). *Origins and destinations: family, class and education in modern Britain.* Oxford: Clarendon Press.

Jarausch, K.H. (1983) (ed.). *The transformation of higher learning, 1860–1930.* Stuttgart: Klett Cotta Press.

Kaelble, H. (1985). *Social mobility in the Nineteenth and Twentieth centuries.* Leamington: Berg Press.

Marsden, W.E. (1987). *Unequal educational provision in England and Wales: the Nineteenth Century roots.* London: Woburn Press.

Miles, A. (1993). 'How open was nineteenth-century British society? Social mobility and equality of opportunity, 1839–1914', in A. Miles and D. Vincent (eds), *Building European Society.* Manchester: Manchester University Press.

Miles, A., M. Savage and D. Vincent (1996). *Pathways and prospects: the development of the modern bureaucratic career in Britain.* Cambridge: Cambridge University Press.

Muller, D.K., F. Ringer and B. Simon (1987) (eds). *The rise of the modern educational system: structural change and social reproduction, 1870–1920.* Cambridge: Cambridge University Press.

Perkin, H. (1989). *The rise of professional society: England since 1880.* London: Routledge Press.

Ringer, F. (1979). *Education and Society in Modern Europe*. Bloomington: Indiana University Press.

Scudamore, C. (1976). *The social background of pupils at the Bridge Street Higher Grade School*. Birmingham: MEd. Thesis, University of Birmingham, UK.

Seaborne, M. and R. Lowe (1977). *The English school: its architecture and organisation, 1870–1970*. London: Routledge and Kegan Paul.

Thernstrom, S. (1964). *Poverty and progress*. New York: Athenaeum Press.

Thernstrom, S. (1973). *The other Bostonians*. Cambridge, MA: Harvard University Press.

Van Leeuwen, M.D.H. and I. Maas (1992). *Long-term social mobility in a European city: Berlin, 1835–1957*. Trento: Paper to the ISA Committee on Social Stratification, University of Trento.

# PART V

# CURRICULUM

## CHAPTER 10

# ETON IN INDIA
## The imperial diffusion of a Victorian educational ethic

J. A. Mangan

*History of Education*, 7, 2, 105–18, 1978

One important consequence of the Mutiny of 1857 for Imperial India was the reassessment of British policy towards the Indian States. Annexation of territory, formerly popular in the interests of the salutary dispersal of sober British role, was now abandoned. The Marquis of Dalhousie's[1] unfortunate annexation of Oudh, a major cause of the Mutiny, was vivid in the memory. There was, in addition, a new awareness of 'the value of the princes' cooperation, and the hold which they still had upon their subjects'.[2] On the one hand, dispossessed royalty, such as the Rani of Jhansi, Begam Hazrat Mahal, Queen Regent of Oudh, and the notorious Nana Sahib, had proved ferocious leaders of the Indian peasant in the struggle against imperialism. On the other, sovereigns like Sindhia of Gwalior, Halkar at Indore and the Nawab of Bhopal had remained steadfastly loyal to the British and thereby made the task of reconquest easier.[3] The lesson seemed clear. In the interests of continued dominion traditional rulers had to be wooed, rather than spurned. There was a further imperative: the need to resist external aggression. A Russian invasion of the sub-continent seemed a real possibility at this time. Loyal Indian States would be useful buffers in such an event.

Symbolic of the change in attitude towards the States was the issue of special 'sanads' of adoption to the major princes by Dalhousie's successor, Lord Canning, Governor-General from 1856 to 1862. On the express condition of loyalty to the Crown, these sanctioned once more the traditional right to adopt an heir. Dalhousie had forbidden adoption in those States dependent on the East India Company. These had then lapsed to the British, which gave rise to understandable resentment, suspicion and insecurity among the indigenous rulers and their subjects. Canning's action meant, in effect, that the India of 1858 became petrified and the result was a 'conglomeration of seven hundred States covering two-fifths of the peninsular, and varying in size from Haidarabad...larger in size than Great Britain, to some tiny Orissan State of a few hundred acres'.[4] In his action, also, was to be found the origin of the policy of 'indirect rule' which spread with the imperial flag and saved men, money and effort. Significantly, its chief apologist in later years, Sir Alfred Lyall, was at this time an influential Indian civil servant.[5]

It was too much, however, to expect stern, ethnocentric moralists like Sir John Lawrence, who became Viceroy[6] in 1864, to abandon a long-held belief in the need to raise the standards of rulers and people. And it was certainly too dangerous to allow the States complete independence from British Rule. The British, while interfering as little as possible and demonstrating their goodwill by such gestures as the reintroduction of the principle of adoption, retained their control. A British Resident was appointed to the principal States as an adviser. The government kept to itself the absolute right to control administration when, in its judgement, cases of gross misrule occurred, to maintain ministers in office, to regulate succession and to depose unsatisfactory rulers. The principle of intervention was eventually given written expression in 1875 in the judgement on the case of Baroda, where the British arrested and deposed the tyrannical ruler, Malkar Rao Gaekwar:

> If gross misgovernment be permitted, if substantial justice be not done...if life and property be not protected, or if the general welfare of the country and people be persistently neglected, the British Government will assuredly intervene.[7]

The Indian States were neither feudatories, protectorates, nor allies, and to explain their curious status a new word – paramountcy – was employed.[8] The combination of imperial seduction and coercion worked. The Indian royal families remained staunch supporters of British rule until independence;[9] for as one Indian commentator has written, 'as long as they danced to the imperial tune, they enjoyed security without struggle'.[10]

During the Mutiny it was not only royalty who had influence. On the outbreak of hostilities in 1857 the tenant farmers of Oudh followed their former landlords with enthusiasm on to the battlefields of Upper India against the imperial forces.[11] The British concluded that the peasantry preferred life under their frequently oppressive local squirarchy, which had been dispossessed by the Benthamite liberals of the East India Company in the years before 1857, to freedom to own their own land. In the changes which followed the Mutiny, therefore, the aristocracy was not overlooked. The Government set about reestablishing the land-owning class, so laboriously disestablished in the pre-Mutiny years. *Zamindars* in Bengal, *sirdars* in the Punjab, *talukdars* in Oudh and *mulquzars* in the Central Provinces, now found themselves in favour. They were appeased, courted and ultimately given a part in local administration.

There was paradox in all this. In the 'orientalization'[12] of British rule in the years after 1857, imperial values were to remain distinctly superior, and were diffused with total conviction. Expedience might dictate political compromise but observation demanded moral indoctrination. By a process of unceasing reiteration, the British had convinced themselves by now of their civilizing role. The idea of a Messianic mission had become detached from the multiplicity of motives which had brought them to India,[13] and had been elevated to the level of an exclusive rationale. The imperialists were sure of their own moral strength; firm in the conviction of oriental moral infirmity; certain of the gifts of character they had to bestow. To the confident and uncomprehending European eye, Indian culture in its many guises, often appeared degenerate, lascivious, revolting and cruel.

The ultimate contribution of the benevolent imperial despot, therefore, was to bring the indigenous peoples of India to moral maturity:

> It was a message carved in granite, hewn out of the rock of doom.[14]

Curiously, one tangible symbol of both political expedience and moral conviction was the creation of a system of 'public schools' for royalty and nobility. The ideological purpose behind this step was quite unambiguous. By means of this system the British hoped to win over some, at least, of the traditionally influential minority and so succour a band of political evangelists sympathetic to the gubernatorial standards of the imperial race.[15]

The establishment of public schools was equally an attempt at 'indirect rule'. This aspiration is well described by Captain F. K. M. Walter, the agent of the Bharatpur Agency, in his annual report of 1869–70:

> I think we ought in future, without fear of consequences on the score of prejudice or misinterpretation of our intentions, to insist upon the youth (of Indian royalty) being brought up as a gentleman should be. But to carry this into effect we must first establish an Eton in India...If we desire to raise the chiefs of India to the standard which they must attain in order to keep pace with the ever advancing spirit of the age, if we wish to make clear to them that our only object is to perpetuate their dynasties and to make them worthy feudatories of the crown of England, we must place within their reach, greater facilities for bestowing on their sons a better education than they can possibly now attain. Then and not till then can we hope to see the native princes of India occupying the position they ought to hold as the promoters of peace, prosperity and progress among their own peoples and hearty supporters of British authority.[16]

Later Lord Curzon spelt out the requirements of the Indian States in more detail:

> Young Chiefs...to learn the English language, and become sufficiently familiar with English customs, literature, science, modes of thought, standards of truth and honour, and...with manly English sports and games...[17]

These alumni, Curzon added, while not forgetting their own heritage, would proudly acquire in their own public schools the attractive physical, moral and executive accomplishments of the English gentleman to the lasting benefit of their subjects.[18] It was a theme, taken up again and again by Viceroys in the remaining decades of the century. Prize Days at Mayo College, eventually the most famous of the schools, saw them regularly preaching the necessity of 'English habits of thought and action'.[19]

In time two grades of public school emerged, the one for the leading and the other for the lesser, chiefs and nobles. Five major 'Chiefs Colleges', as the first grade schools were known, were eventually established: Rajkumar College (1870), Rajkot, for Kathiawar and later all the Bombay Presidency, Mayo College (1872), Ajmere, for Rajputana, Rajkumar College (1872) at Nowgong for Bundelkhand,[20] Daly College (1876), Indore, for Central India and Aitchison College (1886) at Lahore for the Punjab.[21]

By virtue of their preeminence the first grade colleges were the cynosure of government attention. Consequently their development is more fully documented than the lesser institutions which included such schools as the Talukdari School at Sadra in Gujarat and the schools for Girasias at Wadhwan and Gondal, all in the Bombay Presidency, a school for the descendants and relatives of the Nawab of Murshidabad in Bengal, Colvin School, Lucknow in the United Provinces, Rajkumar College in Raipur[22] in the Central Provinces and Nizam College in Hyderabad. The Chiefs Colleges also served as models for the less august schools and concentration in the following pages on the four colleges at Rajkot, Ajmere,

Indore and Lahore[23] will provide insight into the early evolution of the Indian public school.

All four colleges were subject to the general control of the Indian Government and each was governed by a Council or Committee, responsible for general administration and made up of distinguished British and Indian members. For example Mayo College Council comprised:

President:        His Excellency, the Viceroy
Vice-President:   The Hon'ble Agent to the Governor-General of Rajputana
Members:          The Commissioner of Ajmere Seventeen Chiefs of Rajputana.
                  The political officers to the several States
Secretary:        The Principal of the College[24]

As regards the day to day organization of the schools, in the early years Mayo and Aitchison Colleges divided internal control between a military officer (the Principal at Mayo, the Governor at Aitchison) and a European headmaster. In both schools the officer held overall responsibility for administration while the headmaster was

*Table 10.1* Finance*

| College | Rs |
| --- | --- |
| *Mayo College* | |
| Interest | 25,488 |
| Govt. contribution | 12,000 |
| Nat. states | 4,728 |
| Other receipts | 5,610 |
| | 47,826 |
| *Aitchison College* | |
| Fees (Nat. states) | 36,629 |
| Govt. grant | 9,000 |
| Interest | 8,256 |
| Other receipts | 5,862 |
| | 59,747 |
| *Rajkot College* | |
| Fees and misc. receipts | 44,000 |
| Interest | 9,000 |
| Govt. grant in aid** | 5,000 |
| | 58,000 |
| *Daly College* | |
| Fees | 13,941 |
| Interest | 850 |
| Rent*** | 2,520 |
| | 17,311 |

Notes:
In 1903 the exchange rate for the rupee against £1 sterling was 15 rupees.
  * *Progress of Education in India, Fourth Quinquennial Review 1897–98 to 1901–02* (1904), 186.
  ** Grant in aid varied between Rs 3,000 and Rs 5,000.
  *** Paid by Principal, students and Holkar House.

responsible for the teaching. At Rajkot and Daly Colleges on the other hand, the European headmaster (the Principal) was the sole official in charge during the whole period of British administration of India.

While the colleges were certainly founded on the initiative of the British,[25] they were financed initially by large contributions to endowment funds by the native chiefs themselves as well as by less considerable government support. And, as numbers increased, the Indian royalty and nobility gave generously to provide extra classrooms, houses and sports facilities. By 1903 the financial arrangements of the colleges were as described in Table 10.1.

As may be seen clearly from Table 10.1, fees made up the bulk of annual revenue in all the colleges except Mayo, where the munificence of the Chiefs' endowment fund made this unnecessary. The fees were paid by the individual State or the estate of the family and were generally determined by the political officer according to means. The cost of educating individual pupils was by no means standardized as in the public schools of England, and could vary considerably.[26] There were also substantial differences in educational costs between the four colleges:

| | |
|---|---|
| *Mayo* | *Aitchison* |
| Rs 4,300 (Ruling chief) | Rs 1,250 ave. (Moslems) |
| Rs 2,940 (Wealthy Thakur) | Rs 1,300 ave. (Hindus) |
| Rs 780 (ordinary boy with horse) | |
| *Rajkot* | *Daly* |
| From Rs 5,000 to 2,200 (no details) | Rs 2,250[a] |

Note:
a *Progress of Education in India, Fourth Quinquennial Review 1897–98 to 1901–02* (1904), 186.

The salaries of the staff at the various schools reflected both the relative wealth of the institutions and interesting differences in the assessment of professional worth as Table 10.2, clearly demonstrates.

In the internal organization of the schools, the British clung faithfully to the familiar educational blueprint which served their own upper classes so well. For example, throughout the late nineteenth century the Mayo timetable set out below was virtually indistinguishable from its British counterpart.

| *Mayo College Timetable* | |
|---|---|
| 6.15 a.m. | First morning bell |
| 7.00 a.m. | Roll-call (taken by monitors) |
| 7.00 a.m.–7.30 a.m. | Morning P.T. |
| 7.30 a.m.–8.30 a.m. | Prayers and preparation |
| 8.30 a.m.–10.00 a.m. | Breakfast |
| 10.00 a.m.–1.00 p.m. | Classes |
| 1.00 p.m.–2.00 p.m. | Recess (free time) |
| 2.00 p.m.–4.00 p.m. | Classes |
| 4.00 p.m.–6.00 p.m. | Recreation |
| 6.00 p.m.–7.30 p.m. | Prayers and evening meal |
| 7.30 p.m.–8.30 p.m. | Preparation |
| (Wednesdays and Saturdays were half holidays)[a] | |

Note:
a Ian Malcolm, *Indian Problems and Pictures* (1907), 65.

*Table 10.2* Salaries of staff*

| College | Rs |
| --- | --- |
| *Mayo College* | |
| Principal* | 1,250 |
| Headmaster* | 500 |
| 9 Assistant Masters | 50–150 |
| 3 Drill Instructors | 27 (ave.) |
| Total annual cost of staff and establishment | 41,500 |
| *Aitchison College* | |
| Governor** | 400 |
| Principal** | 500–50–1,000 |
| Vice-Principal** | 400 |
| 4 Assistant Masters | 50–100 |
| Science Master | 70 |
| Drawing Master | 75 |
| 3 Oriental Teachers | 30–60 |
| Gymnastic Instructor | 25 |
| 2 boarding house Musahibs | 40 |
| Assistant Musahib and Riding Master | 35 |
| Assistant Musahib | 25 |
| Total etc. | 33,000 |
| *Rajkot College* | |
| Principal* | 1,166 |
| Chief Ass. Master | 250 |
| 8 Assistant Masters | 50–100 |
| Cricket coach | 75 |
| Gym Teacher | 50 |
| Riding Master | 15 |
| Total etc. | 35,424 |
| *Daly College* | |
| Principal** | 750–50–1,000 |
| Superintendant | 180 |
| 4 Assistant Masters | 30–100 |
| Riding Master | 35 |
| Drill Instructor | 10 |
| Total etc. | 24,000 |

*Notes:*
  i  Most of the Indian masters had low educational qualifications; a few however, were graduates of Indian universities.
  ii  For the value of the rupee against £1 sterling see Table 10.1.
  *  *Progress of Education in India, Fourth Quinquennial Review 1897–98 to 1901–02* (1904), 183.
  **  European staff.

Then there were boarding houses, housemasters and tutors. In the early years, however, the shortage of European staff ensured that the house system was not quite as in England. Houses were supervised, not by English housemasters, but by musahibs or motamids, native staff who were rarely teaching staff. They were responsible for such matters as tidiness and general behaviour. There were ten houses at Mayo, organized on a territorial basis. At Rajkot there were two houses, wings of the main building, and the boys simply took rooms as they became available. The arrangements at Daly were similar and Rajputs, Kalthis and Moslems were mixed together in four houses. At Aitchison on the other hand, the three houses were for Moslems, Hindus and Scholars respectively. As at Eton, private tutors were a feature of the schools. Their role, influence and numbers, however, varied from college to college. They served as instruments of British rule. In all cases they had to be approved by the Government, and were frequently selected by political officers. Occasionally, when the pupil's status merited it, they were Englishmen.

The character of the academic work in the schools was similar to that of the state high school, and in several respects not unlike their English model. Details of a typical week's work is set out in Table 10.3.

English was a vital element in the curriculum in all the Colleges as Table 10.3 illustrates. Differences of ability, and motivation and facility with English meant that the pupils completed their studies at varying speeds. At Mayo it took about eight years to complete the curriculum and pupils remained from about the age of ten to eighteen. At Rajkot six or seven years were sufficient to complete the course and pupils arrived at eleven and remained until their late teens. Aitchison pupils spent between eight and ten years at their studies, arriving at eleven and often remaining until they were in their early twenties. At Daly ten years was the usual period in residence: pupils arrived at between eleven and seventeen and remained until their mid-twenties.

Academic standards in the schools left much to be desired.[27] This was the result of professional complacency on the part of the staff and idleness on the part of both masters and pupils. Much of the curriculum was of dubious relevance to the education of Indian princes, the English teaching was not as thorough as it might have been and general studies suffered from a want of definition of aim. There were further reasons for the poor intellectual standard. These were described boldly by a Mr E. Giles, education inspector of the Bombay Northern Division, in a report on Mayo College. He found a tendency to idleness and indifference

*Table 10.3* A typical week's work[a]

| Subject | Mayo | | Aitchison | Rajkot | Daly |
|---|---|---|---|---|---|
| | 1st Class | 2nd, 3rd Classes | 1st, 2nd Classes | 1st, 2nd, 3rd Classes | 1st, 2nd, 3rd Classes |
| English | 9 | 15 | 9 | 9 | 6 |
| Vernacular language | — | — | — | 6 | 4 |
| Class language | $4\frac{1}{2}$ | $4\frac{1}{2}$ | $2\frac{1}{2}$ | — | — |
| Maths | $10\frac{1}{2}$ | $4\frac{1}{2}$ | 7 | 5 | 8 |
| History | — | $4\frac{1}{2}$ | 3 | 5 | 6 |
| Geography | — | $4\frac{1}{2}$ | 3 | 5 | 2 |
| Science | 9 | $4\frac{1}{2}$ | $2\frac{1}{2}$ | 4 | — |
| Drawing | — | — | $1\frac{1}{2}$ | — | — |
| Total (in hours) | 33 | 33 | 25 | 29 | 26 |

*Note:*
a *Progress of Education in India, Fourth Quinquennial Review 1897–98 to 1901–02* (1904), 187.

due to the lack of necessity to learn, pupils' prolonged absences from the college (they were dilatory about returning at the end of vacations) and antagonism towards the school in the boys' homes.[28]

He was not unduly dispirited, however, by this state of affairs. He reminded his readers that, in estimating the value of the institution as a whole, attention ought to be directed 'not so much to what pupils learn as to what they are'. And he was greatly impressed by their admirable training in discipline, truth, manliness and uprightness, which sent out the boys 'honest and straightforward gentlemen, who may become worthy rulers of their own people, and the loyal and enlightened subjects of the Empire'.[29] In short, Giles' sense of proportion was due to the fact that, while a certain casualness represented the schools' approach to intellectual matters, there was one area in which thoroughness was most evident – character training for leadership. In this connection, as in the English public school, the games field was the instrument of achievement.[30] Offended by the frequently vicious idleness of the native ruler, the British wished above all to develop physical and moral robustness in the allegedly effete sons of chief and noble.[31] The *Report of the Commission on Indian Education* of 1883, for example, stated that it was not, of course, desired to make the young chiefs great scholars, but to encourage in them a healthy tone and manly habits.[32]

Morality, as every English schoolboy of the period was aware, grew out of muscular effort! Thus it was written of the Rajkumar College at Rajkot that...'the promoters and founders of this institution deliberately selected the English Public School system as its model and sought to reproduce its most salient features here'. This meant closely following the lines of an English public school on athletic matters to which the English sensibly attached a great deal of importance.[33] One devoted Old Boy wrote admiringly of his college, 'The moral value of properly organized games is strongly upheld by the (European) teacher of all grades'.[34] And it is true that the ideal of manliness was patiently pursued in all the schools by generations of public school masters imported from England for the purpose.[35]

In an Indian setting, these men built up the facilities, encouraged the mannerisms, enacted the rituals and created the symbols of the English public school. No one is a more apt archetype than Chester Macnaghten (1843–1896), the now forgotten 'pioneer of the public-school education of the feudatory chiefs'.[36] Macnaghten came from a family with a long history of service in India.[37] After an English education he returned to the sub-continent in 1867 and became, initially, tutor to the son of the Maharajah of Darbhanga, and then in 1870, principal (headmaster) of Rajkumar College in Kathiawar, the first of the Chiefs schools. It may be said fairly that he took to heart the words of Sir James Peile[38] pronounced at the opening ceremony:

> We shall discipline their bodies in the manliness and hardihood of the English public schoolboy.[39]

Macnaghten attached 'the utmost value to games as a training in character'.[40] In his view they developed 'energy, promptitude, judgement, watchfulness, courage, generous emulation, appreciation of the merits of others and the highest standards of truthfulness and duty'.[41] In short, he taught his boys the value of manly exercise because it was conducive to manliness – an explicit moral condition. He liked to read his Indian princes the passage from *Tom Brown's Schooldays* in which the

Captain of the Eleven (Tom Brown himself) kept his team steady and faced his work bravely in a match crisis. On one occasion Macnaghten followed the reading of the extract with the exhortation:

> In hours so spent you will learn lessons such as no school instruction can give – the lessons of self-reliance, calmness and courage, and of many other excellent qualities, which will better fit you to discharge the duties and face the difficulties, which the future must bring.[42]

Macnaghten was a typical late Victorian public school headmaster, homilist and athlete. He gave the standard addresses on Duty, Courage, Zeal and *Esprit de Corps* and clung to the common belief of the time that moral and physical improvement were more remarkable than the mental; because though scholarship was important, behaviour was far more so.[43] In implementing his games system, he appears to have possessed the pragmatism of G. E. L. Cotton of Marlborough together with the idealism of Hely Hutchinson Almond of Loretto. As *The Times* reported, 'He (Macnaghten) introduced education on the lines of the English public school model for the sons of chiefs who did not want it, and who clung tenaciously to their old traditions'.[44] His pupils were fractious and unenthusiastic; they viewed each other with the open hostility of traditional enemies.[45] Like Cotton, therefore, he used games as an expedient to create order out of disorder. Eventually he established an amiable and enthusiastic climate in which 'boylike simplicity' ultimately prevailed, and in a spirit of comradeship, the school 'played cricket and rounders and football together'. To achieve this state of affairs, like Almond, he inspired both by example and precept: he constructed playing fields, gave their upkeep his constant attention, joined in all the boys' games and, as we have seen above, lectured them constantly on the moral value of exercise.

Macnaghten was no eccentric zealot. He was followed at Rajkot, for example, by C. W. Waddington, who was quite in the Macnaghten mould, 'sportsman, scholar and gentleman'.[46] His predilections are evident from a speech celebrating his virtues recorded in the impressive history of the early years of the school. After making the required, brief obeisances to Waddington's concern for academic standards, the speaker, a local ruler, thrust to the heart of the matter:

> Not neglecting the progress of the Kumars in their studies, Mr Waddington was unremitting in his exertions to bring the Cricket of the College up to the mark from the time when he was placed in sole charge of the Institution, and his labours were crowned with well merited success.

All this was in pursuit of moral excellence, as the same speaker made clear:

> ...it is often in the playground that the schoolmaster's greatest triumphs are won...It is on the cricket ground that a master gets to know the boy as he is out of school, becomes acquainted with his character and has perhaps the most favourable opportunities of moulding that character as he desires. Mr Waddington, himself an expert at all games and sports, has from the first recognised their educational value.[47]

Waddington's successor at Rajkot was J. C. Mayne,[48] another enthusiastic and able sportsman, who joined with his Kumars in all their games and sports. Mayne wrote for the college the obligatory, moralistic song of the period – so typical that it slips smoothly over the edge of banality.

> Here many a happy year we spent.
> Here many friendships made;
> And school-boy friends are life-long friends
> Through sunshine and through shade.
>
> We owe her these – and more beside
> That none can e'er repay –
> The lesson we have daily learnt
> In classroom and at play.

Headmasters such as Macnaghten, Waddington and Mayne were loyally supported by their assistant masters. An outstanding (and tragic) example was Francis John Portman,[49] who excelled in running, tennis, cricket and racquets. Conscientious to a fault, he quite literally ran himself to death racing with his Kumars before breakfast during their training for the school sports – an ill-advised activity for a European in the Indian climate. The English public school fraternity saw only nobility in his devotion to duty:

> Young India needs training in the spirit of chivalrous manhood, and that is exactly what her sons have learnt from contact with Francis Portman.[50]

The eventual success of Macnaghten and his proselytizing successors in smoothly translating an educational ethic from England to India, may be estimated from complementary sources. The first is a photograph of the Mayo College cricket eleven of 1906,[51] who gaze out upon the world in their elegant striped blazers and immaculate white flannels with the calm self-confidence that membership of a public school eleven brought, in those halcyon times, to boys, who were physically talented as well as wealthy and well-born. The second is this assessment of Mayo College at the same period by a local inspector of schools:

> On the whole, the instruction given throughout the classes appeared to be careful and thorough ... In the games there was every indication of keenness and proficiency, and I do not think that the most captious critic would have any fault to find with the general arrangements for recreation and physical instruction, which are in my opinion admirable. The boarding houses appear to be excellently managed, and the whole college, with its large numbers, approaches more nearly to the model of a good English public school than any institution I have seen in India. I have only to add that, throughout the college, the manners and bearing of the boys are excellent. They appear to be gentlemen in every sense of the word.[52]

At about the same time, Ian Malcolm, a visiting journalist from England, found, to his delight, at the school, 'three cricket and football elevens, each with a capital ground' and wrote magnanimously, 'it would be difficult to have a prettier cricket field than the match ground, with its views of trees and distant mountains'.[53] The facilities, he further discovered, included a racquet court, lawn tennis courts, a running track and a gymnasium. A quintette of energetic English games masters ensured there was not a loafer in the place! Malcolm concluded complacently, '... in the matter of public schools, India is following closely in the footsteps of England'.[54]

The arrogance of the British inception was enormous. Ancient Indian educational practices and long-established hedonism ensured that the relatively spartan, games-orientated public life was viewed by many upper class Indians as a most unpalatable alien oddity. Both Hindu and Moslem possessed their own educational systems long before the arrival of the British.[55] Schools of learning were dutifully supported by rulers, nobles, the wealthy and the religious. These were to be found in mosques, temples, in the open air and in the homes of the rich. Pupils entered at the age of twelve and continued to study for a period of up to twelve years. The teaching was predominantly oral and the discipline exceedingly harsh.[56] While Hindu schools concentrated on the teaching of literature, law and logic, the Moslem schools, for their part, taught forms of correspondence, legal processes and Persian and Arabic.[57]

It is not at all clear, however, how many of the leading chiefs and nobles took advantage of the indigenous education prior to, and during the British occupation of India.[58] But several authorities have expressed a poor opinion of the attitude to education of the offspring of the more powerful princes and aristocrats. One British observer wrote of the Indian princeling:

> From his boyhood everything about him combines to thrust education into the background. The influence of the zenana (that part of the house in India reserved for the women) is generally opposed to any enlightenment. Early marriage brings with it hindrances and distractions... in some cases hereditary instinct leads him to regard education as scarcely better than a disgrace![59]

An even harsher critic of the local prince was the Anglophile Indian, Narullah Khan, an old boy of Mayo College and a Cambridge graduate. He wrote caustically of the education of royalty before the coming of the Raj: 'a great deal may be said but not of a pleasing nature'.[60] It was, he explained, in the hands of hereditary servants, called durbaries, neither educated nor enlightened, who supplied only flattery. Others were of a similar opinion. Major R. H. Keatinge considered a prince's education comprised exclusively of 'ruinous habits' from contact with slaves, opium eaters, drunkards and fawning, self-interested native tutors.[61] In consequence, it has been argued that despite British efforts to set up schools for their benefit 'the cadets of the aristrocratic and opulent Indian families were frequently brought up to lead idle lives'.[62] Certainly, while some indigenous leaders proved enthusiastic supporters of the Chiefs Colleges,[63] many were indifferent or antipathetic towards them. It was noted frankly in the Fifth Quinquennial Review: 'On the whole the Colleges have not been cordially supported by the distinguished class for whose benefits they are maintained'.[64] By the turn of the century after some twenty years in existence, the schools could only muster between 180 and 190 pupils between them.[65] At Mayo College, which drew on a possible clientele of eighteen ruling chiefs and three hundred aristocratic families, the situation was hardly reassuring:

| Places available | Numbers at school | Highest number at one time |
| --- | --- | --- |
| 150 | 50 | 80[a] |

Note:
a  Sir Thomas Raleigh, *Lord Curzon in India: Being a Selection from his Speeches as Viceroy and Governor General 1898–1905* (1906), 251.

The college roll from 1875 to 1895 reveals how unsatisfactory the response had been down the years:

| 1875–6 | 1876–7 | 1877–8 | 1878–9 | 1879–80 | 1880–81 | 1881–2 | 1882–3 | 1883–4 | 1884–5 |
|---|---|---|---|---|---|---|---|---|---|
| 23 | 31 | 39 | 37 | 32 | 45 | 62 | 62 | 68 | 74 |
| 1885–6 | 1886–7 | 1887–8 | 1888–9 | 1889–90 | 1890–91 | 1891–2 | 1892–3 | 1893–4 | 1894–5 |
| 80 | 76 | 71 | 70 | 79 | 73 | 68 | 63 | 57 | 68[a] |

Note:
a Herbert Sherring, Mayo College, Ajmere 'The Eton of India': A Record of Twenty Years 1875–1895 (1897), I, 161.

Both the low numbers and the status of entrants produced disappointment. In 1897, for example, it was noted with acute regret: 'As regards rank and numbers, the chief drawbacks are that no heirs or ruling chief from the three first class States of Udaipur, Jodhpur or Jaipur has attended the College, nor has any prince or *thakur* been entered from the States of Bundi or Dungapur.'[66] By 1902 the Viceroy, Lord Curzon, was complaining that only twelve out of thirty-two ruling chiefs of Kathiawar had been educated at Rajkot.[67] It was no better elsewhere. Most chiefs of the Punjab failed to send their sons to Aichison College and Daly College never received the sons of the larger central States such as Gwalior, Bhopal and Dewa. A state of affairs which earned the families concerned a public rebuke from the Viceroy.[68]

Self-respect as well as self-indulgence no doubt played its part in the widespread rejection of English upper class education.[69] And the crude ethnocentricism of the education – drill, gymnastics and cricket would scarcely have impressed the traditional Hindu and Moslem – must have had its effect; but there were other important reasons for lack of support. By the turn of the century complaints about standards in the colleges circulated widely.[70] Curzon was therefore, under no illusion about the chiefs' dissatisfaction with the high cost and general irrelevance of the education provided there. He shared much of this dissatisfaction himself and felt compelled to usher in reforms.[71] They included more European staff attracted by greatly increased salaries, the introduction of political economy, political science and elementary law and revenue into the curriculum, a leaving examination and a diploma, the introduction of regular inspections, the abolition of dual command at Mayo and Aichison, the abolition of the system of private tutors and the allocation of boarding houses to European house masters.

Curzon's aims were several – to improve academic standards, to make the curriculum more relevant to the needs of future Indian rulers and at the same time to make the colleges even more like the English public school and thus raise their tone. It appears that his efforts were remarkably successful. One of Curzon's actions in 1903 was to reduce Daly College to the status of a feeder college for Ajmere, yet his reforms improved things so much that in 1905, at the request of the local chiefs, who provided the land and much of the money, Daly was enlarged and raised once more to the level of a major college.[72] Again, on the introduction of Curzon's reforms Mayo College immediately increased its intake. By 1912 numbers at the colleges had risen to a total of 413.[73] A large building programme was mounted and there was a considerable expansion of facilities. In 1921 a fifth college, Raipur, was admitted to the ranks of Chiefs Colleges. In 1928 Aichison College announced that it had been in full working existence for forty-one years, had amassed many public school traditions and now considered itself sufficiently established to aspire to a proper register of its old alumni.[74] Shortly afterwards Mayo College claimed to be 'widely supported by Ruling Chiefs ... The attendance of Ruling Princes and Old Boys at the recent prize gathering was, except for the jubilee celebrations, a record and is a happy augury for the future'.[75] It is clear from statistics and statements such as those above that the system of public schools in India was now established. Against the odds the British had persisted. They had planted in tropical soil a foreign seed, which slowly grew into a sturdy miniature of a much larger English plant.[76]

The Indian public school, was created out of a hotch potch of Victorian motives – imperial calculation, ethnocentric self-confidence and well-meaning benevolence. It is interesting to reflect on the possible course of events had the British courted the urban professional, industrialist and entrepreneur, the backbone of the nationalist movement, as sedulously as it attempted to win over the royalty and aristocracy, and had established a larger system of public schools embracing academic, merchant, landlord and prince. Even in its more socially restricted form, however, the early Indian public school system provides a fascinating illustration of the cultural diffusion of an educational ethic arising out of imperial conquest. And in only gently modified form it has survived the imperialist.[77]

## Notes

1 Sir James Andrew Brown (1812–1860); educated at Harrow and Oxford; tenth Earl and first Marquis of Dalhousie; Governor-General of India 1847–1856. Annexations during his period as Governor-General included, an addition to Oudh, Lower Burma, Nagpur and Jhansi.

2 E. Thompson and G. T. Garratt, *Rise and Fulfilment of British Rule in India* (1934), 468.

3 Thomas R. Metcalfe, *The aftermath of Revolt: India 1857–1870* (1965), 219–26.

4 Thompson and Garratt, op. cit., 468.

5 Sir Alfred Comyn Lyall (1835–1911); educated at Eton and Haileybury; held various posts in the Indian civil service. His *Rise of the British Dominion in India* was first published in 1893. The third edition (1915) contains the following significant passage:

> . . . the true frontier of the British dominion in Asia . . . does not by any means tally with the outer edge of the immense territory over which we exercise administrative jurisdiction . . . The true frontier includes not only this territory, but also large regions over which the English crown has established protectorates of different kinds and grades, varying according to circumstances and specific conditions . . . whatever may be the particular class to which the protectorate belongs, however faint may be the shadow of authority that we chose to throw over the land, its object is to affirm the right of excluding a rural influence and the right of exclusion carries with it the duty of defence. The outer limits of the country we are prepared to defend must be called our frontier.
>
> (328–9)

Interestingly, Lyall laid the foundation stone of Mayo College, Ajmere in 1878.

6 The title, Governor-General, was changed to Viceroy after the Mutiny.

7 Quoted in R. C. Majumbar, *The History and Culture of the Indian People*, IX (1963), 966.

8 Sayid Ghulam Mustafa, *English Influences on Indian Society*, unpublished MEd Thesis, University of Durham. This is a massive (522 pages), elegant and erudite work written by a Muslim Indian educated at an Indian public school. It provides one Indian's view of the Westernisation of the Indian upper classes.

9 Metcalfe, op. cit., 226.

10 Mustafa, op. cit., 208.

11 Metcalfe, op. cit., 136–7.

12 The term is usefully employed in G. Hutchins, *The Illusion of Permanence: British Imperialism in India* (1967), 154.

13 B. Parry, *Delusions and Discoveries: Studies on India in the British Imagination 1880–1930* (1972), 26. For a typical twentieth century example of such attitudes see James Halliday, *A Special India* (1968), 231–3. Halliday is the nom de plume of David Symington, Cheltenham, Oxford and I.C.S. (1926–1941).

14  Rev. J. Johnston, *Abstract and Analysis of the Report of the 'Indian Education Commission' with Notes and Recommendations in Full* (1884), 92.

15  Michael Edwardes, *High Noon of Empire: India under Curzon* (1965), 141.

16  Quoted in Surendra Mohan Mehta, *Public Schools in India*, unpublished MA Thesis, London University, 1961, 79–80.

17  Sir Thomas Raleigh, *Lord Curzon in India: Being a Selection from his Speeches as Viceroy and Governor General 1898–1905* (1906), 245.

18  Ibid., 246.

19  See, for example, Herbert Sherring, *Mayo College, Ajmere 'The Eton of India': A Record of Twenty Years 1875–1895* (1897), I, 181ff.

20  In 1898 Nowgong College amalgamated with Daly College, Indore.

21  Mayo, Daly and Aitchison Colleges were named after distinguished British administrators in India. The fourth Earl of Mayo (1822–1872) became Viceroy in 1869 and it is recorded in the *Dictionary of National Biography* (1886, VI, 23) 'he encouraged the establishment of colleges for the education of the sons and chiefs in the native states. The Mayo College at Ajmer and the Rajkumar College at Kathiawar were the result of his efforts'. Sir Henry Dermot Daly (1821–1895) after a distinguished military career in India, became Agent to the Governor-General for Central India at Indore in 1861 and worked for the establishment of the college there. Sir Charles Umpherston Aitchison (1832–1896) entered the Indian civil service in 1855; by 1882 he was Lieutenant-Governor of the Punjab and was largely responsible for the development of the Chiefs College at Lahore.

22  Raipur would appear to be the closest of the second grade colleges to the Chiefs Colleges. It was created for the sons of the Chhattisgarch Feudatory States and had 13 pupils in 1896. By 1902 numbers had risen to 22. It had a European headmaster – a mark of superior status. In 1921, in fact, it was recognized as a Chiefs College.

23  For reasons which are not wholly clear Nowgong received little attention in the literature about the schools at this time.

24  *Progress of Education in India, Fourth Quinquennial Review 1897–98 to 1901–02* (1904), 182.

25  For a detailed description of the origins of the college at Rajkot and the role of the British in its inception see, for example *Forty Years of the Rajkumar College 1870–1910* compiled by H. H. Sir Bhavsinhji, Maharaja of Bhavnagar, and prepared and abridged from the papers of the late Chester Macnaghten, II, 2ff. Curzon summed up the general situation as follows:

> It has become apparent that neither private tuition, nor the practices and institutions of Native States or territories, succeed altogether in giving the sons of Chiefs and Nobles, that all-round education, particularly in relation to character, that is admittedly the product of the English public school system. To many of the Indian nobility, the discovery has come slowly; to some perhaps it has not come at all. Nevertheless, of the general existence and steady growth of this feeling among the upper classes of Indian society, there can be no doubt, and it was partly to meet this demand, where it has existed, partly to anticipate it where it had yet not found expression, that Government has interested itself in the foundation of a small number of colleges, directly designed to provide a superior type of education for the sons of the princely and aristocratic families of India.
>
> (*Fourth Quinquennial Review*, op. cit., 181)

26  V. A. Stow in his *A Short History of Mayo College 1869–1942* tells of the Maharajah of Kotah, who in the early days of the college arrived with two hundred followers, for whom a special village was built, and of the Maharajah of Alwar, who had a stable of over twenty polo horses and four carriage horses!

27  *Fourth Quinquennial Review*, op. cit., 187.

28  Sherring, op. cit., 79ff.

29  Ibid., 86.

30  See J. A. Mangan, *Athleticism: A Comparative Study of the Emergence and Consolidation of an Education Ideology*, unpublished PhD Thesis, University of Glasgow, 1976.

31  *Cambridge History of India* (ed. H. H. Dodwell), VI, 34–6.

32  *Report of the Commission of Indian Education* (1883), 482.

33  Bhavsinhji, op. cit., I, 158.

34  Ibid., 159.

35  Three of these Indian public school headmasters were assistant masters at Marlborough at one time or other. F. A. Leslie-Jones was a Marlborough master from 1897 to 1904. He left to become Principal of Aitchison College and was subsequently Principal of Mayo College from 1917 to 1929. V. A. Stow was at Marlborough from 1905 to 1906 and was first Principal of Rajkumar College, Rajpur, and then for several years Principal of Mayo College. E. C. Marchant was at Marlborough from 1931 to 1938. In 1939 he became Principal of Daly College, Indore.

36  *The Times*, 11 May 1895, 5. Macnaghten taught cricket to the famous Indian batsman Ranjitsinhji, as the *Second Quinquennial Review* was quick to note as a point in the College's favour.

37  See the introduction by Robert Whitelaw to Macnaghten's *Common Thoughts on Serious Subjects: Addresses delivered between the years 1887–9 to the elder boys of Rajkumar College in Kathiawar* (1912, revised edition). These 'Addresses' were translated into native languages for use in state schools!

38  Sir James Peile (1833–1906) was a distinguished Indian administrator. He held a variety of posts in India including that of Director of Public Instruction, Bombay (1869–73) in which role he made his speech at the Rajkumar College, and that of Political Agent of Kathiawar (1874–78). He eventually became a member of the Indian Council in London (1887–1902).

39  *The Times*, 11 May 1895, 5.

40  Bhavasinhji, op. cit., I, 334.

41  Ibid.

42  Macnaghten, op. cit., XXII. Macnaghten wrote to one pupil 'for whom he feared': 'Be temperate and pure and do not be idle...Take plenty of outdoor exercise – riding, running, walking, cricket, lawn tennis, shooting...and begin the day with that'.

43  Ibid.

44  *The Times*, 11 May 1895, 5.

45  The anonymous author of 'a Run through Kathiawar' in *Blackwoods Magazine* of October 1876, furnished exotic details of sentries guarding the cricket pitch and wild-looking gentlemen sleeping close to their princes for fear of attack from traditional enemies.

46  Bhavasinhji, op. cit., I 410. Charles Willoughby Waddington (1865–1946) was educated at Charterhouse and Oxford. He became Vice-Principal of Rajkumar College, Rajkot in 1892 and Principal in 1896. In 1903 he was appointed Principal of Mayo College, Ajmere, a post he held until 1917.

47  Ibid., 409–10.

48  Ibid., 412. J. C. Mayne was educated at Tonbridge and Oxford. He taught at Brighton College from 1891 to 1898, then in several Indian schools before becoming Principal of Rajkot in 1903.

49  *Radleian*, 3 March 1906, 314.

50  Ibid.

51  Malcolm, op. cit., facing page 64.

52  *Fifth Quinquennial Review 1902–1907* (1909), 250–1.

53  Malcolm, op. cit., 65.

54  Ibid., p. 67. Clearly the earlier request of Captain Walter had been met namely, that the Indian public schools should be staffed by 'thoroughly educated English gentlemen not mere book worms but men fond of field sports and out of doors exercises'. (*Report of the Commission on Indian Education*, 451.)

55  Johnston, op. cit., 21–2. There is some controversy as to the extensiveness of the indigenous system, however, see for example Sir Philip Hartog, *Some Aspects of Indian Education, Past and Present* (1939), 3.

56  Syed Nurullah and J. P. Naik, *A History of Indian Education in India (During the British Period)* (1957, 2nd ed.), 38ff.

57  Majumbar, op. cit., 20–1.

58  Some were privately educated. Sir Syad Khan, for example, the famous Moslem educational reformer, came from an ancient family of Oudh and was educated at home. He was one of the first, incidentally, to recognize the inadequacies of the old Moslem educational practices for modern society and in 1875 established the College at Aligarh for the Moslem aristocracy. Mustapha, an old boy, claimed its purpose was to inculcate loyalty to British values (op. cit., 224–9). It was certainly run on the lines of an English

public school. How closely it resembled this institution may be seen from Wilfred Scawen Blunt, who, in his report of a visit in 1883, enthused over both the public school image and the facilities created for its implementation. He was more than satisfied to find the boys playing cricket under the benevolent tyranny of a sporting master (*India under Reform: A Private Diary* (1909), 156).

59   Johnston, op. cit., 83. Bahavasinhji with first hand knowledge stated that large numbers were uneducated (op. cit., (Vol. II) 3).
60   Narullah Khan, *The Ruling Chiefs of Western India and the Rajkumar College* (1898), 8.
61   Bhavasinhji, op. cit., Richard Harte Keatinge (1825–1904) was educated at private schools in Dublin. He joined the Bombay Artillery in 1842. After a distinguished military career during which he won the V.C. in the Mutiny, he held a number of civil posts including Political Agent at Kathiawar and later, Chief Commissioner, Central Provinces. He was one of the early advocates of the Chiefs Colleges.
62   *Cambridge History of India*, VI, 346.
63   There are numerous instances of individual support by Indian royalty but perhaps the most exotic is the visits to his palace, some distance from the school, arranged by the Maharaja of Bhavnagar for the whole of Rajkumar College. He supplied his own trains for the journey! He was, incidentally, the first, and for some time the only pupil at the College and arrived by elephant on the opening day.
64   *Fourth Quinquennial Review*, op. cit., 181.
65   Raleigh, op. cit., 251.
66   Ibid.
67   Raleigh, op. cit., 244.
68   Ibid., 253.
69   In her study of Bengal in *Education and Social Change: Three Studies on Nineteenth Century India*, Vina Majumdar points out that the richer classes clung to their own culture and were far from keen to give their children an English education. Only when the large size of the family or declining returns from the land reduced their wealth so that the sons had to earn a living, were they sent to schools run on English lines.
70   For example, His Highness the Gaekwar of Baroda criticised the standards of the schools in *East and West* in January 1902. His criticisms were reproduced in the *Voice of India* and synopsized in the *Kathiawar Times*.
71   Curzon called a Conference at Calcutta in 1902 to discuss the reform of the constitution and curriculum of the Chiefs Colleges. It lasted four days and was attended by the principal political officers, representatives of the native chiefs and the heads of existing colleges. There was a further Conference at Ajmere in 1904. The reformation of the colleges followed.
72   Raleigh, op. cit., 234ff.
73   *Sixth Quinquennial Review* 1907–1912 (1914), 227.
74   *Aitchison Chiefs College: Old Boys Register* (1928), i.
75   *Report of the Mayo College, Ajmer for 1932–33*, Appendix F.
76   By 1970 there were some twenty-seven public schools in India.
77   For a statement of the ideals of the Indian public school in the second half of the twentieth century, see *The Indian Public School. Essays Outlining the Aims of Members of the Indian Public Schools Conference* (1942).

## CHAPTER 11

# CATHOLIC INFLUENCE AND THE SECONDARY SCHOOL CURRICULUM IN IRELAND, 1922–1962

Thomas A. O'Donoghue

*History of Education Review,* 28, 2, 16–29, 1999

Throughout the nineteenth century the Catholic Church expressed deep opposition to the great increase in state intervention in education internationally and it mounted resistance wherever possible. However, by the 1920s there was a small number of countries where it was satisfied with the school system. Ireland was one such country. Here a unique situation arose in that successive governments between the 1920s and the 1960s left management of the schools in the hands of their owners, namely, diocesan authorities and religious orders, while accepting financial responsibility for their operation. In return, the schools were obliged to provide a required number of school subjects and conform to requirements regarding facilities and teachers. This is the broad background to the following paper which arises out of a research project concerned with the manner and scope of Catholic Church influence over the secondary school curriculum in Ireland in the first four decades of Independence, namely, 1922–1962.

The chapter is in four parts. First, the general background is outlined. Second, four major propositions are detailed regarding how the Church pursued its interests through the secondary school curriculum. Third, an historical explanation for this situation is proposed. Finally, an overview of the major changes which have taken place in the secondary school curriculum in Ireland since 1962 is presented, with particular reference to changes which have taken place in the influence of the Church.

## General background

From the early days of the Tudor conquest, schooling in Ireland became intimately bound up with the process of colonisation, with the consequent ascendancy of the English language.[1] The Irish, however, maintained their Catholicism. By the mid-nineteenth century, the Church was a powerful interest group pressing its claims in educational matters with great tenacity. Its efforts, along with those of the Presbyterian Church and the (Anglican) Church of Ireland, ensured that the National schools, which had been intended to provide a multidenominational primary school education, were attended mainly by pupils from one particular denomination and managed by local clergymen.[2]

The Catholic Church, along with the other churches, also sought to keep the secondary schools free from State control. What evolved was a mechanism to support denominational schools which were privately owned, managed and staffed. The State provided no funds directly for the building or equipping of schools and it did not concern itself with their uneven distribution on geographical and social class lines. The qualifications, salaries and conditions of employment of secondary teachers were determined by individual managers and the teachers they employed.

In independent Ireland from 1924 onwards, the State's responsibility for almost all kinds of education outside of the universities was vested in a Minister for Education operating through a newly created Department of Education. Money was now paid to secondary schools as capitation grants for school maintenance and as increments of salary to recognised teachers in schools fulfilling certain conditions.[3] Provision was made also for a special bonus grant to schools in which the Irish language was the medium of instruction. As a condition for recognition, secondary schools had to employ a certain number of recognised teachers, each (if not a priest or a member of a religious order or teaching community) with a contract of employment and an entitlement to a minimum salary paid by the school manager. The Church was happy since the arrangement provided state subvention while preserving Church managerial control. The State, for its part, wanted no controversy with the Church. While the Department of Education inspected schools and exercised a certain degree of supervision through its powers to make grants to secondary schools as a result of inspection, it was not concerned with founding secondary schools or financing their building.

Two new examinations, the Intermediate Certificate Examination (taken at the end of a three year course) and the Leaving Certificate Examination (taken after another two years) were established, and became the focus of the secondary school curriculum. The notion that the curriculum should largely be concerned with the Gaelic development of pupils was central to the programmes for the examinations. This was a major departure from the lack of recognition given to the Irish language in the curriculum of pre-Independence days. Equally radical was that history and geography were now compulsory subjects and that they had an Irish orientation. A national programme of religious instruction for secondary schools which was prescribed by the Irish bishops was also operative and the teaching of it was inspected by each diocese's own religious inspector. These inspectors, who were priests, had free access to schools at all times and the full co-operation of the State authorities.

Satisfied that its educational interests were safeguarded by the administrative and curricular structures, the Church, in turn, supported the State's gaelicisation policy in the schools. Undoubtedly, many of those in religious life had a genuine understanding, love and appreciation of the Irish language and Gaelic culture. However, a curriculum which emphasised a 'glorious' past rather than future progress also appealed to a Church opposed to liberalism, material progress and modernity. The reasons for this opposition and for its support by the Irish people had its roots in the catastrophe of the Great Famine during the middle of the previous century; reasons which will be taken up in detail in the next section of this chapter.

The provision of secondary schools in Ireland from the 1920s to the 1960s was meagre and attendance was poor. In the 1920s, only 5 per cent of those completing primary school were progressing to complete five years of secondary schooling and by 1960 this figure had increased to a mere 16 per cent.[4] The major political parties showed little enthusiasm for the notion of free secondary education for all, preferring to continue with a very limited scholarship system designed to allow only very bright children of poor parents to progress beyond primary school. As late as 1961, however, while only 13 per cent of the work force were professionals, managers and employers, in the secondary schools their children heavily outnumbered those from lower status occupations.[5]

The lack of provision of secondary schools and the fact that only a small percentage of those who left primary school went on to secondary school each year was of little concern to either the Catholic Church or the State, since the numbers involved were sufficient to fulfill their respective expectations of secondary education. The State looked to the secondary schools to produce an adequate number of suitably prepared individuals for the professions and for a variety of public and private occupations. The Catholic Church cooperated with the State in the pursuit of these objectives and, in turn, was afforded great latitude in the pursuit of its interests through the schools, and particularly in the manner in which it was able to saturate the curriculum with a religious ethos.

## The Church's pursuit of its interests through the secondary school curriculum

The Church's primary concern was with 'the salvation of souls' and it saw the control of the schools as being vital in this task. It was especially concerned about maintaining control of the secondary schools in order to generate a loyal middle class whose members would perpetuate the Church's influence in Irish society. The secondary schools also constituted fertile ground for the direct recruitment of priests, religious brothers and religious sisters. During the period 1922–1962, not only was this process successful in producing the required personnel to administer to the 'faithful' at home and to the great number of Irish Catholics who had settled in Britain, the United States, Canada, Australia and New Zealand, but the Church was also able to send large numbers of missionaries to Africa, Asia and Latin America. These missionaries brought their Irish brand of Catholicism to all of these places and contributed to the development of their various Catholic education systems.

Because the Catholic Church controlled Irish secondary schools, staffed them largely with priests, religious sisters and religious brothers, and had the power to employ the lay teachers of its choice provided they met basic academic requirements, it was well positioned for the pursuit of its interests through the curriculum. Four major propositions have been developed regarding how it met these interests.[6] First, the secondary school curriculum was characterised by a religious atmosphere which was all-pervasive. The school day was punctuated with formal and informal religious instruction. The daily religion class was the norm in all schools and there was a strong religious flavour to the manner in which the other school subjects were taught.[7]

Second, while the Church supported the pronounced emphasis which successive governments placed on the Irish language and Gaelic culture in the curriculum, it also successfully opposed some initiatives in this sphere which it considered overzealous. The opposition arose largely out of a fear that English and the Classics, particularly the study of Latin, might become marginalised as curriculum subjects.[8] English, of course, was the language required by the great number of Irish religious who went to minister overseas every year, while Latin was the official language of the Catholic Church.

Third, from the early 1920s through to the 1960s, the secondary school curriculum was concerned with the development of the individual in only a very narrow sense. The development of critical thinking was neglected because of the great deal of effort concentrated on preparing students for the Intermediate and Leaving Certificate examinations and because the assessment of higher order cognitive skills was largely ignored in these examinations. Training for occupational tasks was also excluded. The expectation was that those who did not have leanings towards an academic education but nonetheless desired a second-level education would go to a vocational rather than an academic secondary school. However, the Church restricted the development of the vocational school system in order to protect its own management and curricular interests in secondary education.[9]

Fourth, the Church played a major part in marginalising, if not completely neutralising, other educational interest groups, most notably parents, from contributing to the development of curriculum policy and practice.[10] In particular, the Church cooperated with successive governments to stifle attempts aimed at the establishment of a national forum wherein various curricular and management proposals could be discussed by representatives of the different interest groups within the education system.

## An historical explanation for the Church's great influence over the secondary school curriculum

The acceptance by successive Irish governments of the major influence which the Catholic Church had over secondary school education was one of the ways in which they demonstrated throughout the period 1922–1962 that they did not espouse a revolutionary and secular republicanism. They made it clear it was not their intention to become involved in the founding of secondary schools or in financing the building of them. They also avoided confrontation with the Church on curricular issues. At one level, this avoidance can be attributed to the commitment which the great majority of politicians had to Catholicism and an awareness of the political danger in questioning Church influence. More significant, however, was the prevailing anti-modernist world-view and dread of the confusion inherent in liberalism.[11] At a time when mainstream Catholic social teaching had come to terms with modernism, Church leaders in Ireland continued to fear change in education, as in other areas, because of its potential to disrupt traditional religious practices and values. Equally, they and the middle class from which they were largely recruited, feared change because it had the potential to threaten middle-class dominance of Irish political, social, economic and educational life.

The historical roots of this situation are to be found in the nineteenth century. Immediately prior to the Great Famine of 1845–1848, Irish Catholics comprised two main classes, a middle class and a marginal class.[12] The middle class consisted of farmers and rural merchants. They were threatened with demands for land redistribution from the more numerous and frequently hostile marginal class of labourers, cottiers and farmers with holdings of less than thirty acres. However, this marginal class was devastated by the Great Famine. As a consequence, the middle class was able to impose its own values on society, values which, as Lee has put it, 'sanctified the primacy of property in the rural status system'.[13]

The small holdings of many who died or emigrated were acquired by the middle class in order to consolidate their farms. They now had to take steps to ensure that subdivision into small holdings, which allowed the marginal class to thrive and become a serious threat in pre-Famine days, never happened again. The manner in which this was achieved has been depicted by Lee as follows:

> In order to pass on the farm intact, the father had generally to ensure that only two children married locally, the son who inherited the farm, and the daughter who would marry into a neighbouring farm or into a shop, whose assets had been sedulously investigated. Other children had to be largely disinherited. Children who chose to stay at home could not marry within the rural status system. They could usually survive only as 'relatives assisting', to linger through life, half indulged, half despised, as the maiden aunt and uncle, members of that legion of stunted personalities scattered throughout rural Ireland, where wealth accumulated and 'relatives assisting' decayed.[14]

The outcome was that the proportion of the middle class remained constant as the 'safety valve' of emigration continued to keep the numbers of the marginal class below the threatening level.

Emigration was also one of the safety valves in the inheritance system of the middle class, the other being the cloister; there was a great increase in the numbers entering religious life in the second half of the nineteenth century. Even though the overall Catholic population of the country fell by 27 per cent between 1861 and 1901, there was an increase of 137 per cent in the number of priests, monks and nuns in the country.[15] This great clerical 'army', drawn primarily from the ranks of the middle class, played its part in preaching the values necessary for maintaining the new 'hard, calculating, materialistic society'[16] which developed.

A characteristic of the 'new' Irish Catholicism which came to dominate by the middle of the nineteenth century was the great effort which was put into popular renewal. The result was people 'moulded into a thoroughly sacramental and Mass-going Church'.[17] This condition was reinforced by a vast range of new rituals, mainly imported from the Continent.[18] Structures were also in place to ensure that the spiritual leadership and guidance provided was overseen by religious drawn primarily from the middle class of Irish society. For example, social class divisions were maintained amongst the religious sisters within the convents. While religious orders recruited girls from both classes, only those who paid a dowry were permitted to become 'choir sisters' and train to become teachers or nurses. Those from poorer homes became 'lay sisters', wore more humble clerical garb and were restricted to domestic work within the confines of the cloister. In the case of some orders, they were not even allowed to sit at Mass with the choir sisters, but had to remain hidden from their view in dimly-lit corridors leading off of the main body of the church. In this way, life in the convent reflected life in the general society, thus reinforcing the view that the existing social structure reflected the natural order.

Social class divisions also existed within the priesthood. Priests for the diocese were trained in diocesan seminaries under the jurisdiction of the bishops. Because they charged fees, access to these seminaries was restricted to those who could pay. Occasionally, a sponsor came forward with the necessary finance but it was more normal for poorer boys to join one of the many religious orders in the country since they did not charge fees. On the other hand, after they were ordained, priests attached to religious orders were likely to find themselves ministering in Britain, America, South Africa, Australia or New Zealand, rather than in Ireland. In these other lands, many of the Irish religious imposed their Irish Catholicism through an ecclesiastical model mirroring that which they had experienced at home. Others, however, found an outlet for radical ideas arising out of their own early experiences of poverty, their interpretation of the gospels, and the injustices they perceived around them. Here they could preach social change without disturbing the social order on the home front.

Post-independence Ireland was 'marked by a profound continuity with the social patterns and attitudes of the nineteenth century'.[19] Economic output and employment were dominated by family farming, with the bulk of the population living in the countryside and small towns.[20] Regarding their condition, Hannan and Commins contend that by the beginning of the 1920s, 'the mass of small-scale and middle-sized farmers were witnessing significant improvements in their living standards',[21] along with improved status, security and wellbeing. By contrast, 'the life chances and the local reproduction opportunities for non-inheritors painfully contracted'.[22] As Kennedy argues, the weakest classes suffered severe hardship, being 'forced to emigrate, or remain poor, unemployed and often celibate for life'.[23]

Catholicism and conservative nationalism, 'the two pillars on which Irish political culture rested'[24] were the dominant ideologies. Both traditions were committed to a 'rural fundamentalism which was suspicious and fearful of the industrial city'.[25] Thus, as MacDonagh[26] argues, this was a society disinclined to contemplate any change other than the political change brought about in 1922. Rather, the first four decades of Independence saw an intensification of frugality and puritanical mores. Certain features of the Catholic moral code were enacted into law, particularly in the areas of sexual morality and family relations. There was a refusal to legalise divorce, strict censorship regulations relating to films and books were introduced, and advertising for the import, sale and use of contraceptives was banned.[27] Also, the Church was allowed to consolidate its position in the area of social services, including hospital services and the care of orphaned and homeless children. Viewed against such a background, the great influence which the Church had over education was but another strand in its overall level of influence over Irish family and social life in general.

The secondary school curriculum for the privileged minority reflected a concurrence between the interests of both Church and successive governments in a number of ways. Both favoured the reinforcement of the Catholic world-view prevalent in the wider society through the teaching of religion as a school subject, the promotion of the Catholic position in the teaching of the secular subjects on the curriculum, and the permeation of school life with a Catholic ethos. There was a great emphasis on the certainty of answers, strict discipline and unquestioning obedience, while critical thinking was neglected. Also, both groups succeeded in marginalising other educational interest groups, particularly the lay teachers and parents, greatly obstructing any attempts by them to contribute to the development of curriculum policy and practice. In this, the Church was motivated by fear that a new curricular pattern unsuited to the pursuit of its interests might emerge, while successive governments sought to minimise opportunities for questioning the gaelicisation policy. The effect of the Church and State combination in education in this way has been characterised thus by Hornsby-Smith:

> The religious socialisation of young Catholics was ensured, differentiation from Protestants and an ethnic sense of identity reinforced, the threat of secularising influences countered, hierarchical clerical control over the laity maintained and the power of the church to define morality extended. In exchange the church provided legitimation for the state.[28]

The combination reflected the alliance of both groups in the wider society to maintain a political culture which, in its constant stress on Catholic nationalist uniformity and homogeneity, 'proved quite hostile to any notion of politicising internal social divisions'.[29]

At the same time, it would be wrong to give the impression that there was no disagreement within clerical ranks in the South about the secondary school curriculum. There was indeed disagreement, but it did not reveal itself publicly because of the nature of Church organisation and protocol. The Catholic Headmasters' Association (CHA) and the Christian Brothers were the only Catholic managerial bodies consulted by the Department of Education for most of the period under consideration, with the CHA being seen 'as the major voice representing the educational views of Catholic secondary schools'.[30] However, as O'Buachalla[31] points out:

> In the exercise of its functions the CHA would seem to have been hindered if not frustrated at times by the knowledge that on the central issue of policy, a superior body, the hierarchy, was operating in the same field, a situation rendered all the more sensitive by the existence within the CHA of religious orders whose authority structure was independent of episcopal rule.

The influence of the convent secondary schools was likewise restricted for much of the period since they were represented by the CHA. The Conference of Convent Secondary Schools, in the early decades after its foundation in 1929, 'would not respond to any departmental initiative or undertake any negotiations independent of the CHA'.[32] Throughout all of the period under consideration, it was usually represented at overseas functions by members of the CHA, while its annual meeting was presided over by a senior clerical nominee of the Archbishop of Dublin.

The Church's approach in making representation to the State in secondary education reflected its practice in the wider arena of presenting a united front on all issues, with the bishops either being the main spokespersons or giving their sanction to those claiming to speak on behalf of the institution. This practice had its foundation in the authority structure solidified in the second half of the nineteenth century. In tightening ecclesiastical discipline and ensuring greater uniformity in religious observances, the bishops were responding to pressure from Rome for the Church to become a much more organised and hierarchical institution throughout the world. However, the new authoritarian structures were also attractive to all in religious life in Ireland as a force for marshalling popular support if there was ever any threat of a return to the days of religious persecution. For that reason, a tradition developed whereby public dissent became unknown amongst the bishops, the religious orders and congregations, with the bishops accepted as the public voice of the Church.

The maintenance of the tradition after Independence meant that in the field of education the curriculum ideas of those religious orders concerned primarily with the education of the lower classes were stifled. Thus, they were prisoners of the power of the Bishops. It is clear, for example, that the Christian Brothers were unhappy throughout the period with the lack of emphasis on science as an experimentally-based activity; a matter which is not surprising given their significant success in this quarter under the British administration.[33] Also, they felt that the State should give greater incentives to secondary schools to provide practical subjects, including drawing and manual work, and that the allocation of higher marks to Latin and Greek than to history, geography and science for the award of scholarships was not educationally sound.[34] Members of the Conference of Convent Secondary Schools also debated the academic secondary school curriculum and concluded that the great majority of the girls attending their schools would benefit from more practical courses.[35] Church protocol and internal politics dictated, however, that none of these misgivings were expressed publicly. To have done so would have meant implicit criticism of the bishops, who clearly were not prepared to accept anything other than an academic secondary school curriculum. The powerful tradition which emphasised the importance of presenting an image of a monolithic Church was thereby maintained.

## Changes since 1962

By the mid-1950s, Ireland was going through 'a dark night of the soul'.[36] The decade 1948–1957 was characterised by economic stagnation, continual balance of payments' crises, rising unemployment and 400,000 emigrants. The situation was approaching crisis proportions when the Fianna Fail party was returned to office in 1957, replacing the coalition government of the previous three years.

Fianna Fail created a new spirit of hope, enterprise and innovation. The party advocated much greater state investment in productive industry and incentives to encourage foreign investment. This view was endorsed in 1958 in the first of a series of national economic plans. From then until the oil crisis in 1973, the country enjoyed a period of sustained economic recovery, with an annual growth rate of around 4 per cent. Agriculture declined in importance and urbanisation increased greatly with the migration of workers from the land and peripheral regions to the towns, and particularly to the greater Dublin area where one third of the population now lives.[37] After 1973, however, the economic situation deteriorated and was accompanied by rising public and foreign debt, and high taxation. It was not until the late 1980s that the country made a major economic recovery, which has turned into quite dramatic growth since 1994.

Over the last thirty-five years there have also been significant educational changes. In the late 1950s, T.K. Whitaker, the Secretary of the Department of Finance, argued that economic progress depended to a considerable extent on a broad scientific education among the population at large.[38] In line with international trends, others also argued strongly for a greater emphasis and improved programmes in science and modern languages in the secondary schools. Yet others again held that educational reform should be wider than simply addressing the lack of alignment with the State's industrialisation policy.[39] They advocated engaging in educational surveys to facilitate curriculum planning, catering for different abilities in second level schools and reducing the dominance of the public examinations over secondary schooling.

The first sign that significant change was likely to take place in education was the publication in 1966 of the report, *Investment in Education*.[40] This was a major analysis of the education system, initiated in 1962, by the Department of Education in co-operation with the OECD. It has been summarised as follows:

> *Investment in Education* was a study of trends in the use of the human and material resources in the Irish educational system that sought to estimate the demands that were likely to be made on these resources in the light of the needs of the economy in the years ahead. The report began with a description of the educational system and of the number of qualified people that it was likely to produce if no changes, other than those officially announced at the time, were to be made. This was followed by an examination of employment patterns and a forecast of the number of people with various levels of qualifications expected to be required to meet the projected needs of the economy. Contrasting these indicators of supply and demand the report considered the possible alterations that were required if the adaptation of the system to changing economic needs was to be facilitated.[41]

All of the members of the survey team were Irish. However, its sponsorship by the OECD conferred authority and legitimacy on the stated need to replace 'personal development with the human capital paradigm as the institutional rationale for education'.[42]

From the mid-1960s onwards, and in line with this new rationale, there were major developments geared towards achieving greater provision of education at all levels and greater equality of educational opportunity. At the second level, these included providing free post-primary education, introducing building grants, providing free transport to schools, establishing common secondary and vocational courses and examinations, establishing comprehensive and community schools and, in some cases, organising for the sharing of facilities between adjacent vocational and secondary schools. The extent to which these developments resulted in compromise and conflict between Church and State constitutes a major story in itself. The fact that there was compromise, however, is evident in the existence at the present time of five types of second-level schools, in contrast to the two types which had existed for so long. At the end of primary school, almost all students now proceed to one of these five types of schools and almost 92 per cent of those remain on in the five or six year cycle after the compulsory age of 15 years; in 1991, some 89 per cent of 16 year olds, 69 per cent of 17 year olds and 42 per cent of 18 year olds were in full-time education.[43]

Secondary schools, which 'belong to the tradition of classical grammar schools but have been steadily broadening and modernising their curricula in recent years',[44] still account for two-thirds of all second-level schools. The vocational schools now offer the complete range of secondary subjects. A small number of comprehensive schools, controlled by the Department of Education, have been set up since 1966 to provide second-level education in geographical areas where no school was available and they offer 'a wide ranging curriculum, including technical and vocational subjects'.[45] Several community schools also exist and come under the influence of the Department of Education. They offer the same broad curriculum as the comprehensive schools and, 'like the North American model, are designed to serve as centres for all neighbourhood educational and cultural activities'.[46] Finally, the designation of community college is now being used to describe new or expanded vocational schools.[47]

The decision by Jack Lynch and Dr Hillery, the ministers for education during the period 1957–1962, that a new approach should be taken in the development of educational policy, was significant in breaking the mould. Until then there had been no prime mover in education. Soon, however, the Department of Education became more directive, making it known that it favoured steering second-level schools in a direction which would ensure the provision of a comprehensive curriculum composed of practical and academic subjects for all children of the nation in order to cater for the technological and employment needs of the country. Mulcahy[48] summarised the outcome as follows:

> Substantial content of a technical and applied kind has been introduced into the one-time secondary sector. This has been achieved by introducing subjects like building construction, engineering workshop theory and practice, accounting, and business organisation into the Leaving Certificate examinations list of subjects. At the same time substantial additional content of an academic nature has been introduced into the one-time vocational sector through the introduction into the vocational schools programmes of Intermediate and Leaving Certificate subjects like history, geography and modern languages.

Much effort also went into the improvement of the pedagogical skills of teachers as well as into the introduction of multi-syllabus subjects which offered alternative content.

These educational changes, part of the drive for economic development, were facilitated by other major changes also taking place in Irish society. The introduction of a national television station is 1962 was important 'in opening up the Irish consciousness to the social and cultural changes which were taking place elsewhere and especially in Britain'.[49] A greater openness to external influences also resulted from the debate on Ireland's impending membership of the EEC. The emergence of individual consumerism 'with its attendant motor cars, foreign holidays and new houses', coupled with 'a more cosmopolitan range of leisure pursuits'[50] was likewise an important promoter of change.

Most significant of all, however, was the change within the Catholic Church. As Bryk, Lee and Holland remind us, it was to universal surprise that Pope John XXIII announced the convening of a second Vatican Council which, between 1962 and 1965, brought together bishops from around the world to deliberate. The end result 'was nothing short of revolutionary, profoundly affecting virtually every aspect of Catholic life'.[51] Hornsby-Smith[52] sums up as follows:

> The strategy of suppression or intransigence which had been ruthlessly followed for over half a century since the condemnation of modernism was beginning to break down. The Vatican Council's emphasis on collegiality and participation by all the 'people of God' can be seen as indicating a shift within a changing world to an 'organic' management structure with far more emphasis on lateral consultation than vertical command. There was a movement away from the legalistic following of institutional rules and regulations to a concern with how Christians were to live fully human and liberated lives.[53]

Ireland experienced the full brunt of the reform movement.[54] Ironically, the new outlook led to a dramatic decline in the number of priests, brothers and religious sisters.[55] Accordingly, while major developments took place in education and social services, the dominance of the religious orders in these areas shrank. Various concessions were made by the Church, particularly in education. A ban on Catholics attending Trinity College Dublin, bastion of Anglicanism in Ireland for centuries, was lifted. Early objections to community schools and multi-denominational schools were resolved. Parents also become involved in the management of schools.

At the same time, the Church continued to be very much involved in education. Private consultations were still carried on between the bishops and the Department of Education and, because they were better organised than before, any proposals which were likely to cause public difficulty are negotiated by the parties beforehand.[56] However, in concentrating much of its energy on ensuring that new management structures allowed it to maintain a major foothold in education, the Church has lost much of its influence in the curriculum. Certainly, religion continued to be taught in second-level schools, while the almost total disappearance of Latin was of little concern as the Church had moved to using the vernacular in the Mass. However, one is prompted to speculate that the expansion of technical knowledge, particularly in the curriculum for senior pupils, would not have been so great if the religious orders had continued to dominate the teaching force. What happened at the senior level was that the sciences and commercial subjects began to dominate at the expense of history, geography, art, music and continental languages other than French. There was also an almost complete absence of social scientific education through the non-representation of sociology, social administration, anthropology, political science and media studies in the curriculum. Accordingly, there was little room for meeting the Church's new interest in emphasising social justice, raising consciousness and safeguarding against inequities associated with uncontrolled forms of western capitalism. Instead, the educational experiences for many young people continued 'to be depressingly rigid and examination oriented'.[57]

The curriculum emphasis was largely on the creation of a relatively small technical elite. The dominant examination-oriented mentality rewarded competitive individualism rather than caring and sharing, encouraged docility and unquestioning conformity, sacrificed creativity and imagination for the regurgitation of knowledge, and promoted the notion that pursuing one's own advancement was more important than developing human relationships. Also, second-level education continued to function for the benefit primarily of the middle and upper classes, with pupils from these classes being the most likely to stay on to obtain a Leaving Certificate and attend third-level colleges.[58] As Ireland entered fully into the industrial era, the State appeared to have replaced the Church as the orchestrator of the reproduction of class inequities through the educational system. It is ironic that at the very time when the religious orders in particular were concerned about stressing the importance of reciprocal rights, dialogue and consultation, and working for the rights of the marginalised and the oppressed, they no longer had the critical mass in the classroom – the educational arena where, as history demonstrates, they once held unquestioned sway.

Events during the 1990s clearly indicate the emergence of yet another phase. Against a background in which the Irish economy is growing at a faster rate than most OECD countries, the education system is in the throes of substantial structural reform. As a recent OECD report put it, the 'nation is currently at the crossroads, as the White Paper (1995), which was drawn up following the Green Paper (1992) and the Education Convention (1993) is, piece by piece, translated into legislation'.[59] The report goes on to argue that when the reforms have been achieved, Ireland will have one of the most parent-participative education systems in the world. This, however, is but part of a wider thrust in education at all levels in Ireland towards participation by all major stakeholders. It 'came of age' when the National Education Convention[60] took place in Dublin Castle from 11 to 21 October 1993, bringing together representatives from forty-two organisations to engage in structured and sustained discussion on key issues of educational policy in Ireland. This thrust towards openness in discourse and a partnership model of policy formulation continued in the White Paper of 1995, with its commitment to five new policy principles: pluralism; equality; partnership; quality; accountability.[61] Notably, it also took place at a time of shifting power relations within the Church. In particular, there was a decline of ecclesiastical influence, largely because of revelations of a number of scandals, while at the same time there was an increase in new religious voices for the marginalised.[62]

The move towards a partnership model in policy formulation was also accompanied by certain tensions. Some commentators, for example, criticised that part of the Green Paper which they saw as over-emphasising utilitarian and individualist values and underemphasising cultural, moral, artistic and civic elements.[63] This led to the articulation of a government response emphasising a liberal conception of 'enterprise' and 'a much more enriched view of the arts as part of a balanced education'.[64] The indications now are that this view is beginning to have an impact. For example, a new compulsory subject, 'Civic, Social and Political Education' (CSPE) was introduced into the curriculum in 1997. Also, a new Religious Education syllabus, with a shift of emphasis from transmission of doctrine to exploration of religious traditions, was developed for commencement in 1998. How these and further changes will influence the nature and extent of the Church's influence on the school curriculum in the twenty-first century only time will tell.

## Notes

1  S. Dunn, 'Education, religion and cultural change in the Republic of Ireland', in W. Tulasiewicz and C. Brock (eds), *Christianity and Educational Provision in International Perspective*, London, Routledge, 1988, p. 95.

2  D.H. Akenson, *The Irish Education Experiment: The National System of Education in the Nineteenth Century*, London, Routledge and Kegan Paul, 1970. See also, John Coolahan, *Irish Education: History and Structure*, Dublin, Institute of Public Administration, 1981, pp. 3–52.

3  SPO. Dublin. Cabinet Files. File S.3092 entitled 'Intermediate Education Commissioners' Order, 1923'.

4  *Investment in Education – Report of the Survey Team*, Dublin, Stationery Office, 1966, p. 51.

5  *Investment in Education.*

6  I have given a detailed exposition on these propositions in T.A. O'Donoghue, *The Catholic Church and the Secondary School Curriculum in Ireland, 1922–1962*, New York, Peter Lang, 1999.

7  I have dealt with this in detail in T.A. O'Donoghue, 'The Roman Catholic ethos of Irish secondary schools 1924–62 and its implications for teaching and school organization', *Journal of Educational Administration and History*, vol. 22, no. 2, 1990, pp. 27–37.

8  For an expression of some of this opposition by the Catholic clergy and Hierarchy see *The Times Educational Supplement*, 7 January 1933; *The Irish Times*, 18 May 1936; *Irish Press*, 21 December 1936; *Irish Press*, 19 January 1937.

9  See J.H. Whyte, *Church and State in Modern Ireland, 1923–1970*, Dublin, Gill and Macmillan, 1971, pp. 37–38.

10  S. O'Buachalla, *Education Policy in Twentieth Century Ireland*, Dublin, Wolfhound Press, 1988, p. 320. For a detailed outline of Church involvement in the politics of Irish education see S. Farren, *The Politics of Irish Education, 1920–1965*, Belfast, The Institute of Irish Studies, The Queen's University of Belfast, 1995.

11  See D.H. Akenson, *A Mirror to Kathleen's Face: Education in Independent Ireland, 1922–60*, Montreal and London, McGill-Queen's University Press, 1975. See also E.B. Titley, *Church, State and the Control of Schooling in Ireland, 1900–1944*, Dublin, Gill and Macmillan, 1983.

12  E.O. Hanson, *The Catholic Church in World Politics*, Princeton New Jersey, Princeton University Press, 1987, p. 39.

13  J.J. Lee, 'Continuity and change in Ireland, 1945–70', in J.J. Lee (ed.), *Ireland 1945–70*, Dublin, Gill and Macmillan, 1979, p. 166.

14  Lee, pp. 166–167.

15  See T. Fahey, 'Catholicism and industrial society in Ireland', in J.H. Goldthorpe and C.T. Whelan, *The Development of Industrial Society in Ireland*, Oxford, Oxford University Press, 1994, pp. 249–250.

16  J.J. Lee, p. 167.

17  J.J. O'Riordain, *Irish Catholics: Tradition and Transition*, Dublin, Veritas Publications, 1980, p. 74.

18  O'Riordain.

19  T. Brown, *Ireland: A Social and Cultural History 1922–1985*, London, Fontana Press, 1985, p. 18.

20  T. Fahey, p. 246.

21  D.F. Hannan and P. Commins, 'The significance of small-scale landholders in Ireland's socio-economic transformation', in Goldthorpe and Whelan, p. 95.

22 Hannan and Commins.
23 K.A. Kennedy, 'The context of economic development', in Goldthorpe and Whelan, p. 16.
24 M.P. Hornsby-Smith, 'Social and religious transformations in Ireland: a case of secularisation?', in Goldthorpe and Whelan, p. 268.
25 Fahey, p. 262.
26 O. MacDonagh, *Ireland*, Englewood Cliffs, NJ, Prentice-Hall Inc., 1968, p. 120.
27 D.W Miller, *Church, State and Nation in Ireland 1898–1921*, Dublin, Gill and Macmillan, 1973, p. 494.
28 Hornsby-Smith, p. 275.
29 P. Mair, 'Explaining the absence of class politics in Ireland', in Goldthorpe and Whelan, p. 404.
30 O'Buachalla, p. 147.
31 O'Buachalla.
32 O'Buachalla, p. 142.
33 This is a recurring theme in W. Bracken, A study of the contribution of the Christian Brothers to the development of Irish education, 1803–1975, MEd Thesis, Trinity College Dublin, 1981.
34 Bracken.
35 See CCSS Records. UNISON Offices, Dublin. File entitled 'Conference Commission-Final report'.
36 T.K. Whitaker, 'Economic development – The Irish experience', *The Irish Times*, 20 September 1982.
37 Hornsby-Smith, pp. 268–269.
38 Department of Finance, *Economic Development*, Dublin, Stationery Office, 1958, pp. 110–115. See also, T.K. Whitaker, 'Capital formation, saving and economic progress', *Journal of the Statistical and Social Inquiry Society of Ireland*, vol. 19, 1955–56, pp. 185–188. Here he promoted the contention that economic improvement necessitated certain educational developments. He argued that a declining population retarded the growth of national production, that emigration would not be controlled until there was a high rate of economic development and competitive efficiency in production, and that increased capitalisation would not be sufficient to improve productivity.
39 See P. Birch, 'Co-ordination in education', *University Review*, vol. 11, nos 3–4, 1958, pp. 66–71; S. O'Cathain, *Secondary Education in Ireland*, Dublin, Talbot Press, 1959; T. O'Raifeartaigh, 'Education in the USA', *Studies*, vol. 50, 1961, pp. 57–74.
40 Investment in Education, *Report of the Survey Team, Investment in Education*, Dublin, The Stationery Office, 1963.
41 D. O'Sullivan, 'Cultural strangers and educational change: The OECD Report "Investment in Education" and Irish educational policy', *Journal of Education Policy*, vol. 7, no. 5, 1992, p. 448.
42 O'Sullivan, p. 445.
43 OECD, *Reviews of National Policies for Education-Ireland*, Paris, Organisation for Economic Cooperation and Development, 1991, p. 29.
44 OECD.
45 OECD.
46 OECD.
47 OECD.
48 D.G. Mulcahy, *Curriculum and Policy in Irish Post-Primary Education*, Dublin, Institute of Public Administration, 1981, p. 35.
49 Hornsby-Smith, p. 269.
50 Dunn, p. 91.
51 A.S. Bryk, V.E. Lee and P.B. Holland, *Catholic Schools and the Common Good*, Cambridge, MA, Harvard University Press, 1993, p. 46.
52 Hornsby-Smith, p. 271.
53 Hornsby-Smith.
54 Fahey, p. 255.
55 Fahey, p. 256. Here we are told that 'Male clerical orders, congregations of sisters and congregations of brothers have dropped between 25 and 44 per cent in numbers over the period 1970–86. Intake of new members has fallen even more sharply'.

56  Dunn, p. 111.
57  K. Williams, 'Plus ca change? Recent curriculum change in Ireland', *Curriculum*, vol. 13, no. 2, 1992, p. 127.
58  See also, A.E. Raftery and M. Hout, 'Maximally maintained inequality: expansion, reform, and opportunity in Irish education, 1921–75', *Sociology of Education*, vol. 66, no. 1, 1993, pp. 41–62.
59  OECD, *Parents as Partners in Schooling*, Paris, Organisation for Economic Co-operation and Development, 1997, p. 141.
60  The National Education Convention Secretariat (J. Coolahan, ed.), *Report on the National Education Convention*, Dublin, National Education Secretariat, 1994.
61  Government of Ireland, *Changing our Education Future: White Paper on Education*, Dublin, The Stationery Office, 1995.
62  Conference of Religious of Ireland (CORI), *Religious Congregations in Irish Education: A Role for the Future? A Reflection Paper*, Dublin, CORI, 1997.
63  The National Education Convention Secretariat, p. 149.
64  The National Education Convention Secretariat, p. 150.

# PART VI

# TEACHERS AND PUPILS

# CHAPTER 12

# THE SYMBIOTIC EMBRACE
## American Indians, white educators and the school, 1820s–1920s

### Michael C. Coleman

*History of Education, 25, 1, 1–18, 1996*

We are proud of the Indian men and women who have received a good education... These are the people we need to lead us – men who are good Christians, who are educated, and who will fight for the Indians.

(Howard Whitewolf, Comanche, 1917)

Summing it all up, it depends upon the caprice of the Indians whether children are secured.

(George W. Scott, Superintendent, Chilocco Indian Industrial School, 1889)

Adaptive American Indians such as Whitewolf believed that their peoples needed the school to survive in modern life. Harassed educators such as Scott knew they needed Indians to fill their schools and justify their own professional existence.[1] Thus in the nineteenth and early twentieth centuries such Indians and white educators found themselves drawn into relationships of symbiotic interdependence.[2]

Large numbers of white Americans needed only the Indians' lands, and looked to the final vanishing of the tribes. Yet, from colonial times there were Euro-Americans who, for a mixture of idealistic and other motives, attempted to reconcile just treatment of Indians with expansion of white settlement into their lands. Drawing on colonial missionary examples, officials of the new United States and Christian missionaries embarked upon a crusade which to them appeared both humane and politically practical. Indians would be Christianized, 'civilized', turned from nomadic 'savages' into farmers (which many in fact already were) and absorbed into the American population, thus freeing vast areas of supposedly surplus land for new settlers. Fortuitously, the method for achieving this ambitious assimilative programme appeared to be at hand, in the form of the school. 'From the period of the Revolution onwards', writes Andy Green, 'education was held to be uniquely important for the cultivation of a national identity, for the maintenance of social cohesion and for the promotion of republican values, especially in a country of dispersed and heterogeneous communities, and in the early years of a new and fragile republic'. Through the school, 'savage' tribal children would be brought under constant surveillance and taught the self-control they supposedly lacked. Suitably transformed they would become mediators (cultural brokers, in modern parlance) to spread Christian civilization and American values among their peoples.[3]

Responding to this pragmatic humanitarian rationale, in 1819 the United States Congress set aside the first 'civilization fund' of US $10,000 to employ 'capable persons of good moral character, to instruct them [Indians] in the mode of agriculture suited to their situation; and for teaching their children in reading, writing and arithmetic'.[4] At that time the War Department exercised oversight of Indian affairs, and in 1824 Congress established a unit within it, called the Office of Indian Affairs or the Bureau of Indian Affairs (BIA). Headed from 1832 by the Commissioner of Indian Affairs, the BIA was transferred to the new Department of the Interior in 1849. From its inception the BIA used the civilization fund to help finance existing missionary efforts. By 1824 there were 32 schools, enrolling more than 900 tribal children.[5]

Thus began a century-long experiment in federal–missionary cooperation for the 'uplift' of Indian people. Although Congress discontinued the civilization fund in 1873, three years earlier it had appropriated $100,000 for Indian education and thousands of Indian children were enrolled in schools. By 1882 the sum had risen to $150,000 and by 1887 to about $750,000. Moreover, from the 1870s the government began to dominate the educational effort, quickly pushing the missionary societies, Catholic and Protestant, to the margins. The BIA built day schools, on-reservation boarding schools, and large, off-reservation boarding schools enrolling pupils from many tribes. By 1900 the BIA was spending $3 million per year on Indian education (300 times the 1819 civilization fund), and enrolled over 20,000 children. By 1930 this figure had risen to 34,000; as few as 6000 attended missionary schools. Only in the early twentieth century did Indian children begin to attend state public schools: by 1930 over 38,000 did so.[6] And only at the end of the period under review did the BIA inaugurate a new policy of respect for tribal cultures, after a century-long crusade to destroy them and force Indian assimilation into white American civilization.[7]

A popular image of the 'Indian schools' – missionary and BIA – sees them as harsh institutions of imperialism, little better than prisons. Recent academic scholarship does much to corroborate this image. Their goal, writes K. Tsianina Lomawaima in a passage with which many scholars would concur, was 'to destroy Indian tribal communities and erase individual Indian identity'. She and others have shown how the schools systematically separated children from kin and cultures and forbade them to speak their own languages. Military-style discipline was common, and staff, including Indian 'officers' and disciplinarians, could be capricious or even brutal. Pupils of both sexes and all ages were forced to labour to support the schools. Some children spent years at such establishments without as much as a holiday at home.[8] The objective of this assault on Indian personality and culture, as Commissioner William A. Jones characteristically expressed it in 1903, was to 'exterminate the Indian, but develop a man'.[9]

Yet the same scholars who have provided us with such a negative picture have simultaneously argued for a more complex understanding of school reality for Indian children. Influenced by New Social History emphases upon the adaptive coping strategies of the oppressed, and perhaps also by postmodernist concepts of empowerment, these scholars show that supposedly passive and powerless students could sometimes acquire a surprising amount of power. Lomawaima argues that pupils 'made Chilocco [Indian School] their own'. By their resilience and adaptability they created 'relatively free spaces' to resist the authorities, built their own subcultures, and often gained intellectual and vocational satisfaction from their experiences. Ironically, some Indian pupils achieved a heightened sense of tribal and pan-Indian identity from their times at the schools. Indeed, claims Lomawaima in an extreme expression of the empowerment view, the Chilocco school culture 'was created and sustained by students much more than by teachers or staff'.[10]

Having rightly moved beyond viewing minorities as passive victims, however, scholars thereby risk retrospectively 'over-empowering' Indians. During the nineteenth century United States demographic, economic and military power increased dramatically, and in numerous contact situations Indians had far more adapting to do than white Americans. The men, women *and* children of the tribes nevertheless retained some freedom of action. Focusing first on the missionary schools, then on the BIA schools and finally upon Indian responses, I want to argue that shifting symbiotic relationships of interdependence developed within an educational arena which no group entirely controlled.

## I

Inspired by the evangelical revivals of the Second Great Awakening in the early nineteenth century, Protestant Americans established church-sponsored and nondenominational missionary societies to spread 'Christian civilization' throughout the world. American Indians were not ignored. By mid-century Presbyterians, Friends (Quakers), Congregationalists, Moravians, Episcopalians, Methodist and Baptists had begun missions and schools to many of the Southern, Eastern, Mid-Western and even Far-Western tribes. Roman Catholics also expanded their Indian missions during these decades.[11]

Symbiosis also characterized missionary–federal relationships. Religious societies in part depended upon government co-operation and protection. And, unable to embark upon a school-building programme, the BIA was initially dependent upon the missionaries to 'civilize' and pacify Indians. With the famous 'Peace Policy' of President Ulysses S. Grant (late 1860s to early 1880s), the government actually invited Protestant and Catholic churches to nominate agents and other reservation personnel, including teachers.[12]

Yet the government soon began to dominate the relationship, providing direct grants and other forms of subsidization. Its patronage had 'been of very great importance to the success of the attempts, made for the benefit of the Cherokees and Choctaws', declared a grateful American Board of Commissioners for Foreign Missions (ABCFM) in 1823. Besides the $300 per quarter each of its two schools received, the support of the President, 'whom the Indians are accustomed to call their great Father', was a significant morale-booster to the Presbyterian-Congregational ABCFM.[13]

After 1869, as educational appropriations expanded dramatically, the government subsidized mission schools through contracts; by 1886 the rate was established at $108 per pupil per annum in most areas. But with increasing financial support came accountability. Missionary teachers and superintendents had to report to the BIA and to subject their establishments to inspection. An agent visiting the Jesuit day school on the Flathead reservation in 1864, for example, ordered the school closed because of inadequate attendance and academic performance. Even after the government ended most of its subsidization of religious schools in 1900, many remained under its 'supervisory care'.[14] Religious educators also had to justify their actions to missionary society headquarters and to those who donated money, and during the century began to publish voluminous reports, tracts and magazines to publicize and sustain the crusade.[15]

To satisfy all these groups, the missionaries had to run successful schools, and for this they needed Indian co-operation. The precarious sense of dependence is conveyed by a report on changing Cherokee attitudes in 1835, on the eve of the forced removal of the 'Five Civilized Tribes' – Cherokees, Choctaws, Chickasaws, Creeks and Seminoles – from their southern lands to the Indian Territory in present-day Oklahoma. The political situation of the Cherokees had been 'in such a state as to render the situation of the missionaries extremely perplexing and discouraging', reported the ABCFM:

> The people, believing themselves to be oppressed and spoiled of their dearest rights by a nominally Christian nation, have, to a great extent, imbibed a deep prejudice against our religion and nation, and against Christian missionaries as citizens of the United States, and as being therefore, in their apprehension in some degree accessory to the injuries done themselves.

The writer could not know that the missions to these tribes would begin again in the Indian Territory. He concurred with a colleague that 'never before has the Board, or those labouring under its patronage, been so little esteemed by the Cherokees, or had so little influence with them, as the present time'.[16] Yet these missionaries were fortunate compared with colleagues elsewhere. In 1847 Marcus and Narcissa Whitman and others at the ABCFM mission at Wailatpu, in the Washington Territory, became celebrated evangelical martyrs after their murder by Cayuse Indians.[17]

Some of the financial support for missionary schools actually came from treaty funds, money paid to tribes for the surrender of their lands. In such cases the missionaries were especially dependent upon Indian goodwill. After removal to Oklahoma, the part-white leadership of the Choctaws invited the Presbyterian Board of Foreign Missions (BFM) to open a school. 'Be it enacted by the General Council of the Choctaw Nation here assembled', declared the tribal legislature in 1845, 'that *Spencer Academy* shall be placed under the control and direction of the Board'. The school would be supervised by Choctaw-appointed trustees, and the BFM had to accept complicating conditions such as a prohibition upon educating the black slaves of the Choctaw leaders. Similar conditions forced the ABCFM to withdraw from the Choctaw field on the eve of the Civil War.[18]

Even when missionaries succeeded in winning broad tribal acceptance for their schools, they remained dependent upon the willingness of individual Indian adults to send their children, and of those children to attend regularly and to participate actively in the learning process. Empty or half-filled schools implied a waste of government, missionary society or benefactor money. When Alexander Reid, BFM principal of Spencer Academy, wrote in 1851 that he was 'at his wit's end' because of Indian runaways, he expressed more than the frustration of a teacher staring at empty desks. He also conveyed his dependence upon Choctaw children to keep the ambitious school functioning. BFM Missionaries among the semi-nomadic Omahas were especially chagrined by the annual buffalo hunt, which lured many pupils away from the school.[19]

The insistence that children perform manual labour could also lead to dependence upon them. Missionary and government schools employed the 'half and half' system. Pupils worked half the time in the classroom, on some kind of 'English education' which included the 3Rs, history, geography and religion. The other half they spent in character-forming labour supposedly appropriate to the sexes: boys worked on the school farm, at the blacksmith's or in the tin shop; girls cooked food, worked in the laundry, darned and sewed. The large off-reservation boarding schools and some missionary schools taught an impressive range of academic and vocational subjects to potential citizens, and at many schools, as we shall see, the young Indians actually received small payments for their labour. Isaac White, BFM missionary to the Omahas, indicated a danger of the system, however. 'Last Sabbath five of our boys fled', he wrote in 1864. 'This leaves the mission with but one boy large enough to plow or drive a team.'[20]

The frustration at Indian non-co-operation was especially great because of missionary belief in the school as the gateway of the Gospel into the tribe. Using words which colleagues at many missions would have echoed, the ABCFM noted in 1819 how its Brainerd School was to be 'a Primary Institution, to serve as a center of operations for evangelizing and civilizing the Cherokee Nation'. In 1821 the society hoped that pupils would soon 'be mingling with their countrymen, and imparting their acquired character to others, and they to others still, in a wider and wider range'. Further, the school would train new religious leaders who, as cultural brokers, would mediate between peoples and continue the teaching process, at first under missionary supervision, and then perhaps independently. Acknowledging the delicacy of the situation, however, the missionaries accepted the need for a nuanced but manipulative approach to secure the necessary Indian co-operation. 'Their habits and feeling must not be disregarded', declared the ABCFM in 1823. They 'must be led kindly and cautiously to understand the reason and utility of missionary proceedings'.[21]

The missionaries, therefore, became dependent upon many groups, and especially upon their supposed charges.[22] Edward Goodbird, a Hidatsa who attended a Congregational mission school in the 1870s, came close to a truth not many religious or lay teachers wished to admit. After he played truant to attend a scalp dance, his teacher was upset. But 'she never punished me', he recalled, 'for she knew if she did I would leave the school'.[23]

## II

Many of the same factors operated for government administrators and teachers. They too generally advocated Christian – mostly Protestant – values.[24] They also utilized the child to penetrate Indian society. 'It is only from the minds of the young and rising generations', wrote Superintendent Barclay White in 1873, 'that we can hope to eradicate the plants of superstition and ignorance which now so darkly shadow the intellect, and to plant there instead the seeds of virtue, knowledge, and truth'.[25]

As at mission schools, young Indians were exploited in other, more immediate ways. BIA educators made massive use of pupil labour. For every dollar spent by the government on a student, boasted the principal of Carlisle Indian School in 1910, the student produced nearly a dollar in return.[26] Although not the original intent, this system sometimes degenerated into crude exploitation.[27] But it also increased school dependence upon pupils. Large numbers of absentees or runaways – or even a handful, as BFM missionary White discovered – could seriously threaten the effective functioning of the institution, and might call down the wrath of higher authorities.

The interrelated dynamics of bureaucratization and professionalization also worked to intensify dependence upon Indians. The assimilative goals of the educational campaign implied that the BIA should work itself out of a job. 'Its success', claimed the Board of Indian Commissioners in 1901, 'is to be shown not in self-perpetuation but in self-destruction'.[28] The Bureau, however, grew and grew. In 1824 the superintendent of the new BIA had the services of two clerks. His duties included administration of the civilization fund and annuities (payments to tribes), of other expenditures, deciding upon land claims and handling Indian correspondence. In 1873 an education division was established within the BIA, and by 1888 the school service alone employed 757 white and 137 Indian men and women in almost 60 distinct job categories, and sub-categories, such as superintendents, teachers, matrons, cooks, clerks, farmers and labourers. By the end of the century the BIA employed about 1480 whites and 695 Indians (not including pupils) at its schools. In 1902, 77,000 letters were processed by 132 headquarters employees. By 1911 the number of letters had almost trebled. But, complained Commissioner Jones, there was less than a doubling of the same headquarters staff, to 227. By the same decade there were 6000 employees, half of whom were involved in education. By 1926 the Bureau's activities involved 13 major classifications, such as allotment of Indian lands in severalty, custody of Indian money, medical relief, industrial advancement, policing of reservations, suppression of the liquor trade, supervision of attorneys and, of course, education. By 1937 the BIA had become one of the largest federal bureaucracies. Instead of self-destructing, then, it had grown into a huge, but sometimes poorly organized bureaucracy which 'dominated every aspect of the Indians' lives'.[29]

It also dominated the lives of its employees. The Commissioner was responsible to the Secretary of the Interior, and members of the educational division struggled to justify their expenditure of Congressional appropriations. As early as 1819 school administrators were required to send in reports, and from 1837 agents had to make at least a yearly check on schools in their jurisdictions. In 1873 Congress authorized the appointment of five inspectors of BIA field services, including education, and in 1882 an Inspector, later Superintendent of Indian Schools, was appointed. In 1889 the energetic Commissioner Thomas Jefferson Morgan attempted to systematize the widely separated and disparate schools into one, hierarchical system, and produced a detailed questionnaire for prospective teachers. During the 1890s more and more educational personnel came under civil service protection – but aspirant teachers also faced entry examinations. In addition, the BIA began to encourage staff to attend summer 'institutes' of lectures and discussions to upgrade their skills. After she passed the civil service examination in 1901, for example, the young Gertrude Golden faced a year's probation before appointment as a BIA teacher, and felt herself at the mercy of the principal. 'Our being retained or promoted depended entirely upon the reports sent to the Indian office', she wrote. 'These reports dealt with our efficiency, obedience to established rules and our general fitness for the position.'[30]

Even by the 1920s teachers in the Indian service had not become fully professionalized, in the sense of having undergone pre-service training, or of having established professional autonomy and their own standards and organizations. Indeed the high influential 'Meriam Report' of 1928 decried the 'disastrous effect of lack of training standards' in the BIA's educational division.[31] But many field employees took obvious professional pride in their work. Some wrote only a few lines in their reports. Others, especially from the large schools, provided highly detailed descriptions of curricula, books and teaching methods. 'The object of the whole course in science', according to a teacher of 'normal school' Indian students at Hampton Institute, Virginia, in 1892, 'is not to cover a certain amount of ground, or to crowd the student with facts, but to teach him to think, and to reason from what he observes to definite conclusions; in short, to develop in him a scientific habit of mind'. Whether or not such goals were achieved, the tone was self-consciously professional.[32]

The sense of security within the bureaucracy and of professional self-worth depended heavily upon Indian adults and children, who so often acted in ways that brought disrepute upon the schools and their staffs. In 1870, for instance, Nathan Tinson resigned as superintendent of the Kaw Manual Labour School because he could not persuade enough Indians to send their children. Complaining in 1889 of how inadequate attendance could cause a superintendent to forfeit part of the bond posted to secure the job, George W. Scott of the Chilocco Indian School vividly related his problems. 'The present plan requires all the energy of a man throughout the year, subjecting him to liability under his bond if he fails to keep up his average attendance. Even one less than the appropriate attendance robs the school of its share of the appropriation made by Congress. Summing it all up, it depends upon the caprice of the Indians whether children are secured'. Scott thus found himself at the mercy of those whom he supposedly served: 'The superintendent must visit reservations, council [sic], plead and coax a lot of untutored Indians for children...'[33]

Others expressed similar frustration. Edward E. Reardon, teacher at the Sac and Fox Day School, complained bitterly in 1895 that attendance averaged 10 – out of 120 school-age children! Even with those who chose to attend, 'no discipline can be exercised, nor authority executed,' he wrote. 'The Indian children come when they please, do about as they please, and go when they please. Should any attempt be made to correct them, they answer you in the Indian language, drop their work, and disappear "to return no more".' Worse still, Indian mothers and old women often entered the classroom, interfered with the teaching, and enticed children out of school. Only if 'these obnoxious intruders' could be kept away would it be possible 'to accomplish good'. First Lieutenant V. E. Stottler, acting Mescalero Apache agent, on the other hand, achieved 100% attendance at his school in 1896. But he admitted that it took 'firmness and a judicious use of the guardhouse and starvation of the parents'.[34]

In order to fill the schools, many educators agreed on the need for compulsory education. Congress passed a number of acts permitting some forms of compulsion, but the whole issue remained highly controversial. No fully comprehensive federal policy or universally effective methods of enforcement emerged. But at many reservations agents and tribal police overrode adult protests, rounded up Indian children, and carried them off to school.[35] At the turn of the century Commissioner Jones dramatically conceded the enduring problem. 'These pupils are gathered in from the cabin, the wickiup, and the tepee', he wrote, 'partly by cajolery and partly by threats; partly by bribery and partly by fraud; partly by persuasion and partly by force'.[36]

A powerful need to control Indians underlay the demands for compulsion and the whole educational campaign. Curricula, teaching methods, military regimentation, all were imposed from outside the Indian community. Although teachers were forced to realize their dependence upon Indian co-operation, they made little attempt to involve adult Indian participation – the goal was separation of the child from all tribal influences. 'The sooner we stop consulting the Indian about his welfare', wrote E. M. Yearian, agent on the Lemhi reservation in 1900, 'the better for the Indian'.[37]

From the later nineteenth until the early twentieth century the boarding school appeared the ideal method of establishing the desired control. Occasionally an educator advocated the day school for more immediate penetration of tribal culture. But the manual labour boarding school offered the possibility of quarantining the child from 'heathen' kin and surroundings. Upon no other subject was there 'such entire agreement of opinion', wrote Commissioner Edward P. Smith in 1873. 'The Indian has no regular habits or hours...It is also well nigh impossible to teach the Indian children the English language when they spend twenty out of every twenty-four hours in the wigwam using only their native tongue.' The off-reservation boarding school, especially,

> ...takes the youth under constant care, has him always at hand, and surrounds him by an English-speaking community, and above all, gives instruction in the first lessons of civilization, which can be found only in a well-ordered home.[38]

Or, he implied, in the surrogate home which a boarding school would become.

Whether day school, reservation boarding school, or the large, distant, off-reservation boarding school such as Hampton, Chilocco or Carlisle in Pennsylvania, all were total institutions, designed to give complete control of the lives of the students. Yet even at the most regimented, Indians misbehaved, resisted, often fled. And many children never entered a school at all. Sometimes it became so difficult to fill the classrooms that institutions competed with each other to attract pupils. At other times, admittedly, overcrowded schools had to refuse pupils. But as late as 1920 the BIA conceded that of about 82,000 eligible Indian children, over 20,000 remained outside all schools.[39] Thus the drive to control coexisted with an anguished realization that its full achievement was impossible.

Even when children willingly attended, they continued to present their educators with problems which called into question their professional competence. Despite continual efforts at improving health standards, large numbers of children sickened and died at the schools.[40] Even those who survived often began with little English, thus deeply complicating the educational task. 'The Indian teacher must deal with conditions similar to those which confront the teacher of the deaf and dumb', claimed Estelle Reel, Superintendent of Indian Schools, in 1903. She recommended starting with the 'objective method': the teacher held familiar objects in front of the pupils who repeated the English names. Therefore it was 'only by constant repetition and ceaseless grinding away that the child acquires a working knowledge of English'. The widespread punishment of pupils for speaking their own languages was only in part the expression of an ethnocentric desire to stamp out the languages of 'savagery'. It also reflected the frustration of teachers thrown against a language barrier – and yet continually subject to judgement on how effectively their charges were absorbing the ways of civilization.[41]

Teachers obviously needed pupil application beyond that of white children who, unless non-English-speaking immigrants, understood the classroom language. Many Indians could not or would not give such application. But even those willing to learn have left moving accounts of the demands, especially in the beginning. 'For me, it was very hard', recalled Belle Highwalking, a Northern Cheyenne. Her group knew no English, and thus 'couldn't understand the white people when they spoke to us'. And Luther Standing Bear, a Lakota (Sioux), initially thought that by sleeping in a white man's house he would awake speaking English. He soon discovered that he 'must learn one word at a time'.[42]

## III

Yet Standing Bear persisted. For, just as white educators became dependent upon the co-operation of Indians, many tribal members also began to feel the need for schools. Not all Indians, obviously. Those adults who refused to surrender their children felt no such need. And even pupils who attended often resisted or later fled the schools. However, many Indians developed their own highly pragmatic reasons not only for accepting, but for becoming dependent upon schools.

The 'Five Civilized Tribes', as we have seen, did so. Due to the influence of the part-white élite, the 1827 Cherokee constitution declared that 'schools and the means of education shall forever be encouraged in this Nation'. Cherokee girls attending the ABCFM Brainerd mission school in the late 1820s strongly reflected this conviction. Mostly of part-white ancestry but strongly identifying with the Cherokee Nation, they mixed pride and anxiety in letters to Eastern benefactors and, in one case, to President Andrew Jackson: pride, because they saw themselves privileged to receive a 'civilized' education; anxiety, lest they or their people not live up to the missionary goals. Nancy Reece worried that racial ancestry might hold them back, but happily accepted her teacher's assurance that 'people in the North think that the Cherokees have as good a genius to learn if it was only cultivated'. And Lucy A. Campbell noted how 'The Cherokees are improving fast in learning, they send there [sic] Children to school, and they think about Religion more than they did'. Elizabeth Taylor castigated 'the unenlighted [sic] part of this nation', and she pointed with pride to the enlightened, and to her own progress at school: 'Father is very well satisfied with my improvement last season.' The girls and their parents hoped to convince white Americans of Cherokee capacity, and so prevent the state of Georgia from removing them to the West. In this hope they were disappointed, but they deeply appreciated the opportunity of attending school.[43]

After removal, the 'Five Civilized Tribes' set up their own public school systems in the Indian Territory, which functioned under tribal control until 1906, when taken over by the federal government. At the top of its educational pyramid the Cherokee Nation established seminaries for boys and girls, dedicated to teaching only white culture. Intended for the élite of the tribe, the girls' seminary also accepted 'fullblood' and less-acculturated children, whose kin believed schooling necessary for success. These tribes made the new educational institution their own, and for their own reasons.[44]

So too did Indian pupils of Hampton Institute, all 80 of whom wrote to Senator Charles Curtis in 1912, pleading that Congress continue its appropriation for their education at the school. 'We all plan, so far as we are able, to remain at Hampton', they wrote, 'but we wish you, and all other friends of the Indian, to know that we have received at this school more than we can put into words'. They managed, nevertheless, to put those benefits into words, and assured the Senator they would face with courage any adverse decision of Congress. They concluded by pointing to 'the opportunities which Hampton alone offers for the training of Indian leaders who will really help their people to be good, Christian citizens'.[45]

Teachers no doubt influenced the writing of this letter; but, in light of Indian pragmatism and of the ambitious Hampton curriculum, we cannot assume that the pupils were merely signatories. Ex-pupils of government and missionary schools, no longer under teacher surveillance, also wrote appreciatively about their experiences. Large numbers carefully completed the 'Record of Graduates and Returned Students' sent home to them by Carlisle Indian School. 'I am glad that I have attended Carlisle and have received an education', wrote Norman Cassadore, a San Carlos Apache, in 1913, 'for I can now read and understand those things, that will help me and my people and I tell them about this'. Festus Pelone, also an Apache, wrote: 'I find that I can use to good advantage. [sic] all the things I learned while at Carlisle, and I regret that I did not absorb more.' In a letter to 'My Dear School Carlisle' Ralph Naltway declared, 'I wish I could come see my old school, I still feel for my heart for it [*sic*]'. And in long, articulate letters, Nicodemus Billy pleaded with Commissioner Francis Leupp to readmit him to Carlisle after his expulsion.[46]

The Indian narrators of published autobiographies were also far-removed from teacherly domination – both in time and space. Yet many also acknowledged Indian need for white education. Some of the most memorable expressions come from narrators *denied* adequate schooling. 'My father was wrong concerning education', said Aschie Tsosie, a Navajo, in a long lament about a life he believed was wasted. 'I wish I had gone to school. It is difficult to get a job or go to a place where no one understands your language.' Mountain Wolf Woman was devastated when kin suddenly ended the new experience. 'Alas, I was enjoying school so much', the Winnebago told her interviewer:

> ...and they made me stop. They took me back home. They had let me go to school and now they made me quit. It was then that they told me I was going to be married. I cried but it did not do any good.[47]

Other Indian families experienced no clash between their own needs or tribal loyalty, and the school: like white educators, they too saw the children as cultural mediators. One of the last hold-outs against white civilization, Geronimo chose his nephew Asa Daklugie to attend Carlisle. The older Apache insisted to the deeply reluctant Daklugie that the people needed leaders who knew the ways of the white man. This manipulative pragmatism later bore impressive fruit, as Daklugie and other Apaches learnt about cattle-raising, a useful economic alternative on the new reservation. They also learnt about white laws and lawyers, and began a legal process which in 1971 produced a successful claim of $16 million against the government.[48]

Similarly, Thomas Alford recalled how a Shawnee elder encouraged him to learn reading and writing to help the people understand treaties and other documents necessary for their survival: 'it would enable us to use the club of the white man's wisdom against him'. In 1879 chiefs sent Alford to Hampton Institute so that through him the people would know 'how to understand all that was written and spoken to and about our people and the government'. Sanapia, a Comanche medicine woman, told how her grandmother recognized the utility of the new skills for preserving knowledge of the *old* ways: 'She tell [*sic*] me always to remember what she tells me and I did. She tell me I should write it down, but at the time I didn't even know what writing is, but my grandma did.'[49]

In my sample of 102 published autobiographical accounts, about one half of the 69 who supplied information were sent to school by parents or kin, a decision which sometimes lead to bitter intra-family divisions.[50] The adaptive kin did not necessarily internalize missionary or government belief in the Christian civilization. Sending their children to school was a coping strategy. Many believed, as did Howard Whitewolf, the Comanche quoted at the beginning of this article, that the new forms of education could be exploited to ensure personal and ethnic survival. 'The Indian young men and women who fail to get an education are like the warriors of the old days', he wrote in 1917, 'their arrows do not reach as far as the white man's bullets'. Whites were 'trained to do business. If the Indian does not take this training...he will be cheated and lose money and land'.[51]

Even in retrospect, Indian autobiographical narrators do not claim they themselves possessed such clear-sightedness when they first began school. The small number who enrolled voluntarily did so for a mixture of personal reasons such as curiosity, sibling influence or an interest in learning English. Polingaysi Qoyawayma listened enraptured as her playmates told her about the food available at the local day school, which she soon entered, against the wishes of her Hopi kin. She was not the only narrator who ran away *to* school.[52] Once pupils overcame the shock of arrival, the forced haircutting (mostly of boys), the insistence that they cease speaking their own language and the loneliness, many children began to see positive sides to schooling and to exploit the situation for their own and family needs.[53]

Jason Betzinez, an Apache, found Christianity at Carlisle.[54] Others discovered less profound but nevertheless powerful attractions. After a near-traumatic arrival at boarding school around 1920, Mildred Stinson, an Oglala Sioux, was won over by the food:

> And one thing I will remember to my dying day, at four o'clock we got a great big bun...And everybody waited for this four o'clock time to come – just couldn't wait.

Helen Sekaquaptewa (Hopi) was impressed by the school clothing, and James McCarthy (Papago) remembered his own and classmates' pride as they drilled in their bright new military-style uniforms in front of local white people. Schooling could also produce a sense of superiority over 'savage' Indians – an unhealthy but sometimes real incentive to continue.[55]

Ironically, in light of the harsh regimen and the manual labour requirements, Don Talayesva and Edward Goodbird both regarded school as an escape from more demanding aspects of their tribal cultures: from the Hopi work ethic and the Hidatsa sun dance, respectively. And even school chores could become positive incentives when students gained financial reward. 'The dollar paid me was a small fortune', recalled Lucille Winnie, a Haskell School student of mixed Iroquoian and white ancestry. Further, such duties sometimes involved stimulating challenges. Not only did Helen Sekaquaptewa receive payment, the Hopi was put in charge of the laundry at Keams Canyon Boarding School: 'The teachers and matrons gave us responsibility', she noted proudly, 'and *depended upon us* as we grew older' (emphasis added). She became so used to life at one boarding school that she connived with the principal to attend a second without getting the mandatory consent of her parents.[56] Other narrators also voluntarily transferred to later schools with or without kin consent.[57]

For some pupils the varied and officially sanctioned extracurricular activities became major positive incentives. Even as a bitter Apache, Asa Daklugie grudgingly admitted how the sports activities helped pull him through Carlisle, and looked back with pride on the achievements of the football squad against Ivy League teams. For all his resentment of 'white eyes' he attempted to send his daughters to Carlisle. Luther Standing Bear, at the same school, and Fred Kabotie, a Hopi at the Santa Fe Indian School, gained great satisfaction from playing in the school bands.[58] Girls appear to have been more carefully supervised than boys, and as women had less to say about sports and music. But Lucille Winnie enjoyed the achievements of the Haskell football teams, and especially the athletic performances of her brothers. Once Irene Stewart began to play basketball and sing in the glee club at Haskell, life became easier for her there and she grew less lonely. She deeply regretted her failure to graduate, but voluntarily continued her education at other institutions before final return to her Navajo homeland.[59]

Further, unofficial pupil sub-cultures sometimes evolved. Francis la Flesche and Omaha pupils at a Presbyterian Boarding school in the early 1860s formed gangs, each employing its own ritual and offering protection to its members. Allen James (Pomo) participated in similar gang-building at Sherman Institute, California. Sub-cultures could also involve the ritualistic setting up of fights among pupils, or the establishment of secret student courts. At Chilocco the sub-cultural activities gave a sense of control and meaning to the lives of the pupils – indeed helped them take over large areas of the school, in Lomawaima's view.[60] Enjoyed out of sight and earshot of teachers, these activities expressed fundamentally ambivalent responses to the schools: they provided the spice of resistance, while simultaneously allowing students to continue the education to which they had become accustomed.

Historians must sceptically approach teachers' self-serving claims for impressive pupil performance.[61] But Indians sometimes reported how, once they began to master the new language, they could thrill to the new knowledge. While at Brainerd Mission School in 1828–29, Nancy Reece bubbled with curiosity about the world outside her Cherokee Nation. Visiting the Moravian mission she 'saw the piano and was very much pleased to hear such music. I never saw one before but [the teacher] Miss Ames says they are very common among the ladies at the North [*sic*]'. Elsewhere she wrote: 'I can see things when Miss Ames is telling me about them.' Francis La Flesche gained immense personal satisfaction from his progress in English and his entry into higher school grades. Ely S. Parker's experience at a New York academy was 'among the happiest days of my youthful existence'. His schooling helped prepare him for a distinguished army career, and from 1869 to 1871 this Seneca served as Commissioner of Indian Affairs. Later in the century Thomas Alford, Asa Daklugie and Charles A. Eastman (Santee Sioux) also thrilled to the new learning. 'I absorbed knowledge through every pore', wrote Eastman, who finally graduated as an MD from Boston University. Lucille Winnie, Helen Sekaquaptewa and Anna Moore Shaw, a Pima, also gained strong satisfaction from their school learning.[62]

As younger children these ambitious Indians felt little need for white ways. But once enrolled voluntarily or by parents or tribal police, and once acclimatized, they accepted the school as central to their lives. Rarely did real meetings of minds occur between teachers and even such students as these. Yet they realized that to continue learning English and the ways of the whites, they needed the school as surely as their teachers needed their co-operation. They manifested an intense curiosity about, and openness to different cultural experiences, which in later life made them willing cultural brokers between the white world and their own.[63]

## IV

New Social History/empowerment understandings of Indian–white contact and especially of schooling rightly insist that Indian adults and even children were not passive victims. They did influence events. But I have sought to warn against a triumphalist empowerment argument in Indian history and in the history of confrontations between western powers and colonized peoples, one which portrays the erstwhile victim as now the near-controller of the contact situation. Indians did not control the schools; nor, as much as they hoped, did the teachers, despite their access to the economic and military power of the United States.

Complex and shifting power relationships thus characterized the educational arena. Indians could and did manipulate the schools to their own advantage, just as white educators manipulated Indians. Once the schools were built; once the bureaucracy began to evolve; once careers and professional pride depended on successful transformation of Indian children; once individual Indians or groups of tribespeople realized the importance of the school for personal, kin and ethnic advantage – then groups of American Indians and white educators became locked into symbiotic relationships of interdependence.

## Acknowledgements

I wish to thank John Bannigan, Sirkka Coleman, Courtney Fairweather, Francis Paul Prucha, SJ, Allan Winkler, and the anonymous readers for *History of Education*. Also the University of Jyväskylä, Finland; Miami University, Ohio; The Newberry Library, Chicago; The National Anthropological Archives of The Smithsonian Institution, Washington, DC; and the National Archives, Washington, DC.

## Notes

1 Howard Whitewolf, 'A short story of my life', *The American Indian Magazine* 5 (January–March 1917), 31. Indian responses to schooling in the present essay are based heavily upon published autobiography, listed in Michael C. Coleman, *American Indian Children at School, 1850–1930* (Jackson, 1993), bibliography, 203–8. On the problematic nature of long-term autobiographical recall, see note 19; George W. Scott, 'Report of School at Chilocco, Indian Territory, Aug. 10, 1889, in *Annual Report of the Commissioner of Indian Affairs* (Washington, 1889), 357. Henceforth ARCIA, followed by citation. Available ARCIAs appeared in different publications or separately.

2 David Cowart points to different kinds of symbiosis, in *Literary Symbiosis: the Reconfigured Text in Twentieth-Century Writing* (Athens, GA, 1993), 4. I use the term in the 'mutualistic' sense, indicating a relationship of interdependence in which both organisms or groups benefit, or believe they benefit.

3 Andy Green, *Education and State Formation: the Rise of Education Systems in England, France and the USA* (London, 1990), 171 and ch. 5. The civilizing and educative goals of US Indian policy are a central theme of Francis Paul Prucha, *American Indian Treaties: the History of a Political Anomaly* (Berkeley, 1994), especially 9–14. On Colonial schooling, see Margaret Connell Szasz, *Indian Education in the American Colonies, 1607–1783* (Albuquerque, 1988). Few Euro-Americans accepted that Indian peoples possessed institutionalized educational forms, on which forms see ibid., ch. 1; and Coleman, *American Indian Children*, ch. 2.

4 For the text of the act, Report of the Indian School Superintendent, ARCIA (Washington, 1885), LXXVII–LXXIX. An account of the expenditure was to be 'laid annually before Congress'.

5 ARCIAs; Francis Paul Prucha, *The Great Father: the United States Government and the American Indians*, 2 vols (Lincoln, NE, 1984), I, chs 5 and 6, statistics, 152; Theodore Fischbacher, 'A study of the role of the federal government in the education of the American Indian', unpublished PhD dissertation, Arizona State University, 1967, ch. 4, appendix E.

6 ARCIA (Washington, 1885) LXXIX; ARCIA (1900), *House Document*, No. 5, 56 congress, 2nd session, serial 4101: 12–44; ARCIA, *Annual Report of the Secretary of the Interior* (Washington, 1930), 26–7. Such descriptions and statistics must be approached critically: Fischbacher, 'Study', 85–9, 146. Few of the Indian autobiographical narrators (note 1) attended state public schools.

7 ARCIAs; Margaret Connell Szasz, *Education and the American Indian: the Road to Self-Determination Since 1928* (Albuquerque, 1977); Prucha, *Great Father*, II, chs 36–9; Coleman, *American Indian Children*, 50–3. By 1945 the BIA was returning to assimilationist policies.

8   K. Tsianina Lomawaima, *They Called it Prairie Light: the Story of Chilocco Indian School* (Lincoln, NE, 1994), quotation 98. See also, for example, Coleman, *American Indian Children*; Sally Hyer, *One House, One Voice, One Heart: Native American Education at the Santa Fe Indian School* (Santa Fe, 1990); Robert A. Trennert, Jr, *The Phoenix Indian School: Forced Assimilation in Arizona, 1891–1935* (Norman, 1988); David Wallace Adams, 'Fundamental considerations: the deep meaning of Native American schooling, 1880–1900', *Harvard Educational Review*, 58 (February 1988), 1–28; Sally McBeth, *Ethnic Identity and the Boarding School Experience of West-Central Oklahoma American Indians* (Lanham, 1983); and Robert F. Berkhofer, Jr, *Salvation and the Savage: An Analysis of Protestant Missions and American Indian Response, 1787–1862* (1965; repr. New York, 1972), ch. 2. For recent historical overviews, see David H. Dejong, *Promises of the Past: A History of Indian Education* (Golden, 1993); and John Reyhner and Jeanne Eder, *A History of Indian Education* (Billings, 1989).

9   ARCIA (1903) *House Document*, No. 5, part 1, 58 Congress, 2nd session, serial 4653: 3.

10  Lomawaima, *Prairie Light*, quotations 167, 130, xii–iv. See also note 8, especially works by Coleman, Hyer, Trennert and McBeth. Focusing on an Indian-controlled school but also emphasizing complex and often positive pupil responses is Devon A. Mihesuah, *Cultivating the Rosebuds: The Education of Women at the Cherokee Female Seminary, 1851–1909* (Urbana, 1993), especially chs 5 and 7. See also, Szasz, *Indian Education*, especially ch. 9.

11  See for example, the Board of Foreign Missions of the Presbyterian Church in the USA (BFM), *Annual Report* (New York, 1838–93), henceforth, BFM, AR, and date; American Board of Commissioners for Foreign Missions (ABCFM), *First Ten Annual Reports* (Boston, 1834), *Annual Report* (Boston, 1821–40), henceforth, ABCFM, AR, and date; and *Memorial Volume of the First Fifty Years* (Boston, 1861). See also Carol Devons, *Countering Colonization: Native American Women and Great Lakes Missions, 1630–1900* (Berkeley, 1992); Michael C. Coleman, *Presbyterian Missionary Attitudes Toward American Indians, 1837–1893* (Jackson, 1985), 9–17; and Berkhofer, *Salvation*. On Catholic developments, see Prucha, *Great Father*, I, 145, 395; and John J. Killoren, *'Come, Blackrobe': De Smet and the Indian Tragedy* (Norman, 1994).

12  See optimistic comments by Commissioner Ely S. Parker, a Seneca Indian, in ARCIA (1870), *House Executive Document*, No. 1, 41 Congress, 3rd session, serial 1449: 474; and later ARCIAs. See also, Coleman, *American Indian Children*, ch. 3; Prucha, *Great Father*, I, ch. 20; and Robert H. Keller, Jr, *American Protestantism and United States Indian Policy, 1869–1882* (Lincoln, 1983).

13  ABCFM, AR (1823), 99–100. In the pre-Civil War decades, nevertheless, direct government funding accounted for perhaps less than 10% of the money used to 'civilize' Indians; mission societies raised some of the money; Indian treaty stipulations supplied the bulk of it; Fischbacher, 'Study', 65–7.

14  Fischbacher, 'Study', 95–7, 102, 133–8; see ARCIA (1900), *House Document*, No. 5, 56 Congress, 2nd session, serial 4101: 22–8, on the phasing out of mission subsidization. Large numbers of reports from mission schools were appended to the ARCIA. Jesuit school: Chas. Hutchins, Indian agent, to Commissioner W. P. Dole, Oct. 15, 1864, Letters Received 1824–1881, Schools, 1824–73, Microfilm 234, reel 794: 96–102. In Records of the BIA. Record Group 75, National Archives, Washington (henceforth RG 75, NA).

15  See for example, Coleman, *Presbyterian Missionary Attitudes*, bibliography, sections A2 and A3.

16  ABCFM, AR (1835), 89. On the rebuilding of the missions, see ABCFM, ARs; BFM, ARs; Prucha, *Great Father*, I, 287; and Coleman, *Presbyterian Missionary Attitudes*, 13–14, 61–2.

17  Alvin M. Josephy, Jr, *The Nez Perce Indians and the Opening of the Northwest*, abridged edn (New Haven, 1971), 241–3. Indian resistance to missions is a major theme of Devons, *Countering Colonization*.

18  Copy of an Act Passed at the Twelfth Session of the General Council of the Choctaw Nation, box 9, vol. 2, American Indian Correspondence, Presbyterian Historical Society,

Philadelphia (henceforth 9: 2, AIC); New Laws (of Choctaws, 1853), 10: 2, AIC; Coleman, *Presbyterian Missionary Attitudes*, 72, No. 20; William G. McLoughlin, 'Indian slave-holders and Presbyterian missionaries, 1837–1861', *Church History*, 42 (Dec. 1973), 535–1. The BFM 'seemed to be walking on eggs', 358; Prucha, *American Indian Treaties*, especially 11–13.

19 Alexander Reid to A. L. Wilson, 12 April, 1854, 12: 1, AIC. Also, William Templeton, List of scholars, 12: 2, AIC, on Annie Hardridge. Omaha hunt: for example, Isaac Black to Respected friend, July 15, 1862, 4: 1, AIC; Robert Burtt, Report of the Omaha Mission, ARCIA (1863), *House Executive Document*, No. 1, 38 Congress, 1 session, serial 1182: 359. Cf. corroborating autobiographical account by Francis La Flesche, *The Middle Five: Indian Schoolboys of the Omaha Tribe* (1900; repr. Madison, 1963), 84–5. Many scholars question the credibility of long-term memory, but see my *American Indian Children* and 'The historical credibility of American Indian autobiographical accounts of schooling', *Irish Journal of American Studies*, 3 (1994), 127–50.

20 Reports appended to ARCIA often detailed mission and government school 'half-and-half' curricula. See also, BFM AR (1857), 17, and (1863), 7; Berkhofer, *Salvation*, 37–40; and La Flesche, *Middle Five*, 68–9. Quotation: Isaac Black to Walter Lowrie, March 2, 1864, 4: 1, AIC.

21 ABCFM, AR (1819), 236, (1821), 49, and (1823), 101. See Michael C. Coleman, 'American Indian school pupils as cultural brokers: Cherokee girls at Brainerd Mission, 1828–1829', in ed. Margaret Connell Szasz, *Between Indian and White Worlds: The Cultural Broker* (Norman, 1994), 122–35.

22 Cf. Clayton G. McKenzie, 'Demythologizing the missionaries: a reassessment of the functions and relationships of Christian missionary education under colonialism', *Comparative Education*, 29 (1993), 45–66. 'In essence missionary educators were more the pawns of colonial regimes than the agents of imperialist conquest; and they were considerably at the mercy of the indigenous populace as well' (p. 63).

23 Edward Goodbird, *Goodbird the Indian: His Story*, ed. Gilbert L. Wilson (1914; repr. St Paul, 1985), 41.

24 For example, ARCIA (1899), *House Document*, No. 5, part 1, 56 Congress, 1st session, serial 3915: 29. 'Although sectarian teaching is forbidden in the schools, they are not godless institutions. The broad principles of the Bible, of religion, and morality are taught...'; Prucha, *Great Father*, I, 290.

25 Barclay White to Commissioner Edward P. Smith, ARCIA (1873), *House Executive Document*, No. 1, part 5, 43 Congress, 1st session, serial 1601: 556. Also, for example, W. E. Cullen, Report of the Winnebego Manual Labor School, ARCIA (1860), *Senate Executive Document*, No. 1, 36 Congress, 2nd session, serial 1078: 302–3; M. B. Kent, Report of Fort Peck Indian Agency, ARCIA (Washington, 1977), 142.

26 M. Friedman, 'Annual Report of the Carlisle Indian School, 1910', *The Red Man*, 3 (Oct. 1910), 61–2. And see detailed statistics on the profitable production of the farm, tailor shop, etc., 52–60. Pupils played a large part in producing this magazine. Examples of BIA academic/manual labour curricula: Report of Carlisle School, ARCIA (Washington, 1883), 162–4; Report of School at Chilocco, ARCIA (Washington, 1888), 258–63; Report of Hampton Normal and Agricultural Institute, ARCIA (1890), *House Executive Document*, No. 1, part 5, vol. II, 51 Congress, 2nd session, 2841: 314–23, and see detailed Course of Study, CLVI–CLXII; ARCIA (1913), (Washington, 1914), 23–5. Teachers' accounts: Janette Woodruff, *Indian Oasis* (Caldwell, 1939), 28; Gertrude Golden, *Red Moon Called Me: Memoirs of a Schoolteacher in the Government Indian Service* (San Antonio, 1954), 8, 209. Indian recollections: for example, Noah White, in eds Joseph H. Cash and Herbert T. Hoover, *To Be an Indian: An Oral History* (New York, 1971), 105; Frank Mitchell, *Navajo Blessingway Singer: The Autobiography of Frank Mitchell, 1881–1967*, eds Charlotte E. Frisbie and David P. McAllester (Tucson, 1978), 62. Also, Lomawaima, *Cultivating*, especially chs 3 and 4.

27 Institute for Government Research, *The Problem of Indian Administration* [The Meriam Report] (Baltimore, 1928), 31, 375–8, 382–91, for example. 'The labor of children as carried on in Indian boarding schools would, it is believed, constitute a violation

of child labor laws in most states', 376. Also, Robert A. Trennert, Jr, 'From Carlisle to Phoenix: the rise and fall of the Indian outing system, 1878–1930', *Pacific Historical Review*, 52 (Aug. 1983), 267–91, on the placement of pupils in working Positions outside the schools.

28   Prucha, *Great Father*, II, 779. The Board of Indian Commissioners was established by President Ulysses S. Grant in 1869 to oversee disbursements and appropriations of the Indian service, Fischbacher, 'Study', 76. See also ARCIA, *Reports of the Department of the Interior* (Washington, 1908), 11. Commissioner Francis E. Leupp acknowledged the desirability of 'going out of business at no very distant date', but conceded that 'for the next few years it is going to take more men and a higher class of men to wind up the affairs of the Indian service...'.

29   On the BIA bureaucracy see Prucha, *Great Father*, esp. I, chs 5, 6, 11, 12, 18, 19, 23, and II, chs 28, 30, 32, 33, 36. On 1824 situation, I, 164; on 1926 responsibilities, and on domination of Indians, II, 796, 759. Also Fischbacher, 'Study', especially chs 4–8, and 89 on education division. Developments can also be followed in ARCIA. Statistics: ARCIA (Washington, 1888), xx–xxi; ARCIA (1900), *House Document*, No. 5, 56 Congress, 2nd session, serial 4101: 30; ARCIA *Reports of the Department of the Interior* (Washington, 1911), 28; ARCIA, *Reports of the Department of the Interior*, vol. 2 (Washington, 1912), 3; ARCIA (Washington, 1937), 242.

30   Fischbacher, 'Study', 55–9, 89–92, 123–5; ARCIA (Washington, 1888), xxi–iv, ARCIA (Washington, 1889). See questionnaire, 5; ARCIA (1890), *House Executive Document*, No. 1, part 5, vol. II, 51 Congress, 2nd session, serial 2841: especially CXLVI–CLXIII. On institutes and civil service status, for example, ARCIA (1897), *House Document*, No. 5, 55 Congress, 2nd session, serial 3641: 19, 322–4. Also Prucha, *Great Father*, II, 700–7. Teacher experiences: Golden, *Red Moon*, xi, 16, 209. Also Lucille (Gerry) Winnie, *Sah-Gan-De-Oh: the Chief's Daughter* (New York, 1969), 61.

31   Institute for Government Research, *Indian Administration*, 360, see 359–70. By the beginning of the twentieth century, writes Bruce Kimball, the term 'profession' meant 'a dignified vocation practised by "professionals" who professed selfless and contractual service, membership in a strong association, and functional expertise modelled on the natural sciences', *The 'True Professional Ideal' in America: a History* (Cambridge, MA, 1992), 303. Jurgen Herbst sees education, and individual and collective autonomy in the performance of their tasks as central to the status of professionals, *And Sadly Teach: Teacher Education and Professionalization in American Culture* (Madison, 1989), 6–7.

32   ARCIA (Washington, 1892), 700. Forty-eight Indians, along with 'colored students', took this modified 'grammar and English high-school course'. During the later nineteenth-century, writes Kimball, 'the cultural ideal, the fundamental source of cultural inspiration and legitimation, shifted from polity to science', *The 'True Professional Ideal'*, 200, ch. 4. Science thus became the 'architechtonic' of the era, 10–17.

33   Nathan Tinson (?) to Mahlon Stubbs, 12 Dec. (?), 1870, Letters Received 1824–1881, Schools 1824–1873, M234, reel 798: 130, RG 75, NA. For example of teacher report, see Report of Indian School at Grand Portage, Minnesota, 1865, same collection, M234, reel 794: 924–6; Report of School at Chilocco, ARCIA (Washington, 1889), 357. On bonding, Fischbacher, 'Study', 102. See also Report of the Indian Industrial and Training School, Sitka, Alaska: 'Their crude ideas are so vague', wrote Superintendent W. A. Kelly, 'that they think they are doing us a great favour and placing us under lasting obligation by giving us a child to support and educate', ARCIA (Washington, 1887), 234.

34   Report of Teacher of Sac and Fox Day School, ARCIA (1895), *House Document*, No. 5, vol. II, 54 Congress, 1st session, serial 3381, 169–70; Report of Mescalero Agency, ARCIA (1896), *House Document*, No. 5, vol. II, 54 Congress, 2nd session, serial 3489, 211. By 'starvation' he may have meant reduction of government-supplied rations, see 213.

35   Coleman, *American Indian Children*, 45; see 61–3 for Indian memories of forced attendance, corroborated by each other and by white accounts; Fischbacher, 'Study', 125–31.

36   ARCIA (1901), *House Document*, No. 5, 57 Congress, 1st session, serial 4290: 1–2.

37 Report of Agent for Lemhi Agency, Idaho, ARCIA (1900), *House Document*, No. 5, 56 Congress, 2nd session, serial 4101: 221.

38 On day schools, W. N. Hailman, Report of the Superintendent of Indian Schools, ARCIA (1897), *House Document*, No. 5, 55 Congress, 2nd session, serial 3641: 333. Quotation, ARCIA (1873), *House Executive Document*, No. 1, part 5, 43 Congress, 1st session, serial 1601: 376–7. Also, Commissioner Rowland E. Trowbridge, ARCIA (1880), *House Executive Document*, No. 1, part 5, 46 Congress, 3rd session, serial 1959: 85; Commissioner Thomas J. Morgan, ARCIA (Washington, 1892), 48–50.

39 On the mixed, ambivalent responses of pupils at many government and missionary schools, see Coleman, *American Indian Children*, especially chs 5–9; on competition, Report of School at Hampton, ARCIA (1903), *House Document*, No. 5, 58 Congress, 2nd session, serial 4615: 437; Prucha, *Great Father*, vol. 2, 816–17; Fischbacher, 'Study', 107. Overcrowding: Report of the School at Phoenix, Ariz., ARCIA (1896), *House Document*, No. 5, 54 Congress, 2nd session, vol. II, serial 3489: 364–5. Statistics: ARCIA, *Reports of the Department of the Interior* (Washington, 1920), 147.

40 ARCIA (Washington, 1892), 46; ARCIA (1900), *House Document*, No. 5, 56 Congress, 2nd session, serial 4010: 22; Institute for Government Research, *Indian Administration*, 392–4. On sanitation, W. N. Hailman, Report of the Superintendent of Indian Schools, ARCIA (1897), *House Document*, No. 5, 55 Congress, 2nd session, serial 3641: 330–2. Superintendent T. C. Bradford was relieved to report 'only three deaths' out of 200 pupils, Report of School at Chilocco, ARCIA (Washington, 1888), 258. Cf. relieved comment of missionary in BFM, AR (1851), 5: 'Not one of our children died during the year.' Indian recollections: Luther Standing Bear, *My People the Sioux*, ed. E. A. Brininstool (1928; repr. Lincoln, NE, 1975), 162–6; La Flesche, *Middle Five*, ch. 16. See also Coleman, *American Indian Children*, 162–4.

41 Report of the Superintendent of Indian Schools, ARCIA (1903), *House Document*, No. 5, part 1, 58 Congress, 2nd session, serial 4615: 384. For a teacher's account, Woodruff, *Indian Oasis*, 166–7. For an Indian account, Jim Whitewolf (pseudonym), *The Life of a Kiowa Apache Indian*, ed. Charles S. Brant (New York, 1969), 85–6. Punishments: for example, Report of Superintendent of Omaha School, ARCIA (1896), *House Document*, No. 5, 54 Congress, 2nd session, serial 3489: 200; La Flesche, *Middle Five*, xvii; Ah-nen-la-de-ni, 'An Indian Boy's Story', *The Independent*, LV (July 30, 1903), 1783; Neola Walker, in eds, Cash and Hoover, *To Be an Indian*, 79.

42 Belle Highwalking, *The Narrative of a Northern Cheyenne Woman*, ed. Katherine M. Weist (Billings, 1979), 3; Standing Bear, *My People*, 155–6. Elsie Allen rarely spoke to teachers *or* pupils, almost all from other tribes, during her first year at boarding school, Allen, *Pomo Basketmaking: A Supreme Art for the Weaver*, ed. Vinson Brown (Healdsburg, 1972), 10–11.

43 Constitution of the Cherokee Nation (1827), Article VI, section 10, in Emmett Starr, *History of the Cherokee Indians and their Legends and Folklore* (1921; repr. New York, 1969), 63. Cherokee girls' letters: John Howard Payne Papers, VIII, 1–62, Newberry Library, Chicago (henceforth JHPP, VIII). 'Originals' in same hand, yet most likely verbatim copies. I cite from typed copies (all written in 1828– 29, so I omit dates but give typed page numbers): Nancy Reece to Respected Madam (10); Lucy A. Campbell to Respected Sir (40); Elizabeth Taylor to Dear Cousin (3), and to Dear Miss Abigail (13–14). See also Coleman, 'American Indian school pupils', in Szasz, *Between Indian and White Worlds*, 122–35, 320, n. 12.

44 John D. Benedict, Report of Superintendent of Schools for Indian Territory, ARCIA, *Reports of the Department of the Interior* (Washington, 1907), 349–55; Mihesuah, *Cultivating the Rosebuds*; Prucha, *Great Father*, II, 909–11.

45 To Hon. Charles Curtis from all the Indian students of Hampton Institute, April 23, 1912, Central Classified Files, file 229, RG 75, NA.

46 Student files, in School Records, Records of Carlisle Indian Industrial School, Records of Nonreservation Schools (henceforth, School Records), RG 75, NA: Cassadore (file no. 69), Pelone (108), Naltway (103); Nicodemus Billy to Hon. Francis E. Leupp, Aug. 31, and Sept. 22, 1908 (Central Classified Files, file 826, RG 75, NA).

47 Ashie Tsosie, in ed. Broderick H. Johnson, *Stories of Traditional Navajo Life and Culture by Twenty-Two Navajo Men and Women* (Tsaile, Navajo Nation, 1977), 113–15; Mountain Wolf Woman, *Mountain Wolf Woman, Sister of Crashing Thunder: The Autobiography of a Winnebago Indian*, ed. Nancy O. Lurie (Ann Arbor, 1971), 29.

48 Asa Daklugie et al., *Indeh: An Apache Odyssey*, ed. Eve Ball (Norman, 1988), 135–6; on cattle, 84, 145, 274; on legal claim, 290–1.

49 Thomas Wildcat Alford, *Civilization and the Story of the Absentee Shawnees*, as Told to Florence Drake (Norman, 1936), 73, 90; Sanapia, *Sanapia: Comanche Medicine Woman*, ed. David E. Jones (Prospect Heights, 1972), 21.

50 Coleman, *American Indian Children*, 60–1. Ten children of the 69 volunteered to attend school; 17 were coerced by authorities; 9 recalled overlapping influences. I do not claim the whole sample as representative, but it is diverse: coming from about 30 tribal groups, two-thirds of the 102 were male, one-third female. I have also attempted to corroborate narrator experiences; see note 19. Family division: Irene Stewart, *A Voice in Her Tribe: A Navajo Woman's Own Story*, ed. Doris Ostrander Dawby. Anthropological Papers No. 17 (Socorro, 1980), 15; Charles A. Eastman (Ohiyesa), *From the Deep Woods to Civilization: Chapters in the Autobiography of a Indian* (1916; repr. Lincoln, NE, 1977), 24–8.

51 Howard Whitewolf, 'Short Story', 31.

52 Coleman, *American Indian Children*, ch. 4, and note 51; Polingaysi Qoyawayma (Elizabeth Q. White), *No Turning Back: A True Account of a Hopi Indian Girl's Struggle to Bridge the Gap Between the World of Her people and the World of the White Man*, as Told to Vada F. Carlson (Albuquerque, 1964), 20–6. Ernest Nelson also fled *to* school, Johnson, *Stories of Traditional Navajo Life*, 231–2.

53 Coleman, *American Indian Children*, especially ch. 5.

54 Jason Betzinez, *I Fought with Geronimo*, with William Sturtevant Nye (1959; repr. Lincoln, NE, 1987), 156.

55 Stinson, in Cash and Hoover, eds, *To Be an Indian*, 95; Helen Sekaquaptewa, *Me and Mine: The Life Story of Helen Sekaquaptewa*, as told to Louise Udall (Tucson, 1969), 134–8; James McCarthy, *A Papago Traveller: the Memories of James McCarthy*, ed. John G. Westover (Tucson, 1985), 29. Also, Betzinez, *I Fought*, 153; George Webb, *A Pima Remembers* (Tucson, 1959), 85. Superiority: Goodbird, *Goodbird*, 43; Jim Whitewolf, *Life*, 95.

56 Don Talayesva, *Sun Chief: The Autobiography of a Hopi Indian*, ed. Leo W. Simmons (1942; repr. New Haven, 1970), 100; Goodbird, *Goodbird*, 58–9, on the vision-seeking sun dance; Winnie, *Sah-Gan-De-Oh*, 50; Sekaquaptewa, *Me and Mine*, 124, 139. Changing schools, 132–3. Payment, also McCarthy, *A Papago Traveller*, 43; ARCIA (Washington, 1888), xxi.

57 For example, Albert Yava, *Big Falling Snow: A Tewa-Hopi Indian's Life and Times and the History and Traditions of His People*, ed. Harold Courlander (Albuquerque, 1978), 14–16.

58 Daklugie, *Indeh*, 144, 146–7. On daughters, letter in his file (72), Wm. Light (?) to Mr Lipps, Aug. 31, 1916, School Records, RG 75, NA; Standing Bear, *My People*, 148–9, 171–2; Fred Kabotie, *Fred Kabotie, Hopi Indian Artist: An Autobiography Told with Bill Belknap* (Flagstaff, 1977), 32–3.

59 On supervision of girls, Lomawaima, *Prairie Light*, especially ch. 4. Sports: Winnie, *Sah-Gan-De-Oh*, 53–5; Stewart, *Voice*, 30, 34.

60 La Flesche, *Middle Five*, 36, 70–1, ch. 13, for example; Allen James, *Chief of the Pomos*, ed. Ann Connor (Santa Rosa, 1972), 40–41; Anonymous Choctaw, in *Nations Remembered: An Oral History of the Five Civilized Tribes, 1865–1907*, ed. Theda Perdue (Westport, 1980), 130–2; Lomawaima, *Prairie Light*, especially ch. 6, and on gangs, 112–15, 154–8; Coleman, *American Indian Children*, especially 154–9.

61 For example, Report of School at Carlisle, Pa., ARCIA (1900), *House Document* No. 5, 56 Congress, 2nd session, serial 4101: 506, 'Pupils are strengthening in scholarship, power of independent research, and application; in fondness for study; in ideals and aspirations, and in eagerness for higher training'; Report of Normal and Agricultural Institute at Hampton, Va., ARCIA (Washington, 1892), 700.

62 JHPP, VIII, Nancy Reece to Respected Madam, 17, 8. See note 43; La Flesche, *Middle Five*, 13–14; Ely S. Parker, 'Writings of General Parker', *Publications of the Buffalo Historical Society*, VIII (1905), 530–1; Alford, *Civilization*, 80, for example; Daklugie, *Indeh*, 144–5, on 'desperately' wanting to learn to read, and on his first fascinated discovery of an atlas; Eastman, *Deep Woods*, 54, and chs 2–5; Winnie, *Sah-Gan-De-Oh*, esp. 53; Sekaquaptewa, *Me and Mine, passim* and 93–5, 134–8; Anna Moore Shaw, *A Pima Past* (Tucson, 1974), 140–2, for example.
63 Margaret Connell Szasz, Conclusion to Szasz, ed., *Between Indian and White Worlds*, 294–300. She sees curiosity and receptiveness as major characteristics of cultural brokers.

## CHAPTER 13

# CLASSROOM TEACHERS AND EDUCATIONAL CHANGE 1876–1996

Philip Gardner

*Journal of Education for Teaching*, 24, 1, 33–49, 1998

## Three generations of teachers

One of the defining experiences of life in the twentieth century has been schooling. Schooling has distinguished our own century from the greater part of the previous one – as it may also from the next (Hamilton, 1990; Hargreaves, 1994). From 1876, every generation of parents in England and Wales has been obliged by law to provide for the formal education of their children, and for the great majority, this has meant compulsory attendance at schools regulated and provided or aided by the state (Sutherland, 1973: 125–145).

The habituation of the people of England and Wales to the regime of state-sponsored schooling was hard won but once achieved, it has proved to be deep-rooted and resilient (Philpott, 1904; Rubinstein, 1969; Gardner, 1984, 1991). That this has been so has been largely due to the work of those generations of classroom teachers – just three in number, if we take a notional career length of 40 years – responsible for teaching the nation's children over this period. In 1876 there were, including pupil–teachers, just 56,875 such teachers (Committee of Council, 1877: 339). By 1903, the figure had grown to 150,884 (Board of Education, 1903: 30). In 1926, there were 165,000 (Board of Education, 1927: 47, 158). In 1947 there were 191,819 (Ministry of Education, 1948: 162). In 1962 the figure was 279, 420 (Department of Education and Science, 1968: 17); and in 1990 385,177 (Department of Education and Science, 1996: 2).

Through the hands of this steadily growing army of men and women have passed every cohort of the twentieth century's children. And yet, historically, we know relatively little about them. This is highly paradoxical. As children, our entire understanding of formal education was constituted through the agency of teachers (Pollard, 1974: 114). They stood at the centre of the educational world. Historians have tended to reverse this emphasis. Classroom teachers become not agents of educational change but one of its effects. Whether the history of the teaching profession in the twentieth century is written in terms of broad consensus – as for example in the work of Gosden or Tropp, or in terms of underlying conflict – as for example in the work of Grace or Lawn, the individual classroom teacher seldom has more than an implied or peripheral role (Tropp, 1957; Gosden, 1972; Grace, 1987; Lawn, 1987).

This ascription of role may be wholly legitimate if the aim is expressly to illuminate the development and implementation of policy or to trace the changing relation of the state and the teachers' representative associations. But what we cannot afford to assume is that the attitudes of classroom teachers have been mirrored in, or can be read off from what are, in effect, accounts of change in dominant educational ideologies and institutional structures (Lawn, 1985: 3–4; Barber, 1992: 60; Brehony, 1992: 215–217).

These factors have implications for the ways in which we approach the concept of professionalism, widely seen in many influential accounts as the central analytical issue at stake in the development of the teaching profession in the course of the twentieth century (Barber, 1992: 92–97).

The notion that the idea of professionalism in this period has been deeply contested between teachers and the state is both telling and persuasive. Its strength is diminished, however, to the degree that the concept of professionalism is reified; an object over which, at any given moment, one side or the other has relatively greater or lesser control. In such a perspective, professionalism becomes a fixed currency through which the state endeavours to manage its domination over the teachers and the teachers seek, through their collective associations, to defend and advance their status and independence (Lawn, 1987).

The historical development of teacher professionalism is, however, more complex and more variegated (Helsby, 1995). Attention to the voices of classroom teachers demonstrates this and begins to offer us some understanding not only of how professionalism has been contested, but also some sense of how it has been constructed.

Classroom teachers' constructions of professionalism certainly drew upon the developing relation between their representative bodies and the state. But they drew on much else besides. Institutional factors may not comprise the only, or indeed, the principal elements from which teachers have constructed their professional identities. Similarly, those landmark national events which punctuate the familiar documentary record of educational change – the Hadow Report of 1926, the 1944 Education Act, the national strikes of 1969–70 and the mid-1980s – may not figure to quite the same extent in chronologies of change as recorded in the memories of classroom teachers.

Every term, in schools up and down Britain, the farewell speeches of retiring teachers to their colleagues are a testament to this plurality of influences, as are the longer-term recollections of those who have been retired for many years. In such recollections, official reports, legislation and industrial confrontations take their place alongside more mundane, immediate and local determinants of life in schools. Sometimes the former may be perceived to dominate the latter but very often it is the other way round; the second is seen to have the capacity to ameliorate, absorb or overwhelm the impacts of the first. That is why, when asked if education had seen relatively little change in her many years in the classroom, a Pembrokeshire teacher, Alice Daly, born in 1887 and successively pupil, pupil–teacher and teacher in the same elementary school for an unbroken 43 years, could respond:

> Oh no, it changed. They had a piece built on, because more people were coming to our school, and the school was made bigger.

Changes in the structure and organisation of educational provision since 1876 have, of course, been profound and have been charted many times (Middleton and Weitzman, 1976). But what is the history of the relation of classroom teachers to such change? What has change meant to the insider rather than to the policy maker or the commentator?

One way of grounding this question is to think in terms of a dialogue between the three notional teaching generations of the modern period: 1876–1916; 1916–1956; 1956–1996. If such an exchange were possible, what would its participants find that they could recognisably share in common? And what aspects of their, working experience would separate them?

The voice of the first generation is now beyond our direct questioning; that of the third is not and has been increasingly sought in many studies in recent years (Gibson, 1973; Ball and Goodson, 1985; Sikes *et al.*, 1985; Nias, 1989; Goodson, 1992). The second generation voice is not yet lost, though it is fast disappearing. In many respects, this is the voice to which we should particularly attend because, in concentrating upon it we can seek the connections it makes both backwards and forwards in time, to the experiences of the teachers of the late nineteenth century and the late twentieth century alike.

## Classrooms and pedagogies

The classical site of the teacher's daily work, the classroom, despite many changes in design, layout and capacity, would at every stage of its development be immediately familiar to any teacher since 1876. Throughout, the common experience of a single teacher interacting with a group of children in the pursuit of learning remains the enduring and fundamental characteristic of that confined and private space that we know as the classroom (Hargreaves, 1996: xiv). For example, the experience of Philip Ballard in meeting a new class in the 1890s, leaving aside hallmarks of period style and nuance, is one which would be familiar across all three generations.

> My first lesson with a class was always of the same nature – always serene and sympathetic, and highly flattering to myself as a teacher. The students listened to my instruction gravely and respectfully, and seemed to take a keen interest in everything I said. It did not however, take me long to discover that the interest was illusory. It was not my lesson that interested them; it was myself. They were reckoning me up...
>
> (Ballard, 1937)

But if the difficulties of establishing a workable classroom relationship have been a constant feature of teachers' professional practice, the form of such relationships has seen dramatic change. Distance, formality and predictability have been the dominating qualities to which teachers have most commonly aspired during our period. Closeness between teacher and pupil, though increasingly commended by teacher trainers and school inspectors alike from the earliest years of the twentieth century, was eschewed by the majority of classroom teachers for many years (Selleck, 1972).

The favoured regime drew upon the traditions established in the elementary schools of the school board period (1870–1902), when the incomes of schools and the salaries of teachers were largely dependent upon the results of annual tests administered by Her Majesty's Inspectorate (HMI).

The results were generally uninspiring. In the words of elementary teacher, Elizabeth Trafford:

> Well, you stood in the classroom and they sat in front of you and you talked – chalk and blackboard.

Elementary teacher Edith Norton, when asked how she taught a class of 55 (pupils) replied:

> How can you? I don't know. Just stand up and talk. There's not much more you can do. You can't do anything with individual children.... There would be chanting of tables when it came to arithmetic, but mainly it was just talking at them, I'm afraid.

The corollary of such a pedagogy, given further definition by the pressures of overcrowded classes, fixed classroom furniture and limitations in books and equipment, was a characteristically rigid discipline which maintained its hold until the middle of the twentieth century (Clegg, 1972: 26–37; Gardner, 1996).

Thereafter, this rigidity began to dissipate. Those who taught through these years noted the change and recognised its wellspring as the collective experience of total war from 1939 to 1945. In the words of Beatrice McIver, elementary teacher:

> The discipline was very good. Very good. It was good until, oh, it was after the (Second World) War.

Nora Crawford, infant teacher, returning to teaching in 1965:

> There were quite a lot of changes. I found there was a lot more freedom. I found the children weren't expected to, sort of, settle down and sit at their desks and work all day.

The recollections of teachers in the 1940s and early 1950s suggest that many of the changes which policy makers, teacher trainers and administrators alike had enjoined them to embrace throughout the inter-war years were in fact ultimately brought about through other, less calculated means; through the exigencies of war itself (Clegg, 1972: 50; Lowe, 1988: 4–8; Lowe, 1992: 5–11).

The earlier failure of less formal methods and approaches to root themselves in the inter-war classroom dramatises two central issues in respect of pedagogical cultures. In the first place, it illustrates the power of the mechanisms of internal transmission within such cultures (Gibson, 1973: 238–274). Ultimately, entrants to the profession came to depend upon pedagogical models which, if increasingly stripped of the most brutal elements of corporal punishment, nevertheless continued closely to resemble those of the school board period.

In the second place, it shows that reform in the characteristic practices of a profession such as teaching is immensely difficult to achieve solely through the application of external sanction, injunction or encouragement. As a recent *Times* editorial, citing the words of Tony Blair, subsequently to become Prime Minister, put it, '...no worthwhile reform can take place without the positive engagement of teachers' (*The Times*, 10 January 1997, p. 16).

Reform is likely to succeed only where its central justification accords with a consonant moment of transformation within the profession itself. Just such a moment seems to have arisen as a consequence of the experience of teachers during the Second World War. Thereafter, if progressivist pedagogies were not translated in any straightforward way into classroom practice, they nevertheless became the basis for a new professional ideology far removed from that which had dominated the inter-war years (Cunningham, 1988).

## Practical autonomy

The time lag between change in official and practical ideologies of teaching in the inter-war years had a still larger effect. Increasingly, teachers in these years came to assume as normal a more general dislocation of perception between themselves and those who shaped policy and the regimes of teacher training. Such a perception celebrated the notion of symbolic distance between those in the classroom and those outside it. The latter might be seen to be sympathetic or helpful to a degree. But they could never fully understand what classroom life was truly like or what were the real requirements for its effective daily maintenance. This perception imbued teachers' professional feeling and became deeply rooted in the 1920s and 1930s and was passed, in some degree, from the second-generation to the third. For second-generation teachers, however, the perception could be carried into practice and expressed in a way which would later, with the nationalisation of the curriculum and the tighter regulation of classroom activity, become much more difficult.

Resistance to external pressures for change in the earlier period, especially in the typically smaller schools of the 1920s and 1930s, could be successfully mounted either by incorporating such pressures or simply by ignoring them in favour of traditional practice and precept. Classroom teachers from these years, freed from the curricular directives which governed their forebears and their successors alike, express this as a kind of natural professional autonomy whose only limitations were set by local rather than national educational authority. In the words of Grace Bartholomew, elementary teacher:

> We just got on with the teaching. We didn't seem to be interfered with in any way.

Edith Norton, elementary teacher, commented:

> I think we were more conscious, much more conscious, of our local authority and working with their ideas than we were of the government.

Gwyneth Tomlinson, secondary teacher, recalled:

> Every time I'm talking about school to friends and colleagues – 'Weren't we lucky to be teaching when we were. We knew where we were going, we weren't harassed by, you know, people breathing down our necks and suggesting doing all sorts of daft things. We knew what we had to do and we did it as far as we could.... We had no interest in what the government did. When I was a teacher (in South Wales), I was there for seven years. I didn't see an HMI.

When HMIs did appear, their threat might be circumvented in much the same spirit that the Board of Education itself was relegated or ignored. In the words of Miriam Harford elementary teacher:

> Then there were the HMIs. You never knew when they were coming. They just came. I was really afraid of them.... Generally a ruler was sent round...by somebody, and a ruler arriving meant, 'Look out! The Inspector's here!' Nothing was said, but if the ruler came, you knew what it meant.

The degree of practical classroom autonomy available to second-generation teachers was greater than that experienced by their first-generation predecessors, labouring under the curricular constraints of the centrally imposed Revised Code (Batho, 1989: 33). For third-generation teachers, in a new period of central control over the curriculum and increasingly over pedagogy, the erosion of professional autonomy has been perceptible, though expressed most commonly as a more defensive version of the same kind of turning inwards which classroom teachers in the 1920s and 1930s found to be such an effective strategy. The latter position, ironically, was actually founded upon a relatively confident sense of forward direction, whilst the former betrays its uncertainties in the language of 'getting back', of identifying 'what went wrong' (Helsby, 1995).

> The voice of the teaching profession at the end of 1996 is cynical, pessimistic and profoundly weary.... A deep sense of impotence...declining professional status...and what they perceive as constant 'teacher-bashing' by the Government, the Opposition and the press has destroyed confidence.... Passion has been replaced by a sort of fin de siecle fatalism.
>
> (Gardner, 1991: 8)

'Teacher-bashing' is not new. Certainly, in the early decades of the twentieth century, the professional status of elementary teachers was rising perceptibly. This was a consequence of the incremental pressure of the National Union of Teachers, together with explicit government policies designed to increase the numbers of recruits from non-working-class backgrounds and to secure progressive improvements in the quality and duration of teacher education and training (Aldrich, 1996: 58–76).

These developments led to a widening of public respect for teachers. But it did not make them liked or insulate them from that popular distrust and disregard which had its roots in the first-generation years. This had been the period, in the late nineteenth century, when the education of the working class was taken from its own hands and reconstituted as a formalised and compulsory schooling in basic skills and social discipline designed as appropriate for the industrial masses in a not yet democratic society.

Elementary school teachers were at the leading edge of the long battle to win the agreement of the working class to be schooled in this way. In these early years, physical as well as verbal assaults on teachers were not uncommon and many teachers lived marginalised and sometimes dangerous lives in the communities in which they taught.

This isolation was often magnified by a characteristic professional formality – extending across the second as well as the first generation – which distanced many teachers from each other, sometimes within the same school. Amy Grant, infant teacher, recalled that she:

> Never knew what the teachers' Christian names were in the first two schools I was in because you never heard them. That didn't come until after the evacuation.

Edith Smart, elementary teacher, remembered:

> Always the full name. Never Christian name.... We were always Miss Smith, Mrs Holding, Mr Heath, but the men would use one another's Christian names. They were more pally. And if we were really friends, apart from being on the same staff, in private we would use our first names, you know.

By the turn of the century, the school attendance battles had been won (Rubinstein). Parental resistance was replaced by acceptance, and often a measure of new respect for local teachers as the legitimate educators of their children. But if, as a result, the teacher's life was now less fraught and his or her job easier to carry out, the social and cultural gulf between teachers and local communities remained very deep. There was seldom much closeness around shared interests and little notion of those ideas of partnership which would increasingly prevail in the third generation. Just as inter-war teachers were generally untroubled by the machinations of central government, they were also left substantially unmoved by the parents of the children they taught (Clegg, 1972: 72–73). As a result, school teachers in these years could draw upon a greater measure of practical autonomy at the workplace than either before or since. In their words:

> The attitude then...was, We're the teachers, you're the parents, and never the twain shall meet. There was no contact...
>
> (Harford)

> There was a great gap between the teacher and the parent; the teacher knew, and the parent didn't.
>
> (Walsh)

> They didn't come up to the school. There were no occasions for them to come to school, you know. no parents meetings or evenings. They came if there was anything they didn't like and they came if they were sent for.
>
> (Norton)

> I remember once, a little boy stole some money out of my drawer. (The head-teacher) was very good, because she made the father come up and she made him smack the boy.
>
> (Grant)

> (The mothers) stood at the railings (around the playground). They weren't allowed in and the children weren't allowed to go out. And they would feed them through the railings, like a zoo.... Well, I think the parents were stupid to come. The children didn't need drinks. But, you see, the mothers weren't working. Until after the War, the parents did very little complaining.
>
> (Grant)

> There's far more co-operation between schools than there used to be, far more. (Before the War), they were a bit scared of coming to the school in case they put their foot in it, as you might say.
>
> (Venee Blatch, elementary teacher)

## Post-war change

For those teachers whose careers extended over both the pre-war and the post-war years, mid-century changes in education seemed particularly striking and intense. Sometimes this finds expression in that typically reflective and regretful language through which an older generation assesses its own achievements and passes judgment on its successors, and in which nostalgia, commemoration, critique and perceptions of decline are all mingled. More rarely, it takes the form of an acknowledgement of generational improvement and a recognition of broad progress in education over the years.

The whole attitude of the young teachers today is totally different from ours. I mean (in the 1950s), you'd get a young probationer sitting on a table swinging her legs and children coming up and saying, 'Have you got a boyfriend Miss?', and all this sort of thing, and chatting to them like that.

(McIver)

Oh, it was a big change, yes. In some ways it was a great improvement. I didn't agree with all this standing in the front and having children in rows.

(Bartholomew)

But whatever their degree of overall pessimism or optimism, teachers able to compare the experience of teaching after the war with that which had preceded it, felt the extent and depth of change in the classroom as something profound. Attitudes, expectations and behaviour were all beginning to move, and for teachers used to practising their craft in the relative stability and predictability of the pre-war years, this could be hard to bear. In their recollections, the comparisons are often starkly drawn. The words of Marion Mortimer, elementary teacher, on returning to teaching in 1952 illustrate the changes graphically.

Oh, it was dreadful. I thought I would never cope; I thought I would never cope. I only went in the mornings but I was so exhausted; absolutely exhausted I was. And I thought, 'I'll never cope', because by that time, of course, there was a, sort of, different attitude between the children. They just didn't sit still and be told what to do. They'd got minds of their own and very often their minds were very different from what we expected them to be.... In fact I gave up. I couldn't cope. It was no good staying there and getting ill and that sort of thing.... I do understand a bit about teaching because of my daughter, who's teaching now. It's far, far more difficult now than it was for me – if you do the job properly. I mean, I was still at the stage when children did as they were told without question. You did as teacher said. Therefore, in a way, it was much easier. Now, children are inclined to question, which I think is a good thing, but it's the way it's done that makes teaching difficult I think, these days.

Dorothy Tanner, elementary teacher reminisced:

I mean, we weren't oppressed by all these changes that the government is bringing about. We seemed to sail along very smoothly compared with what they do nowadays. I wouldn't like to be teaching now. For one thing, of course, discipline comes into it these days. That never did in the old days, and interference by parents and all kinds of things happen now that we didn't have to deal with.

As the second generation of teachers gave way to the third, and as the pressures of change multiplied and accelerated, many of those approaching retirement could look back to their early years in the profession as constituting a kind of golden age for the classroom teacher. Undoubtedly, such a construction was, to a degree, a romanticised one (Humphries, 1981). But if the pre-war elementary classroom was not always as devoid of disciplinary problems as teacher recollection sometimes portrays it to be, the claims of former second-generation teachers to a high degree of professional independence in their teaching are difficult to challenge. The years of the post-war social democratic educational consensus – extending into the 1970s – are sometimes described, by comparison with the years that were to follow, as a high point both for the collective political influence of the teaching profession and for the extent of workplace autonomy (Gordon *et al.*, 1991: 275–276; Crowley, 1995; Hoyle and John, 1995).

If the former may be true, the latter is not. The practical autonomy of school teachers was at its zenith in the inter-war period. If this was the case, why was it then that this potentially empowering aspect of their professional inheritance was not drawn upon in some way by teachers of the third generation? Why did such teachers not utilise this tradition as a foundation upon which to build sustained resistance to the erosion of their professional autonomy in the years of post-war expansion?

Part of the answer lies in the fact that initially – that is, in the years immediately following the War – changes in the construction of teachers' professionalism were driven not by intrusive new demands on the part of the state, but primarily by the building of new kinds of relationships between teachers and parents and teachers and children (UNESCO, 1949). Rooted in the shared experience of the war years, this was a change which found expression in ways that were local and organic. Cumulatively, if imperceptibly, it impinged in a very direct way upon teachers' freedom of action at the workplace. Teachers' new concern for the independent interests of parents and children contrasted markedly with the isolation and professional reserve which prevailed in the interwar years. A detailed assessment of the extent and consequences of this grass-roots transformation will require much further research. But it is clear that the change was a highly significant one.

Relationships between teachers and parents from the 1870s through to the 1930s had been dominated either by mutual ignorance or outright hostility. Before the 1870s, there had certainly been close and co-operative teacher–pupil relationships, but these were confined to the operation of working-class private schools – which were to be suppressed in the years following the 1870 Education Act (Gardner, 1984). Thereafter, it took three-quarters of a century and the emergence of a unified national system of education for relationships of this kind to re-emerge. But when this did happen, the closeness was of a different kind. Instead of a foundation in cultural isolation and a segmented educational market place, the roots of this new relationship lay in a common acceptance of the ideology of meritocracy and the principle of a national schooling which, if not yet common, was publicly-provided. Where nineteenth century teachers of working-class private schools had been concerned principally to satisfy the expressed demand of local markets for the elements of learning, their mid-twentieth century successors were shaped by post-war citizenship ideals of service to nation and local community. Such ideals were embodied in closer ties with pupils and parents and embellished in new and initially more positive media representations of teachers and their work (Cunningham, 1992).

The anchoring of teachers' educational and social commitment in the interests of the local parental constituencies they served stimulated a new preparedness to accept wider local scrutiny, debate and participation in matters formerly seen as the exclusive professional preserve of teachers. The balance of interest in education was changing. As it did so, it created the conditions whereby the state, from the 1960s onwards, could contemplate a more intrusive, centralising role in educational policy making which, in the circumstances, could appear legitimate to parents, to public opinion and, if with some qualification, even to the teachers themselves.

In other words, a changed relationship between teachers and the state was legitimated by the earlier changed relationship between teachers and parents at the local level. The dismissive attitude of pre-war teachers to the role of central government could not be sustained in this new climate. It became progressively easier for governments to associate any teacher recalcitrance in the face of policy change with a betrayal of pupils and parents. And if teachers, as was shown in the strikes of the mid-1980s, could still feel driven to challenge the state, they found it far harder and far more painful to maintain such a challenge when it also generated the antipathy of many parents and sustained the attention of an increasingly critical press (Lowe, 1987: 14–15).

The claims of parents and their children impinged upon teachers' historic class-room autonomy from the late 1940s onwards. From the 1970s on the principal impact of policy on teacher autonomy culminated in the removal of collective bar-gaining rights, the imposition of new conditions of service, the introduction of the National Curriculum and new regimes of testing and inspection (Grace, 1987; Aldrich, 1992; Barber; 1992).

The inter-war legacy of relative professional autonomy was a historic resource upon which teachers might have drawn at this moment. But its potential force was diminished both by the distance of time and still more by the incremental effects of the new and closer working relationships established with parents and pupils in the preceding decades (Aldrich, 1996: 72). As these relationships deepened, the old pre-war autonomy could come to represent, especially for younger teachers, not so much a professional asset, but more a symbol of social isolation and a token of localised elitism.

## The second-generation legacy

One of the persistent weaknesses of the teaching profession in the twentieth century – along with the endemic divisiveness of its professional associations – has been its inability or its unwillingness to utilise its own collective past in compiling a vision for the future. Taken as a totality, the pre-war professional legacy was not one which organised teachers of the third generation saw much reason to regard in positive terms. Teachers themselves strongly reflected the national mood for post-war reconstruction based upon the recognition of a historic break with the past. In this perspective, the pre-war years could be presented as the final version of a flawed and failed educational blueprint. Though it had shaped the working lives of the first two generations of teachers, the vision of education at its heart was nar-row and divisive. Most notably, despite the piecemeal local reorganisations of edu-cation contingent upon the Hadow Report of 1926, the majority of pupils and teachers in the inter-war period had continued to labour in an educational ghetto labelled 'elementary' (Lowe, 1987: 5–8). This was a label officially rescinded both in the language and in the provisions of the 1944 Education Act. Former elemen-tary teachers were glad to see the back of it. Re-invented either as primary or sec-ondary modern teachers, they could thereafter present themselves as the notional equals of all other school teachers in a truly national system of education, unified for the first time. In this light, the model of the old elementary system could be despatched without regret, lock, stock and barrel. In policy terms, it could fairly be characterised as part of that 'depressing inter-war period of the 1920s and 1930s, when everything seemed to grind to a halt' (Simon, 1991: 16).

Against such a background, it was not difficult to disregard the importance of the genuine workplace autonomy of these years in denouncing its narrowness, iso-lation and unheroic spirit. There seemed little or nothing that this earlier world could teach the new. Workplace autonomy of this particularly enclosed kind, seen in retrospect, did not seem such a great prize when it applied to work that had been seen by the rest of the educational world as essentially third-rate, effectively unconnected with the higher concerns of genuine learning.

The demonstrable practical expertise, assuredness and self-confidence of the old elementary teachers looked less like a basis from which to reach towards a new professional identity for the future and more like an intellectual dead end. That same social and professional isolation which had underpinned the relative freedom of action of teachers in the classroom now spoke only of the low status and enormous occupational constraints which it had also entailed.

If the will of the elementary teacher had dominated the small world of the classroom, it had seemed to count for little in the wider corridors of power. Teachers in the inter-war years were inured to their relative powerlessness to raise or even defend their modest salaries, to repair ramshackle buildings, to improve poor facilities, to secure adequate teaching materials, to end overcrowding, to widen restricted promotion prospects or to abolish the operation of the marriage bar. Though their professional associations campaigned on all of these issues, at the grassroots, many classroom teachers felt a sense of impotence and resignation.

Experiences of the marriage bar offer one example of this feeling. Nora Crawford infant teacher recounts her experience:

> A vacancy came up in the village a mile away from my home ... (The head) persuaded me to put in for it. But mind, at that time I was engaged to be married and already having a house built in Melton Mowbray where my husband-to-be worked. And I put in an application for this post but, of course, unless you had special reasons you couldn't stay in school after you were married. You couldn't teach. They wouldn't employ married teachers. Now whether this was because there were plenty of teachers around, I don't know. And the chairman of (the school) managers came to see me and said, 'We've all had a meeting and we've sorted out the applications and we're very, very pleased with yours, but', he said, 'I've come to tell you that we couldn't possibly engage you because, for one thing we all know you're having a house built and you'll be married within the next few months. So', he said, 'they've asked me to come to see you personally and just tell you this. We'd have liked to have given you the job, but it just isn't feasible'. Well, I wasn't surprised.

Amy Grant, an infant teacher, provides further examples:

> If you got married, you finished. In the 1920s we were all courting but at that time, of course, it was very bad unemployment. The boy I was fond of didn't have a job until 1939 and so I just couldn't afford to leave to get married. A girl I was in college with was engaged to somebody on a tanker when the tanker runs were four and five years. She was teaching in our school and one Friday afternoon she was very excited. Her fiancee's tanker ... had come into the Tyne. And so they managed to get a special licence and get married. She came back on the Monday morning with a wedding ring. She was sent straight to the (Education) Office. We never saw her again.

## New expectations

The marriage bar came to an end in 1944, together with the entire edifice of elementary education (Oram, 1989: 29). A new relationship between the interests of teachers and society was emerging and the expectations of each were rising. There was a greater demand for schools to be opened up to the public gaze and for teachers to be more accountable for their practices. Politicians and public were increasingly unwilling to be excluded from what went on in the classroom. Moreover, teachers of the new primary schools found that the parents of their pupils were no longer made up primarily from a quiescent working class. In a newly integrated national system of schooling, teachers had to learn to respond also to more voluble lower-middle-class and, increasingly, middle-class parents anxious for the success of their children in the competitive transfer to secondary schools at 11-plus (Simon, 1991: 150–151).

In tune with this trend, by the early 1960s, David Eccles, the Conservative Minister of Education, could talk about the need to open up the teachers' 'secret garden of the curriculum' (Simon, 1991: 312). Forty years before, the metaphor would not have been thought of. In that earlier period:

> The only uniformity that the Board of Education desires to see in the teaching of Public Elementary Schools is that each teacher should think for himself and work out for himself such methods of teaching as may use his powers to the best advantage...
>
> (Board of Education, 1918: 3)

On the teachers' side, there was an anticipation that a revivified interest in the perceived importance of their work would be paralleled by a political willingness to ameliorate the poor conditions of service under which they had laboured for decades. To the extent that this did not happen either to the degree or at the pace that many had hoped for, teachers increasingly began to look to their professional organisations not only to focus and to represent, but also, if necessary, to mobilise their discontents, as in the national industrial actions of 1969–70 and in the mid-1980s. Such action represented a resumption, in the third generation, of a preparedness to contemplate, on a much grander scale, forms of collective action witnessed in the first generation but almost wholly repudiated in the second.

From the perspective of the third-generation classroom teacher, this revived militancy was to invoke a radical new role for their associations. The first recorded teachers' strike had taken place in 1907, in West Ham, London (Burke, 1971: 15–16; Coates, 1972). Thereafter, teachers' strikes became familiar occurrences in the industrially troubled years immediately before and after the First World War (Lawn, 1987; Seifert, 1987). They were, however, essentially localised small-scale events and it is hard to see them in terms of a developing national perception at the grass roots of the union as primarily an instrument of industrial conflict.

The outbreak of local strikes which marked the end of the first generation of teachers was coming to a close as the second generation began and, despite the deepening hardships of the 1920s and 1930s, industrial action was off the agenda. Through their unions – the breakaway National Union of Women Teachers was established in 1909 and the National Association of Schoolmasters in 1922 – many teachers pursued the grievances raised by the marriage bar and by unequal pay and promotion prospects with great vigour (Partington, 1976; Oram, 1989; Copelman, 1996). The majority, reflecting the mood of their wider social and professional isolation, did not. Among this group, however, there was often a very deep, almost tribal allegiance to the NUT as both the national standard bearer of the profession and the only realistic protector of the individual teacher in the face of the kind of localised bullying by school managers or parish priests which many first-generation teachers had endured. But the majority of teachers, as now, did not participate in the affairs of the union or attend routine meetings.

Teachers of the second generation demonstrated an ambivalence to their professional associations which has also had a profound impact on those of the third generation. They joined the union in much the same way that they entered training – as part and parcel of the customary route to becoming a teacher. Once in the union, they thought of it much as the apocryphal Londoner looks upon the Tower of London: a source of pride in tradition, a symbol of security, a token of distinctive identity – but not something to visit. At the root of this ambivalence there was, of course, that enduring tension between teaching conceived as a profession or as waged labour, a distinction which has, from the first, been deeply etched in teachers' struggles over their collective perception (Lawn, 1987; Hoyle and John, 1995).

The surviving voice of second-generation teachers – though its memories are filtered through later and usually highly critical perceptions of subsequent national teachers' strikes – seeks chiefly to celebrate the professional end of the spectrum. This does not mean that trade unionism was repudiated. Neither does it mean that elementary teachers were blind to the realities of their lowly status by comparison with the established professions or their collective weakness in influencing policy. What it does speak of, however, is a real sense of perceived autonomy as a central resource in the construction of a grass-roots professional sensibility among classroom teachers. In their words:

> We didn't talk in terms of strikes or anything like that, not in those days.
>
> (Olive Walsh)

> Yes, there were some in favour of strikes but anyway, most of us were shocked at the idea of striking – never do that. We talked about it and said, 'Oh no, we can't go on strike'; no that was beneath the teachers' profession.
>
> (Ellen Barton)

> We wouldn't stoop to it. That sort of attitude.
>
> (Dorothy Tanner)

> The word strike didn't exist in those days. No one thought of striking. (The teachers) I knew well, you know, they were all red-hot Conservatives.
>
> (Beatrice McIver)

> Never, never, never. I wouldn't strike. It was never mentioned. Even the socialists said, 'What's the good of striking? We don't make anything. Nobody cares whether we strike or whether we don't.
>
> (Miriam Harford)

> Oh, a professional organisation, very much.... The trade union aspect of it didn't come in 'til years later.... I don't think there's the same professional feeling about teachers amongst the general public today as there was at one time.... Nearly all the things that are being imposed on teachers today are being imposed by people who are not practising teachers. The medical profession wouldn't stand for it...
>
> (Edith Norton)

The sentiments expressed in the last extract are particularly complex. Coupled with a profound reluctance to engage in industrial action as both professionally undesirable and individually painful, there is here a realisation, equally painful, that teachers' professional sensibilities have been historically misunderstood and regularly impugned by those outside. In this perspective, the construction which teachers have sought to place on their professionalism has been challenged less by legitimate calls for accountability and more by a kind of enduring public disregard for teachers which, in some degree or other, has been expressed from the time of the first generation onwards.

At the close of the third notional generation of teachers to serve in the nation's schools since 1876, it becomes clear that the next generation has a very mixed legacy upon which to draw as it contemplates continued change in education. In one sense, this can be seen as both a strength and a weakness. It is a strength because it reflects the flexible range of teachers' responses to dealing with change over the twentieth century. These responses have moved between the cultivation of closer local links between themselves and the communities they serve, the opening of the profession to external scrutiny, direct resistance in the form of union pressure or industrial action and private, internal resistance in the form of the manipulation of policy reform within the classroom.

It is a weakness because it rests upon deep historical divisions between different groups of teachers – men and women, graduate and non-graduate, elementary and grammar, primary and secondary headteachers and classroom teachers – which have militated against the achievement of a unified profession in the twentieth century (Griggs, 1991: 325). This has been a weakness compounded by the enduring conflict between teachers' long-standing aspirations to be regarded as professionals and the realities of their treatment as employees in the workplace.

In the face of such internal divisions, it has proved particularly difficult for teachers to balance their claims to professional expertise against the increasing demands of government and society for professional accountability. Following a period of real, if often sterile and unimaginative, practical autonomy in the inter-war years, the nation's teachers embarked on the second half of the century in search of a new and more satisfying social contract. In return for opening up their classrooms and ceding, bit by bit, to parents and then to government their claims to determine what went on there, teachers expected to achieve greater public recognition, higher status and improved material reward.

It will be up to the next generation of teachers to judge how the terms of this exchange commend themselves and are creating the kind of profession to which they aspire, or whether they will wish to rediscover and revisit their collective past to explore different ways forward.

## Interviewees

Bartholomew, Grace: elementary teacher; b. 1906, Essex; f. postman; m. at home.
Barton, Ellen: elementary teacher; b. 1898, Glamorgan; f. colliery electrician; m. at home.
Blatch, Venee: elementary teacher; b. 1909, Liverpool; f. clerk; m. governess.
Crawford, Nora: infant teacher; b. 1908, Nottinghamshire; f. farmer; m. cheese maker.
Daly, Alice: elementary teacher; b. 1887, Pembrokeshire; f. blacksmith; m. at home.
Grant, Amy: infant teacher; b. 1904, Newcastle-on-Tyne; f. cabinet maker; m. at home.
Harford, Miriam: elementary teacher; b. 1901, Birmingham; f. toolmaker; m. at home.
McIver, Beatrice: elementary teacher; b. 1912, Liverpool; f. accountant; m. at home.
Mortimer, Marion: elementary teacher; b. 1905, Derby; f. master plumber; m. dressmaker.
Norton, Edith: elementary teacher; b. 1906, Kent; f. draper; m. draper's assistant.
Smart, Edith: elementary teacher; b. 1904, Burnley; f. blacksmith; m. at home.
Tanner, Dorothy: elementary teacher; b. 1897, Stockport; f. block-cutter; m. dressmaker.
Trafford, Elizabeth: elementary teacher; b. 1901, County Durham; f. colliery manager; m. at home.

Tomlinson, Gwyneth: secondary teacher; b. 1903, Swansea; f. businessman; m. at home.
Walsh, Olive: elementary teacher; b. 1907, Wigan; f. postman; m. at home.

I am most grateful to all the above for their help, and to the Nuffield Foundation
and the Leverhulme Trust for their generous support in financing the projects from
which the interview data derive.

## References

Aldrich, R. (1992) Educational legislation of the 1980s in England, *History of Education*,
    21(1), pp. 57–69.
Aldrich, R. (1996) *Education for the Nation* (London, Cassell).
Board of Education (1903) *Report for the Year 1902–1903* (London, HMSO).
Board of Education (1918) *Suggestions for the Consideration of Teachers and Others
    Concerned in the Work of Public Elementary Schools* (London, HMSO).
Board of Education (1927) *Education in England and Wales 1925–26* (London, HMSO).
Ball, S.J. and Goodson, I.F. (1985) *Teachers' Lives and Careers* (London, Falmer Press).
Ballard, P. (1937) *Things I Cannot Forget* (London, University of London Press).
Barber, M. (1992) *Education and the Teacher Unions* (London, Cassell).
Batho, G. (1989) *Political Issues in Education* (London, Cassell).
Brehony, K. (1992) What's left of progressive primary education?, in: A. Rattansi and
    D. Reeder (Eds) *Rethinking Radical Education: Essays in Honour of Brian Simon*,
    pp. 196–221 (London, Lawrence and Wishart).
Burke, V. (1971) *Teachers in Turmoil* (London, Penguin).
Clegg, A.B. (Ed.) (1972) *The Changing Primary School: Its Problems and Priorities. A statement
    by teachers* (London, Chatto and Windus).
Coates, R.D. (1972) *Teachers' Unions and Interest Group Policies* (Cambridge, Cambridge
    University Press).
Committee of Council (1877) *Report of the Committee of Council on Education and
    Parts I–IV of Appendix 1876–1877* (London, HMSO).
Copelman, D.M. (1996) *London's Women Teachers: Gender, Class and Feminism 1870–1930*
    (London, Routledge).
Crowley, K. (1995) Teacher autonomy under siege?, in: J. Bell (Ed.) *Teachers Talk About
    Teaching: Coping with Change in Turbulent Times*, pp. 19–29 (Milton Keynes, Open
    University Press).
Cunningham, P. (1988) *Curriculum Change in the Primary School since 1945: Dissemination
    of the Progressive Ideal* (Brighton, Falmer Press).
Cunningham, P. (1992) Teachers' professional image and the press 1950–1990, *History of
    Education* 21(1), pp. 37–56.
Department of Education and Science (1968) *Statistics of Education 1989 and 1990*
    (London, HMSO).
Department of Education and Science (1996) *Statistics of Education 1966*, vol. 4 (London,
    HMSO).
Gardiner, J. (1997) Apathy and the death of the idealistic teaching profession, *The Times*
    10 January.
Gardner, P. (1984) *The Lost Elementary Schools of Victorian England* (London, Croom Helm).
Gardner, P. (1991) 'Our schools or theirs? The case of Eliza Duckworth and John
    Stevenson', *History of Education*, 20, pp. 163–186.
Gardner, P. (1996) The giant at the front: young teachers and corporal punishment in
    inter-war elementary schools, *History of Education*, 25, pp. 141–163.
Gibson, T. (1973) *Teachers Talking: Aims, Methods, Attitudes to Change* (London, Allen Lane).
Goodson, I.F. (Ed.) (1992) *Studying Teachers' Lives* (London, Routledge).
Gordon, P.A., Aldrich, R. and Dean, D. (1991) *Education and Policy in England in the
    Twentieth Century*, Dennis (Ilford, Woburn).
Gosden, P.H.J.H. (1972) *The Evolution of a Profession* (Oxford, Oxford University Press).
Grace, G. (1987) Teachers and the state in Britain: a changing relation in M. Lawn and
    G. Gerald (Eds) (1991) *Teachers: The Culture and Politics of Work*, pp. 193–228
    (Brighton, Falmer Press).

Griggs, C. (1991) The National Union of Teachers in the Eastbourne area 1874–1916: a tale of tact and pragmatism, *History of Education*, 20, pp. 325–340.

Hamilton, D. (1990) *Learning About Education: An Unfinished Curriculum* (Milton Keynes, Open University Press).

Hargreaves, D. (1994) *The Mosaic of Learning: Schools and their Teachers for the Next Century* (London, Demos).

Hargreaves, A. (1996) *Changing Teachers, Changing Times: Teachers' Work and Culture in the Postmodern Age* (London, Cassell).

Helsby, G. (1995) Teachers' construction of professionalism in England in the 1990s, *Journal of Education for Teaching*, 21, pp. 317–332.

Hoyle, E. and John, P. (1995) *Professional Knowledge and Professional Practice* (London, Cassell).

Humphries, S. (1981) *Hooligans or Rebels?* (Oxford, Blackwell).

Lawn, M. (Ed.) (1985) *The Politics of Teacher Unionism* (London, Croom Helm).

Lawn, M. (1987) *Servants of the State* (London, Falmer).

Lowe, R. (1988) *Education in the Post-War Years: A Social History* (London, Routledge).

Lowe, R. (1987) Primary education since the second world war, in: R. Lowe (Ed.) *The Changing Primary School*, pp. 1–16 (London, Falmer Press).

Lowe, R. (1992) Education in England during the Second World War, in: R. Lowe (Ed.) *Education and the Second World War: Studies in Schooling and Social Change* (Brighton, Falmer Press).

Middleton, N. and Weitzman, S. (1976) *A Place For Everyone: A History of State Education from the Eighteenth Century to the 1970s* (London, Gollancz).

Ministry of Education (1948) *Education in 1947* (London, HMSO).

Nias, J. (1989) *Primary Teachers Talking* (London, Routledge).

Oram, A. (1989) A master should not serve under a mistress: women and men teachers 1900–1970, in: S. Acker (Ed.) *Teachers, Gender and Careers*, pp. 21–34 (London, Falmer Press).

Partington, G. (1976) *Women Teachers in the Twentieth Century* (Windsor, HEER).

Philpott, H.B. (1904) *London at School: The Story of the School Board 1870–1904* (London, Fisher Unwin).

Pollard, M. (1974) *The Teachers* (Lavenham, Eastland Press).

Rubinstein, D. (1969) *School Attendance in London 1870–1904: A Social History* (Hull, University of Hull).

Seifert, R. (1987) *Teacher Militancy: A History of Teachers' Strikes 1896–1987* (London, Falmer Press).

Selleck, R.J. (1972) *English Primary Education and the Progressives* (London, Routledge, Kegan Paul).

Sikes, P., Measor, L. and Woods, P. (1985) *Teachers' Careers: crises and continuities* (London, Falmer Press).

Simon, B. (1991) *Education and the Social Order 1940–1990* (London, Lawrence and Wishart).

Sutherland, G. (1973) *Policy Making in Elementary Education 1870–1895* (Oxford, Oxford University Press).

*The Times* (1997) *Editorial*, 10 January.

Tropp, A. (1957) *The Schoolteachers* (London, Heinemann).

UNESCO (1949) *The Education and Training of Teachers* (Paris).

# PART VII

# EDUCATION, WORK AND THE ECONOMY

# ENTERING THE WORLD OF WORK

## The transition from youth to adulthood in modern European society

### John Springhall

*Paedagogica Historica*, 29, 1, 33–52, 1993

In 1919 fourteen-year-old Robert Roberts left school in the north of England aspiring to be a journalist. He was told by a young woman at the Juvenile Labour Exchange in his native Salford, near Manchester, that journalists were not in demand, although they wanted a lad in a local brass-finishing shop. On his way home, after getting a seven-year engineering apprenticeship, young Roberts tore his headmaster's reference into shreds: 'That was school done! I was entering the world of men.'[1] The school-to-work transition is actually far more complex than this account suggests but the curious will look in vain for further clarification in most historical texts on youth, despite evidence that, until fairly recently, the vast majority of working people entered their full-time wage-earning lives during childhood or adolescence in nearly all modern European societies.

This transitional experience was and is crucial because, within a relatively short period of leaving school, adolescents were and are expected to discard the role of dependent child and to assume the role of independent working adult. Thus youth's termination, that mysterious development whereby the adolescent 'ugly duckling' emerges transformed into the 'swan' of the well-adjusted working adult, will be the main focus of this exploratory essay. The individual in transit signifies an important stage in the life-cycle because he or she is not only required to choose an occupation, to find and apply for work, but also to learn the norms and values of the new world of work, to learn the intricacies of a new job and to become successfully integrated into a new institution. Hence the shifting process whereby young people achieve adult status through work clearly merits more attention from the historian than it has so far received.

On the other hand, the view of adolescence as a transitional phase between two known statuses of childhood and adulthood is fast becoming obsolete. Major class, gender and regional differences, in terms of length of education and age of entry into formal employment, make it problematic to offer any universal defini-tion of what constituted adolescence in the past or of where it began and where it ended. Thus in 1919 boys from middle and upper-class homes resident in fee-paying boarding schools experienced a much more protracted adolescence than did Robert Roberts, simply because their schooling extended until sixteen, seventeen or even eighteen. Equally, because of the lack of consensus about just when the stage of adulthood is reached in modern European societies, the task of analysing the process in history whereby those in their mid to late teens were identified as no longer dependent on their parents is rendered problematic. Our criteria for measuring this particular plateau do not appear to be very constant over time: leaving school, entering the work force, leaving the household of origin, getting married, or establishing one's own household? In modernizing Western societies, moving from the parental home was very closely linked to age at marriage but in pre-industrial Europe there were many other economic and cultural factors influencing the proportion of children at home.[2] For the sake of brevity, leaving school and entering the work force will be used here to denote the transition from youth to adulthood in modern Europe, particularly Britain and Germany, although clearly other maturational factors also apply. For in adulthood, almost by definition, the majority of people in past societies were expected to work; an experience deferred or avoided only in the case of the aristocracy, seminarists and the indigent poor.

Unlike historical writing, the sociological study of both occupational choice and the transition from youth to adulthood has an extensive, highly developed and sophisticated literature. Implicit in many sociological accounts of youth transition, however, is the assumption that adjustment to the world of work involves some kind of 'culture shock', compounded of simultaneous anxiety, pleasure and confusion, deriving from the clash of values between pre-work expectations and the realities of the work situation.[3] That the shift from school to work was a sudden move for the large majority appears quite unrealistic, if only on the basis of the British historical experience with which I am most familiar. Images of 'culture shock' hardly reflect the reality of wage-earning within the English working class, particularly before the First World War. Paid and unpaid employment was undertaken by large numbers of girls (child-minding, domestic tasks) and boys (running errands) long before puberty and certainly did not coincide neatly with the end of schooling. Thousands of boys took 'part-time' or 'half-time' jobs while still at school and, in consequence, when they left the classroom for good, there was no sudden entry into an alien adult world of work.

In a poor English family, or where the father was out of work, the eldest son could in the 1900s take his school-leaving certificate at the age of ten or eleven, to help support the youngest members of the family. Not even the 1918 Education Act was effective in eliminating child employment in Britain, despite introducing the compulsory schooling until age fourteen of which Robert Roberts was a prominent beneficiary. The 1921 Census of England and Wales indicates that a sizeable proportion of children in the industrial north simply fell through the supposed safety net provided by compulsory schooling. In Rochdale, Lancashire, 45% of all twelve and thirteen year-old girls and 47% of boys of the same age were in full-time employment in that year. Despite local bye-laws, there were still over 6,000 schoolchildren in Manchester working between twenty and forty hours a week for wages in 1922. The labour of schoolchildren is not confined to ancient memory, in 1991 a survey of ten to sixteen year-olds in a spread of Birmingham schools found that 43% of them had a job (nearly three quarters of them employed illegally), while a quarter of those working were under the age of thirteen, the minimum age for legal employment.[4]

**I**

Any discussion of the changing social and cultural conditions of youth during the nineteenth and twentieth centuries, with special regard to the end of adolescence, must confront the cumulative effects of urbanization and industrialization. It was the convention for children in much of pre-industrial Western and Northern Europe to leave home under the age of puberty to work in another household, as either apprentices or servants. The disappearance of this transitional, semi-autonomous, stage is generally accounted a significant change in the lives of young people both during and after industrialization. Thus the movement from pre-industrial, traditional methods of service and apprenticeship to the cash-nexus, wage-labour conditions for the majority of young people in urban-industrial society has generally been interpreted as marking a significant break in historical continuity. The labour of the young in urban-industrial societies is interpreted as being effectively commodified for wages. Boys and girls were likely to stay in the parental home far longer than in rural societies, walk or travel to work at the local factory or workshop, and contribute their earnings to the family or household unit. Yet whereas apprenticeship, or the first job, provided almost a ritual entry into manhood for most males, factory work or domestic service for young women was usually only a temporary strategy – a necessary duty to supplement the family income. Only marriage secured a final sense of the working-class woman's adulthood and femininity throughout much of the nineteenth century. Women in textiles who kept on working after marriage were a rarity; overall only 10% of all married women worked in late Victorian Britain. The typical female factory worker in England before 1914 was an unmarried young woman.[5]

The changing relationship of young people to the world of work as a result of industrialization has emerged as a significant historical factor in some of the more recent problem-based or regionalized studies of European age relations. Colin Heywood's important survey of *Childhood in Nineteenth Century France* (1988) challenges conventional historical wisdom regarding child labour and the introduction of the factory system by arguing for continuity between rural and industrial labour among children, particularly regarding age of entry and hours of work. He contends that industrialization did not radically transform the composition of the labour force in France and, specifically, did not produce a significant growth in the incidence of child labour. In the long run, industrialization brought some improvements in the working conditions of French children, but their diet, housing and life expectancy had to get worse before they got better. Contrary to those who stress only the negative aspects of the urban experience, a recent study of Austrian youth by American historian J. Robert Wegs argues that the social networks in working-class districts protected youth from the most destructive aspects of urban life. Further, he maintains that there was a great diversity among working-class youth, which must be taken into account when discussing working-class experience. The comment by the doyen of youth historians John Gillis that 'we should not be surprised to find a variety of youth cultures within a particular locality or even within a particular class' is echoed in this study of everyday working-class life in Vienna between 1890 and 1938. Income, family size, quality of housing, school expectations and employment opportunities varied greatly between the skilled and the unskilled and thus so too did the experience of working-class youth. The lives and attitudes of Viennese working-class youth could also differ widely according to family values, gender, and nearness to the Social Democratic subculture. Wegs adds a significant strata dimension to the Viennese labouring population's experience that improves our understanding of the real diversity and richness of European working-class culture.[6]

Where industrialization was relatively new, as in late nineteenth-century Germany and Austria, young men still exercised a preference for the traditional crafts, parental approval and skilled status. Thus a Berlin shoemaker of the late

1880s urged his own craft profession on his son: 'There is no need to be pressed into factories or to work outside your home and according to the steam whistle.' In shoemaking something of the old craft *Gemütlichkeit* remained. Many French shoemakers also refused to leave their homes to enter the factory, even after machine competition severely reduced wages. They valued their freedom, seeking not only to work at their own pace but also such simple pleasures as the freedom to smoke on the job. In 1890s Bremen, Northwest Germany, where competition for apprenticeships was intense, high-paying artisan jobs were still chosen in a community setting. The Protestant pastor helped advise children on their profession and paternal guidance also played a significant role. This traditional pattern of selection was increasingly threatened by the end of the century, since opportunities in the German crafts did not expand as rapidly as the demands made upon them, particularly where trades like cabinet-making were being taken over by factories. Mechanization led to increasing concentration of skills and job opportunities within existing craft families and this in turn meant that more aspirants for craft jobs were disappointed than ever before. The ranks of London dockers, for example, were swelled by refugees from the decaying crafts in the East End of London. In particular, many of the young men who opted for the high wages of factory work in Germany were frustrated journeymen or apprentices suffering from a sense of declining status. The instrumental view of work was forced upon them, not freely chosen, and the work itself was no compensation because it had been reviled in their own upbringing.[7]

German and British state policy relative to childhood, schooling and youth employment was often parallel in intent but different in practice. The 1900s campaign to save young workers from moral corruption in Imperial Germany epitomises these national variations, explored recently in Derek Linton's *Who Has the Youth Has the Future!* (1991). This battle cry, sometimes attributed to Luther, was adopted in turn-of-the-century Germany by a nascent campaign launched by middle-class professional reformers (*Bildungsbürgertum*) to win the hearts and minds of young German workers in urban areas. The youth salvation campaign set out primarily to protect autonomous young men, 'between primary school and barracks', from the degenerate influences of modern urban life, such as beer houses, dance halls, 'penny dreadfuls' and crime; to save them from the 'unpatriotic' socialist influence of the Social Democratic Party; and to promote declining national efficiency by improving their health and industrial skills. Linton traces how young German labourers were constructed as an official social problem and delineates the methods used by the 'youth cultivators' in order to redeem them, linked to the changing image of young urban workers and institutional reform during the rapid period of German industrialization. The centralization and militarization of German youth salvation is variously examined by Linton through the agencies of continuation schools, Protestant and Catholic youth work, the Kaiser's 1911 Youth Cultivation Edict, wartime military training and moral policing.[8]

There are clear parallels to be drawn with the pre-1914 concern of English middle-class reformers for national efficiency, racial deterioration and unemployment in relation to working-class adolescents. Efforts by English 'youth savers' to solve the 'boy labour' problem, that of male working-class school-leavers drifting into dead-end jobs believed to lead inevitably to adult unemployment, have recently been examined in Harry Hendrick's *Images of Youth* (1990). This looks at many of the same institutional agencies for the control of urban youth as are examined in Linton's work on Imperial Germany: youth organizations, the Youth Employment

Service and part-time Day Continuation Schools. Hendrick also argues, contrary to John Gillis, that the popular English understanding of 'adolescence', as a concept which structured the youth problem, had far less to do with the Victorian institutionalization of middle and upper-class youth in boarding schools and age relations within middle-class families than with Edwardian disapproval of working-class youth culture, the child psychology movement and the debate on working-class 'boy labour'.[9] Nonetheless, German society before 1914, despite some analogies with British experience, exemplified a much greater conformity and willingness to be ruled by conservative Prussian edict, particularly in the Lower Rhine and Ruhr regions and in a Catholic state like Bavaria. Thus the campaign to censor sensational reading matter by state decree, the exclusion of girls from job training or youth services, as well as the increasing militarization and centralization of Prussian youth cultivation schemes.

Whereas mandatory industrial continuation schools became virtually universal in German cities after 1900, an English Board of Education Report of 1916 on *Juvenile Education in Relation to Employment After the War* concluded that most young people in England were discouraged and disillusioned by their transition 'on the threshold of adult life'. This was labelled one of the gravest menaces of the times ('is the civilisation for which the English have fought to be made a civilisation worth fighting for?'), a contributory cause to permanent and intermittent unemployment and to juvenile delinquency. This wartime report recommended establishing a uniform school-leaving age of fourteen, the ending of partial-exemption ('part-time') schooling in the northern textile districts and provision for local authorities to open compulsory part-time day continuation classes for all fourteen to sixteen year-olds not otherwise engaged in full-time secondary education.[10] The 1918 Fisher Education Act passed all these recommendations but, before the majority of English local education authorities could submit their continuation school schemes for departmental approval, within a few years a combination of factors forced the closure of the half-dozen or so continuation schools which had already opened.

The English voluntary system, and a general disinterest in post-school training, ensured that employers and local authorities were able to thwart all measures for a national and compulsory system of day continuation schools. Perhaps demonstrating the much stronger ethos of individualistic liberalism in England than in Germany and a more jealous guardianship of exclusively local control over educational policy. Yet the long-term effect of this failure in the interwar years was to make the British labour force both less skilled and less competitive in world markets. Even today 80% of young British men and women receive no further training or education after the age of eighteen. Linton claims that German continuation schools were thoroughly modern institutions, under liberal middle-class hegemony, designed to integrate young workers into the Wilhelmine polity, urban life and the industrial order.[11] This may help to explain why German youth are today subject to a much more traditional, standardized, bureaucratic, and hence socially approved, transition between schooling and paid work than their British counterparts.

Unlike Germany, the advent of industrialization in Britain meant the rapid phasing out of the patriarchal craft-apprenticeship system. The Elizabethan Statute of Artificers (1563) was abolished by parliament in 1814, leaving the recruitment of labour entirely to the free working of capitalist market forces. Textiles and mining, industrial skills *par excellence*, did without apprentices. The indentured system survived in Victorian Britain, especially in the handicraft trades, but mostly without prescribed legal forms. George Howell estimated in 1877 that less than 10% of trade union members were 'properly' apprenticed. We are clearly faced here with a problem of definition. Thus Charles More, historian of skill, and the English working class before 1914 usefully distinguished between old-style indentured or 'proper' apprenticeships, workshop-artisan trade apprenticeships, exploitative apprenticeships, new-style apprenticeships, and premium engineering apprenticeships.[12] Increased mechanization and the struggle for union recognition made it increasingly difficult for the new engineering trades to restrict entry to their skills, except those concentrated in a small number of large yards, like ships' boilermakers. By the 1920s, according to Sidney and Beatrice Webb, 'proper' indentured apprenticeship regulations were practically out of use in the British trade union world. Consequently, in March and April 1937, thousands of young engineering and ship-building apprentices on the Clyde, in Middlesbrough, Newcastle and Manchester, went on strike demanding wage increases, union recognition and better training.[13] These spontaneous but little celebrated industrial strikes are not only indicative of large-scale youth mobilization but also demonstrate how far the British apprenticeship system had degenerated into little better than a form of cheap labour by the 1930s.

A study of the life-style of young wage-earners in interwar Manchester draws attention to the above apprentice strikes in order to argue that juveniles actually displayed a considerable degree of autonomy in the labour market. David Fowler also claims that the determinants of job choice were not so restricted as previous commentators have tended to suggest by over-estimating the influence of parental advice and example on job choices. Opportunities open to teenage wage-earners appear to have been much less circumscribed in English cities, as opposed to small towns and villages, although there is some evidence to suggest that parents were initially a guiding influence. A wealth of contemporary evidence in most large urban areas, such as that supplied by juvenile employment bureaux, draws attention to frequent job changes among teenage wage-earners and thus the independence shown by young people in the 'adult' world of work. Local juveniles often decided for themselves what was 'suitable' work, making certain preconditions such as short hours, good pay, and good working conditions before accepting employment deemed fitting by parents and youth employment officers. The belief that those in 'blind-alley' jobs were trapped in work leading nowhere except to unemployment is also depicted as misleading, since many boys deferred apprenticeships for two or more years in order to secure high earnings in van boy and warehouse work at fourteen. Contemporaries understated the buoyancy of the juvenile labour market which made movement from 'blind-alley' occupations into apprenticeships possible for large numbers of urban juveniles. All of this suggests that the job choices of young English wage-earners at this period were far less circumscribed and more autonomous than previously claimed.[14]

## II

We lack any sustained historical analysis of European youth transitions in the postwar period, so I shall attempt a preliminary survey focusing on the English working-class experience. A review of sociological writing on the passage from school to work in Britain over the past fifty years (history as past sociology) presents a gloomy picture of gender and class-structured expectations, wasted working-class talents and the commodification of the young on the labour market. In 1942, when Britain had more than two million working youth under eighteen, a study of girls growing up by Pearl Jephcott concluded that

> great changes will be essential after the war if boys and girls are to make a less haphazard and unsatisfactory entrance to their careers. They will be changes that will make it possible for young people to work for the benefit of the whole community and themselves, and not primarily for the dividends of a limited number of shareholders.

Twenty years later, Michael Carter's study of two hundred working-class school-leavers in Sheffield concluded that neither school nor work meant a great deal to a large number of secondary-modern schoolchildren: work was no more of a challenge to them than school had been. Unsurprisingly in such an industrial city, two fifths of local boys entered the steel and engineering industries, twice as many as had aspired to do so; the same proportion of female school-leavers went into clerical jobs.[15]

Much of the British literature on job opportunities consists of the impressions of teachers, personnel managers, and youth employment agencies which, although invaluable in themselves, provide only a partial insight into the problems of young people on leaving school and are loaded with moral judgements and evaluations. In 1970 Joan Maizels published an important questionnaire-based study of the transition from school to work based on interviews with 183 boys and 147 girls who had left school and were now employed in Willesden, north London. She argued that schools and youth employment services colluded with the requirements of the juvenile labour market and did not meet adolescent needs. British society, through its education system, 'sifts and sorts children into manual and non-manual positions according to their social class rather than their basic endowment'.[16] Maizels felt there was a cultural and linguistic conflict between the attitudes, values and expectations of working-class children and the values, aims and assumptions of middle-class bias in schools. Schooling appeared both irrelevant and authoritarian, thus helping to make the prospect of routine jobs more acceptable for the children most likely to enter them. This conclusion is a damning indictment of the 1944 Butler Education Act, which set up a less than radical tripartite structure of secondary modern, technical and grammar schools, entry to one or the other determined by selective examination at age eleven. The 11+ was abolished in most English counties (but not in Northern Ireland) with the introduction of comprehensive schooling in the late 1960s and 1970s.

Sociologists have testified that most young people in England (if not Wales, Scotland and Northern Ireland) develop a realistic, low-expectation assessment of the job choices open to them. Poverty of aspiration severely restricts the ambitions of young men and women from working-class cultures. Twenty years ago, even the fantasy choices of secondary-modern schoolboys were at a distressingly mundane and realistic level, few selecting the more exciting occupations such as pilot, professional footballer, pop singer, or even the old-fashioned train driver. 'Instead we have the boy who expects to be a labourer at the brickyard choosing the very same job in fantasy, and the potential rubber moulder, who, when offered the whole world from which to choose, still wants to be a rubber moulder', according to a 1974 account of working-class life chances. 'Looking at the occupational expectations of these children, one is struck by their utter realism.'[17] Sociologists invariably appear depressed by the continuing ability of English working-class school-leavers to reconcile themselves to unskilled, careerless, low-paid jobs. However upsetting to the detached academic observer, the expectations of school-leavers tended to reflect the employment opportunities available locally. On the other hand, because the aspirations of so many English school-leavers were incredibly low, the transition from school to work did not generally involve disappointment or dissatisfaction with the jobs eventually obtained; unlike their American counterparts whose aspirations did not adjust so readily to the available job opportunities.[18]

Only twenty years ago, studies of adolescence were overwhelmingly concerned with biological and sexual development, failing to take any account of the realities of the social structure in which the 'problem' of this age group was situated. A reaction against this approach was the neo-Marxism of the University of Birmingham Centre for Contemporary Cultural Studies (CCCS) which dominated youth cultural studies of the 1970s and early 1980s, reinstated class analysis as a major explanatory tool, and is still seen by many in Europe as the only British tradition of youth research. In retrospect, much of the CCCS, new criminology and youth subcultural approach to ethnographic analysis underplayed both a middle-class and a female-transition perspective. The 1980s saw a sociological renaissance of the school-to-work transitions mode of youth research in Britain which can be attributed not only to the application of theories of social and cultural reproduction in the study of schooling, but also to high levels of youth unemployment. Conservative government measures to contain unemployment, caused by their own dogmatic monetarist policies in the fight to curb inflation, resulted in the introduction of Youth Training Schemes (YTS) and the Youth Opportunities Programme (YOP), in effect changing the formal mechanisms of school-to-work transitions.[19]

In the mid-1970s a sociologist of the CCCS school, Paul Willis, became interested in what is now termed 'the process of cultural reproduction' among the working classes and how this contributed to a sense that 'posh jobs' were not for the likes of them. 'The difficult thing to explain about how middle-class kids get middle-class jobs is why others let them', he explained in aphoristic form. 'The difficult thing to explain about how working-class kids get working-class jobs is why they let themselves.'[20] Willis argued in his influential ethnographic study *Learning to Labour* (1977) that the transition process for working-class kids was often smoothed by the close approximation of family, work and neighbourhood, so that it was the middle-class values of school rather than the work-place which appeared alien and unreal. Their own rejection of academic conformism and culturally-induced linguistic backwardness most effectively prepared some working-class males for manual labour. Hence there was and is an element of self-damnation in working-class school-leavers taking on a subordinate role in western capitalism.

Willis was subsequently accused of being overly deterministic and of overlooking gender in his emphasis on how working-class masculinity is defined. The feminist response was that working-class girls 'resisted' the official middle-class ideology of school just as much as boys, by placing a greater emphasis on a culture of femininity and attracting the opposite sex. Unfortunately, this response to schooling also reproduced existing class and gender inequalities. In her 1984 CCCS study of girls in six Birmingham schools Christine Griffin found no female equivalent to Willis's counter-school culture of white working-class 'lads', with their gang-based male groups. Nor could she find any straight links between female school cultures and waged work, largely because the pressures to secure a man by 'going steady' undermined the basis of female networks outside of school. Family life and domestic commitments, such as unpaid housework and child care, played a more important role for girls in shaping entry to the labour market.[21]

Class-based approaches to the transition from youth to adulthood are less fashionable than once they were among European sociologists. 'Critical modernization' theory, which has taken hold in Germany, argues that the separations, and arguably the inequalities, between the situations of young people according to class origin, ethnicity and gender are gradually disappearing. Exponents of this postmodern theory place an emphasis on the process of destructuring and 'individualisation', based on consumer choices, labour market diversity and changing family patterns. Pressure of competition and the complexities of modern urban life-styles have supposedly isolated young people even among their peers and so they increasingly have to take on responsibility for themselves. 'Individualisation' and the diversification of life styles since the 1960s have supposedly made leisure as important as work in terms of the life goals of the young (a proposition strongly denied by Joan Maizels even in 1970). Young people today supposedly approach and experience their lives, in the present and in planning for the future, essentially as individuals responsible for and with the freedom to make their own decisions, *to construct their own biographies* on their own account. Life and career choices thus become a 'biographical project'. 'Critical modernization' theory proposes that young people are growing up today in a socially open space, where few things are certain, where many choices are possible, and where it is unclear which options can be maximized and for whom.[22] Under these conditions, can it be argued that a common experience of 'youth', as classically understood, still 'exists'?

There has been some resistance to this approach, given the importance which radical sociologists attach to the significance of continuity in social reproduction, often to the neglect of an age perspective. According to their alternative analysis, long-standing forms of class and gender inequalities are simply being reproduced in new ways and new divisions are being created among young people themselves, between the employed and the unemployed, between trainees on different types of YTS programmes, or between students and the nonacademic. Thus 'while an individualization of expectations may have taken place, an individualization of destinations remains an implausible sociological proposition'. On the other hand, in North America and most of Western Europe since 1945, the years of mass higher education stand out as a distinct and almost guaranteed phase in the middle-class developmental process. So perhaps students *enmasse* need to be differentiated from adolescents and young adults by the application of the life-stage concept 'youth'?[23]

Opponents of 'critical modernization' theory, such as the radical British and West German contributors to Lynne Chisholm e.a., *Childhood, Youth and Social Change* (1990), argue that patterns of ambition and motivation are not individually constructed but take place within the framework of a social structure, reflect complex social relationships and are subject to historical change. Paths to adulthood and marriage, far from being individualized, can still to a great extent be predicted from social class origins in both Britain and Germany. In other words, there is little evidence of fundamental shifts in structured inequalities or in gendered existence.[24] Only those with no sense of history would want to disagree with the proposition that social structure and historical change, rather than individual consumer choice, still crucially determine the destinies and values of young people.

# III

How did young people select the particular occupations which best suited them on leaving school? The personal recommendations of relatives or 'string-pulling' probably assumed a more important role in small towns and villages than in large industrial cities, with the important exception of skilled workers proposing their sons for apprenticeship, albeit only oral testimony can elicit the true extent of family involvement in job selection. Although there is no agreed sociological theory of youth transition or occupational choice, there was a broad agreement until the mid-1970s that national differences led the majority of French school-leavers to aspire to handicraft occupations and small farming; socially-mobile Americans to expect white-collar jobs; and British, German and Polish working-class adolescents to hope for work in skilled trades.[25] More sophisticated American approaches to career and vocational choice postulated that individuals made their decisions on the basis of 'exploration, crystallisation and specification', or thought that the process was essentially one of developing and implementing a 'self-concept'. Both these 'developmental' theories were and are invalid for the large majority of working-class youth who, like the school-leavers in 1960s Sheffield, rarely selected jobs but simply took whatever was available according to the nature of the local economy. The whole notion of explaining job choice in terms of realizing a 'self-image' would have been just as foreign to the children of labouring or peasant families in the nineteenth century.

Although it may have some validity for a middle-class careerist, the job experience of a typical industrial worker cannot really be regarded as an opportunity for 'self-actualization' and the implementation of a 'self-concept'. Even university graduates can now only expect to become part of a vast army of white-collar 'knowledge workers', managerial staff rather than self-actualizing professionals. The adoption of a 'developmental approach' to career guidance would probably exacerbate rather than overcome the difficulties faced by ordinary school-leavers seeking to enter the world of work, raising their hopes and expectations to a level which in a declining Britain could not be matched in the real economic world of limited opportunities and rising unemployment. Kenneth Roberts has proposed an alternative theory of occupational choice based on the key concept of 'opportunity structure', that is career guidance should be restricted to adjusting individuals to the localised employment to which their education and attainments grant access. The drawback to this pragmatic alternative theory, conveniently reconciling adolescents to the jobs available in their localities, is that it ignores the dynamics of rapidly changing European societies and also discourages rising expectations.[26]

Entry into the world of work has been a problem throughout the greater part of industrial history and the difficulties of recent school-leavers are not without precedent. In the 1950s and 1960s the vast majority of school-leavers found jobs with little difficulty but, with economists becoming more pessimistic about growth, such decades of smooth transition are now seen as exceptions to the general rule. The young are sought in periods of labour shortages and denied jobs during recessions. Market economies have always needed peripheral workers, a sub-proletariat, whether of young people, women or immigrants. The young have always been cheap and therefore useful to marginal businesses, accepting conditions of employment that adults reject. In the mid-1900s, for example, English schoolboy Harry Brown, from a poor home in Enfield, Middlesex, took on numerous part-time jobs outside of school hours in order to help supplement his family's income: delivering on a tricycle, running errands, working long hours for a milkman and running a stall outside a draper's shop until nearly midnight on Saturdays. In retrospect, interviewed nearly seventy years later, he came to believe that before 1914 school-children were very much exploited as cheap labour by the local employers.[27]

Great Britain today is a multinational, multiracial and multiethnic society, quite apart from major regional, class and gender differences. Germany, even after unification, appears on the surface to be more culturally homogeneous, partly because it has managed to institutionalize the school-to-work transition more successfully. British and German youth hence experience entry into the labour market and adulthood in significantly different ways. For example, the basis of a much stronger German tradition of craftsmanship and industry lies in their 'dual system' of education in which specialized training for a particular trade or other career still accounts for those two thirds of pupils who stay on to the higher grades of the 'Grundschule' (primary school), followed by three years' attendance at a 'Berufsschule' or vocational training school. Alternatively, after only four years of elementary education, students may elect to attend the traditional secondary track which runs alongside and consists of the tripartite structure of 'Gymnasium' (grammar school), 'Realschule' (technical grammar) and 'Hauptschule' (secondary modern). In Britain, where schools are also highly stratified, according to social class, ethnic, neighbourhood and gender differences, educational experience is determined as much by the type of school attended as by ability: 'comprehensive' (non-selective), 'grammar' (selective) or 'public' (fee-paying). Academic training still dominates British schools to a misguided extent, largely to meet university entrance requirements, although efforts have recently been made to prioritize technical and vocational education. This may be an uphill struggle in a society where practical skills receive little recognition or status.[28]

The school-to-work transition in modern European nations varies according to family, class, gender, ethnicity and region, factors which condition the occupational choices of young men and women as much today as in past centuries. The social mechanics of transition between Britain and Germany have been shown to differ quite markedly, particularly in regards to apprenticeship, as the contrasting historical experience of day continuation schools might suggest. In 1980 half of all West German school-leavers entered some form of apprenticeship, in France and Britain only 14% each (France had some 40% in post-school vocational education, Britain only 10%). Modern Germany provides highly-regulated mechanisms for the transition process which reflect historical experience and contrast with the more *laissez-faire* attitude current in Britain which has only recently introduced a national curriculum. Yet the large-scale German vocational training sector and the inordinate length of the entire German education process also helps to contain the consequences of mass youth unemployment. Radical sociologists argue that the German system of relatively smooth transition mechanisms is locked just as tightly into the social reproduction of gender and class inequalities as is the British.[29]

In present-day Britain, sixteen-year-old school-leavers unable to find full-time work face a multiplicity of government training schemes, work-related courses and temporary jobs paying youth wages, but few of these so-called opportunities offer guaranteed roads to adult employment. The rapid pace of technical and occupational change is also undermining traditional, life-long working careers based on qualifications and skills acquired prior to entering adult jobs. Changes of occupation during adulthood are becoming the norm rather than the exception and this calls for a versatility that most European educational systems signally fail to provide. Traditional gender roles and the monogamous pattern of family life are also being challenged so that, rather than basing life styles upon stable occupational and domestic statuses, many individuals now appear to spend their entire lives in a process of transition from youth to adulthood.[30]

## Acknowledgements

I would like to thank Harry Hendrick of Oxford Polytechnic and Lynne Chisholm of the University of Bremen for their useful suggestions.

## Notes

1   Robert Roberts, *A Ragged Schooling: Growing Up in the Classic Slum* (Glasgow, 1978 edn.), pp. 157–158.

2   John Springhall, *Coming of Age: Adolescence in Britain, 1860–1960* (Dublin, 1986), pp. 7, 47; Kathleen Alaimo, 'Childhood and Adolescence in Modern European History', *Journal of Social History*, XXIV (1991), 3, pp. 591–602.

3   Peter Brannen, 'Industrial and Economic Change and the Entry Into Work: An Overview', in: P. Brannen (ed.), *Entering the World of Work: Some Sociological Perspectives* (Her Majesty's Stationery Office, 1975), p. 115.

4   John Burnett, *Destiny Obscure: Autobiographies of Childhood. Education and Family from the 1820s to the 1920s* (London, 1982), p. 99; David Fowler, 'The First Teenagers: The Lifestyle of Young Wage-Earners in Interwar Britain', University of Manchester, D.Phil. thesis, 1988, pp. 44–50; Seumas Milne, 'Child Workers Put At Risk By Employers', *The Guardian*, 8 March 1991, p. 2.

5   Richard Wall, 'The Age at Leaving Home', *Journal of Family History*, III (1978), 2, pp. 181–202; Peter N. Stearns, 'Working-Class Women in Britain, 1890–1914', in: Martha Vicinus (ed.), *Suffer and Be Still: Women in the Victorian Age* (London, 1973), p. 110.

6   Colin Heywood, *Childhood in Nineteenth Century France: Work, Health and Education Among the 'Classes Populaires'* (Cambridge, 1988), pp. 144–145, 321; J. Robert Wegs, *Growing Up Working Class: Continuity and Change Among Viennese Youth, 1890–1938* (Pennsylvania, 1989), pp. 1–10, 139–147; John Gillis, *Youth and History: Tradition and Change in European Age Relations. 1770–Present* (New York, 1981 edn.), p. 219.

7   Peter N. Stearns, *Lives of Labour: Work in a Maturing Industrial Society* (London, 1975), pp. 45–84.

8   Derek S. Linton, *'Who Has the Youth Has the Future': The Campaign to Save Young Workers in Imperial Germany* (Cambridge, 1991), *passim*.

9   Harry Hendrick, *Images of Youth: Age, Class and the Male Youth Problem. 1880–1920* (Oxford, 1990), pp. 9–10, 83–84. In the 1900s about sixty British books and pamphlets, ninety-three periodical articles and thirty-nine official publications were devoted to the 'boy labour' topic.

10   *Final Report of the Departmental Committee on Juvenile Education in Relation to Employment After the War*, PP (1917), pp. 325–338; P.I. Kitchen, *From Learning to Earning* (London, 1944), p. 12.

11   D.W. Thomas, 'The Emergence and Failure of the Day Continuation School Experiment', *History of Education*, IV (1975), 1, pp. 36–50; Hendrick, *Images of Youth*, pp. 213–249; Linton, *'Who Has the Youth Has the Future'*, p. 97.

12   W. Knox, 'Apprenticeship and De-skilling in Britain, 1850–1914', *International Review of Social History*, XXXI (1986), Pt. 2, pp. 166–184; George Howell, 'Trade Unions, Apprentices and Technical Education', *Contemporary Review*, XXX (1877), p. 854; Charles More, *Skill and the English Working Class. 1870–1914* (London, 1980), pp. 41–52, 104–105.

13   Alan McKinlay, 'From Industrial Serf to Wage Labourer: The 1937 Apprentice Revolt in Britain', *International Review of Social History*, XXXI (1986), Pt. 1, pp. 1–18; John Gollan, *Youth in British Industry: A Survey of Labour Conditions Today* (London, 1937), pp. 313–315; Fowler, 'The First Teenagers', pp. 136–149.

14   David Fowler, 'The First Teenagers', pp. 37–53.

15   Pearl Jephcott, *Girls Growing Up* (London, 1942), p. 97; Michael Carter, *Home, School and Work: A Study of the Education and Employment of Young People in Great Britain* (Oxford, 1962), p. 211.

16   Joan Maizels, *Adolescent Needs and the Transition from School to Work* (London, 1970), p. 316.

17 Carter, *Home, School and Work*, p. 134; John and Sylvia Jewkes, *The Juvenile Labour Market* (London, 1938), pp. 30–31; William Leversidge, 'Life Chances', in: W.M. Williams (ed.), Occupational Choices (London, 1974), p. 65.

18 Kenneth Roberts, 'The Entry Into Employment: An Approach Towards a General Theory', *Sociological Review*, XVI (1968), 2, p. 180.

19 Stuart Hall and Tony Jefferson (eds), *Resistance Through Rituals: Youth Subcultures in Post-War Britain* (London, 1975); C. Cockburn, *Two-Track Training: Sex Inequalities and YTS* (London, 1987); P. Brown and D. Ashton (eds), *Education, Unemployment and the Labour Market* (London, 1987); D. Lee, D. Marsden, P. Rickman and J. Duncombe (eds), *Scheming for Youth: A Study of the YTS in the Enterprise Culture* (London, 1990).

20 Paul Willis, *Learning to Labour: How Working Class Kids Get Working Class Jobs* (London, 1977), p. 1.

21 Christine Griffin, *Young Women and Work: The Transition from School to the Labour Market for Young Working-Class Women* (Birmingham CCCS, 1984), *passim*. See also: Peter Aggleton, *Rebels Without a Cause: Middle Class Youth and the Transition from School to Work* (London, 1988).

22 U. Beck, *Risikogesellschaft. Auf dem Weg in eine andere Moderne* (Frankfurt, 1986); Lynne Chisholm, Peter Büchner, Heinz-Hermann Krüger and Phillip Brown (eds), *Childhood, Youth and Social Change: A Comparative Perspective* (Basingstoke, 1990), pp. 6–7, 36–38, 112–113.

23 Lynne Chisholm and Manuela du Bois-Reymond, 'Youth Transitions, Gender and Social Change', Mss. loaned by authors; Hugh Klein, 'Adolescence, Youth, and Young Adulthood: Rethinking Current Conceptualizations of Life Stage', *Youth and Society* XXI (1990), 4, pp. 446–471.

24 Gill Jones and Claire Wallace, 'Beyond Individualization: What Sort of Social Change?', in: Lynne Chisholm, e.a. (eds), *Childhood, Youth and Social Change*, p. 139.

25 E.T. Keil, C. Riddell and B.S.R. Green, 'Youth and Work: Problems and Perspectives', in: Williams (ed.), *Occupational Choice*, p. 78.

26 Kenneth Roberts, 'The Entry Into Employment: An Approach Towards a General Theory', in: Williams (ed.), *Occupational Choice*, pp. 138–157; P. Drucker, *The Age of Discontinuity* (London, 1969); Michael West and Peggy Newton, *The Transition from School to Work* (London, 1983), pp. 7–8, 183–184.

27 Cited: Springhall, *Coming of Age*, pp. 74–75.

28 Russ Russell (ed.), *Learning About the World of Work in the Federal Republic of Germany: A Collection of Papers* (Bristol, 1982), pp. 5–6; Philippa Andrews (ed.), *The German Vocational Education System* (Bristol, 1979), pp. 8–9.

29 Lynne Chisholm, e.a. (eds), *Childhood, Youth and Social Change*, pp. 11, 49.

30 Kenneth Roberts, *School-Leavers and Their Prospects: Youth in the Labour Market in the 1980s* (Milton Keynes, 1984), pp. 1–10.

## CHAPTER 15

# POLITICIANS AND ECONOMIC PANIC

Alison Wolf

*History of Education*, 27, 3, 219–34, 1998

## Introduction

We are currently, in the late twentieth century, so accustomed to education being discussed in terms of its economic relevance that any other reference point strikes us as curious. To read Newman[1] on the idea of a university is to enter another world; but the same is true of writings far closer to us in time. Hadow, Spens, Crowther and Newsom on secondary and 'adolescent' education,[2] or Russell on adults,[3] all make us aware of today's obsessive concern with economic relevance by reminding us of a world with wider concerns, and, indeed, a more sophisticated understanding of the relationship between education and economic welfare.

Education policy in the last fifteen years has been driven by an economic panic among politicians, which has also been associated with an unprecedented willingness to hand policy making over to the official representatives of 'the business community'. This article describes beliefs about economic failure and its remedies which, during the 1980s, became the consensus view among the political and business establishments; it also illustrates the degree to which, in response, 'business' was given control and influence over education and training policy.[4] It then compares recent developments with another period of panic, this time in the late nineteenth century: a period which produced two government reports with very familiar themes, but also very different analyses and prescriptions from those of our own time. Finally, it offers some hypotheses about why the ends of two centuries should be alike in their concerns, but also so markedly different in their actions.

## The current panic: players and panaceas

The current obsession with education as a supposed driver of economic growth gathered pace in the United Kingdom from the early 1980s on. The general climate at that time was one of extreme anxiety about the state of the British economy and its prospects.[5] Youth unemployment was very high, and the government felt under enormous pressure to develop policies which would reduce unemployment rates generally, and youth unemployment in particular. At the same time, the then Conservative government was firmly set against any attempt to tackle unemployment through demand expansion and/or government spending, policies it saw as discredited and ultimately destructive.

In this context, a number of academic analyses of Britain's relatively poor rates of postwar economic growth had a major impact. The most important were a series of detailed comparisons of British and European training policies and of sector-specific productivity (e.g. in retail, construction, hotel trades) carried out by the National Institute of Economic and Social Research. The NIESR authors, and especially Professor Sig Prais, argued that British productivity was markedly and consistently lower than that in comparable firms in Germany, France and The Netherlands. The researchers painstakingly documented differences in the numbers of workers obtaining vocational and technical awards in the two countries and argued that a large part of this productivity difference could be ascribed to the inferior education and training of British workers.[6] One of them summarized the results of the programme of studies comparing Germany and the UK as having shown that:

> German productivity is linked to strong vocational skills among the labour force.... The lower educational standard of...British school-leavers makes it difficult and more costly to train them to become skilled workers in comparison with their German counterparts.... The higher skill of the German operator reduces the number of indirect staff needed.... If British manufacturers do not want to lose business a great effort has to be undertaken to improve the skill base of their labour force.[7]

By the mid-1980s the link between, on the one hand, training policy and vocational qualifications, and, on the other, economic growth was becoming standard doctrine in policy circles. The growing consensus on the importance of skills and qualifications influenced and was in turn greatly strengthened by the activities of the Manpower Services Commission (MSC). This government quango was established by the government in the 1970s, largely to run the emergency programmes for the unemployed which were expanding rapidly at that point; but one consequence was the creation of a distinct cadre of government professionals whose main concern was training policy. Under the leadership of a number of politically astute and policy-oriented directors, the MSC soon was promoting widespread change in the education and training systems of the country, designed to make them far more 'friendly' to entrepreneurship, business and technology and so, supposedly, conducive to future economic well-being.

One of the MSC's early collaborations was with the National Economic Development Office, which, like the MSC itself, was a 'corporatist' body, with top-level representation of the major social partners. Two reports were published by MSC and NEDO[8] which a sympathetic author has described as the beginning of 'a sustained assault on two centuries of industrial indifference'.[9] Both reflected the growing consensus that skill levels had a major independent effect on productivity and growth, and that the way to increase both of these was to increase the numbers of people obtaining vocational and technical qualifications.

The Review of Vocational Qualifications was set up by MSC in 1985, and chaired by a businessman, Oscar de Ville. Its view of the problem was one which was becoming increasingly familiar:

> Future economic competitiveness will depend in large measure on improving the adaptability and competences of our workforce at all levels. A coherent

system for the assessment and certification of vocational competence is an important factor in achieving this and in providing adequate opportunities for satisfying personal aspirations.[10]

Its major recommendation was the creation of a National Council for Vocational Qualifications with the brief to produce a national system of vocational qualifications around which would be organized the desired increase in qualification rates. The basis of these qualifications was to be sets of industry 'standards' developed by each occupational sector through its own 'Lead Industry Body', and so encapsulating industry's own view of what vocational awards should contain. The NCVQ was duly established in 1987, and over the next decade huge amounts of public money and effort were poured into trying to persuade firms to underwrite and individuals to work for NVQs (National Vocational Qualifications). Although the government was unwilling to make training compulsory for firms, or institute a training levy, the Training and Enterprise Councils responsible for local training programmes offered and continue to offer financial incentives for NVQ adoption, while assessment and certification costs can be met through the franchising arrangements with FE colleges underwritten by FEFC.[11]

By the end of the 1980s the consensus that economic competitiveness was directly and strongly related to education and training levels was firmly in place, as was the continuing belief that Britain was lagging in this respect. A 1988 article by Finegold and Soskice, which reached and convinced a wide academic audience, elaborated on the NIESR analysis and argued that the British economy was stuck in a 'low skill equilibrium' which doomed it to low productivity, low wages, and low-tech industries compared with the 'high skill equilibrium' of economies such as Germany's.[12] The MSC, now renamed the Training Agency, argued that:

> ...in order to maintain its competitiveness in the international market place, British business must raise the skills profile of its workforce. Insofar as other countries are already ahead, Britain will need to improve its education and training performance even faster than its competitors.[13]

A combination of academic and corporatist networks helped to spread these views beyond the world of training professionals and labour economists. Sir Bryan Nicholson, for example, was Chairman of MSC; Chairman of CNAA; Chairman of NCVQ.[14] Sir John Cassels was the Director of MSC and then Director of NEDO; he followed this with a period as Director of the National Commission on Education (funded by the Paul Hamlyn Foundation). He endorsed the view of crisis, arguing in 1990 that 'Britain does then have a real widespread and severe skill shortage. The implications are very serious'.[15] A few years later, the National Commission's own report advanced similar arguments:

> In the United Kingdom much higher achievement in education and training is needed to match world standard...we have not yet developed the concept...that nearly all jobs, including many humble ones, require skill and will be much better done by a trained than an untrained person. The work of the National Institute of Economic and Social Research has shown that treating jobs as skilled and training accordingly, has led to great benefits in terms of higher productivity, of quality of output and of adaptability to change both in Germany and in other European countries. Direct comparisons with our own practice demonstrate how seriously our performance has lagged.[16]

The mid-1990s have been the period of Sir Ron (now Lord) Dearing, whose own background had exposed him to very much the same influences and arguments as Cassels.[17] Called in quite explicitly as a 'fixer', Dearing has been happy to oblige; first to sort out mainstream schooling (the National Curriculum); then education for 16–19-year-olds; and finally, higher education. His reports are masterpieces of compromise, placating warring players rather than offering visionary solutions, and as such they too reflect clearly the assumptions of the political classes.

Thus, in the Review of Qualifications for 16–19-Year-Olds, the underlying rationale for decisions in this area is offered under the title 'National targets and needs'. It is also couched almost entirely in terms of employment needs – universities get an occasional mention, but beyond that, the whole section is conceived in terms of workplace requirements:

> There is much concern in all quarters about current standards of achievement...(E)mployers are looking for a high level of skill in oral communication.... They feel entitled to look to school and college education to provide this. Employers recognise the growing importance of competence in the use of information technology as a life-time skill. In addition they value certain general skills...These include: Skills in working effectively with other people; Presentational skills; A problem-solving approach; The ability to manage one's own learning....[18]

The report on Higher Education makes some slight obeisance in other directions: thus in the preface, Dearing writes:

> Much of our report is concerned with material things and with the central role of higher education in the economy. It would be surprising were it not so. But throughout we have kept in mind the values that characterise higher education....[19]

This may indeed be the case; but without the avowal in the preface one would be hard put to deduce it. The inquiry's terms of reference conceive of higher education's functions in a primarily economic way; in this respect the major principle to which committee members are directed is that 'learning should be increasingly responsive to employment needs'.[20] The government emphasizes that 'the UK must now compete in increasingly competitive international markets...many of our international competitors are aiming to improve the contribution their higher education systems make to their economic performance';[21] and the Dearing report responds in kind. The 'learning society' it envisages is discussed almost entirely in terms of its contribution to 'a competitive economy', 'competitive pressures', 'demand from industry and commerce'. The Japanese have participation rates 10% higher than ours; therefore, the inquiry concludes, more of our young people must go to university. 'The economic imperative is to resume growth.'[22]

Most of the examples given to date and below concern periods of Conservative government under Thatcher and Major; who at an organizational level gave responsibility for large amounts of *education* funding, as well as training responsibilities, to first the Manpower Services Commission and then the Department of Employment. Major's decision to merge Employment and Education into one department, which was generally applauded, also underlines the unquestioned dominance of a workplace perspective on education. The White Paper which followed Dearing's review of 16–19 education is called 'Learning to Compete'.

However, there is no reason to expect any changes from the Labour government whose pre-election 'Road to the Manifesto' lifted its name and objective, namely the 'skills revolution', directly from the CBI, and identified it as one of the 'four pillars of new Britain'. The document involves a wholesale adoption of policies to be discussed further below, including NVQs and Investors in People, takes Germany as its major comparison point, and quotes the NIESR researchers with approval. 'If we are to face the challenge of creating a high-tech, high-added-value and high-wage economy, we can only do so by skilling [*sic*] our people to be able to provide quality products and quality services',[23] it concludes.

The fact that an entire political and policy-making class has reached a consensus on something does not, of course, automatically mean that they are wrong. As discussed further below, there is, in fact, good reason to believe that there are important links between education and prosperity, although these are a great deal less direct and simple than most of the above would suggest, or than our politicians currently believe. What the simplified analysis and concurrent panic have meant, however, is that 'British business' has been identified as the major legitimator of the content and structure of post-compulsory education.

At first sight, this seems curious. The origin of the campaign for more vocational training and qualifications was the perception that economic growth was lower than in other developed economies, that is, that business was not delivering. While training might be part of the answer, it has never been seen, even by its most enthusiastic proponents, as the only answer. Equally, while it might be argued that there were inevitable market failures justifying increased expenditure on training by governments, it has also been argued consistently that British businesses have been shortsighted and culpable in their failure to train. Marquand, for example, argues that this is linked to the more general failure of British managers to understand the nature of technological change, human learning and productive organizations. 'Lack of training was endemic in industry' prior to the early 1980s she argues. 'The low importance attached to being able to structure thought and its related action had led to lack of coherent thought about the nature and content of training.'[24]

So why entrust the design of training and education systems to exactly the people who are seen as largely responsible for the mess in the first place? There are, I would suggest, a number of reasons for the move. The first is that, once politicians had accepted the argument that specific vocational education and training were directly related to productivity and growth, it was difficult to see educators and civil servants as adequate curriculum designers. The only people who could, logically, provide information on what was required became the employers.

Second, and equally important, was the dominant place accorded to Germany as the role model as well as the quintessential economic competitor. The emphasis in academic research on Germany and other European countries was certainly very important here. (In fact one of the puzzles of the last fifteen years is the lack of academic attention paid to the US economy, which has hardly a national vocational qualification to its name.) Using Germany as the main point of reference encouraged a reform policy based on the formal involvement of the 'social partners', as represented by their own official organizations. However, the Conservative government was generally at loggerheads with the unions, which meant that the entire social partner 'space' was available to be filled by business representatives.

Excluding every group other than business was also entirely consistent with the general attitude of the Conservative government to organized groups; and this, in turn, was the third element tending to enhance business influence in the education and training field. Under Mrs Thatcher, the Conservatives took a consistently hostile attitude towards organized 'provider' or professional groups, regarding them as essentially a conspiracy against the public interest. They attacked not only unions but also local authorities and the organized professions. Businessmen, however, were seen as people who succeeded in the market-place, by responding to individuals' wishes, and therefore as repositories of expertise and efficiency. The general pro-business assumption pre-empted any queries related to their supposed ineffectiveness as trainers in the previous decades or century, and meant that business organizations became the exception to the government's generalized hostility.

## Education and the CBI

Although up to now we have referred to 'business' in a general way, the single largest influence came from one particular organization: the Confederation of British Industry. The CBI represents the big battalions of British industry. (Small companies affiliate to the Institute of Directors which rarely agrees with the CBI on anything.) The CBI headquarters in London's Centre Point building includes a considerable staff devoted to policy analysis; in the last decade, the CBI has organized a number of task-forces and committees, whose members are senior industrialists but whose reports are, inevitably, largely drafted by the CBI staff who service the meetings. The CBI is, in other words, an organization staffed by career bureaucrats, and its behaviour is consistent with its nature.

Large and small firms had been alike in criticizing the Industrial Training Boards, established in the 1960s, supported by compulsory levies on the industry, generally agreed to be inefficient and bureaucratic, and abolished in the early 1980s. However, during the 1980s, the CBI had become extremely interested in education and training policy, responding to the general intellectual climate and both contributing to and benefiting from the enhanced role for business offered by the MSC and the new National Council for Vocational Qualifications. It established a Vocational Education and Training Task Force, chaired by Sir Bryan Nicholson (a past Chairman of the MSC, a future Chairman of NCVQ), with twenty other business representatives and staffed by four senior members of the CBI's Education and Training Directorate. In 1989, this Task Force published a report, 'Towards a Skills Revolution'.

The CBI report wholeheartedly endorsed the analytical position summarized above, quoting as a major source for its position the findings of the NIESR researchers.[25] The report was greeted enthusiastically by the government, but not much studied by education and training professionals. Few, therefore, recognize the extent to which the major education and training policies of the last decade follow, in detail, the detailed recommendations of the CBI. This is partly because the CBI adopted an already prevailing consensus; but it is far from the whole explanation. Having accepted and promulgated arguments which made 'industrial need' the rationale for the nature and content of education, politicians and, indeed, civil servants accepted the implications of their own arguments and showed a consistent tendency to follow CBI recommendations on quite specific matters of policy.

To illustrate this argument, there follow six excerpts from *Towards a Skills Revolution*. The first frames the last ten years' general emphasis on education and training as the saviours of an embattled economy; the following five involve the main planks of post-compulsory education and training during that same period.

## Quotation 1

> Skills shortages are a significant constraint on business efficiency.... There is inadequate and insufficient education and training of young people to meet skills needs. The prospect of more young people entering the labour market directly at age 16 or receiving narrow foundation training is simply unacceptable at a time when German employers, for example, are calling for further strengthening of their own system. Employers believe there must be a quantum leap in the education and training of young people to meet the needs of the British economy and to face the competition on even terms, while continuing the effort to improve, the skills and competences of the existing workforce.

This quotation could just as easily have come from any one of the other reports cited in this chapter – not least in its emphasis on German practice. (As noted earlier, American habits, by contrast, are virtually never alluded to in this literature.) There is, however, an indication that it is an *employers'* federation that is writing in the call for a 'quantum leap' in public expenditure, in contrast with 'continuing the effort' to train existing workers. The implication is that, whatever may be wrong, it is not the employers' fault: a position which is made explicit elsewhere in the same document:

> Continued public investment in skills training is essential, especially when employers are having to deal with deficiencies of the education system which will take time to be remedied.

## Quotation 2

The argument that most of the problem lay with the schools was made repeatedly by the CBI; both the last and the current government certainly give the impression of believing that UK schools are extraordinarily poor, failing to give industry what it 'needs', and themselves in need of ever-tighter central direction and control. However, the CBI did make one suggestion for action by its members rather than by the education sector:

> Education and training are at the top of nearly everyone's agenda for action. The skills of the United Kingdom workforce compare poorly with those of our principal competitors.... Our ... report seeks to bring about a skills revolution by improving the foundation skills of young people as a basis for continued learning throughout working life and by urging all employers to become '*Investors in training*' for all their employees.... (emphasis added)

Their suggestion was accepted, although 'Investors in training' became 'Investors in People'. The CBI's recommendation also became a flagship programme of the Employment Department and its TECs.[26] Strengthening this programme is one of the main concrete proposals in the Labour Party's pre-election document on 'The Skills Revolution'. A firm which is designated an 'Investor in People' must meet criteria which have been developed with public funds as a 'quality standard', and there are financial incentives for involvement. Nonetheless, firms do put a considerable amount of effort and resources into the programme, and a large proportion of CBI members are now 'Investors in People'.

## Quotation 3

> The Task Force believes that it is necessary to set world class targets....
> The...targets will have to be reviewed and raised until the United Kingdom is
> on a par with its main competitors.

The CBI's ideas on 'Investors in training' were relatively happy ones: the same
cannot be said of their endorsement of targets. While they were hardly the only
group promoting targets at this time – reforms everywhere in the public sector,
including, notably, the NHS, were all target-driven – their support for the concept
in education and training was vital in securing its centrality and its continuing and
largely pernicious effect on policy.

Given that they are representatives of companies in market economies, the
enthusiasm of CBI personnel for centrally set targets is extraordinary. The most
superficial analysis of, say, the Russian or the Chinese economy in the postwar
period indicates how much their economic failures were related to central target
setting. If governments set quantitative targets, and make rewards dependent on
achieving these, then people will, indeed, set themselves to produce the quantities
desired. However, in the process, concern with quality, or any discussion of
whether the numbers make sense, both become irrelevances. The Russian economy
produced vast numbers of tractors; but it produced very few tractors that worked.

The same scenario can be traced in training policy over the last decade.
Employment Department staff, and the network of Training and Enterprise
Councils, all became obsessed with achieving target numbers – especially those for
NVQs. Training schemes were pressed to increase their qualification rates (and so
moved to those NVQs which could be achieved quickly and easily); output-related
funding was introduced to give trainers even more incentive to up the numbers
successfully;[27] TEC staff offered firms financial incentives to adopt NVQs; franchising was encouraged so that FE colleges could help increase the number of
NVQs being assessed and registered. Predictably, there also followed stories of
fraud; of widespread pressure on staff to pass candidates irrespective of attainment; of 'whistle-blowers' being sacked and silenced.[28] One large empirical study
of NVQ assessment[29] found that 38% of assessors, and 48% of external verifiers,
felt that 'many candidates pass who shouldn't'.

The targets still figure large in government policy and in the speeches ministers
deliver, in spite of mounting evidence that, as one would expect, the result has been
detrimental to the quality of training and assessment. As Table 15.1 demonstrates,
however, there have been some modifications in their nature since their first
appearance. Although the CBI recommended them, was instrumental in their creation and continues to support them strongly, between 1991 and 1995 the one target that disappeared from the scene was the one for which business itself was
largely responsible, and on which almost no progress had been made: the spread of
NVQ qualifications throughout the workforce.

## Quotation 4

> The task force recommends that from age 14 individuals should possess their
> own careership profile which records achievement and identifies development
> needs.... One national system of Records of Achievement and action plans
> should be used in both schools and employment pre-16 and post-16. This
> would require a coming together of school records with the National Record
> of Vocational Achievement....All young people would then be treated
> equally, irrespective of the route of their learning....

*Table 15.1* The national education and training targets

| 1991 | 1995 |
|------|------|
| By 1997 80% of all young people to reach NVQ2 or equivalent | By 2000 85% of all young people to achieve 5 GCSEs at grade C or above, an Intermediate GNVQ or an NVQ2 |
| By 2000 50% of young people to reach NVQ3 or equivalent | By 2000 75% of young people to achieve level 2 competence in communication, numeracy and IT by age 19; and 35% to achieve level 3 competence by age 21<br>By 2000 60% of young people to achieve 2 GCE A levels, an Advanced GNVQ or an NVQ level 3 by age 21 |
| By 1996 all employees should take part in training or development activities | |
| By 1996 50% of the workforce aiming for NVQs or units towards them | By 2000 60% of the workforce qualified to NVQ level 2, Advanced GNVQ or two GCE A level standard |
| By 2000 50% of the workforce qualified at least NVQ3 or equivalent | By 2000 30% of the workforce to have a qualification at NVQ4 or above |

A puzzling aspect of the CBI's approach to education and training is that it consistently criticized the schools' performance, at a time when criticism was increasingly associated with rejection of 'progressive' teaching methods, yet at the same time endorsed 'progressive' policies in the post-compulsory sector. This endorsement of careership profiles and Records of Achievement (RoAs) came at a time when the government was reviewing the RoA pilots. NCVQ had just introduced its own vocational equivalent. Two years later, the National Record of Achievement was indeed officially endorsed and launched as a mandatory document for all older secondary pupils. The integrated version recommended by the CBI was adopted; and it was NCVQ, the vocational industry-linked quango, that was given the major responsibility and funding for this new initiative.

### Quotation 5

> The Task Force has concluded that government should fund a credit for all 16 year olds to meet the learning costs associated with courses leading to NVQ Level III or its academic equivalent....

Again, this recommendation was accepted. In spite of sustained criticism from those involved in programme delivery, who argued that the system would create nothing new except a cumbersome administrative superstructure, the government launched an ambitious and expensive pilot of training credits in response to the CBI's recommendations. However, the critics were proved right; and the scheme was dropped quietly without ever becoming national policy.

### Quotation 6

> The success of the National Council for Vocational Qualifications (NCVQ) in its work on standardisation and rationalisation is...important. Higher

priority should be given to establishing a critical mass of fully accredited qualifications.... More strenuous efforts at marketing and raising the status of NVQs are required.... Employer representation on the National Council should be strengthened...individual levels of attainment need more overt recognition across the education and training spectrum.

As described above, the NCVQ was conceived by a committee headed by a businessman; and, throughout the Council's ten-year history, the CBI provided consistent, vocal and very effective support. The deficiencies of the assessment and certification model developed by NCVQ have been documented widely: the narrowness of the qualifications, the over-reliance on highly detailed and opaque 'standards' to promote both validity and reliability of assessment; the huge costs of assessment; the lack of standardization.[30]

The CBI, however, remained resolute in its support, setting itself firmly against any move to make the awards less tightly reflective of workplace practice, to introduce external assessment, or to reduce the extent to which NVQs were based entirely on industrial standards rather than more general and educational considerations. While they were by no means the only barrier to reform, they were a, and perhaps the, critical one. Ironically, however, this firm support of the status quo may ultimately have doomed the Council, as it became apparent to Whitehall that the rising flood of criticism did indeed mean a need for reform. Politically, the easiest way to achieve this was to abolish the NCVQ, merge it with the schools assessment quango (SCAA), and thus reduce both the visibility of vocational qualifications, and the influence of any one interest group. In 1997 this was achieved with the creation of the unified Qualifications and Curriculum Authority.

### Training and growth

This section has discussed in some detail how economic panic, a theory about vocational skills and productivity, and business influence on education policy became intertwined. To a considerable degree they remain so, but it is also becoming clear that the relationship between economic growth and vocational education and training is by no means as simple as was believed. Successful economies operate with a very wide range of training systems; equally, the systems they operate are deeply embedded in their general institutional and labour market structure, and cannot be revolutionized overnight. Cross-cultural borrowing is virtually never a workable option.[31]

At the same time, the continuing dynamism of industrialized economies, and the regular job and career changes which characterize most people's lives, have clear lessons for policy makers. They make the development of courses and qualifications modelled directly on current industries' current needs a dubious use for public money. Individuals, as so often, have proven more clear-sighted than governments. By a large margin, they have chosen to pursue general education, preferably to university level, rather than highly specific vocational qualifications.[32]

### An older panic: the findings of the Samuelson Report

The fifteen-year period now drawing to a close has been unique, in the twentieth century, for its obsession with the relation between education and economic growth. Of course, the relationship has been of *concern* at other times. A succession of civil servants and commentators has promoted the need for more technical education, or more support for technical colleges and schools, or for more science, and maths, and engineering. Worries during the mid-1950s (the Sputnik period) provoked a White Paper on Technical Education (1956) which drew pessimistic comparisons between the UK on the one hand and the USA, Russia and Western Europe on the other, but nothing much happened as a result. A White Paper on Industrial Training in 1962 produced the Industrial Training Act of 1963, which set up the Training Boards. But otherwise, again, very little happened. The activity was elsewhere: in primary education, secondary reform, university expansion.

To find a period comparable to our own recent past, we need to look back a century or so, to first the Select Committee and then the Royal Commission chaired by Sir Bernhard Samuelson.[33] These inquiries and reports also reflected a widespread anxiety about the British economy, British competitiveness and prosperity, and the relationship between education and industry. There was a general consensus among policy makers that all was not well, and that reforms were needed; and a particular concern with German practices – all, in fact, very similar indeed to the situation a hundred years later. Both public debate and comment, and the inquiries themselves, were triggered by a quintessential policy insider. As the 1884 report itself notes, 'the first impulse to an inquiry into the subject of technical instruction was given by the important letter of Dr, now Sir Lyn Playfair, K.C.B., of May 15, 1867, to the Chairman of the Schools Inquiry Commission, in which he called attention to the great progress in engineering and manufactures abroad shown at the Paris Exhibition of that year'. Playfair, playing the role of a nineteenth-century academic analyst, found ready attention; and did so because he encapsulated the responses of many other contemporary visitors to the Exhibition and the more general national mood of economic unease.

The Samuelson Commission has been discussed extensively by historians, most recently, and from a new perspective, by Dr Robin Betts.[34] In the continuing arguments about the causes of English economic decline, and the factors which shaped England's national and public education system, the Commission and its aftermath appear frequently as exhibits – normally for the prosecution.[35] The political and administrative classes of the time are generally blamed for failing to respond adequately to the work of Samuelson and his colleagues; and, consequently, for perpetuating the anti-industrial culture criticized by Wiener and Margaret Thatcher alike.[36]

Here, however, I want to concentrate on a rather different issue, namely the contrast between the views expressed by 'Business' in the late twentieth century and those expressed by businessmen in the late nineteenth. The Commission members and their witnesses provided a far more complex analysis of the relation between education and the workplace than did their modern successors; and this is best demonstrated by quoting their own words.

The first extract is from the Introduction to the summary report, a short document which was widely sold and distributed and effectively sums up the conclusions reached by the Commission:

> During the first half of this century we enjoyed an unchallenged industrial supremacy, the result of many contributory causes. Among them were physical causes, such as our mineral wealth...and our bracing climate; moral and

intellectual causes such as the natural energy and inventiveness of our people; political causes such as the happy union of individual liberty with public order; economic causes such as the gradual accumulation of capital in earlier times.... So conspicuous was the supremacy thus established that some among us came to regard it almost as part of the fixed order of Nature. These good people took the same view respecting their country which a Sheffield manufacturer expressed respecting his town: – 'Sheffield was really a very fine town and he questioned whether any part of the world was equal to it.' Although conceivably we might improve ourselves, yet we were so superior to other nations that improvement was hardly a thing of practical concern.

Our neighbours, however, saw things more clearly. The industrial supremacy of Great Britain appeared to them the effect of definite causes, not of indefinite perfection in the British. England served them as a model of organisation and equipment, but their trained intelligence enabled them to improve upon this model. For some time past, whilst we have advanced, they have advanced faster still; they have driven us from several of their domestic markets, and they are sharply competing with us in the markets of other nations. We find that our most formidable assailants are the best educated peoples....

...The success of our rivals is not to be explained by reference to the low wages and long hours of work general on the Continent.... In so far as the competition between ourselves and foreign nations depends on the workman, it is mainly the sobriety and intelligence of their workmen which give them the advantage. But in that competition it is not only the intelligence of the workmen, it is the intelligence of the foreman, the manager, the master, nay it is the intelligence of the whole people which is of so much weight....

Let us dwell a little longer upon this point for it is of supreme consequence to ourselves. We have begun to see the commercial value of elementary and technical education. But our perception of their commercial value will not help us unless it is joined to a perception of their place and relations in the whole scheme of enlightenment. We must again and again repeat that neither elementary education nor technical education can be perfected apart from education in general, or could by themselves have made Germany so puissant a rival as we now find her. The strength of Germany lies in the culture of the evening class,... in the real love of learning which animates the people and their rulers, in the patient, inquiring and scientific spirit which has transformed every branch of human activity from metaphysics to the art of war....

In Germany the problem of how to educate the whole nation as well as possible has for many years been constantly present to the minds of scholars and statesmen. In England, and still more in Ireland, it is less the education of the people than the advantage which parties can draw from controlling education that has fascinated journalists and Members of Parliament. Education, however, is too grave a concern to be dealt with by men who lack singleness of aim and purity of purpose.... The education of the people is a whole and has a unity.... The education which draws out all the intelligence of the community is a necessary antecedent to the education which draws out the capacity of this or that man for this or that calling.

I have quoted this at length because the whole tenor of the argument is so different from that advanced a century later by the CBI. The guiding principle is that 'The education which draws out all the intelligence of the community is a necessary antecedent to the education which draws out the capacity of this or that man for this or that calling'. The Commission's recommendations had nothing to do with subsidizing firms' own training, or tying vocational qualifications tightly to the particular procedures of contemporary manufacture; nor did they ever suggest that what education most needed was business control. On the contrary, the important requirements for later business success were, in their view, the same as those which fitted people for their role in the community, and for personal development: a broad education, made available to all. They wanted to improve access to elementary education (1868); introduce new subjects into the school curriculum including science for all (1868 and 1884); create art schools (1884); create science schools and increase the pay of science teachers (1868 and 1884); provide free access to further education for artisans (1884); and fund scholarships to secondary schools teaching modern and technical subjects (1884). Yet these were not civil servants; most Commissioners had had active industrial and commercial careers of their own.[37]

It is equally striking that, among the many witnesses called by the Samuelson Commission, the most consistent and vehement advocates of general education are the manufacturers. The headmasters and directors of education, the academics and the public servants discuss training institutes and technical courses. The manufacturers talk about science. Here, for example, is Mr W. H. Ripley, Chairman of Bradford Chamber of Commerce and a third-generation Dyer.

> *Question* (from the Commissioners): Have you found in your own experience that the supposed superior knowledge of foreign foremen and workmen is enabling them to make progress which places our manufacturers at a disadvantage?
>
> *Answer*: I think that the scientific knowledge which has been rapidly progressing in France and Germany has enabled both these countries to progress much more rapidly during the past 12 or 15 years than they otherwise would have done. Speaking with regard to matters which come within my own knowledge, I may mention with respect to the dyeing business, whilst we in England have maintained our superiority in the dyeing of mixed cotton and wool goods, we have attained it by the indomitable perseverance for which the English are so noted and which has led us to fight our way through the difficulties of our want of chemical knowledge....
>
> *Question*: The foreign manufacturers have endeavoured to avail themselves of your experience by importing dyes from this country?
>
> *Answer*: Yes, and applying their scientific knowledge to the knowledge which they are thus gaining, I think they will at no very distant period be able to produce results, in consequence of that scientific knowledge, cheaper than we can do. For many years past I have seen that the waste which goes on among our men from the guesswork to which they have to resort from want of scientific knowledge is perfectly frightful.[38]

Or as Mr Anthony John Mundella, a manufacturer of fancy printed woollen yarns and Chairman of the Nottingham Chamber of Commerce put it:

> In Germany they are all well educated and it is to that fact that I attribute their greater progress. They say 'We are better instructed than you and we do it better because we are more scientific'.[39]

Over a century later, having spent many millions on over-specific NVQs which few people wanted, and which were outdated before they were designed, one must admire these manufacturers' prescience. But why should they have embraced general education while their successors offered detailed recommendations for records of achievement, core skills in the curriculum, and training vouchers, and demanded national targets, Lead Industry Bodies, and day-by-day involvement in education policy?

## The 1880s and the 1980s: why the same – and why so different?

While the parallels between the 1880s and the 1980s are striking, there are, in fact, also some important differences.[40] Taking the similarities first, it is true that both periods coincided with major changes not simply in the relative economic position of different states, but also in the nature of technology and in the importance of different sectors. The late nineteenth century was the period of great revolution in chemicals and chemical-related industries; the period when the German universities' impact on industry was becoming clear, and when research-based products reached a mass public.[41] It was also the period when the modern structure of German industry emerged; so that while UK commentators now agonize over the fact that German employment is still much more heavily manufacturing based than the UK's, contemporary German commentators worry that this indicates the dominance of 'old' industries.

In the late twentieth century a similar phenomenon is evident. There is considerable controversy over whether changes in the labour market (greater wage differentials, higher unskilled unemployment) are the result of technological change, or global competition, or more local institutional factors.[42] However, it is clear that the nature of many industries and sectors is undergoing a genuine and massive shift as a result of modern information and communication technologies: a change considerably further reaching than were the technological changes of, say, 1930–60.

These parallels provide one possible explanation for the long-separated panics discussed in these pages. What of the differences in analysis and prescription? Why did nineteenth-century observers emphasize general education where today's opt for analysis and prescription based on a supposed direct link between specific training and economic growth?

The first possibility, obviously, is that today's commentators are more sophisticated and have more historical experience to draw on; but the evidence is against this. As noted above, the growing body of research on education, training and economic growth indicates that the relationships between them are far more complex and variable than the current political consensus would imply. To reiterate the most important counter-example: if structured vocational training and qualifications on the German model are so important, then why does the United States, with hardly an apprenticeship to its name, have an economy which is the most successful in the world in terms of job creation and technological innovation? One does not need to discount the importance of both education and training to conclude that the policies visited upon British vocational education in the last fifteen years were rigid and simplistic, not the product of superior analysis.

The reason for the differences in approach probably lies instead in the *institutional* differences between late nineteenth-century Britain and today. Of these, the two most important are, first, the far larger share of GNP controlled directly or indirectly by the public sector and, second, the growth of professional lobbyists and full-time sector 'representatives', who play a major part in the policy making and implementation process. It would not have occurred to the Bradford and Nottingham manufacturers quoted above that they could obtain state funding to pay for their in-company training, nor did they envisage the complex tangle of financial incentives, taxes, European-matched funding, regulations and subsidies which encompass modern firms, and give them a permanent interest in government decisions. It certainly occurs to modern industrialists, and, consciously or unconsciously, they have an interest in making a case for their own priorities and concerns against those of other, rival spenders (such as the schools).

It is generally agreed among economists that the one area of training where there is no justification for public subsidy is the highly 'firm specific': that is, training someone to carry out the particular tasks and skills needed by a company or sector. Cynical economists would probably also have predicted that, if you hand the design of qualifications over to business, and also give it a strong influence over funding policy, the net result is likely to be subsidized company training. The cynics would have been right.[43] But business is certainly not behaving any differently from any other group in a society where governmental controls, regulations, subsidies and taxes affect virtually every corner of economic and social life.

The growth of the state provides the background for the differences described, but what is even more important is a corollary of such growth, namely the development of the professional 'representative'. One of twentieth-century governments' largest job-creation schemes has been here, in the fostering of a huge number of lobbyists, and of professional and trade organizations, staffed by full-time salaried 'spokespersons'. They have grown in importance because of government's evergrowing role, and the CBI is a classic example of the species.

In understanding the behaviour of such organizations, however, it is important to note that the interests of their staff are not, in fact, synonymous with those of the group for whom they speak. Institutions such as the CBI, the TUC, the BMA, and their equivalents in other countries have as their *raison d'être* successful influence of government decisions on behalf of their members. They must convince politicians and government officials that they do indeed 'speak for' their constituents. However, they *also* have an additional direct interest, which is *in increasing the number and impact of their own activities*. Thus, in the late twentieth century, it has been the CBI bureaucrats who have actually developed and enunciated policy, and who briefed the senior industrialists whose own knowledge of an NVQ, or a careership profile, was slight to non-existent. As a bureaucratic group, they have a strong interest in advancing the influence and funding of the CBI itself, as any public choice theorist would point out. So while the Bradford manufacturer of the late nineteenth century was predominantly concerned with getting back to running a successful business in Bradford, the CBI official of a century later is making his career in the policy circles of London. Such an individual is strongly motivated to sit on government panels, bid to take over policy-making roles, and generally raise the CBI's public profile by advancing a 'business' view of what is required.

In formulating the education and training policy of the 1980s and 1990s, British ministers would have done better to have skipped lunch at the CBI and retired to their desks with Sir Bernhard Samuelson's report. And indeed many of the policies that the CBI advocated have, now, been modified or abandoned. However, given the nature of modern government, it is very unlikely that this will be the last example of either economic panic or of policy pre-emption by influential and organized interest groups.

## Notes

1   J. H. Newman, *Selected Discourses on Liberal Knowledge* (Dublin: James Liffy, 1852: reprinted 1928).

2 W. H. Hadow, *Report of the Consultative Committee of the Board of Education on the Education of the Adolescent* (HMSO, 1926); W. Spens, *Report of the Consultative Committee of the Board of Education on Secondary Education with Special Reference to Grammar Schools and Technical High Schools* (HMSO, 1938); Sir C. Norwood, *Report of the Committee of the Secondary Schools Examination Council on Curriculum and Examinations in Secondary Schools* (HMSO, 1943); Sir G. Crowther, *15 to 18*, Report of the Central Advisory Council for Education (England) (HMSO, 1959); J. Newsom, *Half Our Future*, Report of the Minister of Education's Central Advisory Council (HMSO, 1963).

3 Sir L. Russell, *Adult Education: A Plan for development*, Report of a Committee of Enquiry appointed by the Secretary of State (HMSO, 1973).

4 The other 'social partners', namely organized labour, were not markedly different in their diagnosis of problems; but they were increasingly unwilling to collaborate with the government of the day in the area of training policy – largely because of their opposition to its general policies towards trade unions. From 1973 to 1988, the unions had three representatives on the board of the Manpower Services Commission (as did employers); and the MSC, a quango carved out of the Department of Employment, had the major responsibility for youth and adult training programmes. The MSC was disbanded in 1988, at the time that the TUC voted not to cooperate with the Employment Training scheme for unemployed adults. Direct union influence on policies was slight.

5 See for example, J. Marquand, *Autonomy and Change: The Sources of Economic Growth* (Hemel Hempstead: Harvester Wheatsheaf, 1989).

6 Reports on the NIESR research appeared regularly over a period of time, largely as articles in the National Institute Economic Review or as NIESR monographs. The most important were later collected together in a book edited by Prais: S. J. Prais (ed.), *Productivity, Education and Training: Britain and Other Countries Compared* (London: NIESR, 1989).

7 Karin Wagner 'Training Efforts & Industrial Efficiency in West Germany', in J. Stevens and R. Mackay (eds), *Training & Competitiveness* (NEDO Policy Issues Series) (London: Kogan Page, 1991).

8 *Competence and Competition* (1984) and *Challenge to Complacency* (1985). Although the reports looked at Japan and the United States as well, it was the German model which was actually emphasized in the policy recommendations, and the MSC activities which followed. This selective reading reflects the already pervasive impact of the view that formally organized vocational training was the key to growth. Neither Japan nor the USA operates such a system, and if they had been taken as the models to follow, the conclusions drawn would have been very different.

9 Marquand, p. 189.

10 *Review of Vocational Qualifications in England & Wales: Interim Report* (Sheffield, 1985).

11 For discussions of NVQ developments, and the reasons why NVQs were not, in fact, the popular success with employers which was expected see especially C. Callendar, *Will NVQs Work? Evidence from the Construction Industry* (University of Sussex, Institute of Manpower Studies, 1992); A. Wolf, *Competence-based Assessment* (Buckingham: Open University Press, 1995); M. Eraut, S. Steadman, J. Trill and J. Parkes, *The Assessment of NVQs* (University of Sussex, 1996); P. Robinson, *Rhetoric and Reality* (London: Centre for Economic Performance LSE, 1996).

12 D. Finegold and D. Soskice, 'Britain's Failure to Train: Explanations and Possible Strategies'. *Oxford Review of Economic Policy*, 4/3 (1988).

13 Training Agency, *Training in Britain: A Study of Funding, Activity and Attitudes: The Main Report* (HMSO, 1989).

14 He was also a member of NEDC.

15 John Casses, *Britain's Real Skill Shortage and What to Do About it* (London: PSI, 1990).

16 National Commission on Education, *Learning to Succeed: A Radical Look at Education Today and a Strategy for the Future* (London: Heinemann, 1993), p. 1, 278 *passim*.

17 Dearing was chairman and chief executive of the Post Office, just as Nicholson had been. The latter's successor at NCVQ was the current Post Office chief executive, Sir Michael Heron.

18 *Review of Qualifications for 16–19-Year-Olds* (London: SCAA, 1996).

19  Sir Ron Dearing, *Higher Education in the Learning Society: Report of the National Committee of Enquiry into Higher Education* (London, 1997).
20  Quoted in Dearing, 1997, p. 3.
21  Quoted in Dearing, 1997, p. 4.
22  Dearing 1997, p. 9.
23  Labour Party, *The Skills Revolution* (London, 1997).
24  Marquand, p. 183.
25  CBI, *Towards a Skills Revolution* (London, 1989), p. 18.
26  The Training and Enterprise Councils run the government-funded programmes for young and adult unemployed, provide financial support for firms offering NVQs, coordinate Investors in People and are also intended to help foster businesses in their area.
27  Trainers offering programmes for the unemployed must offer programmes leading to an NVQ. Their payment is tied to whether the trainee does indeed achieve the award; in fact, it is only possible to break even if a large proportion of your trainees do achieve an NVQ. In the circumstances it is hardly surprising that there have been recurrent cases of fraud. See G. Stanton, *Output-Related Funding and the Quality of Education and Training* (London: Institute of Education, 1996).
28  See, e.g. *Daily Telegraph*, 14 December 1994.
29  Eraut, 1996. Assessment of NVQs is all continuous, with no external examinations, and verifiers are the people responsible for policing the system and ensuring quality.
30  See note 11.
31  See for example, A. Green, T. Leney and A. Wolf, *Convergences and Divergences in European Education and Training Systems* (London: Institute of Education, 1997).
32  A. Wolf, 'Growth stocks and lemons; diplomas in the English market place', *Assessment in Education*, 4/1 (1997).
33  Their full titles were the Select Committee appointed to Inquire into the Provisions for giving Instructions in Theory & Applied Science to the Industrial Classes, which reported in 1868; and the Royal Commission Appointed to Inquire into the State of Technical Instruction, set up in 1881, with a first report in 1882, a second, major report in 1884, and a widely circulated summary report in 1887.
34  Robin Betts, 'Persistent but Misguided? The Technical Educationists 1867–1889', *History of Education*, 27/3 (1998); see also 'The Samuelson Commission of 1881–1884 and English Technical Education', *History of Education Society Bulletin*, 43 (Autumn 1984); 'The Issue of Technical Education 1867–1868', *History of Education Society Bulletin*, 48 (Autumn 1991).
35  See, e.g. Michael Sanderson, *The Missing Stratum: Technical School Education in England 1900–1990s* (London: Athlone, 1994) for the view that there has been a century of policy failure in technical education, and that this has been a significant factor in economic decline.
36  Betts's argument is different and draws attention instead to the increasing unimportance of the traditional industries examined by the Commission and to the issue of commercial education.
37  See Betts, 1984. Samuelson himself had established both a railway works in France and an agricultural machinery factory in Oxfordshire.
38  Royal Commission on Technical Instruction 1st Report paras 4046 and 4047.
39  Ibid., para 4630.
40  This section has benefited greatly from comments offered on an earlier draft at the 1997 History of Education Society conference.
41  See especially J. Ben-David and A. Zloczower, 'Universities and Academic Systems in Modern Societies', *European Journal of Sociology*, 3 (1962); and J. Ben-David, 'The Universities and the Growth of Science in Germany and the United States', *Minerva*, 7 (1968).
42  S. Machin and J. Van Reenan, *Technology and Change in Skill Structure* (London: LSE, 1997); S. N. Broadberry, *The Productivity Race* (Cambridge: Cambridge University Press, 1997).
43  Because of the obsession with targets, a great deal of recent governmental effort has been directed to increasing the numbers of NVQs obtained. TEC subsidies have recently been bolstered by the 'franchising' system, whereby FE colleges undertake all the assessment of NVQs in the workforce, with the cost being paid for through mainstream education funding.

# PART VIII

# EDUCATION AND NATIONAL IDENTITY

## CHAPTER 16

# EDUCATION IN WALES

## A historical perspective

Gareth Elwyn Jones

*The Education of a Nation* (1997), Cardiff: University of Wales Press, pp. 1–11

Paradox pervades Welsh education, past and present. There is even an historical paradox. One of the distinctive features of Welsh education is supposed to be its centrality to our history. It has certainly not been central to our historiography. In the renaissance in historical writing in Wales over the last thirty years attention to the history of education has been marginal. There have been a few excellent theses, articles and monographs, but generally, distinguished Welsh historians have construed educational history as a rivulet feeding the political, religious or economic mainstream.

Is it that the history of education in Wales is seen as 'tunnel' history, a line of development best hived off from the generality of social history? If such is the case it compounds the felony since the only worthwhile history of education assumes its centrality in the wider society. Such an assumption underlies the excellent introductory text of Lawson and Silver[1] for English education. More likely, the history of education is seen as of lesser significance than that of the politics and economics of Wales. This, in turn, may be partly due to the fact that the Whig interpretation of history is especially seductive when it comes to education; whatever the indices, educational provision is better today than it was fifty years ago. School-leaving age, grant aid, provision of materials, proportion of gross national product, training of teachers, teacher–pupil ratios have all improved since the war. When, as now, we regress, the shock is the greater precisely because of entrenched expectations of constant improvement.

The tale of that improvement has been related often in histories of English education or, more tellingly, for Great Britain, in such standard works of not very long ago as those of Curtis[2] and Barnard.[3] Curtis (7th edn, no less) still remains an ideal source to quarry for the facts of acts. It may be that Curtis's title *History of Education in Great Britain* (separate chapters for Scotland) tells a story – perhaps for Welsh historians it has told the whole story. Do we have another paradox, that one of the distinguishing features of Welsh education is that we constantly hear of its superiority to that of England, yet the histories of both countries in the twentieth century have so converged, that the Welsh educational dimension has syncromeshed its way out of existence?

Here, then, may be the difference of perspective in Wales and Scotland. The Scottish education system, as with its law, has always retained a distinctive administrative structure. It has similar proud claims on national sentiment as the Welsh, but fundamental similarities with English developments have been packaged under different labels. The result is that there are at least three orthodox histories of Scottish education. A standard history, by James Scotland,[4] has emerged relatively recently. In Wales we have no standard history, no one who has imposed on events a historically respectable Whig interpretation. England has produced Marxist re-evaluations, particularly in the work of Brian Simon.[5] In Scotland, historians are beginning to counter James Scotland's orthodoxies.[6] In Wales we have no orthodoxies to undermine. We have not reached first base.

This is serious, not only because education is part of the warp and weft of our social fabric in Britain but also, as Welsh nationals, it is fundamental to our under-standing of the nature of Wales and Welshness, myth and reality, past and present. The Welsh are, we all know, at least as educated as they are musical. Despite the occasional dent in the image these days, accumulation of fact and myth since the eighteenth century results in a concept of a nation concerned for education, formal and informal. Inextricably intertwined with the notion of the *gwerin* – rural, peasant backbone of Wales, the true Wales, farmer-poets, philosophers and theologians – the appetite and respect for education is second to none. There is a residual compelling image of a poor society, desperately manufacturing its own culture, leadership and democratic identity in the face of hostility from an anglicized, exploiting gentry through the self-help of response to Griffith Jones, Hugh Owen and, in a changed context, O. M. Edwards. Circulating schools, the university founded and run on the pennies of the poor, and the county schools, provide a potent image of concern for the finer things in life in the face of material deprivation.

More recently, national pride and self-congratulation engendered by this idealized picture would appear to have been dented in the Loosmore report and its aftermath. Doubts have been cast on the performance of Welsh comprehensive schools, espe-cially in their ability to deliver examination results for the middle-ability ranges.[7] Here again, paradox. The researchers concerned suggested that one of the reasons for this worrying disparity in the performance of Welsh and English schools was the inheritance of a grammar-school ethos in the new comprehensive schools, an ambi-ence conducive to concentration on 'academic' subjects, a continuation of the hier-archical structures of the old grammar schools. Certainly there are still speech days which celebrate academic success as they did in the 1900s, if less ostentatiously. There are still photographs in evening papers of pupils destined for punts and glit-tering prizes, not for Salford and Aston. But the perpetuation of such 'grammar-school' practices has not led to popular questioning of the county/grammar-school ethos and practice – far from it. The alleged shortcomings of Welsh comprehensive schools (and even here the picture muddies with each succeeding study) have led, instead, to a nostalgia for the old schools and the old standards and the old days of a secure meritocracy.

There is more than hearsay evidence that, in the absence of professional history, the old stereotypes suffice in the best circles. An English reviewer in *The Times Educational Supplement* adjudged some years ago that 'being Welsh like being Jewish traditionally means respecting education'.[8] The old story of the future Sir Henry Jones walking miles to see a Bachelor of Arts is well known. What is striking is that there are modern equivalents among greater heroes. Barry John, asked in a television interview how he felt on learning that he had been awarded his first Welsh cap, could hardly find words to describe that transcendental moment: 'It was like learning you'd got your PhD' Some might swap.

Such reactions are rooted in a different social history from that of England. Myth-making stems from the historic role of Welsh education in providing economic and social mobility in a society in which both have been restricted compared with England. So, consciousness of the importance of educational opportunity has seared itself into the Welsh psyche, and that opportunity has been most dramatically associated with the county/grammar schools of the first half of the twentieth century. Carwyn James, teacher, littérateur, greatest of all rugby coaches, Welsh to the core, wrote:

> Came, alas, the destruction of one of the best educational systems in the world. Came the levelling down process. A disbelief in Plato's gold, silver and brass. All children are equal and none is more equal than another. Comprehensive. The new in-word. Big and beautiful. Hours of business strictly nine-to-four. Special responsibility allowances a must. Preferably no Saturday morning games.[9]

Perhaps Gwyn Thomas was too close to the chalk face for too long for such an endorsement of the county/grammar system to be so disingenuous. But in a more modified, more realistic form he sees a more distant, thus perhaps more potent, sunlit age:

> From the University College...came a legion of eager harvesters, the shining centurions on a march that was to endow the common folk with a new power and dignity. Seen in our present gloomy penumbra, our cultural mange, the last statement might sound odd, a jape from a dogeared and disavowed comedy script. But there was a day, not too long ago, when the truth of these words rang out like the stroke of a golden bell. Learning was to be mankind's new and magic robe. It would put a new face on the absurdity of endless labour in places from which grace and beauty had been removed as if by surgical excision.
> The early native graduates who staffed the county school during the end of the last century and the beginning of this were a remarkable band of pioneers. They were the first across the Missouri, not yet plagued by a clear view of the Rockies of recalcitrance, failure and breakdown that for many of them lay ahead. They were lucky men. They were in their day anointed princes. They were Tibetan Lamas of infinite wisdom and authority set in the context of shorter mountains and taller pretensions. The teachers in the early days of mass education, if they were a people blessed with a deep vanity, lived in a school climate as balmy as Barbados...Given the often demented pride that parents felt for them, the deep respect instinctively shown them by their pupils, and the wide-spread awe felt for them by neighbours still stuck in their ancient traps, it is wonderful that so many of the native graduates in the post-1870 era remained loyal to the serene egalitarianism of their radical tradition.[10]

Indeed, but their *raison d'être*, their social function in the schools which so many served so faithfully for so long, was to promote inegalitarianism. We even need to be wary about those Welsh Tibetan Lamas. They did tend to remain in a single school for much of their careers, though this might have had something to do with the restricted career opportunities of the day. That same restricted career structure ensured that some of our most eminent scholars served their apprenticeships and more in the secondary schools; they were the best academic posts available. W. J. Gruffydd, most distinguished of scholars, professor of Celtic, playwright, poet of outstanding talent, began his career as a teacher at Beaumaris Grammar School. Historian David Williams wrote: 'his old pupils there still speak with emotion of the undisguised disgust with which he regarded them and his duties'.[11]

It is uncomfortable to question myths. They are especially important to a nation as precariously poised in history as Wales, emanating, as they often do, from that precariousness. Nights of Long Knives help compensate for an oft-felt ubiquitous aimlessness, particularly apparent in contemporary Wales since 1979. And we are allowed our legends since they seem to carry no political or social danger. But myths are dangerous. They develop a life of their own which serves a nationalistic and political purpose as real as the fact which underlies them.

Such a process is not confined to Wales. With all its historiography that same process can be observed at work in Scotland and in that inelegantly labelled entity, England and Wales. Here, too, a strait-jacket of historical interpretation can all too easily be imposed which it becomes almost disloyal to question. There are, for example, some striking parallels between the 1889 Welsh Intermediate Education Act in the Welsh context and the 1944 Education Act in the context of a wider nation. One similarity is that historians interpret both Acts as the enlightened provision of enhanced opportunity and greater egalitarianism by progressive politicians fighting entrenched back-woods attitudes in Treasury and educational establishments. It is almost heresy to question the 'breakthrough' of the 1944 Act in inaugurating free secondary education for all pupils, raising of the school-leaving age and the rest. The steady erosion of the educational consensus, particularly since 1979, has had something of a similar effect on our perspective of the 1944 Act as has the Loosmore Report in Wales on our conception of Welsh county/grammar schools. Where Conservative educational policies since 1979 might have led to questioning of the impact of the 1944 Act and its inadequacies it has instead led to the consensus politicians falling back on the Act as a kind of beacon of educational enlightenment. In the 1980s this was manifest in the debate over the charging of fees for university tuition – its Tory opponents centred their opposition on the breach of the principle of free tuition enshrined in the Butler Act. An idealized interpretation of the 1944 Act serves a political, hence social, purpose now. It can be construed very differently. Its blueprint had been etched before the war, in the Spens Report of 1938. This was rejected, in the time-honoured way of governments, as too expensive, in a refrain which had disguised class ideology of secondary education since the birth of state secondary schools in England in 1902. For Wales, continuity with a pre-war pattern was yet more marked. The main provisions of the 1944 Act echoed trends already long apparent in the Welsh system – particularly that of free entry by ability to a selective system. No debunking of the 1944 Act need obscure the achievement of R. A. Butler in reconciling powerful religious pressure groups which had helped scupper Labour attempts at reform in 1929 and 1930. Even though Butler had to buy off these interests, he required all his considerable political finesse even to create the atmosphere in which money talked. But he was responsible for legislation within which central direction of the education system, often disguised, produced a rigorously enforced bipartitism. The major element in the Act – free secondary education for all up to the age of 15 – was remarkable not for its originality of concept but because it actually happened. The Act provided the framework within which civil servants and educational administrators, with the aid of a succession of Labour and Tory conservatives, could perpetuate the divisions of a society, especially in Wales where they had to work far harder to do so. But succeed they did, in the face of educational and organizational logic. That divide in the system of schooling has been centrally significant since the state began to intervene massively as the forces of change in industrial society became too much for voluntary organizations to handle. Through the nineteenth century and early in the twentieth century the divisions were openly discussed in class terms. From the 1920s it became less acceptable for officialdom openly to comment on the necessity for the superiority of a paid-up middle-class education over that of the working class. Fee-paying had to secure something better, and be seen to be leading to something better – jobs, pay – else economic logic, indeed the fabric of society, would be undermined. Another weapon of discrimination was conveniently at hand, the intelligence test, and its accompanying tests of attainment: the scholarship. In effect these tests performed the same social function as payment of fees – and they operated in tandem until 1944. IQ became a shibboleth; absolute assessment at the magic age of eleven (just when administratively convenient). We now know that the 1944 Act's provision of secondary education for 'age, aptitude and ability' disguised a decision taken in 1941 by the Board of Education's senior civil servants to perpetuate the bipartite discriminatory post-eleven provision. Multilateral schools were accorded merely the most grudging experimental status. The first pamphlet of the new Ministry of Education, *The Nation's Schools*, indicated that 'future employment will not demand any measure of technical skill or knowledge'. The majority would be 'the hewers of wood and the drawers of water'.[12] Labour ministers, though not the rank and file, faithfully followed the mandarins, mystified. Later Conservative governments, naturally, endorsed the system fabricated for them by those civil servants who were the product of the most highly selective educational system in the world. They perpetuated that system in their own image. Yet it was skilfully done in a framework of consensus.

Disillusionment with the system produced by the 1944 Act mounted in the 1960s and the progression to a comprehensive system produced its own backlash. But with the erosion in recent years the 1944 Act has become a kind of touchstone of progressivism and enlightenment. This is dangerous. The historian, as well as the educationalist, has the duty to point out that the author of the 1944 Education Act, when Chancellor in 1953, produced a list of savings for his cabinet colleagues which included levying fees in state schools, raising age of entry to six and lowering the leaving age to fourteen.[13]

In Wales we are, of course, part of this wider scene but we need to be even more conscious that education is part of the fabric of society. The education system is the product of that society and it reflects and helps perpetuate it. But it also helps to modify it. In short, if we are Welsh we must have a Welsh education. An 'English' education (in whatever language) will not do.

> In the Musée du Louvre there is a striking statue of a scribe of the old Kingdom of Egypt. It is about 4,500 years old. He is carved in limestone and painted – hair black, flesh brown, eyes of alabaster, rock crystal and copper – an alert crossed-legged figure, ready with his papyrus scroll. To be so memorialised in stone the scribe must have played an important role in the eyes of his contemporaries. This was because he had mastered the major technique in civilized communication – he could write...Because he could write and cypher he could receive written instructions and eventually but inevitably became the man who could most easily execute them. Thus he became, whether high or low in the scale of royal servants, a member of an educated secretariat that directly or indirectly wielded the power behind the throne.[14]

The interaction of education, social mobility, class, politics, power, if true for ancient Egypt, has never been so easily analysed since. But the fact of that relationship has been fully appreciated by monarchs and governments. The study of the history of education in Wales must take cognizance of this at all points. For example in the eighteenth century in Wales the Society for Promoting Christian Knowledge and Griffith Jones, whose circulating schools made much of the nation literate, expended considerable energy on reassuring their wealthy supporters that they were not educating the poor out of their station.

The social dimension of the history of education tends to disappear from the Welsh historian's view when he has dispensed with Griffith Jones. The graph of state activity, and of state expenditure on education in Wales, seems to proceed ever upwards – grants to British and National Society schools (1847 a watershed), board schools, training colleges, a university, a state system of county schools from the 1890s, Hadow-type reorganization (not such a success story this), the 1944 Act, the excitements of the expansion and reorganization of the 1960s. The detail of that story, based on careful research into the mass of printed and documentary primary sources, would be invaluable both as a work of reference and as a framework within which alternative interpretations might be placed. Our knowledge of those schools which have educated the mass of the Welsh population since the industrial revolution, the elementary schools, voluntary and board, and the primary schools is indeed sparse. Larger issues are rarely treated. There has been little fundamental questioning of processes by which groups or classes in Welsh society have sought to preserve the education system in their own image and to best serve their immediate interests. We have only hints here and there. But the history of modern Wales requires these questions to be asked at every point. While it would be absurd to deny the contribution of the *gwerin* and their pennies to the development of secondary and university education in a Wales transformed by the industrial revolution, and churlish to minimize the efforts expended by Hugh Owen and O. M. Edwards, it is unhistorical to rest content with some residual glow of a golden age, when the sun shone at every sports day. *The Corn is Green* syndrome, so seductive for the playwright, is the hallmark of a relatively poor, inegalitarian, educationally and socially blighted society. It is the stuff of self-sacrifice; it is the stuff of ruthless competition. It evokes community appreciation and help – a transferred *cymorth;* it produces alienation and division. In pre-industrial Wales, indeed for much of the nineteenth century, community flourished in poverty. Wales paid for its centrality to the Industrial Revolution by becoming part of a society in which such community was inevitably transmuted. One of the major agencies of the metamorphosis has been education. And here the situation in Wales gets more complex than that in England, more exciting. The county schools of Wales were no accident. The Industrial Revolution fed on itself. It created the need for vastly increased numbers of literate and numerate people as primary industry, then commerce and service industries, grew apace. Blackcoat jobs were created on some scale. For Wales, a world centre of primary industry in the second half of the nineteenth century, the result was a burgeoning middle class which did not have the appropriate grammar-school education to perpetuate itself as it was doing successfully and exclusively in England, though there, too, there was a thrust towards increasing secondary provision as demand outstripped supply. For reasons of Welsh national prestige and respectability, as well as for wider social and political reasons, the vacuum had to be filled. That it took the form of the Welsh Intermediate Education Act and its schools was due to individuals acting in a particular political and administrative context. That the schools came into existence was due to economic, social and class forces. Welsh historians have yet to explore the interaction in detail.

Such profound social and educational changes forced fundamental questions to be asked about Wales and Welshness. National respectability for the leaders of opinion in Wales, at least since the 1847 Blue Books, had been bound up with the question of education, whether for enlightenment, or social control or industrial and commercial efficiency. National respectability for Welsh leaders of the nineteenth and early twentieth century involved loyalty to Britain and to the Empire along with loyalty to Wales. After all, it was the economic imperatives of the British Empire which were moulding the new Wales. That respectability in Victorian times could only be conferred and cemented by an educated middle class, providing leaders and opinion-formers for the nation. To this process a system of secondary schools was essential. Hugh Owen was acutely aware of the dynamic relationship between education, Welsh society and Welsh nationalism.

The Welsh county secondary schools took in a far wider social mix than the English. On a greater scale than was the case in England the county schools and the municipal secondary schools after 1902, educated the sons and daughters of a working class as well as those of a middle class. But they educated an élite, and that élite was inexorably anglicized, not only in language but also, far more fundamentally, in attitude. Indeed, in one sense, this was part of the purpose. There was then, and remains, no such entity as a distinctively Welsh middle class, as opposed to a middle class in Wales. That term itself is one signifying accommodation into a wider society. The Welshness of the people so designated must lie outside that which makes them 'middle class'. What distinguished them as a middle class tended to extinguish them as Welsh – at least in traditional terms. That élite was concerned not only with creating a Wales after its own image but also perpetuating its distinguishing advantages. The education system was central to this, though in less stark terms than in England. Such a social function of the secondary schools, in a context of a view of Welsh history which highlighted the community and national role of an educated, enlightened, respectable, rural, classless, peasant *gwerin*, led to the Welsh national disease of schizophrenia among educators and social analysts. Owen M. Edwards struggled desperately and, of course, unavailingly, to reconcile the irreconcilable. He, too, saw clearly the interrelationship between education, society and nationalism in the Wales of the early twentieth century.

It is not evident that present-day analysts of education in Wales are aware of the centrality of the relationship, and historians must be held partly responsible. Of course the Welsh language figures centrally in education debate, rightly. Examination results, as in O. M. Edwards's day, can spark off acrimonious exchanges. The point, now as then, seems to have been missed. O. M. Edwards and Major Edgar Jones, the classic protagonists of the 1909/10 controversy over yardsticks of success by which the county schools might be measured, were arguing from irreconcilably different premises.[15]

One of the sadder features of the controversy surrounding the Loosmore Report was that no one seemed to take the O. M. Edwards line – that education was about more than examination results. The meritocratic ethos seems finally to have overwhelmed all else in Wales.

None of this can be adequately and fairly discussed without recourse to the history of a long-standing debate, combined with an appreciation of the centrality of education to the economic, political and social structure of this – or any – nation. It is not the historian's task *qua* historian, to analyse the present predicament in Welsh education. The historian may legitimately indicate that the history of Welsh education, in so far as it *has* been written, leads inexorably to the conclusion that questions about the state of Welsh education are questions about the state of Welsh society. When we ask what sort of education we want in Wales we ask what sort of Wales we want. Myths are no basis on which to start addressing that question.

## Notes

1  J. Lawson and H. Silver, *A Social History of Education in England* (London, 1973).
2  S. J. Curtis, *History of Education in Great Britain*, 7th edition (London, 1967).
3  H. C. Barnard, *A Short History of English Education, 1760–1944* (London, 1947).
4  James Scotland, *The History of Scottish Education*, 2 vols (London, 1969).
5  Brian Simon, *Education and the Labour Movement, 1870–1920* (London, 1965); and *The Politics of Educational Reform 1920–1940* (London, 1974).
6  W. M. Humes and H. M. Paterson, *Scottish Culture and Scottish Education 1800–1980* (Edinburgh, 1983).
7  F. A. Loosmore, *Curriculum and Assessment in Wales. An Exploratory Study* (Cardiff, 1981). This study indicated that in 1977/78 27.6 per cent of pupils left Welsh secondary schools without any qualification. The comparative figure for England was 14.2 per cent; c.f. David Reynolds, 'Schooled for failure?', in *Disaffection in Secondary Schools in Wales* (Cardiff, 1983), pp. 14–27; and D. Reynolds and S. Murgatroyd in *Times Educational Supplement*, 15 February, 1985.
8  *Times Educational Supplement*, 15 April, 1983, 31.
9  Quoted in *Times Educational Supplement*, 21 October, 1983, 6.
10 Gwyn Thomas, 'The First Waves', in Gwyn Jones and Michael Quinn (eds), *Fountains of Praise* (Cardiff, 1983), pp. 123, 124.
11 David Williams, 'Old Man of the Sea: W. J. Gruffydd', in Jones and Quinn, op. cit., p. 102.
12 Max Morris, 'Built to last', *Times Educational Supplement*, 10 August, 1984, 4.
13 Ibid., p. 4.
14 E. B. Castle, *The Teacher* (London, 1970), p. 3.
15 Gareth Elwyn Jones, *Controls and Conflicts in Welsh Secondary Education, 1889–1944* (Cardiff, 1982), pp. 26, 27.

## CHAPTER 17

# 'THERE'S NO PLACE LIKE HOME'
## Education and the making of national identity

Ian Grosvenor

*History of Education*, 28, 3, 235–50, 1999

Firstly I look upon Britain as my homeland...Liberty, the love of home, tolerance and justice – these are some of the things which Britain has infused into most of her sons and daughters....What does Britain mean to me?, I say 'A home and the home of the good things in life'. (HAI.1.)

Britain means to me my HOME. And I use 'home' in the fullest sense as after years spent abroad, it is always the one place I had a secret hankering to come back to (SM1.6)

England is home and there's no place like home. That's what Britain means to me. With all its faults, it means just everything to me (MIL.9.)

(Report on 'What does Britain mean to you', 1941)[1]

In the 1990s 'identity' – social, sexual, gender, 'ethnic', national – has become a keyword, a focus for academic and popular debate. Questions about identity and identity formation have captured the interest of sociologists, political scientists, cultural theorists and geographers. Writings about identity have made links with modernity and postmodernity, have speculated about hybridity, 'difference' and positionality, and have generated reflections about ideas of home and displacement, of frontiers and boundaries, of memory and loss. Historians have not been immune to these debates and 'Englishness' and 'Britishness', once such natural and unquestioned categories, are now being historicized and problematized as never before. The aim of this essay is to engage with the issues around the nature and meaning of identity that are currently being explored by considering the role of education in the making of national identity in nineteenth- and twentieth-century Britain.

The first part of the chapter is structured around a reading of four texts, two each from 1939 and 1998. These texts stand independently of each other but none the less connect and are used to generate questions about the relationship between schooling and the formation of national identity over time.

## Empire Day

'The British Empire means every man, woman and child in it', declared the girl who portrayed Britannia at Whitehall Junior School's Empire Day pageant. So begins the newspaper account of the celebration of Empire Day in Walsall Schools on 24 May 1939. The form of celebration was left to the discretion of respective head teachers. The head teacher at Whitehall Junior School told the *Walsall Observer* that;

> We have had the usual classes in Empire Day subjects, but to focus the minds of the children on various aspects of the Empire I don't think there is anything to compare with allowing them to Portray the colonies and dependencies.

The school's pageant told the story of how the British Empire unfolded. Beginning with 'the tribal unions that laid the foundations of the British nation', the pageant went on to tell 'of how England began to spread her wings and then to recount the exploration, settlement and colonisation that marked the spacious days of Queen Elizabeth'. Pupils read excerpts from Shakespeare, Cowper, Blake and Campbell. Ranging in age from seven years to eleven, some 60 children took part in the pageant, while the platform was flanked by Boy Scouts and Girl Guides who attended Whitehall School. At Chuckery Senior Girls' School, the head teacher and her staff had devised a pageant in which the various Dominions became linked up with Britannia, seated on her throne, 'with streamers of red, white and blue', whilst the figure of Peace, with wings outstretched, gave the gathering her blessing. 'England' and 'Land of Hope and Glory' were sung, and afterwards pupils were asked to describe the pageant in an essay competition. Songs were also a feature of celebrations at Hillary Street Senior School, a teacher spoke to the children about 'the roll of honour' of Empire Builders, and nine pupils recited 'poetical quotations bringing out some particular feature of Empire duty and service'. At Chuckery Senior Boys School a short musical programme was accompanied by a display of physical training to convey 'the idea that physical fitness is an important Empire asset'. The newspaper concluded that 'where careful preparation' was given to the celebration of Empire Day 'it formed a lesson of lasting educational influence'.[2]

This local account of Empire Day raised several questions. How was the curriculum changed to prepare for Empire Day? What were Empire Day subjects? What did teachers think about the celebration? How involved were pupils in decisions about its content and form? Did the experience have 'a lasting educational influence'? Could pupils distinguish between England and the British nation? What did parents think about a celebration that was not a part of their own schooling?

## Images in schools

The second text is from the *London Review of Books*, April 1998, and is an account by the writer and playwright, Alan Bennett, of his involvement in selecting paintings from galleries in the British Isles for the Sainsbury scheme whereby every year four selected paintings are reproduced, framed and sent with an information pack to schools local to Sainsbury's stores. Bennett's account begins with a memory of schooling:

> When I was at school in the late Forties there were two sorts of paintings on the walls. Most classrooms hosted a couple of pictures scarcely above the Highland-cattle level...that had been discarded by the City Art Gallery and palmed off on the Education Committee, which sent them round schools. These uninspired canvasses didn't so much encourage an appreciation of art as a proficiency in darts. However, there was another category of picture occasionally to be seen: reproductions on board of work by modern British

painters – Ravilious, Paul Nash, Henry Moore, Pasmore. These, I think, were put out by Shell.... That I have always liked – and found no effort in liking – British paintings of the Forties and Fifties I partly put down to my early exposure to these well-chosen reproductions.

As the extract suggests, Bennett's account is highly autobiographical; indeed, three of the paintings he selected are directly linked in his essay with childhood experiences.[3] It is the issue of 'exposure' to images in childhood that is particularly striking, especially bearing in mind Bennett's comment that this exposure helped to shape his interests. Bennett's piece also acted as a 'trigger' and propelled me back into my own secondary school days in the 1960s where reproductions of *Derby Day* by Frith (1858) and *The Blind Girl* (1858), *The Boyhood of Raleigh* (1870) and *The Princes in the Tower* (1878) by Millais adorned classroom walls, images that have remained very strong in my mind. Further, photographic evidence shows that reproductions of British paintings were a common feature in Birmingham schools in both the 1890s and the 1930s.[4] How did pupils react to these images? How were they selected? Did teachers use them in their teaching? Who paid for them and how were they made available?

## Children and 'race-thinking'

The third text consists of two brief extracts from essays written by children in 1939. The first essay, written by a 13-year-old girl, is on 'What I Think About The Jews':

Notorious for their supposed meanness, the Jews are now suffering under someone else's meanness. I did not know until recently that the Jews owned the cinemas, and most of the big shops, and hold an important position in the world of finance in England. Also I cannot imagine how they managed to own the diamond mines in South Africa.

The second essay, by a 12-year-old boy, is entitled 'Niggers':

Niggers, or rather negroes [blackies crossed out] are the inhabitants of Africa and numerous small islands in the Pacific. The negroes [blackies crossed out] we find in America are not true inhabitants of that country, they were imported from Africa as Slaves. The negroes [blackies crossed out] who inhabit Australia and New Zealand are Maoris and came from one of the Pacific islands. A black person's teeth are usually white, so are the whites of his eyes. Negroes [niggers crossed out] are keen spiritualists as their songs show us. When the Slaves became free men they did not return to Africa, but were employed in America. A nigger has often [usually crossed out] a very good voice.[5]

The essays were part of a school survey collected by Mass-Observation for an antisemitism project. Mass-Observation believed that childhood was a critical stage in the formation of attitudes towards minority groups.[6] In what contexts had these racist thoughts developed? What contemporary influences shaped the 'race-thinking' of these children?

## Attitudes to Europe

The final text is a survey commissioned by the Runnymede Trust on young people's attitudes to Europe.[7] A total of 550 young people, aged between 14 and 25, were questioned in street interviews in 10 cities between 29 December 1997 and 14 January 1998. The majority of 'ethnic minority youth' referred to themselves as 'Black British' and 'Asian British'. Overall, almost three-quarters of respondents identified their nationality as British. Of the total white population, 73% identified themselves as British, the remaining 27% choosing to designate themselves as something other, including English, Welsh and Scottish. When asked what images came to mind when they thought of the word 'British' there was a strong tendency to mention formal institutions (the monarchy, parliament), to relate 'British' to the land mass of the British Isles in a geographical sense, and to associate it with fish and chips, tea, various sport teams, the former British Empire and Britain as a world power. Some white youth identified 'British' with white people generally and some Black and Asian youth similarly identified 'British' as meaning white. When asked about their sense of European identity, 69% of young people said they thought of Britain as being part of Europe. 'White youth' were less likely to think this, two-thirds stating this compared with 69% of 'black youth' and 74% of 'South Asian youth'. However, when asked if they thought of British people as Europeans, 60% thought this to be the case. In contrast, however, 61% said they never identified themselves as European. Over three-quarters of all those surveyed stated that they did not think that their peers were interested in either Europe or nationality issues. Finally, most of those interviewed said that they did not receive enough information from school, government or the media about how decisions made at a European level affected Britain.

The Runnymede survey points to a range of issues relating to national identity, not least the role of schools in providing information about nationality issues within the European Union, but what is particularly noticeable is the use of the descriptors 'black', 'white' and 'South Asian' to establish and define sub-categories of British national identity. How do these categories relate to one another? How have they emerged?

So far in this chapter I have intentionally built up layers of questions about the nature of national identity and the role of education in its formation. In the second part of the chapter I want to use these questions to frame a series of reflections on the problems and possibilities confronting historians of education engaged in exploring the changing landscape of national identity. To this end, these reflections are presented under four headings: 'Living in an age of anxiety'; 'Home and national identity'; 'The contingency of identity'; and 'Educating the nation'. Finally, history as a subject has the potential to illuminate the human condition both in the past and the present. Historians can aid understanding of the present complexities of life and consequently can influence the framing of the future. It is in this context that the final section of this chapter is headed 'Into the future: national identity and education'.

## Living in an age of anxiety

As we approach the end of the twentieth century we have entered, to borrow Dunant and Porter's phrase, an 'age of anxiety'.[8] We are living in an age where 'a powerful mixture of technology and economics' is dissolving many of the bonds that have traditionally bound together the nation. National identity is being undermined by global economic integration and by the free flow of ideas and images.[9] Communications round the world are now virtually instantaneous. New technologies have expanded choices, but have also served to diminish our sense of control. Space and time have been compressed. People feel threatened by a perceived loss of stability. We read of fragmentation and homogenization, of depthlessness and instantaneity, of shifting labour patterns and structural unemployment, of dislocation, diaspora and displacement.[10] There are moral panics over levels of violence, crime and family breakdown.[11] There is talk of environmental crisis. Scottish and Welsh devolution and the possibility of English assemblies have generated debate about the components of an English identity. At the same time, the European project is perceived as a threat to British institutions: parliamentary democracy, the monarchy, the common law.

We are living in an age where 'whiteness' has become an 'object of popular, political and academic interest' and where white ethnic studies demonstrate that young white males 'seem like cultural ghosts' seeking symbols and emblems that fit 'their' cultural identity, but find very little that fits or, in the case of the Union Jack, find that the emblem itself 'is already a contested battle-ground'.[12] We are in an age where to be black is to engage with a range of identities dependent upon cultural and political contexts:

> How do I identify myself?...at school, you was black,...When it comes to cricket, 'Oh go on West Indies! Give England a thrashing' If England are playing a football match...and if there's four or five black guys, 'Go on England!'. How can I identify myself? Realistically I'm British, black British...I'm trying to look for a word to say what I am. I'm black, that's a fact. I suppose British West Indian. I don't know how you sort it out.[13]

We are in an age where the once perceived monolithic 'Asian community' has splintered 'in the light of a growing recognition of Asian differences in white eyes'. This broadening recognition of difference has occurred parallel with what some observers have identified as multiple paradigm shifts among the second generation of British Asians as they rediscover 'Muslim, Sikh and Hindu identities that parents downplayed'.[14] Indeed, Modood claims that differences between ethnic groups are now more significant than any black–white divide, with Pakistanis and Bangladeshis underachieving and Indians and East African Asians succeeding in education and professionally.[15] At the same time there are fears of further fragmentation of community resulting from 'less knowledge of Asian languages, a weakening of the extended family and young people being educated away from home and becoming successful professionals thus sharing the lifestyles of their peers'.[16]

'Life', in the world of late twentieth-century capitalism, 'can no longer be lived sequentially along a single time line' as each of us enters daily into a multitude of situations – at home, work, leisure, with peer groups – each of which is a world of its own with a distinctive history. We are 'forced to contend with multiple identities and multiple memories'.[17] When we look for certainty from the past we find the emergence of both a school of self-consciously 'British' historians who have begun to undermine traditional interpretations of Britain's past and its origins, and a cultural historical project to unravel the category of Englishness.[18] Thus, 'our' sense of 'our' past and 'our' ability to comprehend 'our' future appear increasingly uncertain. In short, 'we' are in an age where 'we' are less certain about who 'we' are.[19]

These uncertainties are not new. Indeed, it is possible to trace the contours of their development in Britain across the decades since the Second World War.[20] Traces can be located in the 1980s when the New Right embarked on a political project of renewal and policies were pursued which, in Sivanandan's words, 'destabilised people's lives, weaken[ed] the social fabric, fragment[ed] society...[broke] up community, destroy[ed] collectivity, and dissipat[ed] opposition'.[21] It was a period in which black and Asian parents increasingly protested about their being 'outside' the nation, excluded by both the formal and hidden curriculum of schooling.[22] Traces can be mapped in the 1970s when the 'troubles' in Ireland increasingly called into question the legitimacy of the British state and when devolution made its way onto the agenda of Westminster politics in the aftermath of the energy crisis and the boom in North Sea Oil.[23] They can be traced in the 1950s and '60s to the Americanization of culture, the withdrawal from Empire and to the reduction of Britain's economic and political standing in the world. These were decades which also saw the unsettling appearance of colonial 'immigrants' within the metropolitan centre: 'As they hauled down the flag, we got on the banana boat and sailed right into London...to the centre of the world.'[24] Postwar migrations of colonized peoples into British labour markets brought the former periphery to the core, establishing Salman Rushdie's 'New Empire within Britain'.[25] These migrations destabilized traditional definitions of national belonging and stimulated the development of racialized politics and social relations.[26]

Eric Hobsbawm and Terence Ranger's *The Invention of Tradition* (London, 1983), Robert Colls and Richard Dodd's *Englishness* (London, 1986) and the three-volume History Workshop collection *Patriotism* (London, 1989) edited by Raphael Samuel established the period 1880–1950 as central to constructions of Englishness currently in circulation. It follows that if we currently occupy an age of uncertainty – the roots of which we can find in Britain's postwar history – there must logically have been an age of certainty some time between 1880 and 1945, when we knew 'who' we were. Was this age of certainty in the 1930s when, as we have seen, children celebrated the 'wonder' of the British Empire? Or was it earlier, in the era of the First World War when tens of thousands died for 'King and Country' in the fields of Flanders? The answer is elusive, because when we begin to map the nature of the nation and national identity across this time frame, 1880 to 1945, we find fluidity.

For example, in the period after 1880, when Victorian Britain is generally described as entering its most confident and self-regarding phase, when mass schooling began to flourish, where 'really useful knowledge' shaped the school curriculum and popular imperialism was securely established, the idea of the nation was legitimized through invented tradition.[27] These 'invented traditions' included, for example, many of the traditions associated with undergraduate culture:

> ...athletic competitions, the union (or debating) societies, extravagant May Balls, annual examinations for degrees, the Oxford and Cambridge 'manner', and the assumption that an education of this sort fitted one for a position of power....[28]

Students, the product of these traditions, were characterized by an Oxbridge identity that captured 'the best model of the ordinary English gentleman', notably: 'bodily activity, manliness, generosity', 'enthusiasm, congeniality, and a vein of chivalry'. The Oxbridge students might represent Englishness but at the same time they were viewed as 'a people apart. It is not everybody who can understand them.'[29] Identity was clearly differentiated and fractured by class. Further, Winter has shown that the 'most striking feature' of pre-1914 discussions of national identity 'is their vagueness', followed by their subdued and sedate nature. After 1914 'Englishness', according to Winter, was redefined in terms of the wartime and postwar assertion of virtues and values synonymous with masculine 'decency', moral rectitude and martial virtue. Initially, these characteristics were associated with the brotherhood of arms and were generalized to the whole population, but by the 1930s the 'true' expression of Englishness came to be located in 'the sons of the privileged, whose decency, courage and self-confidence took them to war'. 'Englishness' came to mean the values of the officer class.[30] However, Alison Light has argued that in the 1930s the heroic and masculine rhetoric of national identity was superseded by a new emphasis on modes of belonging which were more inward looking, emphasizing the domestic and private characteristics of national life:

> …the 1920s and 30s saw a move away from formerly heroic and officially mas-
> culine public rhetorics of national identity and from a dynamic and missionary
> view of the Victorian and Edwardian middle classes in 'Great Britain' to an
> Englishness at once less imperial and more inward-looking, more domestic and
> more private and, in terms of pre-war standards, more 'feminine'.[31]

The research of Deslandes, Winter and Light clearly demonstrates the relevance of Sir Ernest Barker's observation in 1927 that:

> Not only is national character made; it continues to be made and remade. It is
> not made once, for all, it always remains modifiable. A nation may alter its
> character in the course of history to suit new conditions or to fit new purposes.[32]

There may have been periods of certainty about 'who we were' before 1945, but the components of that identity, at least in the twentieth century, were continually in the process of being re-imagined and reinvented, made and remade. Further, the components of that identity related to collections of individuals rather than the national collective.

## 'Home' and national identity

> The Germans live in Germany;
> The Romans live in Rome;
> The Turkeys live in Turkey;
> But the English live at home.[33]

Home Counties, Home Guard, Home Secretary, homecoming, homeland, home-sick, home-made, home truths; 'Make yourself at home', 'Home sweet home', 'Home is where the heart is', 'Keep the home fires burning', 'There's no place like home', 'England, home and beauty' etc. The word 'home' is rich in associations. Many of these associations are linked to ideas of nation and belonging, of the nation as home. James Donald, in an essay 'How English is it', wrote of the nation as a 'symbolic universe in which we feel at home'.[34] Certainly, in Imperial Britain it was 'home' that was the link between nation and empire, as was recognized in Birmingham in 1908:

> Sure I am that no nobler and more Imperialistic work is being done in
> Birmingham than that which is being done in the gymnasium at Digbeth. And
> in promoting imperialism at home, Digbeth is doing service to the nation and
> the Empire, whose policy Birmingham has done so much to mould.[35]

Male physical fitness, rooted in drill and discipline in school and youth movements, served the nation by promoting 'national efficiency', and equipped the youth of the day to defend 'home' and promote national virtues and ideas overseas.[36]

'Home' was also the domestic space in which women were called upon to help create and sustain the nation. From the late nineteenth century through to the Second World War the schooling of girls was predicated on the assumption that women would be employed only prior to marriage and that formal education should prepare them for temporary employment and for their future role as home-makers and mothers. Education legitimized the sexual division of labour. The elementary curricula insisted that girls learn cooking, needlework, laundering and homemaking.[37] Women, said Eleanor Rathbone, were 'the natural custodians of childhood. That at least is part of the traditional role assigned to us by men and one that we have never repudiated'.[38] Girls were educated to nourish and nurture and in times of war 'to keep the home fires burning'. It follows, therefore, that if 'home' represented the nation, women were allocated a different place in discourses of national identity from men. Further, did girls and women at particular moments in history understand and relate to national identity, and by implication the nation, differently from boys and men? Or, to put it another way, were their experiences of Empire Day celebrations differently felt?

'Home' has also been, and continues to be, 'a rallying ground for reactionary nationalisms'.[39] Domestic metaphors and images of privacy, as Cohen has argued, are frequently used as devices in arguments about exclusion, about those who are 'outside' the nation, about those who 'threaten' national identity. For example, such sentiments were expressed in the 1880s in relation to Jewish immigration into the East End of London:

> This great influx is driving out the native from hearth and home. Some of us have been born here. Others have come here when quite young children, have been brought up and educated here. Some of us have old associations.[40]

Such sentiments similarly informed Evan Gordon's speech to Parliament on 29 January 1902, demanding immediate immigration controls:

> Not a day passes but English families are ruthlessly turned out to make room for foreign invaders. Out they go to make room for Rumanians, Russians and Poles.... The working classes know that new buildings are erected not for them but for strangers from abroad; they see notices that no English need apply placarded on vacant rooms; they see the schools crowded with foreign children...[41]

Similar sentiments – of the nation as 'home' and under siege from strangers – are central to Enoch Powell's racist rhetoric of the 1960s and later. Powell's speeches regularly included references to 'ordinary, decent, sensible...English people' being 'persecuted' in their own 'homes' by immigrants. So, in the notorious 'River Tiber foaming with much blood' speech in Birmingham on 20 April 1968 Powell spoke of the threat posed by 'strangers':

> ...for reasons which they [Englishmen] could not comprehend...they found their wives unable to obtain hospital beds in childbirth, their children unable to obtain school places, their homes and neighbourhoods changed beyond recognition, their plans and prospects for the future defeated...they began to hear...more and more voices which told them that they were now the unwanted.[42]

What is interesting in these constructions of the home as nation is also the reference to schooling as implicitly an extension of home, the site where values and traditions are imparted.

What, then, of those children who were the offspring of 'strangers'? For Powell it was these children who represented the greatest threat to 'England's green and pleasant land'. In November 1968 he gave a speech which began with a flood of statistics about children: the percentages of births to immigrant mothers, the percentages of 'coloured children' in the schools of 'immigrant areas' and then concluded:

> Sometimes people point to the increasing proportion of immigrant offspring born in this country as if the fact contained within itself the ultimate solution. The truth is the opposite. The West Indian or Asian does not, by being born in England become an Englishman. In law he becomes a United Kingdom citizen by birth; in fact, he is a West Indian or an Asian still...he will by the very nature of things have lost one country without gaining another, lost one nationality without acquiring a new one. Time is running against us and them....[43]

For Powell, to be 'of' the nation was to be part of, and share in, common historical experiences, culture, language and religion. Belonging could not be conferred, it could not be given, it was felt. It was a definition of belonging that reflected sentiments expressed during the Falklands War: 'the Falklanders were British...by language, customs and race...more British indeed than so-called "Black Englishmen" living on British soil'.[44] It was a definition of belonging that was central to the New Right's political project of renewal in the 1980s and shaped their vision of the nation and its past. It was a definition of belonging that produced a National Curriculum framework that offered a narrative of the nation which had no space 'for that which is not English, white and Christian'.[45] In short, the invocation of home as nation contributed to the racialization of belonging.

## The contingency of identity

The cultural theorist, Homi Bhabha, has argued that at any one moment a nation can be 'caught, uncertainly, in the act of composing its...image', and that in this process national identity is constituted both from the romanticized 'pleasures of the hearth', the local, and from 'the terror of the space or race of the Other', the global. For Bhabha, the local and the global are constantly soliciting one another.[46] In other words, there is a constant interplay between Self and Other in the construction and reconstruction of national identity. Bhabha's use of the binary Other focuses on colonial and postcolonial encounters. In the present context of nineteenth- and twentieth-century Britain this relationship can be explored productively using the political framework of black/white relations.[47]

White and black relations in the past have developed in a multiplicity of contexts: the transatlantic slave trade, the development of plantation economies and systems of indentured labour, colonialism and imperialism, neo-colonialism and development, and the incorporation of migrant labour in metropolitan economies. Each of these historically specific encounters between 'white' and 'black' groups has seen the construction and reproduction of subordinate racialized black identities. These racialized identities can all be said to constitute representations of 'Otherness'. They are the 'Other', the alterity, in a relationship where the 'Self' is 'what rules, names, defines and assigns' its Other.[48] The history of 'the Other' is therefore necessarily deeply implicated in the history of 'the Self'. Thus, when in the past, for instance, 'the West' produced the 'Orient', it was at the same moment producing and representing itself. Similarly, when politicians, academics, teachers and so forth constructed racialized identities for black migrants in post-1945 Britain, they were at the same time defining, constructing and affirming their own sense of identity. In the process of defining their 'Other' they were defining themselves. The authorial subjects were implicitly the normative referent. By studying the identity of the 'Other' the identity of the 'Self' is brought into sharper focus. Their histories are inscribed within each other; they are not separate.[49]

It follows, therefore, that when we try and map constructions of Englishness and Britishness in the nineteenth and twentieth centuries our focus should be broader than the territorial boundary of the nation state. 'Home' was also *in* Empire: domestic England was transported beyond the home shores of the nation. This journey also shaped national identity; after all, its celebration was a feature of the school calendar and had 'lasting educational influence'. There was a relationship between 'over there' and 'back here', between the 'Englishman abroad' and 'at home'. It was, however, a relationship which, as Bill Schwarz has argued, only become 'fully articulated within English culture itself at the moment of mass immigration' of former colonial subjects from the Indian subcontinent and the Caribbean, and then in 'an exclusivist, racist reflex'.[50]

This relationship between 'over there' and 'back here' constitutes a spatial dimension in Catherine Hall's project 'to imagine a British "post-nation" which is not ethnically pure, which is inclusive and culturally diverse', a project which would involve 'memory-work' where Empire was 're-read', 're-imagined' and 're-remembered'.[51] Her project recognizes that it was in encounters within empire that Europeans ascribed identities to colonial peoples, that black encounters with white racism and British capitalist power did not begin in England but in British colonies overseas, and that current narratives of the national identity are incomplete as, to use Gillis's phrase, they do not offer minority 'admission to national memories'.[52] In narratives of the nation black migrants, whether in the sixteenth or twentieth centuries, continue to be denied both historical agency and cultural strength.

It is, however, not only black populations who have been the object of racialization and exclusion. A comprehensive analysis of the racialization process in Britain would of necessity have to include the experiences of all those migrant groups who have historically been given 'race' identities: Jewish, Irish, German, Turkish and Greek Cypriot, Chinese, East European, Romany and so forth.[53] Each of these groups has, at some time, constituted the 'Other', yet they too are absent from 'national memories' except in the form of stereotypes linked to their place of origin. In this context, it is useful to remember the binary Other when confronted by the stereotypes of foreigners listed in Orwell's celebrated essay on boys weeklies published in 1939. They were as follows:

FRENCHMAN: Excitable. Wears beard, gesticulates wildly.
SPANIARD, MEXICAN etc.: Sinister, treacherous.
ARAB, AFGHAN etc.: Sinister, treacherous.
CHINESE: Sinister, treacherous. Wears pigtail.
ITALIAN: Excitable. Grinds barrel-organ or carries stiletto.
SWEDE, DANE etc.: Kind-hearted, stupid.
NEGRO: Comic, very faithful.[54]

National identity is always contingent and relational and depends for its unity, coherence and security on the construction of boundaries which mark the difference between Self and Other. Further, the subjectivities of the Self were/are at any one time constituted in relationship to a *multiplicity* of 'Others'. It follows, therefore, that in order to fully comprehend the nature and shape of national identity in nineteenth- and twentieth-century Britain historians have to attend to documenting the complex intermeshing of the global and the local, and the intertwined histories of the metropolitan centre and its periphery. Finally, it is in the context of shifting boundaries where differences between Self and Other appear to have become insecure and permeable that the recent academic preoccupation with white English ethnicity can best be understood.[55]

## Educating the nation

A nation, as Benedict Anderson has persuasively argued, is an 'imagined political community':

> ...imagined as both inherently limited and sovereign...imagined because the members of even the smallest nation will never know most of their fellow-members, meet them, or even hear of them, yet in the minds of each lives the image of their communion...imagined as limited because even the largest of them has finite, if elastic boundaries, beyond which lie other nations...imagined as a community, because regardless of the actual inequality and exploitation that may prevail in each, the nation is always conceived as a deep, horizontal comradeship.[56]

National identity can be similarly conceived as 'imagined'; it provides an 'imaginary unity' against other possible unities. The development of the public sector in Britain at the end of the nineteenth century provided a mechanism whereby the state could foster 'communion' and 'comradeship'. The modern classroom was invented, together with a teacher, furniture, texts and aids, to produce a designed effect: the 'separation, segmentation and segregation' of childhood and the inculcation of common values and virtues.[57]

Working-class children shared a similar curriculum to that of their middle-class contemporaries, which promoted patriotic values. History and geography were taught in a way that fostered a 'burning, active love of one's own country'.[58] Joanna Bourke has documented how children learnt in schools that:

> Frenchmen were 'a lot of frogs and were a little sissy as they had a great pull with the opposite sex',...that Germans had square heads, crew cuts, and fancy braces, and were totally without initiative...[that] the violence of 'Chin Chin Chinaman' was frightening, the beards and side-curls of Orthodox Jews eerie, and Polish and Yiddish speech disconcerting.[59]

The forty years leading up to the First World War saw a flood of nursery tales, recitation materials, children's books, juvenile literature and historical novels which flattered the British and stereotyped the world's non-white populations. 'Patriotism, militarism, adulation of the monarchy, and...imperial expansion' came to be the central concerns of school history texts.[60]

The impact of such schooling is, as Paul Goalen has recently written, difficult to assess as the evidence is contradictory.[61] For example, George Orwell could write, 'there is not one working-class boy in a thousand who does not pine for the day when he will leave school. He wants to be doing real work, not wasting his time on ridiculous subjects like history and geography', but also believed that 'all English children' were successfully educated 'to despise the Southern European races'.[62] Oral history has uncovered some evidence that such schooling was successful because stories of popular heroes and heroines 'provided welcome relief from the monotony of the school routine which was dominated by the three Rs'.[63] However, Patrick Brindle has pointed out that in the pre-Second World War classroom, teachers were divided over the goals and methods of history teaching, that the dominant experience was of 'chalk and talk', that there were enormous class sizes, a shortage of books and resources and 'in many rural schools the teacher was the greatest consumer of the history textbook because the teacher would have access to the only copy'.[64] In 1930s Walsall, for example, schooling was characterized by poor accommodation, large classes, poor attendance, low achievement and staying-on rates, and staffing shortages.[65] Indeed, these characteristics were defining features of popular education in Walsall from the 1870s onwards.[66]

I want to argue that, in order to come to some conclusion about the impact of education in identity formation, we need to extend our vision of schooling to consider the cumulative effect of value messages in both the formal and 'hidden curriculum'. After all, it is the latter which research has shown has been critical in excluding black and Asian pupils from school life, from 'our schools'.[67] In other words, our research agenda should be widened to embrace the grammar and the 'choreography', the routines and the rituals, and the symbolic events of everyday schooling: to ask questions about the learning of folk-sayings and proverbs, drill and other exercises that regulated behaviour, memories of collective worship and celebrations involving the Union Jack, the imagery in the hymns that children sang every day – 'England's Green and Pleasant Land' 'Land of Hope and Glory', 'We plough the fields and scatter'.[68] We should look beyond formal school processes to the material culture of schooling and consider the impact of the friezes displayed on primary classroom walls, the history timelines, the 'lantern-slides' in the geography classroom, the wallcharts and maps depicting the Empire, the display of reproduction paintings, the symbols printed on exercise books, the world globe, the units of measurements on rulers and scientific equipment, school magazines, badges and uniforms, images on shields, cups, medals and certificates, class, team and prizeday photographs. The parameters of the research agenda should be expanded to include the culture of the playground where folk memories and myths are recycled through songs and chants, where 'British Bulldog' is played and where comic books and magazines are circulated. As historians we also have to consider the impact of other 'educational' sites and spaces – the home, the church, the youth club, the museum, the war memorial – in shaping and reinforcing identity, in rendering national identity stable, secure and coherent. At the same time we should aim to identify the processes, images and symbols which trivialized and patronized, gave form to the nation's 'Other', and produced racialized identities. Finally, we should also seek to identify those educational spaces and sites where racialized identities were challenged.

## Into the future: national identity and education

This chapter began with a series of questions which, in turn, prompted a series of reflections about the relationship between education and national identity formation. These reflections crystallized around four themes: the fluidity in the components of national identity across time; differential experiences and understandings of national identity formation and categorization; the contingency of identity and the permeable nature of boundaries; and the need for historians of education to extend the research frame in relation to identity formation. Structurally, it would therefore seem appropriate to end with a question: What, then, of the future of national identity?

New Labour's 'stake-holding society' has been presented as a strategy aimed at generating a renewal of a sense of belonging to a national project through combined reform of the constitution, the economy and the welfare state. What conception of the nation accompanies this desire to create a sense of belonging? At the 1995 Labour Party conference in Brighton Tony Blair spoke of the British as 'Decent people. Good people. Patriotic people...these are "our people"....It is a new Britain. One Britain: the people united by shared values and shared aims' a new age. To be led by a new generation.'[69] Blair expanded upon this vision of the nation the following year in a keynote address to conference:

> ...consider a thousand years of British history and what it tells us. The first parliament of the World; the Industrial Revolution – ahead of its time; an Empire, the largest the World has ever known, relinquished in peace. The invention of virtually every Scientific device of the modern World. Two World Wars in which our country was bled dry, in which two generations perished, but which in the defeat of the most evil force ever let loose by man showed the most sustained example of bravery in human history.
>   This our nation.
>   Our characteristics: common-sense, standing up for the under-dog, fiercely independent.[70]

In September 1998, Blair, again at a conference but this time as Prime Minister, placed the nation at the centre of his 'third way' strategy:

> There are three choices. Resist change – futile. Let it happen – *laissez faire* – each person for themselves, each country for itself. Or the third way: we manage change, together. Modernise. Reform. Equip our country for the future. This way we face the challenge together. And if the spirit of the nation is willing, it can make the body of the nation strong. One nation, one community, each and every one of us playing our part...ours is a mission to modernise for a purpose; to build a Britain strong and prosperous. Strong because it is just, prosperous because it uses the talents of all the people. Confident because the challenge is being taken on not by each of us in isolation from each other, but together, one nation, sure of its values and therefore sure of its future.[71]

So, there we have it, the new Britain of this project of belonging is united as One. Blair's conception of the nation is as simplistic and triumphalist as any evoked under Conservative rule. It is a conception of the nation that favours an authentic version of national identity, an identity grounded in over 'a thousand years' of history. It is a conception of the nation and belonging which sits uneasily with the arguments articulated in this paper. Identity, I have argued, is always and continuously being produced. Identity formation is never complete. In 1990s Britain the conjuncture of Self and Other within the bounded nation-state requires negotiation over new notions of national culture and belonging. To imagine new ways of being British means recognizing that the nation is not homogenous but is, and always has been, plural, fragmented and differentiated. It means avoiding looking back with nostalgia to the past, but rather, as bell hooks has written, struggling 'against forgetting; a politicization of memory that distinguishes nostalgia, that longing for something to be as it once was, a kind of useless act, from that remembering that serves to illuminate and transform the present'.[72] It means developing a sense of belonging that is not closed and intole ant. It means shifting the focus away from cultural norms and 'problems of identity' – ethnic, class, gender, nationality – and embracing the hybridity generated through 'the cultural interchange and intervention' that marks Britain today.[73] However, it is Blair's concept of the nation that provides the framework within which education policy for 'a new age' will be developed and pursued. The extent to which education in this 'new Britain' is successful in involving all 'stakeholders' will be a research question for future historians of education, identity and 'home'.

## Notes

1  Mass Observation Archive: FR 878. I wish to thank Kevin Myers for this reference.
2  *Walsall Observer*, 27 May 1939.
3  'Alan Bennett chooses four painting for schools', *London Review of Books*, 20/7 (2 April 1998), 7–10. Bennett chose *The Adoration of the Kings* by Gossaert (*c.* 1510), *Hambletonian, Rubbing Down* by George Stubbes (1800), *Lorenzo and Isabella* by Sir John Millais (1849) and *Southwold* by Stanley Spencer (1937).
4  Birmingham Central Library, Local Studies Department: see, for example, WK/B11/5155; WK/B11/5164.
5  Mass Observation Archive: TC Antisemitism Box 1 File C.
6  T. Kushner, *Observing the 'Other'. Mass-Observation and 'Race'*, Mass Observation Occasional Paper No 2 (University of Sussex Library 1995), 6.
7  *Young People in the UK: Attitudes and Opinions on Europe, Europeans and the European Union* (London: the Runnymede Trust in Partnership with the Commission for Racial Equality, 1998) *passim*.
8  S. Dunant and R. Porter (eds), *The Age of Anxiety* (London: Virago Press, 1996).
9  V. Cable, *The World's New Fissures. Identities in Crisis* (London: Demos, 1994), 20–2.
10  See, for example D. Harvey, *The Condition of Postmodernity* (Oxford: Basil Blackwell, 1989); P. Emberley, 'Places and stories: the challenge of technology', *Social Research*, 5/3 (1989), 741–85; K. Robins, 'Tradition and translation: national culture in its global context', in *Enterprise and Heritage*, edited by J. Corner and S. Honey (London: Routledge, 1991), 21–44; B. Axford, *The Global System: Economics, Politics and Culture* (Cambridge: Polity Press, 1995); A. Brah, *Cartographies of Diaspora* (London: Routledge, 1996).
11  M. Ignatieff, 'Identity parades', *Prospect* (April 1998), 18–23.
12  J. Gabriel, *Whitewash. Racialised Politics and the Media* (London: Routledge, 1998), 18; R. Hewitt, *Routes of Racism. The Social Basis of Racist Action* (Stoke-on-Trent: Trentham Books, 1996), 40. See also, A. Bonnet, ' "How the British working class became white": the symbolic [re]formation of racialized capitalism', *Journal of Historical Sociology*, 11/3 (1998), 316–40.
13  Quoted in M. Chamberlain, 'I belong to whoever wants me', *Frontlines Backyards*, edited by B. Schwarz and P. Cohen, *New Formations*, 33 (1998), 50. See also, E. Pennicott, 'Reading identity: young Black British men', in *Young Britain. Politics, Pleasures and Predicaments*, edited by J. Rutherford (London: Lawrence & Wishart, 1998), 147–53; and A. Faust, I. Grosvenor and J. Schaechter, *Children and Social Exclusion* (forthcoming).
14  M. Kamal quoted in R. Huq, 'Currying favour? Race and diaspora in New Britain', in *The Moderniser's Dilemma. Radical Politics in the Age of Blair*, edited by A. Coddington and M. Perryman (London: Lawrence & Wishart, 1998), 70.
15  T. Modood *et al.*, *Ethnic Minorities in Britain: Diversity and Disadvantage* (London: PSI, 1997).
16  Kamal quoted in Huq, op. cit., 70–1.
17  J. R. Gillis, 'Memory and identity: the history of a relationship', in *Commemorations. The Politics of National Identity*, edited by J. R. Gillis (Princeton, NJ: Princeton University Press, 1994), 15–16.
18  See, for example, Patrick Wright, *On Living in an Old Country. The National Past in Contemporary Britain* (London: Verso, 1985); R. Colls and P. Dodds (eds), *Englishness: Politics and Culture, 1880–1920* (Brighton: Croom Helm, 1986); P. Gilroy, *There Ain't No Black in the Union Jack: The Cultural Politics of Race and Nation*

(London: Hutchinson, 1987); R. Samuel (ed.), *Patriotism: The Making and Un-Making of British Identity*, 3 vols (London: Routledge, 1989); L. Colley, *Britons: Forging the Nation, 1707–1837* (New Haven, CT: Yale University Press, 1992); A. Grainger and K. Stringer (eds), *Uniting the Kingdom? The Making of British History?* (London: Routledge, 1995); B. Schwarz (ed.), *The Expansion of England. Race, Ethnicity and Culture* (London: Routledge, 1996); R. Samuel, *Island Stories. Unravelling Britain* (London: Verso, 1998).

19 For a critique of the nature and impact of this 'time–space compression', see D. Massey, 'A place called home?', *The Question of Home*, edited by A. Bammer, *New Formations*, 17 (1992), 3–15. See also, P. Dodd, *The Battle over Britain* (London: Demos, 1995).

20 See R. Samuel, 'British dimensions: four nations history', *History Workshop Journal*, 40 (Autumn 1995), iii–iv; I. Grosvenor, *Assimilating Identities. Racism and Educational Policy in Post*, 1945 Britain (London: Lawrence & Wishart, 1997), Ch. 5.

21 A. Sivanandan, 'Beyond state-watching', in *Statewatching the New Europe: A Handbook on the European State*, edited by T. Bunyan (London: Statewatch, 1993), 13.

22 Grosvenor, op. cit., 68–9, 86–8.

23 Samuel (1995), op. cit., ii–iv.

24 S. Hall, 'The local and the global: globalization and identity', in *Culture, Globalization and the World System: Contemporary Conditions for the Representation of Identity*, edited by A. D. King (Basingstoke: Macmillan, 1991), 24.

25 S. Rushdie, 'The new empire within Britain', in *Imaginary Homelands. Essays and Criticism, 1981–1991* (London: Granta Books, 1991), 129–38.

26 See S. Joshi and B. Carter, 'The role of Labour in the creation of a racist Britain', *Race and Class* XXV (1984), 53–70 and B. Carter, C. Harris and S. Joshi, 'The 1951–55 Conservative Government and the Racialization of Black Immigration', *Immigrants and Minorities* 6/3 (1987), 335–47.

27 For a discussion of 'invented traditions' see E. Hobsbawm and T. Ranger (eds), *The Invention of Tradition* (Cambridge: Cambridge University Press, 1983), and Samuel (1989), op. cit., Vol. 3, 'Introduction'.

28 P. R. Deslandes, ' "The foreign element": newcomers and the rhetoric of race, nation, and empire in "Oxbridge" undergraduate culture, 1850–1920', *Journal of British Studies*, 37 (January, 1998), 56.

29 Ibid., 61–3.

30 J. M. Winter, 'British national identity and the First World War', in *The Boundaries of the State in Modern Britain*, edited by S. J. D. Green and R. C. Whiting (Cambridge: Cambridge University Press, 1996), 261–77.

31 A. Light, *Forever England: Femininity, Literature and Conservatism between the Wars* (London: Routledge, 1991), 8.

32 E. Barker, *National Character and the Factors in its Formation* (London: Methuen, 1927), 8.

33 J. H. Goring, *The Ballad of Lake Laloo and other Rhymes* (London: Utopia Press, 1909), n.p.

34 J. Donald, 'How English is it?', in *Sentimental Education: Schooling, Popular Culture and the Regulation of Liberty* (London: Verso, 1992), 50.

35 Quoted in M. Blanch, 'Imperialism, nationalism and organized youth', in *Working Class Culture. Studies in History and Theory*, edited by J. Clarke, C. Critcher and R. Johnson (London: Hutchinson, 1979), 112.

36 Ibid., 103–20.

37 See, for example, A. Davin, 'Imperialism and motherhood', *History Workshop Journal*, 5 (1978), 9–65; D. Beddoe, *Back to Home and Duty: Women Between the Wars, 1918–1939* (London: Pandora, 1989); J. Giles, *Women, Identity and Private Life in Britain, 1900–50* (Basingstoke: Macmillan, 1995); W. Webster, *Imagining Home. Gender, 'Race' and National Identity, 1945–64* (London: UCL Press, 1998).

38 Eleanor Rathbone quoted in J. Lewis, *Women in England* (Sussex: Wheatsheaf, 1984), 105.

39 A. Bammer, 'Editorial' in 'A Question of Home', *New Formations*, 17 (Summer 1992), x.

40 Quoted in P. Cohen, *Home Rules. Some Reflections on Racism and Nationalism in Everyday Life* (London: New Ethnicities Unit, 1993), 5.

41 Quoted P. Foot, *Immigration and Race in British Politics* (Harmondsworth: Penguin, 1969), 88–9.

288 *Ian Grosvenor*

42 E. Powell, 'Birmingham Speech, April 20, 1968'. The full text is reproduced in B. Smithies and P. Fiddick, *Enoch Powell on Immigration* (London: Sphere, 1969), 35–43.
43 E. Powell, 'Eastbourne Speech, November, 16, 1968' in Smithies and Fiddick, op. cit., 63–77.
44 J. Casey, 'One nation: the politics of race', *The Salisbury Review*, 1 (Autumn 1982), 25.
45 J. Haviland (ed.), *Take Care Mr Baker!* (London: Fourth Estate), 22.
46 H. Bhabha, 'Introduction: narrating the nation', in *Nation and Narration*, edited by H. Bhabha (London: Routledge), 2.
47 Black and white are the dominant categories associated with the process of racialization in Britain. For a critique of the application of the binary Other see J. M. Mackenzie, 'Empire and national identities: the case of Scotland', *Transactions of the Royal Historical Society*, Sixth Series, VIII (1998), 215–32.
48 H. Cixous and C. Clement, *The Newly Born Woman* (Manchester: Manchester University Press), 207.
49 For fuller exposition of this argument see Grosvenor, op. cit., and M. Green and I. Grosvenor, 'Making subjects: history-writing, education and race categories', *Paedagogica Historica*, XXXIII/3 (1997), 883–908.
50 B. Schwarz, 'An Englishman abroad...and at home. The case of Paul Scott', in 'The question of home', *New Formations*, 17 (Summer 1992), 95.
51 C. Hall, 'Histories, empires and the post-colonial moment', in *The Post-Colonial Question*, edited by I. Chambers and L. Curti (London: Routledge, 1996), 65–77.
52 Gillis, op. cit., 10.
53 See R. Miles, *Racism after 'Race Relations'* (London: Routledge, 1993). Linda Colley also used the concept of the binary Other in her study of the emergence of the British nation in the eighteenth century, Colley, op. cit.
54 G. Orwell, *Collected Essays, Journalism and Letters*, edited by S. Orwell and I. Angus, Vol. 1 (Harmondsworth: Penguin, 1970), 517.
55 See, for example, the introduction to J. Rutherford, *Forever England. Reflections on Masculinity and Empire* (London: Lawrence & Wishart, 1997). Philip Dodd identifies the report over the killing of Ahmed Ullah by Darren Coulborn, a thirteen-year-old white boy, in 1986 in the Burnage School, Manchester as a significant marker in the developing 'crisis of self-scrutiny among the white English'; Dodd (1995), op. cit., 37.
56 B. Anderson, *Imagined Communities. Reflections on the Origin and Spread of Nationalism* (London: Verso, 1983), 15–16.
57 T. J. Schlereth, *Cultural History and Material Culture* (Charlottesville: University Press of Virginia, 1990), 15.
58 W. H. Webb, 'History, patriotism and the child', *History*, 2/1 (1913), 54.
59 J. Bourke, *Working-Class Cultures in Britain, 1890–1960. Gender, Class and Ethnicity* (London: Routledge, 1994), 186.
60 J. M. Mackenzie, *Progaganda and Empire. The Manipulation of British Public Opinion, 1880–1960* (Manchester: Manchester University Press, 1984), 176. See also K. Castle, *Britannia's Children. Reading Colonialism through Children's Books* (Manchester: Manchester University Press, 1996).
61 Paul Goalen, 'History and national identity in the classroom', *History Today* (June 1997), 6–8.
62 G. Orwell, *The Road to Wigan Pier* (Harmondsworth: Penguin, 1989), 107; G. Orwell (1970), op. cit., 473.
63 Goalen, op. cit., 7.
64 Patrick Brindle, 'Mr Chips with everything?', *History Today*, 46/6 (June 1996), 11–14. I wish to thank Dr Stephen Bulman for this reference.
65 T. Harris, *Popular Education in Walsall, 1760–1955* (Walsall: Walsall Local History Centre, 1997), 133, 138–9, 141, 144.
66 Ibid., passim.
67 The Rampton report was entitled *West Indian Children in our Schools* (London: HMSO, 1981).
68 The idea of the choreography of schooling (patterns of discipline, time and order) is borrowed from Betty Eggremont who introduced it in her presentation on visual images at ISCHE, Leuven, August 1998.
69 Tony Blair, 'Speech to the 1995 Labour Party Conference', Brighton, 3 October 1995.

70  I would like to thank David Gillborn for this reference. See his 'Race, nation and education: new labour and the new racism', in *Education Policy and Contemporary Politics*, edited by J. Demaine (London: Macmillan, 1999).

71  Tony Blair, 'Speech to the 1998 Labour Party Conference', Blackpool, 29 September 1998.

72  b. hooks, *Yearning: Race, Gender and Cultural Politics* (London: Turnaround, 1991), 147.

73  H. K. Bhabha, 'Re-inventing Britain – a manifesto, 21 March 1997', British Council website: http://www.britcoun.org/studies/stdsmani.htm. For a discussion of the emergence of hybridity see Grosvenor, op. cit., Ch. 5.

Lightning Source UK Ltd.
Milton Keynes UK
UKOW020702111011

180102UK00003B/44/P